Classical Social Theory

Classical
Social
Theory

Ian Craib

OXFORD UNIVERSITY PRESS
1997

Oxford University Press, Great Clarendon Street, Oxford OX2 6DP

Oxford New York
Athens Auckland Bangkok Bogota Bombay
Buenos Aires Calcutta Cape Town Dar es Salaam
Delhi Florence Hong Kong Istanbul Karachi
Kuala Lumpur Madras Madrid Melbourne
Mexico City Nairobi Paris Singapore
Taipei Tokyo Toronto
and associated companies in
Berlin Ibadan

Oxford is a trade mark of Oxford University Press

Published in the United States
by Oxford University Press Inc., New York

British Library Cataloguing in Publication Data
Data available

Library of Congress Cataloging in Publication Data
Craib Ian, 1945–
Classical social theory / Ian Craib.
Includes bibliographical references.
1. Sociology—Philosophy.   2. Social sciences—Philosophy.
I. Title
HM24.C698   1997   301'.01—dc21   96–24111
ISBN 0–19–878116–4
ISBN 0–19–878117–2 (Pbk)

10 9 8 7 6 5 4 3 2 1

Typeset by Hope Services (Abingdon) Ltd.
Printed in Great Britain
on acid-free paper by
Biddles, Ltd.,
Guildford & King's Lynn

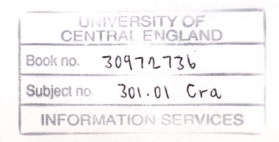

Preface

In this book, Ian Craib compellingly shows the value of studying such classic thinkers as Marx, Weber, Durkheim, and Simmel alongside the more popular contemporary questions of sociology. Providing an account of the key ideas of classical social theory, Dr Craib establishes their relevance today, their enduring significance, and their contribution to understanding contemporary problems.

Written in a direct, personal style, *Classical Social Theory*'s thematic structure helps the reader compare the theorists systematically, and the book-by-book approach pays close attention to each of thinkers' key texts, quoting the most important passages and analysing them in a clear, straightforward way.

Other student-friendly features include:

- Biographical details and an elementary overview of the work of Marx, Weber, Durkheim, and Simmel
- *Dramatis personae* at the end of the book, with brief details of the life and thought of other relevant thinkers
- Glossary covering important terms and phrases used in the text

How to use this book

Classical Social Theory is divided up into three parts, covering methodology (ways of thinking about thinking), conceptions of social structure (answers to the question 'what is society?'), and explanations of the nature of social change and historical development.

Each part contains a chapter on each theorist, so that you can either read the book from beginning to end to develop a comparative understanding of all four thinkers, or you can read the chapters on one individual thinker throughout, concentrating on the development of that thinker's theory.

Before you get to the three main parts, there are introductory chapters about this book and on the biographies and social and intellectual backgrounds of the individual thinkers.

Each chapter has suggestions for further reading at the end. Throughout the book you will find summary boxes, outlining the ideas just discussed and consolidating the different thinkers' views of them.

At the end of the book, there are various resources that you may wish to refer to as you go through. There is a list of other relevant thinkers of the time (the *Dramatis personae*), a Glossary, and the complete references for all the books mentioned in the text. Throughout the text, you'll see that the original publication dates are given for the classical texts along with the dates of current editions, so that you can see the development of the ideas as well as being able to get hold of complete versions of the relevant texts.

Acknowledgements

This book has emerged from several decades of discussion and argument with students and colleagues and I can thank only the most recent contributors to an ongoing process. I would like to thank in particular Ted Benton, David Lee, and John Scott, all of the Essex Sociology Department, for reading and commenting on sections of the manuscript. It would be nice to blame them for the book's deficiencies, but sadly I alone am responsible for those.

Contents

Chapter summaries

1. What's the point?

The purpose of the book: the continuing importance of the founding thinkers—the necessity of general theories—sociology's relationship to the Enlightenment; the two-sided nature of Enlightenment thought and of social theory; the basic dualisms of social theory; the structure of the book and how to read it. *How to think about the thinkers.*

2. The main characters and the main ideas

Brief biographies of the classical theorists (*Marx, Durkheim, Simmel*, and *Weber*), together with an elementary introduction to their ideas and intellectual background. *The social and intellectual background* to the rise of sociology.

PART 1. WHAT IS SOCIETY AND HOW DO WE STUDY IT?

....

Introduction to Part 1

3. Emile Durkheim: the discovery of social facts

Introduction: background; Comte and positivism. *Durkheim's rules*: the objectivity of social facts; considering social facts as things; the use of statistics to identify social facts; the normal and the pathological—the normality of crime. *Suicide as a social fact*: its underlying causes. *What can we take from Durkheim*: criticisms of Durkheim's methodology and discussion.

4. Karl Marx: the primacy of production

Introduction: the problems set by political misinterpretations of Marx; Marx and Darwin. *Marx's methods: the starting point*: the ideology of individualism; the importance of practical, everyday life; the action/structure dualism in Marx; comparison of Marx with Durkheim; dialectical thinking and the separation of analysis and history.

5. Max Weber: the primacy of social action

Introduction: comparison with Marx and Durkheim; Kantian background and the differences between the natural and the human sciences. *The proper object of sociology*: sociology's concern with the individual event and Weber's debate with Marx's ghost; the society/individual dualism; behaviour and action; meaningful social action; further comparison of Marx and Durkheim. *Different types of meaningful action. Understanding social action*: observational and explanatory understanding; causal adequacy and meaning adequacy. *The ideal type*: Weber's individualism and further comparison with Marx and Durkheim; scientific and common-sense knowledge. *Values and value-freedom.*

6. Georg Simmel: society as form and process—the outsider's view

Introduction: Simmel as a herald of postmodernism. *Society and the social*: his conception of society—comparison with Weber and Lukacs; social forms and the life process and the protection of individuality. *The social forms*: society, social relationships, social institutions, and play forms; his methods and organizational principles.

Conclusion to Part 1: the first basic dualism of social theory

---

PART 2. CONCEPTIONS OF SOCIAL STRUCTURE

....

Introduction to Part 2

7. Durkheim: drunk and orderly

Introduction

Social integration and system integration

Types of solidarity: *The Division of Labour*

Mechanical and organic solidarity: repressive law and the *conscience collective*; the function of the division of labour; Durkheim's functionalism; organic solidarity and restitutive law; individualism and dependency in modern societies; Durkheim and modern politics; the use of the organic analogy. *Abnormal forms of the division of labour*: understanding social conflict; industrialism and capitalism; the forced division of labour; managerial deficiencies.

The sociology of religion and knowledge

The nature of religion: the sacred/profane distinction; totemism; religious beliefs as representations of the social; comparison of Durkheim and Marx on religion. *The arguments in Elementary Forms*: Durkheim's causal, interpretive, and functional analyses of religion. Durkheimian analyses of contemporary societies. *The sociology of knowledge*: Durkheim's attempt at a sociological explanation of Kant's categories; the link between social structure and the structure of thought, the problems with Durkheim's sociology of knowledge and comparison with Marx's theory of ideology.

The sociology of morality and education

The conservative and radical Durkheim; the relation of morality to the social; morality in a period of change; sociology and morality; moral education and its aim; spontaneous education and direct teaching; discipline, authority, and power; the rational justification of moral rules; dignity, self-determination, and attachment to society; the humanistic goals of education and the balance of individual and society.

The sociology of the law, state, and politics

The evolution of punishment towards humanist ideals; the developing sympathy for the criminal; the power of the state; the distinction between governor and governed and the definition of the state; the governing of secondary groupings; the state as defender of individual rights; Durkheim and contemporary political debates.

Conclusion

The importance of Durkheim's insights; his contributions to understanding the basic dualisms of sociology.

8. Was Marx a Marxist?

Introduction

Marxism and popular prejudice and simplistic arguments; relationship between Marx's earlier and later works; his starting point in human action; comparison with Durkheim.

Human powers 1: the theory of alienation

Underlying conception of human nature—distinction from a theory of needs; human nature as a transformative power—humans change themselves through changing their environment. The alienation of the worker from the product, from work, and from co-workers and his/her own nature. Marxist idealism and its problems; the empirical study of alienation; the distinction between economic analysis and the analysis of ideas and action.

Human powers 2: commodity fetishism

The continuity between Marx's earlier and later work; commodity fetishism as the alienation of human relationships; the 'free' market.

Marxist economics: a brief and simple introduction

Classical and marginalist economics; the labour theory of value; use value and exchange value; labour power as a commodity with a use and exchange value; exploitation; surface appearances and underlying reality; capitalism as a system of regular crises; the central contradiction of capitalism—the forces and relations of production; Marx's sociological economics.

Social class

The place of class in Marxist theory; class-in-itself and class-for-itself. The peasantry and its need for strong leadership. The bourgeoisie and its different fractions. The petty bourgeoisie, traditional and new. The proletariat—working-class identity and shared experience; divisions in the proletariat and contemporary attempts to understand them. The lumpenproletariat and the underclass. The contemporary relevance of social class.

The state

Marx's political and analytic writings; the conspiracy theory of the state; the state as alienated human power and revolutionary democracy; comparison with Durkheim; economic explanations of the state and the possibility of its autonomy; the peaceful or violent transformation of the state; the class nature of the modern state; class and citizenship.

Ideology

Ideology as false consciousness and as non-science; ideology and social integration; ideas and the life process—parallels with modern sociology and psychology; ideology as alienation; economic determinist conceptions of ideology; ideology as illusion; ideology as imagination; ideology as the accurate perception of one level of reality; ideology and commodity fetishism; representation as ideology—the link with postmodernism; conclusion—the difficulties with deterministic notions.

Marxism and the family

Primitive communism; private property and the development of the pairing family; the linking of people and property; the social organization of sexuality and love; assessment of Engel's work.

Conclusion

Comparison with Durkheim; further development of the basic dualisms.

9. The liberal Weber

Introduction

Weber's complexity; Weber and Marx.

The fundamental concepts of sociology

Legitimacy; conflict; Weber's cautious evolutionism; communal relations based on identity; associative relations based on interest; corporate groups and different forms of control; the nature of politics and the state; power as an end in itself.

Weber's economic sociology

Weber's concern with the sociological preconditions of the capitalist economy; the advantages of the market; formal and substantive rationality; the stability offered by the market to precarious social and political institutions; free disposal over goods and free labour and other preconditions of the development of formally rational accounting in productive enterprises; different types of capitalism and the peculiarity of western capitalism.

Class, status, and party

Weber and a theory of social structure; comparison of Marx and Weber on social class; class situation as market situation and life chances; the possibility of solidary class relations; the complexity of class structure seen in Weberian terms; the possibility of combining Marxist and Weberian conceptions; status as social esteem and lifestyle and the ambiguity of Weber's concept; the relationships between class and status in Weber's and Marx's sense; status groups in contemporary society; status groups and educational qualifications; professional groups and self-interest—comparison with Durkheim; parties and their ineffectiveness—Weber's determinism.

Power, domination, and authority

Types of domination; charismatic leadership—comparison with Durkheim; the routinization of charisma; traditional patriarchal domination and its development into patrimonialism; feudalism and its development; legal-rational domination and the characteristics of the modern state; the absence of any absolute basis for authority; the basis of legitimacy in legal-rational domination; Weber's ideal type of bureaucracy.

Conclusion

The fragility of the social order.

10. Simmel: the social and the personal

Introduction

Simmel's originality; the mutual implications of Simmel and Durkheim.

Society and the individual

The evolution of the individual/group relation from a starting point of near merging; individuation and the development of individual norms; the paradox of the emergence of the individual and the growing power of the group; the development of multiple and conflict roles; similarities between Simmel and Parsons; Simmel's radical critique of universal institutions; the significance of the size of social groups; the dyad and its internal fragility; the move from the dyad to larger groups.

The Philosophy of Money

Value and exchange; human beings as valuing creatures; Simmel and existentialism; the objectification of subjective value; comparison with Marx; the exchange of value and the exchange of representations—Simmel and postmodernism; money as the extension of freedom and its psychological consequences; the growth of objective culture and the decreasing importance of the personality; Simmel's theory of alienation; the ambivalent implications of the division of labour; the decreasing ability to love objects; conclusion—Simmel and Marxism, Simmel and Weber.

Simmel's sociology

Simmel as a sociological impressionist. *Simmel on relationships*: faithfulness in the maintenance of relationships; the renegade; the distinctive nature of Simmel's notion of the life process; Simmel and Freud; gratitude as a cement for and generator of relationships; Simmel and Kleinian psychoanalysis; sociability as a play form and an example of formal sociology; domination as a form of interaction; domination by an individual, by a plurality, and by principle or law; comparison with Weber; conflict as a contribution to integration; the importance of secrecy; the secret society. *Simmel on social types*: the notion of type in literature and social theory; the miser as a seeker of total control; the miser's similarity to the spendthrift; the adventurer as an artist; the stranger as a newcomer and/or outsider; the objectivity of the outsider; objectivity as participation. *Simmel on modernity*: The psychological effects of urban living; the head ruling the heart; the sophistication of the town-dweller; the standardization of social life; the individual's conflicting needs for identification and separation and fashion as satisfying both; the psychological satisfactions of science; class and status differences in fashion. *Simmel on social groups*: the poor; different obligations and duties; the emergence of the poor as a group in modern societies through state welfare systems; modern developments of Simmel—the social construction of poverty; comparison with Marx; the aristocracy—united by the highest status honour; in-group marriage; the possibility of decadent emptiness; women, love, and sexuality: the masculine nature of objective culture; the psychological differences between men and women and comparison with modern gender theorists; the possibility of gender equality in relation to the objective culture; male and female sexuality; flirtation as a play form; Simmel's essentialism; comparison with Engels.

Conclusion

Simmel's compatibility with other theorists; further development of the basic dualisms.

Conclusion to Part 2: The theorists contrasted

PART 3. HISTORY AND SOCIAL CHANGE

Introduction to Part 3

11. Durkheim's organic analogy

Introduction

Durkheim on history and politics.

The organic analogy and Durkheim's theory of history

The explanation of change in the *Division of Labour*; change through population growth; primary and secondary factors in the division of labour; increasing universality of the *conscience collective* and the growing freedom of the individual; the importance of organic and psychological factors in the division of labour; Durkheim's materialism and his increasing concern with cultural patterns. The explanation of change in *The Rules of Sociological Method*; the classification of social types; the primitive horde and more complex combinations; societies as species; the distinction between society and civilization; critique of the species analogy; Durkheim and modern evolutionary theory.

Durkheim's conservatism and Durkheim's socialism

The debate about Durkheim's politics; the importance of placing limits on human nature; his critique of modernity and his critique of socialism as an ideological reaction to industrialization compared to sociology as a scientific reaction—comparison with Engels. Durkheim's liberal/left sympathies; the emphasis on the importance of professional groupings which would control the state (his syndicalism); his support for the Dreyfusards and his individualism—the sacredness of the individual in general; the importance of freedom of thought and the cognitive role of the state; the problem of politics and analysis in Durkheim; his conservative views on divorce and women.

Conclusion

The continuing importance of Durkheim as a theorist of society and social cohesion; the *conscience collective* in the modern world; the importance of his conception of the state as protector of the individual and civil society; his lack of a theory of action; criticism of his theory of history.

12. Marx and the meaning of history

Introduction

Marx's conception of history; Marx and Hegel; dialectical materialism and historical inevitability.

Historical laws and laws of history

Historical laws; Marx's originality; Marx's suggestions as explanation sketches.

Types of society/modes of production

Primitive communism: possible paths of social development starting from the priority of the community over the individual; forms of distributing the surplus; Marx's theoretical ordering of levels of development in terms of the development of individuality. *The Asiatic mode of production*: dominance of communal property and the despot; important role of the state and religion. *The Germanic mode of production*: the inevitable production of traditional relations. *The ancient mode of production*: dominated by the city; development of individual proprietorship; the emergence of the state; transformation brought about by the reproduction of the system. *Feudalism and the development of capitalism*: the ancient and the feudal modes; the town/country division and the division of labour; the development of the towns—the craft guilds—the merchant class—the bourgeoisie; machine production; the money economy; international markets. *Evolution from feudalism to capitalism*: a theoretical understanding of the development; comparison with Durkheim. *The complexities of class analysis of history*: the English Civil War as an example.

Theory and history

Theoretical and empirical distinctions: modern elaborations of the concept of mode of production. *Contemporary notions of evolution*: The nature of historical progress; open-ended conceptions of evolution.

The dynamics of capitalism

The tendency of the rate of profit to fall: living and dead labour and the increasing importance of the latter; countervailing tendencies; the increasing rate of technological change; the expansionist dynamic of capitalism. *Changes at other levels*: *transformations of the crisis*: Habermas on the evolution of modern capitalism; economic crisis—rationality crisis—legitimation crisis—motivation crisis.

Communism

The importance of the French Revolution; the proletariat as a revolution class; violence and revolution; the concept of overdetermination; the state and revolution; earlier and later phases of communism; the importance of utopian ideas; comparison with reality.

Conclusion

13. Weber as a tragic liberal: the rise of the West
Introduction

Weber's ghostly evolutionism.

The sociology of religion

Choices between tradition and progress/differentiation; prophecy and the growth of universality; a class analysis of religions, the latter producing action to change the world.

Chinese religion: Confucianism and Taoism

The power of the family giving power to the countryside over the town; the power of the central government; conflict between central government, its local officials, and local kin groups; the growth of capitalism restricted by the power of the family and the Confucian ethic which devalued economic activity; Taoism as a mystical alternative; comparison of Confucianism and Puritanism.

Indian religion: Hinduism and Buddhism

The caste system; distinction between sects and churches in relation to Hinduism; the Brahmins; the absence of a universal ethic, and of the possibility of social criticism in an eternal order; status conflict in the wider social order; the Brahmin ascetic ideal; the absence of a rationalized pursuit of wealth.

Palestine: ancient Judaism

The importance of positive ethical action and unintended consequences; the history of Israel and its special relationship to Jahwe; the emergence of new ideas on the edge of centres of civilization; prophecy and the prophets; Jahwe as a universal God.

The Protestant ethic and the spirit of capitalism

Introduction: the descriptive and analytic in Weber's work; the 'elective affinity' as an explanation; the work ethic in Weber's history. *The spirit of capitalism*: capitalism based on rational accounting; protestantism not originally associated with the accumulation of wealth association; Benjamin Franklin as the source of the ideal type of the spirit of capitalism; accumulation as the supreme good; the notion of a calling; moralized money-making versus traditionalism. *The Protestant ethic*: Protestantism as the origin of the rationality of European capitalism; Luther's notion of a calling; different forms of ascetic Protestantism; Calvin and predestination; worldly success as a sign of salvation; Calvinism as an ideal type; capitalism as an unintended consequence.

Conclusion

Weber's importance to modern sociology; Weber as a theorist of modernity; his view of socialism; the contribution of his religious studies to the basic dualisms; his theoretical ambivalence; his views on German politics.

14. Simmel: countering an overdose of history?

The decreasing importance of history in Simmel's work; his inversion of Marx; Simmel and Nietzsche; his critique of historicism; history as a genre; Simmel's place in differing existential traditions; his aesthetic perspective.

15. Conclusion: the framework of social theory

A discussion of the dualisms of social theory and what happens when they are ignored or when theorists attempt to transcend them; the necessary problems of social theory.

List of boxes

1 | What's the point?

The purpose of the book: the continuing importance of the founding thinkers—the necessity of general theories—sociology's relationship to the Enlightenment; the two-sided nature of Enlightenment thought and of social theory; the basic dualisms of social theory; *the structure of the book* and how to read it; *how to think about the thinkers.*

The purpose of the book

This is an introduction to the classical social theorists—primarily Karl Marx, Emile Durkheim, Max Weber, and Georg Simmel. There are two ways of treating such a text: it can be a historical survey, a history of ideas, or it can be a contribution to contemporary debates about society and about social theory itself: its aims, its scope, and its intentions. I hope this book will be more of the latter, and that it will introduce the reader as much to contemporary arguments about theory and society as to the nineteenth- and early twentieth-century arguments. We can't help looking at the past from the standpoint of the present, and each generation will see the past in a different way, just as we see our own lives differently as we grow older. It is better that this is explicit, rather than disguised under some attempt to find out what Marx—or whoever—*really* said. Such arguments can be important, but perhaps they do not belong to an introductory book.

A recurrent theme in what I will have to say is the apparently increasing rate of social change, on a technological level as well as in terms of social and geographical mobility and the nature of the labour market. It seems to me that this profoundly affects our sense of history and its meaning and that, at least in contemporary European and North American society, we are finding it increasingly difficult to experience ourselves as the products of what seems to be an irrelevant past. A symptom of this is that in the teaching of sociology at university level thirty years ago there was no question but that the founding thinkers of sociology were important figures and that reading nineteenth- and early twentieth-century sociology was not just a matter of historical interest, but also a way of understanding our own society, in fact a way of understanding all societies. Now this is questioned—there are suggestions that perhaps we don't need to teach the classical theorists any more, that what they say might be of historical interest, but that sociology, social theory, and society itself have developed well beyond the range of their work. It is all different now and the early theorists are of only academic interest.

I will try to make the case for studying them by considering some of the arguments that devalue their importance. It is sometimes argued that society itself has changed and that the old theories are no longer appropriate to changed conditions. This was the impetus behind Anthony Giddens's critique of the classical theorists in *Capitalism and Modern Social Theory* (1971). Such arguments have been around since the Second World War but it has always remained the case that the new 'theories' often reproduced old ideas in partial or disguised form. Many of the ideas that go under the label 'postmodernist' can, for example, be found in the work of Marx in the nineteenth and Simmel in the early twentieth centuries. Unless we are aware of the general theories of society that have framed the development of the social sciences, and profoundly and deeply and unavoidably embedded themselves in our ways of thinking about the social world, we are in danger either of constantly reinventing the wheel or of creating a situation where the wheel needs to be reinvented. It seems to me that this is what Giddens does, but that argument belongs elsewhere.

We should not think that the issues that concern us today have changed beyond recognition since the classical theorists were writing. The ideas that I will be examining are fundamental not only to the sociologist's understanding of society but to our everyday understanding; they have entered into the way we think about our social life and the way we conduct our political arguments, and they are part and parcel of those arguments themselves. I will be referring to many contemporary issues in the course of the book: the role of the state and the extent to which individuals are or should be responsible for their actions and their lives; the issue of crime and punishment; changes in the labour market which create increasing job insecurity; issues of wealth, poverty, and social class; the nature of morality; the modern concern with the 'self' and identity; the fragmentation of contemporary society; modern feminism; issues around multiculturalism; the significance of the market economy—all these will be directly relevant. Just as we cannot but work with some overall theory of society, some way of making moral and epistemological judgements, so we cannot but talk about these issues through the spectacles supplied by these theorists. They must be studied to understand the power that their ideas have over us even when we have not heard of them. They have, as it were, entered the air that we breathe. I will discuss the background of each of these thinkers, but, as I noted earlier, I will be less concerned with the historical development of their ideas than with their structure and meaning and their contemporary relevance.

The early thinkers had very little or absolutely nothing to say about some of the issues that concern us today—the information revolution and the packaging of knowledge and computer technology, for example; they were not fortune tellers. But they have provided us with *ways of understanding* these phenomena, ways of approaching them. This should become clear throughout the book, but especially in Part 1.

Many of the arguments against studying the classical theorists can be found under the label of 'postmodernism', an approach at the centre of modern theoretical debates. One argument is that the classical thinkers, particularly Marx and Durkheim, were offering general or 'totalizing' theories of society, but in fact social life is complex and multidimensional and cannot be grasped by one theory. I will argue in the course of this book that it is true that social life is multidimensional and cannot be grasped by one theory, but at the same time the very process of theoretical thinking pushes us towards general theories and we cannot avoid them. Giddens (1971) is critical of the attempt to see the classical theorists as offering a general theory of society but he spent the next two decades developing his own general theory of society—structuration theory—and the lesson is that we cannot *but* think in terms of a general theory of society; an attempt to explain or understand one social phenomenon will always have implications for understanding others, whether we like it or not. If you think about it, the statement that social life is multidimensional is itself a general theory, applying to all societies, and it raises the general theoretical problem of how different theories might relate to each other. That will be a central concern of this book. We *have* to work with general theory.

Amongst the postmodernist thinkers there is a more radical version of this criticism which has to do with sociology's relationship to the Enlightenment—that period during and around the eighteenth century that saw the growth of modern science and a new faith in the power of reason and the improvement of the human condition. Irving Zeitlin sums up what he calls the 'mind of the Enlightenment' as follows:

For the Enlightenment thinkers, all aspects of man's life and works were subject to critical examination—the various sciences, religious revelation, metaphysics, aesthetics, etc. These thinkers felt and sensed the many mighty forces impelling them along, but they refused to abandon themselves to these forces. Self-examination, an understanding of their own activity, their own society, their own time, was an essential function of thought. By knowing, understanding and recognizing the main forces and tendencies of their epoch, men could determine the direction and control the consequences of these forces. Through reason and science, men could achieve ever greater degrees of freedom, and therefore ever greater degrees of perfection. Intellectual progress, an idea that permeated the thinking of that age, was to serve constantly to further man's general progress. (Zeitlin 1968: 5)

Social theory has always had an ambivalent relationship to the Enlightenment: on the one hand, many would see it as growing out of and extending Enlightenment thought to society as a whole; others have seen it as a conservative reaction to the Enlightenment, emphasizing the power of community and tradition over the power and freedom of the individual (Nisbet 1967). There is an ambivalence in Enlightenment ideas themselves—Zeitlin talks about increased freedom and progress, on the one hand, but also about increased power to determine what happens in society, and therefore increased control over others.

Even the most pessimistic of the four theorists considered here—Weber and Simmel—still followed the Enlightenment course of constant questioning and the search for knowledge as a good thing in its own right. The postmodernist reaction to this questions both the search for scientific knowledge or truth and its relationship to human freedom. A leading postmodernist theorist, Jean-François Lyotard (1984) has argued that all knowledge comes in the form of a narrative—a story—and that there is no such thing as a meta-narrative, a story of stories that we might call Science or Reason. Much nineteenth-century theory, but particularly Marxism, laid claim to being a meta-narrative. The growth in modern communications and the resulting confrontation of alternative stories have finally shown that such theories are no more than further stories, no better or worse than others. This way of thinking is very closely related to a political argument: the Enlightenment, it is argued, was concerned with establishing hierarchies and systems of control over people. The founding thinkers of sociology all assume that there is a clear distinction between knowledge and non-knowledge (the latter category including, for example, the imagination or intuition or feeling), and that the former is more valuable than the latter. Scientific knowledge is continually making distinctions and establishing hierarchies.

These ideas and their sociological import are most clearly worked out in the work of Foucault (especially 1973, 1977, 1979). The Enlightenment thinkers saw a close relationship between knowledge and freedom: the more knowledge we gain the more free we can become. Foucault, drawing on the philosophy of Nietzsche, inverts that relationship. The link is not between knowledge and freedom, but between knowledge and power. The establishment of medical knowledge, or psychiatric knowledge, or knowledge about sexuality, for example, is the means by which those who work with this knowledge—doctors, psychiatrists, sexologists—establish a power over those who are subjects of the knowledge.

In this sense, all the nineteenth-century sociologists were concerned with establishing power, hierarchies of knowledge, and control over the social organization of people. This is most obvious in the case of Marxism, but the postmodernist argument would be that all meta-narratives are concerned with the organization of hierarchies and the exercise of power. Some would go further: the authors or proponents of the meta-theories are white males (some might add middle class to the list) and these theoretical systems exclude women and ethnic and sexual minorities. Against such meta-narratives, people juxtapose

tance of the knowledge of subordinate groups—women or blacks or
which is seen as an assertion of the multidimensional nature of truth and
ial reality, where all stories are equal, and the old white male meta-stories
no longer tenable. These are sometimes summed up in complaints about
having to learn the work of 'dead white men', and dead white men are very much
the subject of this book.

There are a number of counter-arguments to such a case, and importantly
there are counter-arguments that can accept some of the politics of the postmodernists without accepting their philosophical and epistemological position.
There are, I think, two decisive and very similar arguments against the overall
position. The first is that the argument against meta-narratives is itself a meta-
narrative—it is telling us a general story about knowledge, and making claims
about good and bad knowledge; 'good' knowledge on this account recognizes
that it is one story amongst others, and it lays claim to do nothing more than
enhance our experience of social reality. However, this sets up a hierarchy by
excluding knowledge which lays claim to be epistemologically superior; it out-
laws the grand narratives. It seems to me that it is the case that, just as we cannot but imply a general theory of society, so we cannot but engage in
distinguishing between good and bad knowledge, and so setting up hierarchies.
If I say that there can be no grand narrative that is better than all the others, I am
proposing a grand narrative which *I* think is better than all the others.

It is possible to argue that this sort of logical argument must take second place
to political necessity, that it is most urgent to include within social theory the
standpoint of the subordinate and oppressed groups, and in order to do that we
have to jettison the epistemological criteria which reinforce their oppression. I
can understand such an argument, but I think there is a case that this confuses
beyond hope epistemological and political criteria. It would mean that there is
no difference between making judgements about knowledge and judgements
about politics, whereas it seems to me that, whilst the two are closely related
(and the relationship will play an important part throughout the rest of this
book), they are not the same thing. There are ways of thinking about society and
the social world in which we can claim to offer a general theory of society,
together with the criteria which enable us to distinguish between good and bad
knowledge, and include the points of view of subordinate groups, even if those
groups reject epistemology altogether.

In any theoretical argument, or in any other argument come to that, it is a
good rule to be suspicious of either/or alternatives; it is almost invariably the
case that reality is made up of shades of grey. Although it is comforting to think
of the world in terms of heroes and villains, of unalloyed good facing unalloyed
evil, perhaps because it brings back the childhood comfort of fairy stories, it
rarely matches any external reality. The postmodernist argument seems to deal
in either/or alternatives. The starting point is that the Enlightenment, or science,
is seeking an absolute, a certain knowledge; because we cannot obtain such

knowledge, it makes the unreasonable claim that all knowledge clai[
equal status. It seems reasonable to me to suggest that we might not be
find an absolute truth, but we can distinguish between better and worse l
ledge claims; nor are we faced with a straightforward choice between close
hierarchies and open equality. Further, it does not follow that being able to distinguish between better and worse knowledge is the same thing as, or necessarily leads towards, distinguishing between better and worse people. The grounds
on which we judge knowledge are very different from the grounds on which we
judge people; the only indisputable thing is that we judge on every level; it is in
the nature of human thought to make distinctions of fact and value, even
though at times we might like to pretend to ourselves that we don't.

We have already seen that Enlightenment thought itself is ambivalent. The
Enlightenment notion of reason, for example, is double edged. On one reading
it *is* exclusive, narrow, instrumental; on another it is open and inclusive.[1] Both
possibilities are there and they are engaged in a complex relationship with each
other. One way in which the notion of reason, or rationality, may be elaborated
is as a universal human property: we are human beings, therefore we are rational
beings, or (if this strikes you as unlikely or hopelessly optimistic) we have the
capacity for rational thought and action. This and similar notions (such as the
idea that knowledge comes from our sense experience) were central to the
democratic impulse behind the Enlightenment; such ideas meant that knowledge was something each person could arrive at, assess, and understand for
themselves—it no longer had to be handed down and taken on trust from our
social superiors.

From this point of view, rationality can be taken as a standard by means of
which societies can be judged as good or bad; a society, for example, which
excludes some of its members from the political process because they are black,
or because they are women, or because they are disabled, is acting irrationally;
as is a society which provides differential access to political debate. More positively, it is possible to construct models for participation—Jürgen Habermas
(1984, 1987), for example, talks about an 'ideal speech situation' where all participants have equal access to relevant information and equal opportunity to
participate in debate. If we follow these ideas then we end up with an ideal which
combines knowledge, scientific knowledge, and the sort of participation in public debate desired by the postmodernists. In his work in the philosophy of science, Habermas (1972) suggests that the most developed forms of human
science pursue what he calls an 'emancipatory' interest, a desire to free human
beings from avoidable physical and material restraints and a desire to cut a way
through mutual misunderstanding and the exercise of power through exclusive

---

[1] The complexity of Enlightenment thought and its double-edged nature, as well as the radical
interpretation the I am presenting here, has been worked out most clearly over the last fifty years
by the school of thought known as 'critical theory'. See in particular Adorno and Horkheimer
(1972), Held (1980), Habermas (1990).

possession of knowledge. He uses psychoanalysis as an example of such a science: to begin with the analyst possesses knowledge and the analysand is ignorant; at the end of the process they are able to communicate as equals.

My own view is that these two interpretations of the Enlightenment are two sides of the same coin: we cannot have one without the other, and if we try to leave the Enlightenment behind us, we might get away from hierarchies of knowledge but we also lose the possibility of freedom. My account of the founding thinkers of sociology will employ both interpretations as a framework for understanding the founding thinkers, but my emphasis will be on what I shall call the radical rather than the conservative interpretation of the Enlightenment: the ways in which these ideas are steps towards a knowledge of the social world, and, through such knowledge, steps towards some form of human liberation. It is this side which I think modern social theory risks losing.

The double-edged nature of theory will become apparent in other ways. I will argue that we can look at each of the founding thinkers in terms of his approach to four crucial dualisms—four sets of alternatives. Any social theory has to take account of both sides of each dualism and the choice of one or the other side to start with can move the theorist in very different directions; and any attempt to collapse them into one another means that there will be large ranges of phenomena which cannot be discussed. Unfortunately many modern theorists, most recently Anthony Giddens, but in the middle part of this century Talcott Parsons, try to collapse them into each other and I do not think this can be done—each refers to real and different aspects of the world and we have to take account of all of them. I do not think it is possible to develop one coherent, unified social theory.

The four dualisms which provide an organizing framework for social theory are:

1. *Individual/society*: any social theory must say or imply something about individuals and their relationships to whatever it is we call society and vice versa. The crucial question is which takes priority.

2. *Action/structure*: this is slightly different. Any social theory has to say something about human action, whether it be individual or collective, and about social structure—the *organization* of society. Again the crucial question is which takes priority.

3. *Social integration/system integration*: this is a development of the action/ structure dualism. *Social integration* refers to what it is that relates actors or individuals within society; *system integration* refers to what relates different parts of a society. Integration does not mean harmony—individuals and parts of a society may be related through conflict.

4. *Modernity/capitalism–socialism*: the fourth dualism is rather different in that the first three would be relevant whatever society we were studying, but this last is relevant only to modern society since the industrial revolution. It is,

therefore, a secondary dualism. Each of the theorists considered here as well as contemporary theorists has to consider whether the features of contemporary society are the result of one particular form of society—capitalism—and whether they might be transformed by another—socialism—or whether they are the more or less inevitable result of modern society *per se*.

Each of these will become relevant at a different time and I will be elaborating on each of them throughout the book.

The structure of the book

After the introductory chapters, the book will be divided into three parts. Each part will contain a chapter on each theorist. The book can thus be read in two ways: the 'normal' way from beginning to end to develop a comparative understanding of all four thinkers; this will provide the reader with an idea of the scope of classical social theory, its complexity, and the way different ideas interrelate. Or it can be read as an account of one of four different thinkers; the reader could concentrate, say, on the chapters on Durkheim, glossing over the comparisons when they are not relevant and concentrating on the substantive account of the one thinker's theory.

Chapter 2 of the introductory section will tell the story of each of the main thinkers, their biographical details and what we know of their personal lives together with an elementary introduction to their work—this should set the scene for people completely new to the area. There will also be a brief account of the conditions under which sociology developed. This section is complemented by the *Dramatis personae* at the end. Here I offer brief biographies of the other dead white men mentioned in the book, which will give you some further basic historical information. You can refer to this when you come across an unfamiliar name of someone writing in the first part of this century or in the last century.

Part 1 will be concerned with methodology in its broadest sense, on the level not of questionnaire surveys or participant observation, but of ways of thinking about thinking. What is this peculiar thing called theory and how does it relate to what might be called reality? What goes on when we theorize, and how is it different from everyday, 'normal' ways of thinking? Is social theory, in some sense or another, scientific and if so, in what sense? What methodology or methodologies, in the narrower sense, are implied by this particular way of thinking about society? At the end of these chapters it will be possible to map out the levels of social reality and the dualisms with which classical theory was concerned.

Part 2 is concerned with conceptions of social structure—answers to the question: what is society? This is the meat (or, if you're a vegetarian, the nut roast) of sociology. Is society made up only of individual people in different types of relationships, and if so what are these relationships? Are some types of relationship more important than others? Or are social groups, such as classes or status groups, more important than individuals? Or is 'society' something which exists over and above individuals? Who exercises power in society and how? What are the relationships between different parts of society?

Part 3 looks at explanations of the nature of social change and historical development. Is modern society caught in a process of increasing rationalization and bureaucratization, or is it driven forward by economic development or conflict between social classes, or by a process of different social institutions adjusting to each other? Or is it none of these things and is social change a much more haphazard, irrational process than we might suppose? In addition each theorist's work contains a critique of his existing society and a vision of what should be—the society which is possible—and through the way in which each explains social change we can look at how he expected the modern world to develop and what he expected to happen.

How to think about the thinkers

It is tempting to preach about the best attitude to adopt when using this book—so tempting, in fact, that I am going to do it. I suggested earlier that classical social theory has entered into our own way of thinking about issues, whether we know it or not; we cannot *but* look through the spectacles that it has created. If you look at particular areas and particular issues that interest you, you are likely to find a gut reaction: one approach or another will articulate what you are already thinking, or will put into words the way in which you think about society and social relationships. This could be a tenuous toehold on the sheer rock face of social theory—at last something I can understand or get hold of!—or it could be the entrance to a large cave—yes, I can understand and develop this way of looking at things. Either way, this is the starting point for further exploration. If, say, it is Marx's theory of alienation that grabs you first, then you can follow this up by exploring the other sections about Marx, leaving the ones that seem most difficult to the last.

My own way of entering into this immense area when I was a student was to take a partisan attitude: I was a Marxist and later, as my pretensions grew, an Existentialist Marxist—the capital letters give a good idea of how pretentious I was. I know many people who have entered social theory through a similar partisanship, although not necessarily with Marx. This might not be everybody's way of proceeding, but if it becomes important to justify the position you sympathize with, you do an awful lot of thinking about social theory; in fact, you begin to make it a familiar part of the world in which you live.

This stage can be difficult enough, but there is another, more difficult stage. It is sometimes tempting to remain a partisan—and perhaps as a citizen engaged in what passes as a democratic political process it is a good thing to remain partisan—but creative thought in social theory does not come only from partisan arguments. Sometimes sociologists will argue as if the different approaches were contestants in some immense sporting contest which would end with one winner. But theories are not generally eliminated through argument. We still read the nineteenth- and early twentieth-century social theorists, and indeed seventeenth- and eighteenth-century social theorists, because something of what they say corresponds with our experience and our knowledge of contemporary society, and ideas do not survive that long if they are simply wrong. Each of the thinkers we will look at in this text grasps, more or less adequately, some crucial aspect of society and social life; exactly how these aspects are related is another matter, beyond the scope of this introduction and really beyond the scope of this book. Suffice it to say that it is not enough to adopt one thinker and cling to him without moving, however necessary that might be at the beginning. To enter fully into thinking about society, we need to understand and in some way come to terms with the truth of other approaches—we need to spend a lot of time *thinking against ourselves* and changing our ideas. So when you feel comfortable with the thinker who most closely approximates your own prejudices (in the sense of pre-judgements, your gut ways of thinking about the social world), you need to move on to the others—if you are brave, starting with the one furthest away from your gut prejudices.

So when you take up this book, be prepared first for the pleasure of finding out what you already think, and learning to think it, and then for the painful task of changing your mind.

2 | The main characters and the main ideas

Brief biographies of the classical theorists (Marx, Durkheim, Simmel, and Weber), together with an elementary introduction to their ideas and intellectual background. The social and intellectual background to the rise of sociology.

Introduction

When I start setting out the classical theorists in a systematic way I will begin with Durkheim, perhaps the most sociological of the early sociologists and a useful point of comparison. In this chapter, however, I am interested in the historical background and I will start with the earliest of the four, Karl Marx (1818–83), whose political importance and chronological position means that the others are conventionally seen in relation to him. The other three are almost contemporaries, Emile Durkheim and Georg Simmel were both born in 1858, Durkheim dying in 1917, and Simmel a year later, whilst Max Weber was born in 1864 and died in 1920. These are not the earliest social theorists by any means, but they are the ones who have 'stuck' and whose ideas still form the framework for modern social thought. Their ideas have stuck, I would suggest, because they are more coherent and inclusive than those of other contemporaries.

I will set out both biographical details and an elementary introduction to their ideas and the intellectual traditions they come from, and follow this by talking about the social conditions which gave rise to sociology.

Karl Marx (1818–1883)

Marx was born to a large Jewish family—he had seven brothers and sisters—in Prussia; he came from a long line of rabbis, which ended with his father, who was baptized to avoid persecution. In 1836 he went to study law at the University of Bonn, already secretly engaged to Jenny von Westphalen. He is reputed to have led a riotous existence, spending money, drinking, duelling, and writing poetry. A year later he transferred to Berlin, where he became a reformed character, coming under the influence of a group of radical thinkers and deciding to take up an academic career. However, his association with radical thinkers got in the way and, when he left Berlin in 1841, he embarked on a life of radical journalism. The first paper for which he worked was closed after an attack on the Russian Absolutist monarchy, and after marrying Jenny he moved, in 1843, to Paris, living communally with a group with whom he intended to start a new journal. This ran only to one issue, but whilst in Paris Marx began his critiques of the German idealist philosopher, G. W. F. Hegel, and his studies of the British economists, Adam Smith and David Ricardo, and his confrontations with French socialism. In 1845 he was expelled by the French government, under pressure from Prussia, and moved to Brussels, where he began his lifelong collaboration with Friedrich Engels.

In 1847 Marx and Engels attended the second conference of the Communist League in London, out of which came *The Communist Manifesto* (Marx 1848/ 1968*a*).[1] The year 1848 was one first of revolutionary upheavals and then of oppression. As he was being expelled from Brussels for breaking his promise not to engage in political journalism, so he was invited to Paris by the leaders of a popular uprising against King Louis Philippe; he then returned to Prussia, where there were also liberal stirrings. Then later that year a spontaneous uprising in Paris was crushed and the Prussian king reasserted his control and Marx ended up in what was to be a permanent exile in London.

He continued to engage in political organization, writing, and disputes, including the founding of the First International Working Man's Association in 1866 and its demise after he split with the anarchist Bakunin in 1872; and he continued with his scientific work—his research into philosophy and economics, culminating with the three volumes of *Capital*. He earned a living by journalism, which he resented—the 'journalistic muck' which kept him away from his real research. During the 1850s and early 1860s this provided him with an often precarious living. In 1852 his daughter Franziska died and he wrote that he could not afford medicine for his family and they were living on bread and potatoes. In 1855 his son Edgar died. Things slowly improved through inheritance and the support of Engels, who had inherited his father's business in Manchester. During the last ten years of his life he suffered from ill health and he never recovered from Jenny's death in 1881, dying himself two years later.

For present purposes it is most useful to think of Marx's ideas as working on three levels: the philosophical, the economic, and the political, all intimately interconnected. His politics is at the centre. As a young man he was caught up with the ideas of the French Revolution of 1789, which, under its slogan of liberty, equality, and fraternity, had generated a new liberalism, and with exploring the failure of the Revolution to make these ideas reality. The philosophical

---

[1] When I refer to major classical texts I will include the original date of publication or of writing (if they are different) and the date of a recent edition which should be more readily available.

tradition against which he was defining himself was German idealism—particularly the work of Hegel.[2] The simplest—rather, the crudest—definition of 'idealism' is the view that the social world is the product of ideas, that we develop ideas and then make them actual, and that history is the steady realization of thought, of Reason. Marx's critique of Hegel was, famously, to turn him on his head—to argue that ideas grew out of human life, the material basis of society.

It was the attempt to understand the material basis which led to Marx's study of economics. His argument concerned itself with a number of levels. Technology is important—the growth of machine production in large factories, for example, brought together large numbers of workers in one place and enabled the formation of trade unions. The experience of day-to-day production, whether in a factory, in a small workshop, or in the fields, shaped the way people thought about the world and politics. Also important were what Marx called the 'relations of production', property relationships: whether people owned or did not own machines and land, whether they earned their living by selling their ability to labour, whether they employed or did not employ workers. These property relationships allocated people to social classes, and their work experience gave them a shared view of the world. These ideas were developed through a critique of the classical economists, primarily Adam Smith and David Ricardo, and Marx came to argue that the failure of the French Revolution had to do with the level of economic development of French society.

The life of the state and the political life of a society, Marx argued, was a result of the struggle for power which occurred between these classes. The state was the means by which the ruling class established its power over subordinate classes. The most radical class, the class that would be able to realize the liberty, equality, and fraternity that could not be realized by the French Revolution, was the new working class. They could achieve a real equality because there was nobody below them in the social order—they had nothing to lose but their chains.

At the centre of Marx's theory, then, is the idea that the economic organization of society is the most important level of social organization, and the major influence on the political, social, and intellectual life of the society. Economically based social classes are the major forces which push societies forward to an ideal state of communism. All this will be explained in more detail, and with a lot more precision, later.

Emile Durkheim (1858–1917)

Durkheim, too, was born into a Jewish, rabbinical family and was initially expected to follow his father into the priesthood. Biographers seem to agree

[2] You need to be fairly enthusiastic to follow up Hegel's work; the best introduction I know is Charles Taylor (1977); the best starting-point for Hegel himself is *The Phenomenology of Spirit* (1977) but you should approach it with a commentary.

that, although he broke away from the faith and called himself an agnostic, the work habits he learnt at the beginning of his training as a rabbi stayed with him for the rest of his life. Whereas Marx had a comparatively adventurous life, often beset by poverty and chased round Europe by reactionary governments whilst trying to organize revolutionary movements, Durkheim seems to have led the life of a quiet but hard-working and productive academic, touched by tragedy when his only son was killed in the First World War, an event which seemed to hasten his own death a couple of years later.

His academic career was distinguished, although in 1876 it began with two failures to gain entrance into the élite *École Normale Supérieure*, but when he did get there he was recognized as brilliant. He concerned himself with social and political philosophy, in particular Auguste Comte's attempt to develop sociology (although, according to Anthony Giddens (1978), he thought the term was a 'barbarous neologism') and Kantian philosophy, another strand of German idealism. After graduation he taught philosophy in schools and spent a year studying in Germany. On his return in 1887 he took up a post in the University of Bordeaux, marrying in the same year. In 1902 he moved to a chair of education, later education and sociology, at the Sorbonne, where he remained until his death. Soon after his son's death, he suffered a stroke from which he never fully recovered.

He is often wrongly characterized as sociology's conservative thinker, an opposite to Marx. Whilst he seems to have had little time for revolutionary socialism, he was nevertheless a reforming liberal or socialist in political terms. His one public political intervention was in defence of Alfred Dreyfus—a famous case of a Jewish army officer unjustly scapegoated for the misdeeds of the army establishment—and took the form of a liberal defence of individualism. His immediate intellectual background was the work of Comte, who was concerned with the development of social science as the final stage in the triumph of the sciences over metaphysical thought and he thought that sociology in particular would put an end to political debates about how society should be organized. For Durkheim this was a matter of showing that sociology had its own proper object, distinct from the objects, say, of psychology and biology, and that it could be studied by accepted scientific methods. This was the aim of two major works: *The Rules of Sociological Method* (1895/1964) and *Suicide* (1897/1952), where he argued that the job of sociology is to study *social facts*, regularities, which are often identifiable statistically—as, for example, in official suicide and crime figures—and which can be shown to depend not on the will of individuals but on the type of society in which individuals live. His attempt to establish sociology as an independent science was not just an intellectual enterprise but also a practical one. In the same year that *Suicide* was published, he founded *L'Année sociologique*—a famous journal intended to bring together the latest research in the area, and which contributed towards the establishment of his own sociological approach as a school.

A second intellectual focus was on the evolutionary change in society from one form of social cohesion to another and in particular the role of individualism in modern societies. This was the centre of attention in *The Division of Labour in Society* (1893/1984). He argued that, despite the apparent collapse of traditional communities and the growth of individualism, modern society was not falling apart. It was being held together not by shared beliefs, as were traditional societies, but by the division of labour, our economic dependence on each other. However, a shared moral basis was necessary to the social order, and Durkheim saw the religion that provided this in traditional societies being replaced by a philosophy of individualism. His concern with religion, with shared beliefs, produced his last major work, *The Elementary Forms of the Religious Life,* (1912/1915), and guided his concerns with education and moral philosophy as well.

Although the division of labour was important for Durkheim, it was not at the basis of his social theory. Unlike Marx, he did not see the economic level of social organization as providing the basis for all others, and he was much more concerned with shared beliefs. He thought that class conflict was a temporary abnormality in social development, and far from seeing the state as Marx did as the way in which one social class established its role over another, he saw it as a mediator, ensuring smooth development during modernization. In this sense he was not the political opposite of Marx but his theoretical opposite. The Kantian idealist tradition in which he worked, when it is taken into the social sciences, is concerned with the ways in which our thought, our ideas, and our ways of thinking organize the social world.

Georg Simmel (1858–1918)

Georg Simmel was neither a political revolutionary nor a successful career academic—it was only near the end of his life that he was offered the chair of philosophy at the University of Strasbourg, which was not regarded as a major university. He was born in Berlin and directly and indirectly he was the theorist of metropolitan life, attributing much of his achievement to living most of his life in that city. He maintained that nobody in his house possessed an intellectual culture and he put one together for himself at Berlin University. His first doctorate was rejected in 1880. According to Frisby (1984), the examiners were not even impressed with his empirical survey of yodelling. A dissertation on Immanuel Kant gained him his doctorate a year later, and from 1885 he was qualified to teach in Berlin at a level roughly approximate to junior lecturer, and he continued at this level until 1900.

Simmel, to the best of my knowledge, was the only one of the founding thinkers of sociology to have an attempt made on his life (Frisby 1984). He is reputed to have been a brilliant lecturer, thinking spontaneously and on the spot. One of his hearers described him as not a teacher but an 'inciter', (Simmel 1950), and he seemed to have evoked a similar response in his reputation as a thinker. He was proud of the number of students he could attract to his courses and he allowed women to attend as 'guest' students long before they were entitled to become full students. It was, according to Frisby, a combination of this sort of action, plus the fact that he attracted students from eastern Europe, and associated with socialists in the early part of his career, that held back his academic progress. But all commentators seem to agree that above all he was held back by anti-Semitism, by his colleagues' jealousy of his popularity, and by a suspicion of the new discipline of sociology. When he got his chair at Strasbourg he was not terribly impressed with his new colleagues—'a half-witted bunch'. In Berlin he had built up a network of artists and intellectuals, including Max Weber, the philosopher Henri Bergson, the poets Stefan Georg and Rainer Maria Rilke, and the sculptor Auguste Rodin. Amongst his students were the sociologist Karl Mannheim and the Marxist philosophers Georg Lukacs and Ernst Bloch. Compared with such central figures it is not surprising that Simmel found his new colleagues dull.

It is difficult to sum up Simmel's theory in the same way as one can that of Marx and Durkheim. In one sense, one could say that he didn't have a theory, although he had an awful lot of interesting theoretical things to say. He had a highly individual way of looking at the world and he is often compared with Goffman in this respect. However, his range of interests and his knowledge were much wider that Goffman's. In the earlier part of his career his focus seemed primarily to be on psychology and social psychology, then moving on to sociology, but throughout there was an interest in philosophy. His doctoral dissertation was on Kant, but he later developed an important interest in Schopenhauer and Nietzsche. Towards the end of his career, he turned to art and aesthetics.

He developed what he called a formal sociology, coming from his interest in Kant; an investigation into how human beings imposed forms on the world of experience, organizing and making sense of it. This is idealist, in the sense that it sees the world not so much as a product of thought, as did Hegel, but as organized by thought. The particular forms which interested Simmel were those of relationships between individuals and groups. His books were largely collections of essays, but the titles of the translations give a good idea of his subject matter: *Conflict and the Web of Group Affiliations* (1955); *On Individuality and Social Forms* (1971); *The Conflict in Modern Culture and Other Essays* (1968). The comparison with Goffman is often extended to link these aspects of Simmel's work with the development in America of symbolic interactionism.

But at the same time there were Simmel's socialist connections, particularly in the early stages of his career and one of his major books, *The Philosophy of Money* (1900/1990), is much closer to Marxism—particularly the Marx of the *Economic and Philosophic Manuscripts of 1844* and the section of *Capital* on commodity fetishism, of which more later. It is here that Simmel links his ideas of the ways in which relationships between people, and individual psychologies, change with the development of modernity and the money economy. In this book he often seems to come closer to a materialist explanation than to a philosophical understanding of the forms of human relationships and the developments of individual psychology.

Simmel is increasingly seen as a forerunner of postmodernism. I shall argue later that there is a degree of truth in this, but there is also a sense in which Simmel goes beyond postmodernism—but he certainly identified one important process which is often regarded as a recent sociological insight. This is the way in which the development of social forms moulds individual lives into socially acceptable behaviour. It is his response to this which takes him to his concern with aesthetics—it is as if ithe only way in which the individual can save his or her spontaneity is by living life as if it were an art form. Many of these ideas link Simmel to existentialist philosophy as well as to later sociological traditions. I was thinking especially of Simmel's sociology when I warned of the danger of reinventing the wheel in our ignorance that it had already been invented.

Max Weber (1864–1920)

Weber's life, and his psyche, have proved a happy hunting ground for amateur psychoanalysts, since for many of his fifty-six years he struggled with what has variously been called a breakdown or melancholia or what would probably be called depression. He was born in Erfurt in what until recently was East Germany, but the family soon moved to Berlin. The root of his trouble was the contrast between his mother and his father, and it was as if he were trying to mediate between the two, and bring them together in his person, his life, and his theory. His father was a lawyer and liberal parliamentarian and a man of action. According to R. Bendix (1966: 1), 'his mother was a woman of culture and piety whose humanitarian and religious interests were not shared by her husband'. It seems that Weber would occasionally try to become, or think about becoming, the man of action and rapidly retreat. He grew up in an environment of political and academic discussion—the society of professors and politicians.

In 1882 he went to study jurisprudence—the law—at the University of Heidelberg and, like Marx, went through his spell of spending, drinking, carousing, and duelling. After military service, he studied at the universities of Berlin and Göttingen. His academic work began with legal studies, but at the same time, while he was trying to qualify for the bar, he showed an interest in the problems of agrarian societies. In 1893 he married. After a couple of years of teaching in Berlin, he moved to Freiburg in 1895 and then back to Heidelberg in 1896. The following year his difficulties began. Frank Parkin (1982) describes him as spending the rest of his life as though on a kind of prolonged sabbatical, although I am not sure that this is entirely fair. However, Parkin's account of the onset of the problem is worth quoting in full:

His illness occurred soon after the death of his father. Weber senior was by all accounts a bad caricature of the Victorian paterfamilias—a martinet to his children, overbearing and insensitive towards his wife. Shortly before his death, he and Max had quarrelled violently. It was something to do with the son's insistence that his mother be allowed to visit him unaccompanied by his father, whom he regarded as a bit of a lout. The row culminated in Weber junior doing the unthinkable and ordering his father from the house. Max never saw his father alive again. On learning of the old man's sudden death he was consumed by guilt and remorse. He then became virtually catatonic.   (Parkin 1982: 14)

He tried, with some success, to deal with his difficulties by running away from them, travelling around Europe and then to the USA, where he began to return to studying and writing, and then, despite recurrent depressions, he became immensely productive. Parkin suggests that today no one could ever master the fields of law, history, and social sciences in the way that he did. He pursued his studies and his arguments with a care and determination that is rarely matched, and he infused his work with a passion that was also present in his lectures.

During the First World War he directed army hospitals in Heidelberg and served on various government committees. Towards the end of his life he accepted a chair at Munich, but this seemed to throw him back into psychological turmoil. At the same time he longed to be a man of action, and he was a dedicated nationalist, to the extent that he is sometimes accused—at least by left-wing students—of being a forerunner of the Nazis. It will become apparent later that I think that this accusation is mistaken. Of course his political activity was ineffective; when he sought nomination as a candidate for the new German Democratic Party at the end of war, he did not canvass support and was very upset when he did not get the nomination. He seemed to share a fantasy with his wife that the nation would call on him in its hour of need.

Bendix sums up the contradiction of Weber's personality neatly: 'he continuously engaged in the simultaneous effort to be a man of science with the strenuous vigour more common in a man of action, and to be a man of action with all the ethical rigor and personal detachment more common in a man of science' (Bendix 1966: 6).

If Weber's personality and his life were full of paradoxes, then so was his work. It will become apparent that there is a sense in which he does not have a conception of 'society' as a social system at all, although he famously talks about the 'iron cage' of capitalism in which we all become caught. It is certainly true that he had a heightened sense of the precariousness of the social order. His starting point was a variant of Kantian philosophy, which argued that the basis of the human sciences was different from that of the natural sciences. Thus sociology would not be a science in the same sense of physics or chemistry. The social sciences were sciences because people behaved rationally and it was possible to construct rational explanations of their actions. The social order produced in such a way was shaky, not least because of the struggle for power between different groups at the heart of politics, and the market economy was particularly important because it acted as a source of stability, holding people in relationships with each other.

In this respect Weber is the founding sociologist at the liberal end of the political spectrum, and much of what he has to say about politics and social life is still familiar today in the mouth of the proponents of the free market, and there is an important sense in which it imposes rational action upon people. The origin of this type of rational action—Weber sometimes calls it rational calculability and others call it instrumental rationality—is of central interest to Weber the sociologist. He saw such rationality and the development of capitalism itself as a specifically European phenomena. In a series of massive studies of the world religions he tried to demonstrate that what was specific to Europe was a particular development of Christian belief—Protestantism—and its effects on economic behaviour. An equivalent to Protestantism did not exist in the other world religions, even where the other preconditions of capitalist development did exist.

It is often said that Weber was always arguing against Marx's ghost, and one might think from the above account that he was arguing that it was ideas and not economic relationships that determined social development. In fact he was at great pains to point out that social developments had many causes and some aspects of his studies of the world religions could have come just as well from the pen of a sophisticated Marxist. And, in so far as he developed a theory of social structure, he saw it not as dominated by social classes, but as a combination of multiple social classes, status groups, and political parties vying for power. He was not a man to espouse simple causal processes.

There was inevitably a paradox in the way he regarded all this; again Bendix sums it up well: 'He left no doubt that his profound personal commitment to the cause of reason and freedom had guided his choice to subject matter; and his research left no doubt that reason and freedom in the Western world were in jeopardy' (Bendix 1966: 9). Bendix goes on to suggest that Weber's commitment to German nationalism must be understood not in the terms that we might see it after the rise of the Nazis but as a commitment to Germany's mission to protect the reason and freedom set in motion by the Enlightenment. He was ambivalent even about the triumph of reason; the triumph of bureaucratic organization was not something to be welcomed and, with the process of rationalization, contributed to the 'disenchantment' of the world Throughout, I will emphasize the paradoxes of Weber's thought: from individualism to the iron cage; from the free market to political struggles for power between different social groups; from rationality to disenchantment.

The social and intellectual background

Any attempt to divide history into periods can only be very approximate; it is next to impossible to find a beginning to anything and the history of social theory could be said to begin with Greek philosophy; a good, short history can be found in the first couple of chapters of Swingewood (1991). We can say with reasonable certainty that there were important changes in the way that people thought about the world that emerged in the Enlightenment and continued through the eighteenth century, and that the emergence of social theory through the nineteenth and twentieth centuries is the fruition of these changes. We can also say that these changes are parallel to radical changes in the everyday life of people living in Europe, particularly northern Europe, and that these changes are still continuing and have spread throughout the world. The four thinkers discussed here set the framework for making sense of these changes and do so within the framework set for them by the Enlightenment. The division of philosophy into empiricist and rationalist traditions—that knowledge must be based on sense experience or on reason—provides a frame for the divisions and oppositions in social theory.

However, here I want to concentrate on the social changes that transformed so many people's lives. They too go back over the centuries, beginning in northwest Europe and particularly in Britain. The economy had begun to change as early as the thirteenth century, when the Black Death—bubonic plague—had laid waste the labour force, and the habit of paying workers developed as a way of attracting labour. Over a long period the growth of sheep farming, which needs little labour, and the wool trade, set the conditions for a capitalist agriculture to develop—agricultural wage labourers replaced peasants and a developing market system encouraged farming for profit rather than subsistence. By the eighteenth century, the growth of capitalist farming encouraged new very productive technological changes in farming and fed a process of rapid technological change which we now take for granted. Capitalist agriculture produced profits which financed the new forms of production made possible by technological developments; workers were forced off the land and wandered around often in large unemployed groups until they were absorbed into the new factories in the growing towns.

The first change, then, is the growth of capitalism and the primacy of the money economy, which was especially important for Marx and Simmel. The industrial revolution, which was at its height in Britain from 1750 to 1850, was the second change, bringing people together into large groups—larger than ever before, forcing them into closer contact than ever before, and sharing similar living conditions—in the case of the workers, often appalling living conditions. The third change is now known to sociologists as urbanization—the growth of larger and larger towns, eventually into huge conurbations which dominate the way of life of those who remain in the country.

These changes may have taken centuries to develop, but the speed with which they came to fruition and changed lives was new and dramatic, and beyond the understanding of more traditional ways of looking at the world. They demanded new forms of thinking, new ways of seeing the world. To begin with, there was the experience of people moving together into large groups, sharing common conditions. This was most evident in the case of the poor and the new workers, who were often the source of social unrest. People trying to make sense of all this started in the course of the nineteenth century to talk in terms of 'class' and 'social class', a way of looking at the world which was to be developed furthest by Marx and later Marxists.

The process of industrialization brought immense increases in productive capacity, not least through the division of labour that became possible through large-scale factory production. The nature of people's lives was changed in this respect as well. The family lost its status as a productive unit, and work became something which happened outside the home; traditional communities and ways of life were often washed away. Whereas Durkheim was concerned with this change in his elaboration of the way in which the division of labour itself provided a new source of social cohesion, Marx was critical of its alienating potential, and Weber of the rationalizing dynamic behind it all. The division of labour and the market economy produced an individualizing effect as well which paralleled the opposite tendency to grouping people into classes. This is something which Durkheim in particular identified and gave a central place to in his work. Factory production also brought a new discipline to people, who came to be dominated by the clock and the organization of the workplace. For thinkers like Weber, this growing individualism and rationalization provided not only the central topic for social theory but also its methodology.

Living in towns also placed new demands on the individual personality: it demanded the development of a sort of shell to protect against the constant bombardment of new stimuli, and it replaced traditional forms of relationship, few in number and comparatively deep in nature, with a new way of living involving possibly larger numbers of comparatively shallow, surface relationships. This, coupled with the new and increasing interest in the individual, drove the development of psychology and towards the end of the nineteenth century gave birth to psychoanalysis. Of the thinkers discussed here, Simmel was most concerned with this area.

The middle of the nineteenth century saw one further major development in intellectual life that was to add to the framework of sociology and social theory. Rapid change had by itself already opened the way to historical thinking, to seeing social life in terms of a development, at least from the past to the present, if not on into the future. The publication of Darwin's theory of evolution early in the second half of the century saw his ideas immediately and more or less crudely transposed into social theory. All four thinkers work with some idea of social evolution from some primitive state to some more complex and presumably civilized state; however, as well as the benefits of social change, they were able, in their different ways, to see the drawbacks and dangers—the breakdown of traditional life and the loss of community, the increasing organization and control of everyday life to which people were subjected, and the danger of fragmentation—and each developed his own form of social criticism. We shall see that the political debates that their thought generated are still raging today.

Further reading

David McLennan, *The Thought of Karl Marx* (1971), divides Marx's life up into its important periods and gives an excellent account of his activities during each of them, as well as a clear account of his writings over the same period.

For further details about Durkheim's life, see S. Lukes, *Emile Durkheim* (1973), and for Simmel, see D. Frisby, *Georg Simmel* (1984), chapter 2.

The best account of Weber's life, including a psychoanalytic account of his depression, can be found in A. Mitzman, *The Iron Cage: An Historical Interpretation of Max Weber* (1971).

Part 1

What is society and how do we study it?

Introduction to Part 1

Any social theory worth its salt is difficult, for the self-evident reason that it tries to understand a complex object; there is no easy understanding of social structures or social processes, and—in order to make life even more difficult—I am going to start at the hardest end of social theory, that of methodology in the broadest sense. By this I mean the general ways in which we think about what we are doing, the way in which we decide on and define what we are going to study; the way in which we might map out our task as we proceed with our investigations; and the assumptions we make about what we are doing and why we are doing it. Part of this is the question of what we might mean by a sociological understanding or a sociological explanation of what we study.

Each of the thinkers we will be looking at has a different answer to each of these problems, but what they share in common, explicitly or implicitly, is a concern with something called *society* as a proper object of scientific investigation—even though the meaning of scientific is different for each, as is the meaning of society. My intention is to elaborate what each means by the investigation of society and how each envisages society and sociology in the most general terms. Generally these methods are seen as ways of understanding all societies and also of classifying different types of society.

'Ways of looking at' is important: by using the phrase, I do not think that each of the views I will be discussing is of equal worth to the others, or to those I do not discuss. Rather I think it is arguable that one of the reasons that these theories have survived and these thinkers are still read, discussed, and developed is that each manages to delineate and begin to explore and develop an understanding of an essential aspect of the social, without which we could have no understanding of society. These theories sometimes complement each other, sometimes contradict each other, and are sometimes talking about such radically different things that there can be no contact.

I will begin this part by looking at Durkheim, who on one level offers the simplest conception of what a society is and how we should understand it. I will then move on to Marx, who offers a more complicated way of conceptualizing a society and investigating it. These approaches share one important feature: they both see a scientific understanding of society as penetrating below the surface level of appearances and showing us something which we could not otherwise see. In other words, social science is surprising: it gives us news, it tells us things that we do not know simply by looking around us; as Marx points out on one occasion, there would be no need for a science if we could tell what the world was like simply by looking at it. This means that for Marx and Durkheim there is a gap between the language of social theory and sociological under-standing and the everyday language in which we think and talk about our actions. It means also that we do not necessarily know what we are doing—we think we are doing one thing and 'in reality', seen in terms of our relationship to society, we are doing another. I might marry out of love but I also reproduce the family; I might feel desperate and suicidal because my marriage has broken up, but I will also be responding to a form of social integration of which I am unlikely to be conscious.

In the case of Weber, we start with our common-sense notions of the world and we elaborate on these—our understanding of society comes from our inter-pretation of the ideas that govern peoples' actions; central to his approach is a conception of rationality—we can think of social science as scientific because it presents us with a rational understanding not of society but of social action, of the way people act in relation to each other. Simmel presents yet another model, concerned with the formal structures of relationships.

By the end of Part 1 you should have a preliminary idea of the different approaches outlined by the classical thinkers, of how they think about sociology and sociological investigation. This will be developed over the following chap-ters. I said earlier that this is the difficult end of social theory but it is also the end which presents the best overview. You should have a good sense of the pos-sibilities of social theory, and, if you are aware of contemporary debates and alternatives in sociology, you will realize that what is set out here covers most of the options open to modern sociology.

3 | Durkheim: the discovery of social facts

Introduction: background; Comte and positivism. *Durkheim's rules:* the objectivity of social facts; considering social facts as things; the use of statistics to identify social facts; the normal and the pathological—the normality of crime. *Suicide as a social fact:* its underlying causes. *What can we take from Durkheim:* criticisms of Durkheim's methodology and discussion.

Introduction

Durkheim's *Rules of Sociological Method* (1895/1964) is a classic text in the best sense, and for generations of students it has represented their first contact with sociology and provided material for the first essay question they have had to answer: 'Is sociology a science?'. Thirty years ago many sociologists—and many non-sociologists—assumed a fairly simple model of scientific activity and explanation, one which generally goes under the name of positivism, and Durkheim has been taken as the archetypal sociological positivist. There is a degree of truth in this but not the whole truth.

What is positivism? Historically the term is associated with Auguste Comte, the French philosopher who was a central, but not the only influence on Durkheim. Like most nineteenth-century philosophers and social theorists, Comte saw history as progress, in his case through three different stages: the religious, the metaphysical, and the scientific, the last of which he thought we were entering. Each stage rejected and replaced the way of thinking about the world that characterized the previous phase. The religious phase involves, as one might expect, the explanation of the world by the supernatural, and its most developed form is monotheism, the belief in one God as a final cause. The metaphysical stage is a transitional stage—gods are replaced by abstract forces such as nature—and this develops into the positive, scientific stage.

In Comte's view, the problem with the metaphysical stage is that it is negative: it sets itself against the traditional order and leads to a constant questioning of ideas and relations, leading to anarchy, a constant argument about how society should be organized. It is bound up with one strand of Enlightenment thought—that as rational beings we gain our freedom by such constant questioning. It enables us to overcome superstition and irrational oppression. Comte—and much nineteenth-century sociology—can be seen as representing a conservative reaction to this strand of thought, an attempt to stop the process of questioning. Comte argued that there was no solution to the constant argument about what society *should* be like—the negative approach; instead we should find out what it *is* like—the *positive* approach. Hence positivism. There was in Comte the idea that we could gain firm positive knowledge about the world. In the twentieth century the strand of Enlightenment that Comte was arguing against has reasserted itself at the heart of positivist philosophy. The work of Karl Popper (1959) has demonstrated that we cannot positively prove something to be always the case. If, for example, I wished to prove that all swans were white in a 'positive' sense I would have to show that every swan that has existed or does or will exist is white and that of course is impossible. Without such proof, however, it is always possible that we can find a black swan. Popper's response is to argue that science is concerned not with establishing absolute forms of knowledge, but with establishing that knowledge claims are false (in this example by trying to find a black swan). Science should always be questioning knowledge claims.

Comte, however, was unaware of the eventual reversal of his project. His aim, through observation, classification, and analysis, was to find the laws of society. If we know what society *is*, we will no longer need to argue about what it *should be*; knowing the laws of society, like knowing the laws of nature, enables us to predict what will happen and therefore to control what will happen. Then we will be able to restore social order. Although Comte himself can be seen as representing a conservative reaction to Enlightenment thought and to the unrest that followed the French Revolution, such ideas are not *necessarily* conservative: indeed in the nineteenth century they influenced George Eliot and her partner and they can be found at the roots of British reformist socialism through the Fabian Society. I don't think anybody today would go all the way with Comte, but common-sense versions of many of Comte's ideas underlie much bread-and-butter social-policy research—on poverty and crime, for example.

We can also find in Comte's work a notion that became very important to Durkheim, that of society as a *whole*—that no one part of a society can be studied separately from the others but must be seen in the context of its relationships to all other parts.

Durkheim's rules

A social fact is every way of acting, fixed or not, capable of exercising on the individual an external constraint; or again, every way of acting which is general throughout a given society, while at the same time existing in its own right independent of its individual manifestations.

(Durkheim 1964: 13)

SOCIAL FACTS AND OBJECTIVITY

Durkheim sees his first task as stating exactly what it is that sociology is *about*, what it studies. One way of thinking about the social world seems to imply that it includes everything, and many modern approaches that go under the name of 'social constructionism' do precisely this; sociological theories of sexuality or of the emotions, for example, talk as if biology and psychology have no relevance (Craib 1995). This sets in train a sociological imperialism which implicitly makes all other sciences, including the natural sciences, redundant. Durkheim's aims for sociology were much more modest—and rightly so, since when he was writing in 1894, the closest sciences to sociology—psychology and biology— were much more highly developed than the social sciences. We would do well to bear that modesty in mind, because in many ways it is still appropriate. Some modern writers seem to think that sociology must explain everything or it can explain nothing, and that there is no alternative in between.

Durkheim's intention was to distinguish sociology from biology and psychology, particularly the latter. What distinguishes a *social* fact is that it is imposed upon us from the outside, that there is a large degree of compulsion about it. It is worth examining this in some detail. I have often heard people saying things like 'Well, society makes us do this or that, or teaches us to believe this or that.' But if we think about this for a while it clearly is not true—we have some sort of choice. It might be true in one sense that society expects each of us to get married and have children, but lots of people fail to do so or choose not to do so— and they are not excluded from society, and they do not find social life impossible, although they might occasionally feel or be made to feel different or odd. On the other hand, if I decided to speak dog Latin rather than English, I would be unable to continue life as a member of this society for very long. Clearly degrees of constraint and freedom vary and there is always a degree of choice, but there is also a degree of constraint. Social facts exercise a particularly high degree of constraint.

Having defined social facts as the proper concern or object of sociology, Durkheim instructs us to consider social facts as if they were things. By such an instruction, he is trying to distinguish sociological analysis from what we might call speculative theorizing. We all have common-sense ideas about the social world and how it works, and the temptation is to focus our thinking on those and build theories around them. Durkheim's warning here is also a warning to take heed of facts, the reality of the society we are studying which remains independent of our ideas about it. A recent example which struck me is the way in which, for some thirty years, people have argued that living together before marriage is a way of finding our whether a couple are suited to each other, thus avoiding a terrible mistake; yet the most recent available evidence (Buck *et al.* 1994) shows that couples who live together before marriage are much more likely to get divorced than those who don't. It is this sort of simple, but profound, mistake that Durkheim is talking about. He argues that our everyday thinking and speculating about the world are geared to the purpose of making us feel 'in harmony with our environment'. In other words, it is wishful thinking. It is often worthwhile thinking about political arguments in this way, as a means of making people—the speaker and the audience—feel comfortable, protecting them from reality. This is not what sociology is about. Durkheim insists on the difference between scientific concepts and what he calls 'prenotions'—our common-sense ideas and prejudices.

The injunction *to treat social facts as things* is to distinguish them from such ideas, or ideologies. He is not saying that we should treat them objectively, which modern students often assume—thinking of objectivity as a state of mind, a way of looking at what we study. Social facts remain the same, however we look at them; they are objective in the sense that they are like objects, and they do not change if we think of them differently, just as my desk would remain a desk, even if I thought it was a rhinoceros. Objectivity is a quality of objects, not an attitude of mind.

As examples of social facts which are fairly clearly things in this sense, Durkheim cites the law, embodied in codes set out in books, or statistical evidence about, for example, suicide. A social fact cannot be accepted as such until we find some external embodiment or identifying feature; it can only constrain us if it has an existence external to us. A scientific investigation needs to be directed at a limited number of clearly defined facts, and defining facts through our pre-notions does not work. We could, for example, try to define crime by reference to some moral law—a crime is that which runs counter to morality, yet morality varies from society to society, if not from individual to individual. However, all societies have a legal system or at least they have laws, and operate various forms of punishment when those laws are broken. It is here that we find the *external* feature of a crime that enables us to identify it as a social fact—the fact that it is punished. The criminal nature of the act is not some feature inherent in the act itself; it is in the fact that it is punished. The definition meets three of Durkheim's criteria for the identification of social facts. The definition must be clear of common-sense pre-notions—that is why it is surprising; secondly, it must be general: we cannot start from individual manifestations of a phenomenon; and, thirdly, there is external constraint: if I want to kill my grandmother in order to inherit her wealth, I cannot rewrite the law to excuse the action. It is a crime whether I like it or not.

THE NORMAL AND THE PATHOLOGICAL

Even now, a century after Durkheim was writing, I suspect that this way of defining crime is surprising to new students, as it might be surprising to many people who take part in popular arguments about crime and punishment. One implication, for example, is that the same act can be a crime in one society but not in another. A second implication is the idea that crime is normal. When Durkheim goes on to distinguish between the normal and the pathological, his borrowing of an organic analogy from biology becomes most evident. Societies are like organisms, and in this context he talks about types of societies as species, individual members of which can be identified as normal or pathological. Unlike many thinkers of that period, and now, Durkheim took the position that it was possible to argue from *is* to *ought*, that on the basis of an analysis of what exists it is possible to develop an argument about what should exist. Basically something is normal if there is a lot of it about. Of course it is not quite as simple as this. We must take into account the type of society and its stage of development—a social fact is normal when it is 'present in the average society of that species at the corresponding phase of its evolution' (Durkheim 1895/1964: 64). Evidence for this is to be backed up by an analysis which shows how the social fact is bound up with the social life of that type of society.

We can return to the striking idea that crime might be a normal social fact. I say striking because for Durkheim the normal is also the healthy, because it is an important part of a functioning society. The notion that crime might be healthy would not, I suspect, be acceptable to many contemporary political parties who make law and order a central part of their platform. It is normal and healthy because, in the first place, the committing of a crime and its punishment help to mark out and reinforce social boundaries, and so contribute towards a cohesion of a society, and, secondly, because it is a mechanism of social change: it can challenge those same boundaries. A contemporary example would be the public relationship between homosexuals at least one of whom is under the age 18—currently an offence in the United Kingdom, but under a law which, happily, is likely to be changed.

SOCIOLOGICAL EXPLANATION

The purpose of all the life sciences, insists Durkheim, is to describe the normal and the healthy, to distinguish it from the pathological; we discover what the normal body is like and how it works by looking at the bodies around us—there is no point in speculating about what it *should* be like (three legs and two livers, perhaps?). He goes on to discuss, comparatively briefly, how we may classify societies and comes to the conclusion that we should start with the simplest societies—those of one segment, one clan or kinship group; it is as if the simplest society is like a single cell and more complex societies like more complex organisms. The explanation of social facts has two dimensions: we should look for their *efficient cause*, which I would understand as a historical explanation, how and why this education system developed, and for their *function* in relation to the whole of the society, how it contributes to the continuing existence of society. The function of an institution does not explain its appearance—a trap into which modern functionalism too easily falls—but might help account for its continued existence once it has appeared. He outlines a comparative method by means of which the histories of different societies may be studied. In all such comparisons, within or between societies, 'Concomitant variation alone, as long as the variations were serial and systematic rather than isolated and spasmodic, was always sufficient to establish a sociological law' (Jones 1986: 75). For example, if we can establish that the suicide rate varies directly with types of social cohesion (see below), we have a sociological law.

Of course, Durkheim did not always employ his own method of concomitant variation—in fact, much of his later work is concerned with ideas, with a 'collective consciousness', but we shall see that this, too, is a social fact.

Suicide as a social fact

Some of these changes are apparent in Durkheim's study *Suicide* (1897/1952) but with some pushing and shoving it can be used as an example of the methods he outlines in *The Rules*. In the latter, he talks about *social currents* as well as social facts: these are general feelings which can run through a society or a large group. They emerge from the collective and move to individuals rather than the other way around. I suspect that most people have had the experience of being pulled along with the crowd into something they would not otherwise have done—even if it is only into getting drunk at a Christmas party. However, he clearly states all the way through that we must concern ourselves with social *facts*, not wishful thinking, and that social facts must be explained by social facts. Thus in *Suicide* Durkheim sets about showing first that, despite the fact that one might think that suicide is an individual act, it is a social fact. Suicide rates show a remarkable constancy, and they vary in a systematic way over time and from society to society. Here, then, is the first of the criteria by which a social fact can be identified—its externality. One might think that constraint—the second criterion—might be more difficult to establish. How can somebody be constrained to commit suicide, particularly by a society which forbids suicide. It must be remembered that, when Durkheim was writing, it had only recently ceased to be the practice to punish the bodies of suicides. The constraint that Durkheim is talking about here is different from the constraint that, for example, might stop us committing murder; it is the constraint of a 'social current' which pushes the individual towards a particular action. He talks about a 'suicidogenic current' present in each society, to which we are all subjected. The determinant—the social fact—which governs the strength of the suicidogenic current in a society can best be described as the form and strength of the social integration of a society.

He identifies four types of suicide dependent upon different degrees and forms of integration, two pairs at opposite ends of a continuum. The two most virulent suicidogenic currents in European society produced anomic and egoistic suicide. Anomic suicide occurs when the rules that govern social life fail and we are left not knowing how to behave, or what is appropriate; this often happens during periods of rapid social change, which will be reflected in individual lives, perhaps through the sudden gain or loss of wealth. There is nearly always a period of anomie, of greater or shorter length, on the break-up of a long-term intimate relationship, and it is not unknown for suicide to occur in such situations. In any case, the important point is about the comparative absence of social integration, a situation where people do not know what to do because the old rules seem no longer to apply, and there are no obvious new rules. At the opposite end of the continuum we have the situation where the social rules or norms are very powerful and apply rigidly—such as when an Indian widow might be compelled to throw herself on the funeral pyre or her dead husband—the practice of suttee. Durkheim calls this fatalistic suicide.

Egoistic suicide is a matter less of the level of integration than of its type. His argument seems to be that we can be integrated into a society in two ways. In the first we are integrated as individuals who are similar to each other, sharing the same sort of ideas—it is what we share with those around us which is important. An extreme variant of this in modern society—at least in Durkheim's time—would be the army, and it would be here that we would find incidents of what Durkheim called altruistic suicide, putting one's own life at risk to save another.

The alternative form of integration occurs when we are integrated into our society not as sharing common features with others but as individuals, responsible for our own individual fates, our own actions. This is not, as it might appear, a fragmentation of society, but it places greater responsibility for social cohesion on the individual, and Durkheim's argument is that in such societies the individual does not receive the collective support that he or she might receive in others types of society and is more vulnerable to isolation and suicide. The statistics that he looks at in this connection show systematic differences in suicide rates between, for example, Protestant communities, with their emphasis on the individual conscience, and Roman Catholic communities, with their emphasis of confession and forgiveness through the community leader, the priest, and systematic differences between the married and the unmarried.

What can we take from Durkheim?

As Mike Gane (1988) has pointed out, it is customary to dismiss much of Durkheim's methodology in modern texts; from the introductory Lee and

Newby (1983) to the more sophisticated study by Lukes (1973), Durkheim's notion of a social fact is regarded as inadequate, and in the case of suicide his statistical methods have been questioned; through the late 1960s and early 1970s there was a much more systematic attack on Durkheim's whole enterprise, particularly as it was manifested in *Suicide*. It seems to me that these criticisms are well worth looking at, but some of them are too easy.

In the first place it is argued that his criteria for the identification of social facts are vague. The nature of externality, for example, is ambiguous: is language, one of Durkheim's central examples of a social fact, internal or external, and how exactly does it constrain us? I have to speak English if I want most of the people around me to understand me, and there is a sense in which the language limits what I can say, but it also enables me to say things without setting in motion some strict process of determination. I can and do choose the words I put on this page; I might choose them badly, but I am not forced to write them.

There are interesting issues arising around these arguments. First of all, it seems to me that the ambiguity is probably necessary and we need to think about what Durkheim was trying to do and what he was trying to persuade us towards. It is clear, within the context of his general sociology, that one of the things that he was interested in was the way in which a society is reproduced within us or through our actions. In contemporary terms this sort of issue arises in debates about, for example, the way in which the personal is political—in, for example, the feminist argument that the way men and women behave in relation to each other on a personal level reproduces the features of patriarchy, the inequalities of power in the wider society. Society is always both inside and outside—and Durkheim was well able to recognize this, as we shall see later when we look at his conception of the *conscience collective*.

If we turn to modern arguments about *Suicide*, other things emerge. One argument is that suicide statistics do not reflect anything 'real' in the outside world but are themselves a social construction, a result of the procedures by which statistics are collected—the theories which organize them (see Hindess 1973) or the social context in which they are collected. Jack Douglas's *The Social Meanings of Suicide* (1967) pointed out that we might expect lower suicide rates in Roman Catholic communities because suicide is a sin, and officials would be reluctant to identify deaths as suicides. Douglas in fact makes a sweeping critique of Durkheim's methodology, arguing that he appears to be talking about objective phenomena 'out there', but his explanations assume not some simple causal process in which something called 'society' forces itself on individuals but a process of interpretation of shared beliefs—that, if more people commit suicide in an economic crisis, or if more Roman Catholics than Protestants commit suicide, then this is as a result of individuals interpreting the meaning of their situations and beliefs. Douglas is of course quite right, but I think he misses what Durkheim is trying to do: it is not only in respect of statistical regularities that suicide can be seen as a social fact; it is in relation to socially established and shared belief systems—the *conscience collective*. The statistics can be seen as the surface appearance; they are *signs* and, if they show regularities, there might be some underlying social, causal process at work—and that cause could lie in the form of social cohesion and/or in socially established belief systems and/or the construction of the statistics themselves.

What I am suggesting here is that Durkheim is not quite the strict positivist in the modern sense that his critics take him to be. Modern positivism has gone beyond Comte in attempting to root knowledge in sense experience and to establish general laws in a rigorous way. If we read Durkheim as trying to do this, then the criticisms hold, but if we regard him as developing more realist arguments—looking for underlying causes of surface phenomena—he can be defended. In this context, his insistence that social facts should be regarded as things is an insistence on the existence of underlying structures or processes which affect the way in which individuals behave to some degree independently of their will—the structures or processes or beliefs push us in one direction rather than another, limit our choices, and *sometimes* perhaps force us to do things. Not many people can resist the force of, for example, a patriotic war, and not many people become voluntarily unemployed, except in a very limited sense of taking up a redundancy offer. In other words, what is valuable is Durkheim's insistence that there is such a thing as society and that there are various ways in which it imposes itself upon us; it is there and it works on us, whatever we might think about it.

There is something else to be learnt about the nature of argument in social theory: that *precise* definitions are rarely not part of the game and, although we need to be as clear and precise as we can, it is possible to define an idea out of existence. When one writer criticizes another for being imprecise, it is often— but not always—a criticism of somebody for thinking, and there is always a degree of ambiguity in thinking. There are types of theoretical argument which open things up and other types of argument which close things down; it is not always easy to decide which is appropriate, but, in the case of Durkheim's arguments about social facts, the criticism of lack of precision closes down possibilities. The notion of a social fact, in a strong or a weak form, has been at the centre of sociology—even the development of a 'postmodern society' must be explained as a social fact, although not many of its proponents would accept this.

Further reading

From Durkheim's original work, *The Rules of Sociological Method* (1895/1964), chapters 1, 2, and 3 are a good starting point, followed by his preface to the second edition; you should also try to look at *Suicide* (1897/1952)—especially parts 2 and 3—as the classic sociological text.

For an oversimple but important criticism of Durkheim's method, see Jack Douglas, *Social Meanings of Suicide* (1967), and for a more conventional discussion, see S. Lukes, *Emile Durkheim* (1973), chapter 10. For a good modern discussion of positivism in sociology, see C. A. Bryant, *Positivism in Social Theory and Research* (1985).

4 | Karl Marx: the primacy of production

Introduction: the problems set by political misinterpretations of Marx; Marx and Darwin. *Marx's method: the starting point*: the ideology of individualism; the importance of practical, everyday life; the action/structure dualism in Marx; comparison of Marx with Durkheim; dialectical thinking and the separation of analysis and history.

Introduction

The production of ideas, conceptions, of consciousness, is, to begin with, immediately involved in the material activity and the material interaction of men, the language of real life. Conceiving, thinking—the intellectual interaction of men—still appear here as the direct emanation of their material affairs.

(Marx 1846/1977a: 37)

In the social production of their life, men enter into definite relations that are indispensable and independent of their will, relations of production which correspond to a definite stage of development of their material productive forces.

The sum total of these relations of production constitutes the economic structure of society, the real foundation, on which rises a legal and political superstructure and to which correspond definite forms of social consciousness. The mode of production of material life conditions the social, political and intellectual life process in general. It is not the consciousness of men that determines their being, but, on the contrary, their social being that determines their consciousness.

(Marx 1859/1968b: 181)

Before going any further it will perhaps be useful to read these quotations carefully and think about whether you can see any differences between them. I will be returning to them shortly, but I will say now that the difference between them represents one of the central dualisms which have to be balanced by any social theory.

Marx is perhaps the most problematic of all the theorists we will be looking at; there are multiple interpretations of Durkheim, Weber, and Simmel but their theories did not provide a motivating force for the political struggles of the twentieth century, nor did they provide the principles of social organization for societies in much of Europe, Asia, Africa, and Central America. It is impossible to think of Marx without thinking of Marxism and the political debates that it brings in its train; in the English-speaking West, Marxism has entered into popular culture in profoundly distorted forms. These debates will not be the focus for what follows and my advice to the reader would be to try, as far as possible, to suspend any knowledge which you already might have of Marx and Marxism.

Writing some fifty or sixty years before Durkheim but around the same time as Comte, Marx too developed the idea of a society which existed *sui generis*, but he conceived of it in a very different way, emphasizing the material conditions of people's lives and the fundamental importance of history. Marx dedicated his great work *Capital* to Charles Darwin, and he saw himself as the scientist of society and the development of social forms, as Darwin was the scientist of the development of living forms. It has become common to talk about modern scientific ideas as involving the steady displacement of humanity from the centre of the stage. With Galileo comes the realization that the earth is not the centre of the universe, but just one planet amongst many in one solar system amongst many; with Darwin comes the realization that humanity is not the centre of creation but one development amongst others in the course of a long process of evolution; with Marx comes the realization that human beings are not the creators of society but are the creatures of society, the product of the social world into which they are born; and finally with Freud comes the understanding that the human individual is the product of unconscious forces, not fully in control of him- or herself.

Marx's method: the starting point

There is a long history of philosophical debate over Marx's methodology, some of it very abstract indeed. Marx himself was a philosopher and well acquainted with the history of European philosophy—he was no simplistic thinker, but was at the forefront of the development of the thought of his time, and just as his name is associated with ideas of political revolutions, so is it associated with intellectual revolution. Like Durkheim, Marx argued against the acceptance of contemporary common-sense ideas about society, what Durkheim called prenotions, but what Marx and Marxists would be more likely to call ideology. Whereas Durkheim based his argument on psychological reasons—to avoid wishful thinking—Marx based his on sociological *and* psychological grounds. Our wishful thinking derives from the fact that we will see the world through the blinkers of our social class—it is the product, crudely, of our material self-interest, not just our desire for peace of mind.

This is at the heart of his criticism of the classical economists and of the liberal philosopher John Start Mill. They start their analyses with the notion of the isolated individual, somebody separate from the individuals surrounding him or her; I suspect that this is still the first, rather naïve, way in which people think about society as they come to maturity. Despite the fact that from the moment of birth we are part of a social unit, we can see only other individuals, coming together and separating, engaging in economic and social activities through choice, just as we seem to organize our own lives—conveniently but profoundly forgetting that we have no choice about the family, the socio-economic class, the geographical area, or the culture into which we are born, and these are the very things that make us what we are. Marx argued that such a conception of individuality—the 'individuated individual'—was the result of the loss of the social ties of feudal societies and the growth of the capitalist systems of production and the market economy. In other words, it was the product of a specific historic period, whereas the thinkers that Marx was criticizing tended to regard such an individual as having existed throughout history. A constant theme of the Marxist criticism of bourgeois or ruling-class thought is the way in which it turns temporary, historically conditioned and produced features of social lives into eternal truths of human nature.

Marx regarded such notions of the human individual as abstract, and his criticism of this way of looking at the world merged with his criticism of German idealist philosophy, and particularly of Hegel, whose philosophy he famously 'stood on its head'. Hegel's idealism sees the world as the product of ideas working themselves out through history. Against such a starting point, Marx posits real people, acting practically in real social relations. In his *Theses on Feuerbach* (Marx 1845/1968*d*), Marx writes of Feuerbach—a German philosopher who had begun to move away from Hegel, but in Marx's view only half succeeded—that: 'Feuerbach, not satisfied with *abstract thought* wants *empirical observation*, but he does not conceive the sensible world as *practical*, human sense activity' (Ibid. 29), and later: 'All social life is essentially *practical*. All the mysteries which lead theory towards mysticism find their rational solution in human practice and in the comprehension of this practice' (ibid. 30).

Hegel had seen human history in terms of the development of ideas and Feuerbach had gone half-way to inverting that understanding, half-way to seeing ideas and their development as the product of human social history. He had argued that our conception of God does not come from our process of thinking; rather it is an alienation of a human essence: something which is part of us is projected onto an omnipotent being. Marx takes this further—the notion of a human essence is abstract; in fact, it is our power as practical beings working together that we project onto our idea of God—our strength as people collectively acting on and changing the world. It is this practical and sensuous activity that forms the basis of everything else. The first quotation at the beginning of this chapter seems to me to emphasize this aspect of his work, and it belongs to what commentators usually call the 'young Marx'.

There has been much debate at various times among interpreters of Marx about the difference between the 'young' and the 'old' Marx; there is a clear shift of emphasis in his thinking from the humanism of the above quotations, his concern with real people engaged in real activities and relationships with each other, to his later concern with the economic structure of capitalism, pushing people and societies through processes over which they have no control and of which they are ignorant—an attitude which stands out clearly from the second quotation at the beginning of the chapter. I do not think of this as a major problem; rather it is a mark of Marx's greatness as a thinker that he was able to work with both sides of a dualism which still haunts and I think inevitably must haunt social theory—that between action and structure. As many have done since, he begins by talking about human action and moves into an analysis of the structure created by human action, and which in turn determines human action; this is often called a dialectical process and the same idea was being pushed by such non-Marxist sociologists as Peter Berger and Thomas Luckman (1967) well into the second half of this century.

I sometimes think that the history of Marxist thought can be seen as an extended elaboration of the second quotation, and much of it can be understood as a debate about the meaning of the last two lines: 'it is not the consciousness of men that determines their being, but, on the contrary, their social being that determines their consciousness.' For the moment, however, I want to contrast Marx with Durkheim.

A crucial difference is the starting point. For Durkheim it is the search for social facts, features of life which impose themselves upon us. For Marx it is our sensuous everyday activity, the ways in which we make our living, grow food, manufacture artefacts. Whereas Durkheim starts off in a realm of determinism, Marx begins in a realm of freedom, even if he then moves to look at the way in which what we produce through this freedom acts back upon us to determine our lives, to impose itself on us from the outside, this time through our being placed in relationships over which we have no control. It is perhaps common for people to think of Marx as the social thinker who held the most rigidly determinist view of human existence, but this starting point in human interaction has sometimes led to him being compared to that least determinist of all sociological approaches, symbolic interactionism (see Goff 1980). This movement from the freedom of human interaction through to the way in which society and social relations impose themselves upon us is summed up, at least as far as capitalism is concerned, in the theory of alienation (see Marx 1844/1973a; Ollman 1971). So Marx adds a dimension to our conception of social life which Durkheim, at least in his methodological writings, ignores. There is also a difference in the way in which each conceives of the society that imposes itself upon us—although their important similarity is that they *do* see society as something which imposes itself upon us.

Marx's conception is of a more complex arrangement, less like an organism and more like a building, to use his own analogy of an infrastructure and super-structure. Most important in such an analogy is the argument that one part of this structure, the economic base, is more important than the others, that it somehow conditions their existence and determines, at least in the sense of lim-its, what goes on there.

In both thinkers we find an idea of an underlying social structure: in Durkheim forms of social cohesion, and in Marx the forces of production which produce the visible effects and actions that make up peoples' lives. They share the idea that the function of science is to penetrate below the surface of social life to reveal features of our life of which we are not immediately aware, but the way in which we search for these underlying features is different. For Durkheim it is a matter of looking for empirical regularities—he is much closer to the conven-tional picture of the natural scientist. For Marx, however, it is a different matter, a process of analytic thinking rather than empirical investigation. It must not be forgotten that Marx was a philosopher and Terrell Carver's judgement is, I think, correct: 'My conclusion is not that Marx was exclusively (or even primarily) a philosopher and logician, but that he applied the techniques of philosophy and logic . . . [to] the criticism of political economy' (Carver 1975: 177).

One part of this philosophical thinking was to differentiate between the process of thinking about a phenomenon and the process by which that phe-nomenon comes into existence. Our understanding of the historical develop-ment of capitalism is not the same thing as our understanding of the way in which capitalism works—thinking in the social sciences is not the same as telling historical stories, just as discovering the workings of a particular cancer cell is not the same thing as knowing why it should have appeared in the first place. Marx in his introduction to the *Grundrisse* discusses two 'moments' of thinking—an analytic moment, and a synthetic moment which begins and ends with what he calls the 'concrete'. The analytic moment breaks down what we are studying (the concrete) into its component simpler parts. We can begin our ana-lysis, he suggests, with the population of a society, the people who are engaged in the productive process. But if we start in such a way, we are dealing with an abstraction: the concept of 'population' needs to be broken down into its com-ponent parts—for example, social classes—and these too need to be further broken down. This moves us away from the abstraction and closer to the con-crete reality we are trying to understand. But not only do these abstractions have to be broken down; they need to be brought together in a synthesis, showing how they are related to each other: 'The concrete is concrete, because it is the sum of many determinations [and] therefore a unity of diversity' (Carver 1975: 72).

The important point here is the separation of the historical development of a society and our way of analysing that society, and Marx provides us with a model for the thinking process that enables us to produce knowledge, a process of breaking down and synthesizing that is generally referred to as dialectical in a rather more sophisticated sense than was used in connection with Berger and Luckman above. This use of the term 'dialectical' suggests three dimensions to thinking: the first is the notion of the whole or the totality—the idea that our knowledge can be judged by its inclusiveness, the extent to which it gives a knowledge of the totality of what we are studying. This is implied in the second part of the last quotation—the concrete is the sum of many determinations, a unity of diversity.

The second dimension is an elaboration of the development of thought which is usually attributed to Hegel. The crude and oversimplified version is that thought (and for Hegel, history itself) progresses through stages: a thesis, an initial proposition, an antithesis—the opposite to the thesis,—and a synthesis—a result of the argument which combines both thesis and antithesis, which in turn becomes the thesis for a new movement. In fact Hegel was never as crude as this, and the process of analysis and synthesis is more complex, involving more complex concepts and developmental paths, producing a more complex conception of reality, of 'society'. The 'unity of diversity' implies an understanding of social reality as the product of many causes, none of which we understand properly until we find its place in the whole process. This is in contrast to Marx's desire to give priority to the economic structure in the causal process, and this tension between a multi-causal model and a mono-causal model has haunted the history of Marxism, as well as provided the basis for many alternative arguments.

The third aspect of the notion of dialectic is that of contradiction and movement: a society is not a simple entity, but a combination of contradictory elements in a permanent (and with capitalism, increasingly rapid) process of change. Contradiction, conflict, and change are seen as normal and inevitable aspects of social development, and, as we shall see, this marks a real difference between Durkheim and Marx. For Marx, the 'individuated individual' of capitalism could not grasp this aspect of history, and the importance which he attributed to dialectical thinking is summed up in William McBride's translation from his 'Afterword' to the German edition of *Capital*:

In its rational form (dialectic) is a scandal and abomination to bourgeoisdom and its doctrinaire professors, because it includes in its comprehension and affirmative recognition of the existing state of things, at the same time also, the recognition of the negation of that state, of its inevitable breaking up; because it regards every historically developed form as in fluid movement, and therefore takes into account its transient nature not less than its momentary existence; because it lets nothing impose upon it, and is in its essence critical and revolutionary.   (McBride 1977: 68)

Finally, returning to the notion of totality itself, some of the more important implications were brought out by later Marxists and I want to look in particular

at the contribution of Georg Lukacs, a Hungarian Marxist whose most important work was *History and Class Consciousness* (1923/1971*a*). Lukacs elaborated
on these ideas in an interesting way. First he took some of Marx's comments to
argue that the analytic moment of thought—the separation of what we are
studying into its separate components—is in fact an *ideological* moment; the
development of capitalism leads to a way of looking at the world which sees it
precisely in terms of separate entities which are *externally* related. By this he
means that we think of the world as consisting of separate objects related by
simple causal relationships which, in essence, can be measured. Durkheim's
instructions on how to identify social facts through concomitant variations
would be an example of such analytic thinking.

Marxist thought, in contrast, sees each separate entity as part of a network
which comprises a whole, and each separate phenomenon can be understood
only in terms of its relationship to the whole. To develop the example of suicide,
it is not enough to relate suicide rates to a particular religious belief and what
that implies for the form of social integration. The development of
Protestantism, for example, would need to be related to certain aspects of the
economic development of capitalism and in turn might be related to certain
forms of political democracy, and certain types of business organization, a
changing education system, and so on. We gain a full knowledge of, in this case,
suicide only when we have an understanding of the whole network of relationships within which the suicides take place, and this knowledge is produced by
theory as well as by observation and measurement. And Marxist thinking is constantly moving from one level of analysis to the next. This way of thinking, this
method of analysis, was for Lukacs of crucial importance—to the point that he
argued that, even if all Marx's predictions proved wrong, we would not have to
abandon the essence of Marxism: its method.

The same could, of course, be said about Durkheim's more conventional
scientific method; there are all sorts of reasons why the knowledge produced by
any method might be wrong, without invalidating the method; but these are not
the only conceptions of society or of method that can be found in the work of
sociology's founders. If both Durkheim and Marx insist on the way in which
society imposes itself on its members, Weber, at least in principle, if not always
in practice, was concerned to show how people actually created the society they
live in.

Further reading

There is no easy reading on these matters; amongst the original texts, Marx's Preface and
more important Introduction to the *Critique of Political Economy* (*The Grundrisse*)
(1859/1968*b* and 1859/1973 respectively) are worth looking at, perhaps in conjunction
with Terrell Carver's commentary in his *Karl Marx: Texts on Method* (1975).

I first came to understand what was meant by dialectical thinking through reading Lucien Goldmann, *The Human Sciences and Philosophy* (1969), and Henri Lefebvre, *Dialectical Materialism*, (1968), in quick succession. If you want to give yourself a really hard time, try Georg Lukacs, *History and Class Consciousness* (1971a).

5 | Max Weber: the primacy of social action

Introduction: Comparison with Marx and Durkheim; Kantian background and the differences between the natural and the human sciences. *The proper object of sociology:* sociology's concern with the individual event and Weber's debate with Marx's ghost; the society/individual dualism; behaviour and action; meaningful social action; further comparison of Marx and Durkheim; *Different types of meaningful action. Understanding social action:* observational and explanatory understanding; causal adequacy and meaning adequacy. *The ideal type:* Weber's individualism and further comparison with Marx and Durkheim; scientific and common-sense knowledge. *Values and value freedom.*

Introduction

> Sociology (in the sense in which this highly ambiguous word is used here) is a science which attempts the interpretive understanding of social action in order thereby to arrive at a causal explanation of its course and effects. In 'action' is included all human behaviour when and in so far as the acting individual attaches a subjective meaning to it. Action in this sense may be either overt or purely inward or subjective; it may consist of positive intervention in a situation, or of deliberately refraining from such intervention or passively acquiescing in the situation. Action is social in so far as, by virtue of the subjective meaning attached to it by the acting individual (or individuals), it takes account of the behaviour of others and is thereby oriented in its course.
>
> (Weber 1922/1947: 88)

And now for something completely different. Max Weber's most productive years covered the first two decades of the twentieth century and many would think of him, perhaps together with Simmel, as the most contemporary of the four theorists, even as representing the first signs of postmodernism. He has a very different starting point from both Durkheim and Marx and emerges from a very different philosophical tradition. Whereas Durkheim's work came out of

Comte's concern with the unity of the sciences, and directs itself to the natural sciences, and Marx's model of science is Darwin's theory of evolution and involves a notion of underlying structures of social reality to which we do not have immediate access, Weber comes from a tradition which asserts a radical difference between the natural and human sciences.

This tradition was developed through Rickert (1962; see also Burger 1976), who started with a distinction in Kant's philosophy between the phenomenal world, the world of external objects, and the *nuomenal* world, the world of consciousness. The former exists in time and space and can be known through experience and the methods of the natural sciences. Consciousness, on the other hand, is not an object out there in the world. We cannot see it, it does not exist in any particular space or at any particular time out there. However, we do have an experience of what it is to be conscious. I can look around and distinguish between people and animals and objects. It is possible to construct from such experience an understanding of what consciousness *must be* like in order to have such experiences. We are constantly making judgements about the world—that if I cross the road here, that car in the distance will stop before it hits me, or that moving object over there is a dog and not a flamingo, and we can say that one of the qualities of consciousness is to make judgements, or to distinguish between different types of object. This is known as a *transcendental* argument, an argument which transcends—goes beyond—given, empirical reality. It is a form of argument employed recently by Roy Bhaskar (1978, 1979) in his development of a modern realist philosophy for the social sciences.

I do not want to follow this aspect of Kantian philosophy too far, but it does provide an idea of why Weber should think that the process of thought in itself produces knowledge, in addition to the knowledge produced by observation and experiment. I discussed Marx's version of this in the last chapter, but it must be remembered that neither Marx nor Weber thought we could dispense with observation, or, when possible, experiment (at least thought experiments) or measurement; it is just that they gave a greater role to thought than Durkheim (at least explicitly) recognized. It is also important to know that Kant gave a particular role to moral judgement, which appears in Weber's work as a concern with value and value choice.

Now, whereas both Marx and Durkheim were concerned with establishing social laws or general truths about society, the Kantian tradition thought this was only possible in the natural sciences, which are concerned with what is general and common to different phenomena, with the laws of nature. By contrast, the human sciences are concerned with individuals, individual events, individual actors, and the way people express themselves.

In these senses, then, Weber continues the great tradition of German idealism, the concern with the constitutive nature of ideas, compared with Marx, who half a century before had attempted to stand that tradition on its head. It is often said that Weber was engaged in a lifelong debate with Marx's ghost, and, while there is a degree of truth in this, it is, as ever, not that simple. There are many aspects of Weber's substantive sociology which seem to me to be open-ended Marxist studies, and Weber himself, in *The Protestant Ethic and the Spirit of Capitalism* (1904–5/1976) insisted that he was not setting out to replace a one-sided materialist, Marxist argument with a one-sided idealist argument. One of the factors that has made Weber's work such a rich source of ideas right up to the present time has been that, in practice, Weber was never one-sided about anything, even if, in theory, he appeared to be so. Thus his individualism, as we shall see, is never quite as individualistic as it seems, his relativism is never quite as relativist as it seems, his idealism is never quite as idealist, and his rationalism never quite as rationalist as it seems. And, in the comparison between Weber, on the one hand, and Durkheim and Marx, on the other, we have found another central sociological dualism: that between individual and society. Every sociological theory must deal with both, yet the two are very different and can provide mutually exclusive understandings of the social world.

The proper object of sociology

In his methodological writings, Weber is always drawing distinctions. The social sciences are concerned with individual phenomena, events, and people. But if social organizations—societies—are simply collections of individuals acting randomly, there could be no scientific investigation of society. What makes such an investigation possible is that people act rationally, organizing the world in a coherent way; the aim of the social sciences is to arrive at a rational under-standing of human action. But not of all human action. This is where the dis-tinctions begin. First of all there is a distinction between behaviour and action. Behaviour is what we do without attaching a meaning to it. If I sneeze, or cough, or blink, my movements can be understood as the end result of physical processes in the body, as the result of a physical cause rather than as a *meaning-ful* action. Sociology is concerned with the latter. If we take Freud seriously, much action which we think is meaningless might have an unconscious mean-ing, and we will find that, in all these distinctions, the edges are constantly blurred, something which Weber himself recognized. They are not meant to be watertight compartments but rather to bring order from chaos, to offer a way of understanding which can begin to make sense of what at first glance seems a muddle—and if we look at the social world as made up of individual actions, then it does appear to be a muddle.

Sociology is concerned with meaningful action—whether meaning is attrib-uted to an action by an individual or to one by a group of individuals, in which case our knowledge of the meaning is more approximate. We must also take account of the meanings attributed to inanimate objects, which, of course, do not have their own subjective meanings—they must be seen in relation to human action as means and ends. But then comes a further distinction: not all meaningful action concerns sociology, only meaningful action which is directed towards or takes account of other people—meaningful *social* action. Weber's own example here is of a distinction between a collision between two cyclists, which we can look at as an event in the natural world, a result of a causal chain of physical events. Although each cyclist is engaged in meaningful action, their collision was not meant by either. What follows, however, whether an argument or an apology or the expression of concern, is meaningful social action in which each is directing his or her action towards the other. It becomes clear here that Weber is concerned with what we might call *intentional acts of meaning*, rational actions that we deliberately or consciously take in relation to and directed towards other people. Actions into which we are pushed—for example, by the influence of crowds—do not count.

This marks an important difference from Marx and Durkheim. They also deal with human action, as must every social theorist. For Marx, however, human action can be affected by forces of which the actors do not necessarily have any knowledge—for example, our actions are constantly conditioned by economic forces which we don't know about or understand, and to which we do not, therefore, attribute a subjective meaning. In Durkheim's case, the notion of social consciousness implies that meaning itself is social—we are socialized into ways of thinking. The modern British philosopher Peter Winch (1958) arrives at the same conclusion via a rather different course. Social action, he argues, is rule-following, and by definition rules are social constructs: to establish a rule we need at least two people. Thus any meaningful action is rule-following and therefore social. I don't think that many modern sociologists would see Weber's distinction as important.

Different types of meaningful action

Weber goes on to distinguish between four types of meaningful social action which vary in the degree of meaningfulness and therefore of rationality. First he talks about *traditional* action, close to the borderline of the rational : 'For it is very often a matter of almost automatic reaction to habitual stimuli which guide behaviour in a course which has been repeatedly followed. The great bulk of all everyday action to which people have become habitually accustomed approaches this type' (Weber 1922/1947: 116). Thus Weber sees as borderline an area of social reality—everyday routine—which modern sociologists from Garfinkel (1967) to Giddens (1984) regard as central to understanding social cohesion.

Weber's second type of action, that based on emotion, the 'purely affectual', is also on the borderline of the rational; it is not meaningful when it is uncontrollable, but the more control that is exercised, the more meaningful it becomes. The crucial issue seems to be whether the action has an aim outside itself. If I am angry and smash something simply to express and relieve the anger, it is not rational; if I smash the plate in order to intimidate the person I am arguing with, it is an angry action but also a meaningful social action. Again, some contemporary theorists might see emotions as part of the central dynamics of social interaction, but Weber was concerned to limit the range of the study of sociology, to define its proper object.

The third type of action is oriented towards an ultimate value in a self-conscious way; like affectual action, it does not necessarily have an end external to itself but is satisfying for its own sake. If I am a Christian and I go into a church to pray, I am not engaging in a rational action to achieve a practical result but rather I am acting in a way that satisfies my belief in my duties to a Christian God. However, there is a difference from affective action: it might not be rational to believe in a Christian God, but, given that I do so believe, then it is rational that I engage in such actions as church-going and praying. When Weber talks about ultimate values, he is thinking of such values as are enshrined in a religious belief, and, by implication, in, say, atheism or agnosticism, humanism or communism, or indeed the pursuit of scientific knowledge itself—if such beliefs govern our action.

Jean-Paul Sartre, the French existentialist philosopher, argued that human beings were always engaged in choosing how they would live; we cannot do otherwise—we have no choice but to choose and we are always responsible for our actions; they are not forced on us. Weber seems to be saying something like this several decades before Sartre and without the latter's concern with responsibility and everyday life. We have to choose between ultimate values and there is no rational basis for that choice. Once the choice has been made, however, the actions that follow on from it can be understood as rational.

The fourth, most rational, type of action:

> is rationally oriented to a system of discrete individual ends, when the end, the means and the secondary results are all taken into account and weighed. This involves rational consideration of alternative means to the end, of the relations of the end to other prospective results of employment of any given means, and finally of the relative importance of different possible ends.   (Weber 1922/1947: 117)

Weber goes on to make a point which is obvious if you have been thinking about the different types of action as you have read through this: that very few actions are oriented in only one way. Think, for example, about the activity of lecturing in a university. There is a traditional element to it—things have always been done this way in universities, even though there is evidence that it is not the most effective way of teaching. It is also an affectual action, in a not very obvious way: it creates a sense of security for students and staff in what might otherwise be an unstructured and therefore anxiety-provoking situation. We can all feel that we are doing something, even if nothing much is happening in the way of education. Then on many occasions it can be an activity oriented to an ultimate value, with both students and staff committed to the value of learning and education, the growth of knowledge. And finally it is a straightforward instrumental activity: I lecture as a way of securing a salary which in turn secures me a roof over my head, food, and other goods that I feel are useful or enjoyable to me; students come perhaps in the hope of learning what it is expected that they shall reproduce in examinations, in order to make sure that they get their piece of paper at the end of the course which in turn will help them secure a job which in turn will supply them with an income, and so on. This might sound a very depressing way of looking at the world, as well as at your own future, and Weber would agree with you. He talked about a process of disenchantment, of the world losing its magic and becoming steadily more rationalized; in fact, he saw this as the major process of change in the modern world.

So, of Weber's four types of action, only one and a half are fully rational, meaningful forms of social action. His conception of rationality has become known as 'instrumental': it involves a strict relationship between means and ends, each step leading on to the next in a necessary way, until the desired end is reached. Marxist critics (and others) think of this conception of rationality as one concerned with domination: the control and manipulation of the natural world, spreading to the control and manipulation of human beings as if they were things. This is juxtaposed to dialectical rationality, the process of analysis and synthesis which I discussed in the previous chapter. Here, too, we can see the contrast I discussed in Chapter 1 between the view that knowledge is a liberation and the view that it is an enslavement; what is often lost in the modern debate is the idea that there are different aspects of knowledge and different types of rationality. Weber's particular conception of rationality represents the analytic moment of understanding, breaking down, and describing the elements of social reality as it exists at the moment; it is the moment of domination. In contrast, the Marxist conception can be seen as the synthetic movement, which brings together these elements and takes us beyond what exists at the moment to what might exist; it is the liberating moment.

Understanding social action

The next question to answer is how we understand meaningful social action. Weber makes a distinction between what he calls *observational* understanding and *explanatory* understanding. If somebody in the room gets up and opens a window, I recognize that 'he or she is opening the window'. This is observational understanding. Explanatory understanding goes further: it involves realizing that, for example, the room is very hot, or full of cigarette smoke or assorted bodily smells, or—if a lecture is in progress—that people are going to sleep, and that opening the window is a way of clearing the air or waking people up. The explanatory understanding sets out the chain of means leading up to an end; Weber talks about this as a context of meaning and the contexts can be elaborated—waking people up in a lecture can be linked into a broader chain of steps which encompasses the purposes of education from the points of view of the teacher and the student.

Weber uses the German term *verstehen* when he talks about understanding. This often seems to have been taken by English-speaking commentators as closer to empathic understanding, a sort of emotional identification with the actors whom we are trying to understand (see e.g. Runciman 1972), and this has provided an easy target for criticism—empathy might be a useful way of arriving at hypotheses about what someone is doing, but by itself it is entirely subjective and cannot possibly be a way of gaining knowledge. However, there is, as it were, another interpretation of interpretation. Talcott Parsons's version in a footnote to his translation of Weber's methodological writings is rather placid but makes the basic point:

Its primary reference in this work is to the observation and theoretical interpretation of the subjective 'states of mind' of actors. But it also extends to the grasp of the meaning of logical and other systems of symbols, a meaning which is usually thought of as in some sense 'intended' by a mind or intelligent being of some sort.   (Weber 1922/1947: 87)

Diana Leat (1972) makes the same point with rather more verve. We could imagine, for example, a statistical correlation between the birth rate and stork population; it would be amusing, but we would not take it seriously as suggesting a causal relationship. On the other hand, if we are told that there is a correlation between the number of days lost through strike action and the level of unemployment, we do think that there is likely to be a causal connection. We are members of the same society, or type of society, to which the statistics apply, and we can therefore follow the likely reasoning of the actors involved. If there is a high level of unemployment and jobs are hard to find, workers will not strike for fear of being sacked and replaced by others; if unemployment is lower and alternative employment can be found, then they are likely to be more adventurous. In other words, we have understood the rationality of the actors and we can regard the statistical correlation as meaningful—not meaningless, as in the first example.

Weber talks about two criteria by which we can judge that our understanding is adequate—adequacy on the level of cause and adequacy on the level of meaning. By adequacy on the level of cause, he means that we must search for similar situations in which the same outcome might be expected, finding confirmation of our understanding if the same outcome does ensue. Or does not ensue—Weber's argument that a certain sort of Protestantism is necessary for the development of capitalism finds evidence for its adequacy if we can find other situations where all the other preconditions for the growth of capitalism exist but there is no equivalent of the Protestant ethic and capitalism does not develop.

Adequacy on the level of meaning is a matter of the account making sense, being intelligible and comprehensible to us; it must be a believable story. There are all sorts of interesting possibilities here, since novelists too tell believable stories, but the sociologist's stories have to meet more rigorous standards of rationality and also to meet the condition of causal adequacy. Weber did not put himself in the position of many contemporary thinkers and argue that all stories were equal; he clearly thought that some were better than others, that his stories of the rise of capitalism were, for example, better than Marx's.

The ideal type

The tool that we use to understand social events and processes using interpretive understanding is the *ideal type*. Although, in the following passage, Weber describes the ideal type as a *utopia*, he does not mean this in the sense that it is a desirable state of affairs at which we should aim—he means it simply in the sense that the ideal type does not exist in reality. We do not construct an ideal type of, say, a bureaucracy by taking the average or typical components of existing bureaucracies or by trying to construct a model of a real bureaucracy. Rather it is the most rational form of the bureaucracy that we can imagine:

The ideal type is formed by the one-sided *accentuation* of one or more points of view, and by the synthesis of a great many diffuse, discrete more or less present and occasionally absent *concrete individual* phenomena which are arranged according to those one-sidedly emphasized viewpoints into a unified *analytical* construct. In its conceptual purity, this mental construct cannot be found anywhere in reality. It is a *utopia*.   (Weber 1904/1949: 90)

Alfred Schutz (1972) glosses Weber's arguments as setting out to construct concepts and types by a process of typification—of using rational criteria to select out common elements of what we are studying and linking them together in a rational way. He suggests that it is a matter of building—in the mind—a rational puppet theatre, and then manipulating the puppets to see how they would act in different situations. This enables the social scientist not only to understand past events but also to predict future events. The following quotation covers the construction of ideal-type concepts and illustrates some further important points about Weberian methodology:

when we inquire as to what corresponds to the idea of the 'state' in empirical reality, we find an infinity of diffuse and discrete human action, both active and passive, factually and legally regulated relationships, partly unique and partly recurrent in character, all bound together by an idea, namely the belief in the actual or normal validity of rules and of the authority of some human beings towards others. This belief is in part consciously, in part dimly felt, and in part passively accepted by persons who, should they think about the 'idea' in a really clearly defined manner, would not first need a 'general theory of the state' which aims to articulate the idea. The scientific conception of the state, however it is formulated, is naturally always a synthesis we construct for certain heuristic purposes. But on the other hand, it is also abstracted from the unclear syntheses which are found in the mind of human beings.   (Schutz 1972: 99)

There are two significant ways here in which Weber differs from the approaches of Marx and Durkheim. In the first place he is saying that what we call the 'state' does not have an existence in its own right over and above the people whose relationships and actions comprise reality—there is a confused network of relationships and actions that comprises reality, and the concept of the state makes some sense of the confusion. This is so for the sociologist but it is also true for the person he or she studies, and if the people we study think there is such a thing as the state, then we can treat it as existing, because it then figures in their action and they take account of it. The second point is that, in order to understand the state, the sociologist elaborates on and clarifies the common-sense ideas of those he or she studies: there is not that radical break between 'pre-notion' or 'ideology' and scientific concept: they develop out of each other.

Finally, Weber argues that sociology is not concerned with totalizing explanations: only individuals have an *ontological* reality, society does not exist in that real sense, and so sociological explanations must be in terms of individual events and processes. Thus, unlike Marx, Weber would not claim to offer a totalizing explanation of the development of capitalism, prioritizing different causal processes, but would rather offer a series of snapshots, taken from different angles and showing different aspects: *The Protestant Ethic and the Spirit of Capitalism* shows, as it were, the 'ideological' preconditions for the growth of capitalism, but one can also find in Weber studies of the economic preconditions of capitalism and of the legal preconditions—but he does not bring them together into some sort of overall explanation which would link them together in causal processes.

Values and value freedom

There is one final point to be made about Weber's methodology: he raises the issues of value in a way different from that which we find in Durkheim and Marx. For Durkheim, value freedom was the result of shedding 'pre-notions' and sticking to social facts; for Marx, social science itself carried the values of human emancipation and provided the basis for political action. Weber produced a subtle and complex argument which contained elements of both positions. For many years English-speaking sociologists interpreted Weber's injunction to 'value freedom' as implying a sort of simple objectivity on the part of the sociologist—the sort of grey neutrality. That interpretation disappeared during the 1960s in favour of one that is much closer to Weber's real intentions. Martin Albrow lists ten points that Weber makes about values. The first four are particularly important:

1. Science is guided by values, such as integrity, rigour, clarity, truth.
2. Human beings are valuing beings. They live lives through and for values.
3. History only makes sense if it is considered from the standpoint of values.
4. Social scientists choose their lines and objects of inquiry by reference to values. (Albrow 1990: 243–4)

So, if Weber saw values as so central to peoples' lives, how could he talk of value freedom? The answer is that sociology is only value-free in a limited and rather sophisticated way. The choice of a scientific career is itself a value choice—the scientist commits him- or herself to the values of integrity, rigour, clarity, and truth; what I choose to study as a scientist is a value choice, as is the method with which I choose to study it. Once these choices have been made, however, the overarching values of science—integrity, and so on—come into play and it is possible to construct—in the social sciences—a shared rational understanding of what we are studying. Value freedom is always value freedom within the limits of the values of our culture and our personal choices; in fact value freedom is itself a value that we choose.

Weber is adding something important here to our understanding not only of social life but of sociology itself; sociology might produce knowledge (Durkheim); it might produce knowledge which becomes a tool or weapon in political emancipation (Marx), but it also involves the choices of some values over and against other values; it involves what are basically moral choices and the implication is that we need to elucidate the moral choice that we make. Very few sociologists embark on that enterprise.

Further reading

The most accessible and intelligible of Weber's methodological writings are the opening sections of *The Theory of Social and Economic Organization* (1922/1947); his account of the ideal type and of value freedom can be found in *The Methodology of the Social Sciences* (1949)—these are more difficult essays and require a lot of concentration.

6 | Georg Simmel: society as form and process—the outsider's view

Introduction: Simmel as a herald of postmodernism. *Society and the social*: his conception of society—comparison with Weber and Lukacs; social forms and the life process and the protection of individuality. *The social forms*: society, social relationships, social institutions, and play forms; his methods and organizational principles.

Introduction

> How does the raw material of immediate experience become the theoretical structure that we call history? The transformation in question is of a more radical sort than common sense usually assumes. To demonstrate this is to develop a critique of historical realism—of the view that the science of history should provide a mirror image of the past 'as it really was'. Such a view commits no less an error than does realism in art, which pretends to copy reality without being aware of how thoroughly this act of 'copying' in fact stylizes the contents of reality.
>
> (Simmel 1907/1971: 3)

Georg Simmel was a contemporary and colleague of Weber, part of an intellectual group which would meet regularly and included the Marxist Georg Lukacs, whom I discussed earlier. He never quite seems to qualify as one of sociology's founding thinkers of equal status with the other three. Yet he is frequently cited as the most original and seminal of the four (e.g. Levine 1971) with a major influence on early American sociology; he is often also cited as the most difficult, an ambivalent attitude that was common to his contemporaries as well. There is little that is systematic about his work and Coser (1991*a*) talks of the 'almost studied disorderliness of his method'. It is perhaps his disorderliness that sometimes gives the impression that he belongs to the contemporary world. The way in which he bridges the gap between the first and the last decades of the twentieth century can be seen in the above quotation. He begins with Weber's problem: how do we make sense of the complex reality of our experience. But he moves immediately towards the novelist's task, comparing it directly with that of the social scientist and presenting us with a very modern idea: that what we think of as reality is in fact a construction, just as the novelist's 'real world' is a construction. He seems to move to and fro between the realist and postmodern constructionist position. Overall perhaps the latter dominates, but there are interesting elements of the former.

Society and the social

Simmel's conception of society is not as clear as Durkheim's or Marx's but it is there, in some ways clearer than Weber's. Sometimes he writes as if society is the combination of relationships between people, a more or less Weberian position, but he seems to give that combination a reality of its own. In a difficult sentence he talks about society being 'the sum of those forms of relationship by virtue of which individuals are transformed, precisely, into "society" in the first sense'— that is, the combination of relationships between individuals. There is in this the notion of a society producing or reproducing itself by socializing its individual members into more or less determinate relationships which together make up the society in question. In other words, there is also the notion here of a society existing over and above its individual members. But there are good reasons why Simmel does not pursue a more systematic analysis of society.

As might be expected from Lewis Coser's comments, it is difficult to give a coherent account of Simmel's conception of society and his sociological method—not because his own accounts are incoherent but rather because they often seem fragmented, and looking through some of the secondary accounts of Simmel one could almost think that each refers to a different thinker. I have already mentioned the links between Lukacs, Weber, and Simmel, and I want first to try to explore these a little further; I hope that this might make more sense of his fragmentary style of working. All three worked within the conceptual context of a fundamental dualism, between human existence and the natural world, with whatever it is we call 'society' coming in between. For Weber, society was only the relationships between individuals; for Lukacs, working with the Marxist notion of alienation, these relationships could become 'solidified' as a 'second nature' which imposes as many restrictions and limitations on us as the natural world, and which seems to us as unchangeable as the natural world. It is precisely this fear of 'solidification', or 'ossification', or alienation that haunts Simmel's conception of modern society, his conception of what sociology ought to be about, and his own style of sociological work.

One clue to Simmel's method comes from an early and comparatively little known work of Lukacs before he embraced Marxism: *Soul and Form* (1910/1971*b*). This has been described as one of the first great works of European existentialism (Goldmann 1977). Lukacs attempts to explore what might be called the fundamental forms of relationship which are possible between the soul, the human spirit, and its surrounding world, arguing that the 'inauthentic' (my word) relationships are those in which the soul becomes stifled, or allows itself to be stifled by what is around it. Simmel in his own work was afraid of this happening on a world scale—that the modern world would 'socialize' the human spirit, limit and standardize it; Simmel wished to preserve the autonomy of spirit, or mind, or—a word I would prefer but I suspect many wouldn't—the soul.

Systematic sociological theorizing threatened just such a socialization or stifling of, in his case, his own soul. He was insistent that sociology was not and should not be some synthesizing queen of the sciences, regarding the whole of what would now be called the 'social' as its province; the objective realm of nature and the realm of the individual were also suitable subjects for other sciences. Not everything was a social construction and, what's more, it was desirable that we should not think that that was the case and that society should not provide the explanatory base of every aspect of human life. Simmel would certainly not have used this term, but he was arguing against a totalitarian sociological vision.

His style can be seen as a defence against such a vision and a defence against his incorporation into such a vision. This is summed up clearly by Charles Axelrod in a passage worth quoting at length:

For Simmel, his style as method cannot be divorced from his experience of theorizing. Rather, by virtue of his topical preoccupation with the theme of individuality, it produces a conception of method as a consequence of the individuality achieved in theorizing. For Simmel, any method imposed on a member by the scientific community binds that member and restricts his ability to articulate his individuality. That is, method imposed by the community is precisely what the individual must attempt to transcend (even as he is participating in the life of the group). . . . Through his writing Simmel can only become the exemplar of individuality within his scientific community.   (Axelrod 1991: 166)

If, in his method, fragmentation was an attempt to preserve his autonomy, he was less sure about fragmentation in the social being a good thing. According to Levine, Simmel (unlike Marx, whose radical vision presented the possibility of a united humanity) saw

the generation of increasingly specialized cultural products ordered in fundamentally discrete and incommensurable worlds. The Gods who rule these worlds are not at war with one another—any more than colours and sounds are in basic conflict—but each tries to move human accomplishment closer to the universal implementation of its basic principle. (Levine 1971: pp. xvii–xviii)

Allowing for difference in style and concepts (jargon ?) this sounds remarkably like Foucault's critique of modernity, but with rather more profundity.

The social forms

The profundity in the way that Simmel talks about these issues lies in his notion of the human spirit which he wishes to protect from extinction by society, and the way in which he develops the notion of different social forms which comprise and emerge from social interaction. Sociology itself can be seen as part of the enemy. The science arose in the course of the nineteenth century as a consequence of the growing power of social groupings, in particular social classes, and from this power came the idea that the social constitution of life is all pervasive and this is then projected back onto history. It is, therefore, as I said earlier, important for Simmel not to allow sociology to be taken as the most important of the social sciences, and he used the distinction between form and content, which coheres with his Kantian background, to try to establish the nature of sociology as one autonomous science amongst others. The 'contents' of sociology are those aspects of human life which push individuals into association with each other, our needs, our drives, and our aims and intentions. Forms are the means by which we synthesize these relationships in social entities which are over and above the individuals who make them up. There are four forms. We have already encountered the most abstract—'society' itself. The least abstract are the social relationships which individuals enter into with each other to satisfy their mutual and individual needs; we can regard these relationships as the elementary form of society, a sort of molecular structure. What is important is the *relationship*:

Strictly speaking, neither hunger not love, work nor religiosity, technology nor the functions and results of intelligence, are social. They are factors in association only when they transform the mere aggregation of isolated individuals into specific forms of being with and for one another, forms that are subsumed under the general concept of interaction. Sociation is the form (realized in innumerably different ways) in which individuals grow together into a unity and within which their interests are realized. And it is on the basis of their interests—sensuous or ideal, momentary or lasting, conscious or unconscious, causal or teleological—that individuals form such unities'　(Simmel 1907/1971: 24)

In between the molecular structure and society, there are two other forms. There are those activities and relationships which solidify into institutions which are effectively visible and goal-oriented—institutions such as the state or trade unions, the church, the university or college. These become autonomous from the flux of interaction and react back on it to organize it. Secondly, there are those forms which develop for, as Levine (1971) puts it, the sake of the forms themselves, not for practical purposes. These are 'play' forms of association: instead of engaging in economic competition I might compete at football or cricket; instead of having affairs and hurting my wife, I flirt. As Levine points out, 'In all these modes of interaction, the emphasis is on *good form*'—in a peculiarly English fashion, it is playing the game that matters, not winning or losing.

It is clear from our contemporary perspective that the latter form has been subordinated to the former, the instrumental form. Simmel is one of the few sociologists to take play seriously for its own sake—that is, as an activity in its own right rather than as a part of the much more serious process of socialization, as it was for Mead. It is possible to develop a second string to Simmel's critical sociology: not only do certain social developments threaten the imprisonment of the spirit; they also threaten the dominance of instrumentality over play.

Simmel's method is to choose a particular phenomenon from the flux of experience and examine its structure and its history. It is not unlike Weber's ideal-type analysis which I described as producing a series of still snapshots of social reality from different points of view, but Simmel's version is more fragmentary, lacking the cohesion that Weber finds through his concept of rationality. Levine (1971) identifies four principles which underlie all of Simmel's analyses. We have already met the first: each study seeks the form which has imposed a particular order on the world—Simmel sees the form/content distinction as fundamental to human thought. The second is the principle of reciprocity—each phenomenon takes a meaning only through its relationships with others; no event or object has an intrinsic meaning 'in itself'; thirdly, there is the principle of distance—that 'the properties of forms and meanings of things are a function of the relative distances between individuals and other individuals or things' (ibid., p. xxxiv); finally, the world can be understood in terms of dualisms that may involve conflict or may simply be contrasted with each other. Many of Simmel's studies, for example, consist of analyses of different combinations of proximity or closeness.

These principles fulfil the same functions as the notion of rationality in Weber's thought—they link together the apparently disparate nature of his studies and, like Weber's conception of rationality, they are important aspects of the development of the modern world. I have already pointed to Simmel's view that modernity leads to fragmentation—there is no sense in his work of the prospect that Lukacs held out, from a not dissimilar viewpoint, of the transcendence of the dualisms, the achievement of a unity of form and content in the establishment of socialism

Further reading

Trying to make overall sense of Simmel is rather like trying to catch a fish with your hands—it keeps slipping away. As might be evident from my quotations, I found Donald M. Levine's introduction to *Georg Simmel on Individuality and Social Forms* (1971) very useful; the four essays by Simmel in part 1 of this book are the best of the original texts.

Conclusion to Part 1: the first basic dualism of social theory

What emerges most clearly from the four previous chapters is that Marx and Durkheim have one starting point for sociological analysis—society—and Weber another—the individual—whereas Simmel seems to fall between the two although he gives some priority to the individual. This is the first of the basic dualisms with which social theory has to contend—it is a dualism because the starting point is not sufficient. Each theorist of society also has to take account of the individual and in turn Weber and Simmel also have to take account of something called society. Any theory has to choose one as a starting point, but cannot avoid the other.

Perhaps the most important thing to note at this point is that all four were struggling to come to grips with something called 'society', even if they did so in very different ways. In Durkheim there is the notion of society existing over and above the individual and of social facts, and their discovery and explanation through identifying, measuring, and correlating their external manifestations. There is already here a notion of an *underlying* social structure (forms of solidarity) which has surface effects. The consistency of suicide rates indicates that social forces are at work, and it is not a matter of purely individual whims. Different forms of suicide are traced to different forms of social cohesion, so we can predict that rates will increase when, for whatever reason, the rules and norms of a society lose some of their strength or when too much responsibility is placed on the individual ego rather than on the community.

The other three did not talk about suicide, but it is possible to illustrate how they would differ in their approaches. A Marxist would approach the problem through placing suicide in a wider context of an interaction between the individual and society; whereas Durkheim comes close to seeing a suicide as a result only of society acting on the individual, a Marxist would be concerned with this—in particular with what we will discuss in the Chapter 8 as the alienating effects of the capitalist relations of production—but also with the situation and perceptions which are involved in the individual's decision to commit suicide. I think it is fair to say that there would be a more complex social analysis which would lead on to different distinctions from those found in Durkheim. For example, a Marxist might point out that there is a different wider social meaning to the suicide of a Wall Street banker after the 1929 slump than there is to a Buddhist monk publicly burning himself as a protest against the American presence in Vietnam. Durkheim would see the first as anomic suicide, the second as altruistic, but he would miss or underrate these wider social meanings, whereas the Marxist would see them as primary. In the first case suicide would be symptomatic of the isolating and alienating effects of the market; the second would be part of a significant struggle for national liberation.

Box 6.1. **The first basic dualism of social theory**

THE INDIVIDUAL	SOCIETY
Durkheim: the individual is formed and limited by society.	**Durkheim:** society exists over and above the individual.
Marx: the 'individuated' individual is an idea produced as part of the development of capitalism.	**Marx:** society is created by human action but acts back upon individuals as an external power.
Weber: the individual is the only reality and analysis must start from individual rational action.	**Weber:** society is the rather fragile result of human interaction.
Simmel: the individual life is engaged in a constant dialectic with social forms.	**Simmel:** 'society' is an increasingly important form organizing peoples' lives.

A Weberian study of suicide would concern itself with *the social meanings of suicide*. Jack Douglas's book of that name (1967) might not be technically a 'Weberian' study but it concerns itself with the meaning of a suicide to the actors involved; from this he argues that it is possible to build up a picture of the meanings that a particular society gives to suicide. He or she would direct attention to what we might call suicide as a rational action—to avoid further suffering, to take revenge on another person ('you'll be sorry') , to avoid the humiliation of bankruptcy, or to make a symbolic statement about an occupying army; the structural dimensions, forms of social cohesion, relations of production, and so on would not be considered.

Now, turning to Simmel, there are two options. The first, and the least Simmelian, would be to attempt to apply some of the ideas I discussed in Chapter 6; this could involve seeing suicide as an individual's way of resisting social forms, or in a more Durkheimian sense an individual's reaction to a collapse of established forms. A true 'Simmelian' approach, however, would contain something unexpected—perhaps along the lines of an elaboration of the French psychoanalyst Jacques Lacan's reported comment that a person may be kept alive by the possibility of committing suicide, or looking at suicide as a way of maintaining relationships and social cohesion.

What I find most interesting about this discussion is that none of these approaches seems to be mutually exclusive and none of them is complete by itself; yet they cannot somehow be added together into a total view. Each reveals a different aspect of what we are studying, and the disagreement would come in trying to give priority to one form of explanation or another. This, in turn, leads on to a range of philosophical issues which are beyond the scope of this particular text. Further complications will emerge as we come across the other dualisms in future chapters. At this stage it is possible to sum up the individual/society dualism as shown in Box 6.1.

Part 2

Conceptions of social structure

Introduction to Part 2

Strictly speaking, this part is not about *models* of society, in the sense that we have models of aeroplanes, small-scale versions of the real thing. However, it is a useful metaphor for attempts to think about the crucial aspects or components of a society and the way in which these are related to each other. These theories begin life as attempts to understand changes in late-nineteenth and early twentieth-century European and North American society. Inevitably, however, each theorist produces concepts which have a wider applicability and help us to reach an understanding of very different types of society, including, of course, our own. There will be some overlap between Part 2 and Part 3 on theories of social change, and you should bear in mind that the division is arbitrary. But I think that it is a useful division: Part 2 will describe the various models of society offered by the classical theorists, including the mechanisms which hold them together and keep them working; Part 3 will look at different conceptions of history and of further development—their ideas about where we are all going.

As we proceed it should become clear just how complex these thinkers are and how their explicit methodologies considered in the last chapter do not quite contain their work—it often goes beyond what they say they are doing, and it is often when they go beyond their explicit methodology that they are most interesting.

7 | Durkheim: drunk and orderly

Introduction

Social integration and system integration.

Types of solidarity: *The Division of Labour*

Mechanical and organic solidarity: repressive law and the *conscience collective*; the function of the division of labour; Durkheim's functionalism; organic solidarity and restitutive law; individualism and dependency in modern societies; Durkheim and modern politics; the use of the organic analogy. *Abnormal forms of the division of labour*: understanding social conflict; industrialism and capitalism; the forced division of labour; managerial deficiencies.

The sociology of religion and knowledge

The nature of religion: the sacred/profane distinction; totemism; religious beliefs as representations of the social; comparison of Durkheim and Marx on religion. *The arguments in Elementary Forms*: Durkheim's causal, interpretive, and functional analyses of religion. Durkheimian analyses of contemporary societies. *The sociology of knowledge*: Durkheim's attempt at a sociological explanation of Kant's categories; the link between social structure and the structure of thought; the problems with Durkheim's sociology of knowledge and comparison with Marx's theory of ideology.

The sociology of morality and education

The conservative and radical Durkheim; the relation of morality to the social; morality in a period of change; sociology and morality; moral education and its aim; spontaneous education and direct teaching; discipline, authority, and power; the rational justification of moral rules; dignity, self-determination, and attachment to society; the humanistic goals of education and the balance of individual and society.

Sociology of the law, state, and politics

The evolution of punishment towards humanist ideals; the developing sympathy for the criminal; the power of the state; the distinction between governor and governed and the definition of the state; the governing of secondary groupings; the state as defender of individual rights; Durkheim and contemporary political debates.

> Conclusion
> The importance of Durkheim's insights; his contributions to understanding
> the basic dualisms of sociology.

Introduction

in general 'la société' had an intoxicating effect on his mind.

(Ginsberg 1956: 51)

Durkheim is the most sociological of all four thinkers, in the sense that he saw political, social, and philosophical problems as amenable to sociological analysis and solution. He would often refer to 'society' as an explanation, and a change in society as a solution. However, Ginsberg's point that Durkheim was content to use the term 'society' without further analysis is not quite fair. There is much more to his work than a simplistic notion of the social whole.

Chapter 2 discussed social facts, their discovery, and their explanation. Durkheim generally proceeds in the way he prescribes and gives the impression of identifying a social fact and going on to test various hypothetical explanations. Some of these arguments are useful and some seem to have a mainly rhetorical purpose and I will not always consider all his points. My intention is less to trace the detail of his argument than to present an overall picture. There is a change of emphasis as his work progresses which is perhaps best seen as a move between two levels of social organization (although both are present all the time). In the earlier work he concentrates on the level of practical relationship between people and groups; in the later work he moves to a concern with shared ideals and systems of thought. It is useful here to introduce a distinction from modern sociology which follows on the action/structure dualism, a distinction made by David Lockwood (1964) between social integration and system integration. The latter refers to the way in which institutions are bound together, the former to the way in which individuals are bound together, usually through shared values and beliefs. Lockwood takes Marx as being concerned primarily with system integration and Durkheim, and later Talcott Parsons, with social integration. Of course, the distinction appears within each individual theorist and I shall suggest that in the *Division of Labour* Durkheim is closer to a concern with system integration.

If Durkheim was drunk on the concept of society, he still saw society as orderly, not a chaotic jumble. He was trying to understand how different parts of society were related to each other in a functioning whole and he was increasingly concerned with the place of the individual in modern society, as witnessed in my earlier discussion of *Suicide*.

Types of solidarity: *The Division of Labour*

Mechanical and organic solidarity

In his earliest major work, *The Division of Labour in Society* (1893/1984), we find Durkheim contrasting two very different types of society: those that are held together by *mechanical* solidarity, in which there is very little division of labour, and those held together by *organic* solidarity, where the division of labour is highly developed. The way in which one develops to the other is a matter for the next chapter. For the moment we can regard them as two types of society at opposite ends of a continuum.

We can think of the different forms of solidarity as social facts, like suicido-genic currents, not immediately visible but identifiable through an external phenomenon. The 'visible symbol' of the form of solidarity is the legal system, the organization of social life in 'its most stable form'. Mechanical solidarity is distinguished by *repressive law*, which insists on the punishment of the wrongdoer for those actions which offend against the clearest and most determinate moral sentiments held by a society, or its 'average members'. There are gradations of clarity matched by gradations of punishment—murder is fairly clear and is punished by death or life imprisonment; not being courteous to one's siblings brings only mild disapproval, if that. The totality of such beliefs 'forms a determinate system with a life of its own'—the *conscience collective* of a society. Giddens (1978) points out that neither of the two usual English traditions of this term—collective conscience or collective consciousness—is quite accurate. In fact, Durkheim seems to use the term to cover both. In this context he is using it to refer to the collective values and what modern sociologists would call the norms of a society: the strongest values and norms shared by most people and enforced by repressive law. This is close to the collective-conscience translation. Elsewhere—particularly in *The Elementary Forms of the Religious Life* (1912/1915)—he uses it to refer to very basic ways of seeing the world which we all share: the forms of logic that we use and our conceptions of time and space which impose order and sense on the world. This is closer to the collective-consciousness translation.

In a society held together by mechanical solidarity, the *conscience collective* exists over and above individuals and becomes implanted in them. It is a society in which the division of labour remains at a very basic level—no more, perhaps, than the sexual division of labour implied by the different biological make-up of men and women. Mechanical solidarity implies the similarity of individuals. All share the same basic beliefs about the world and about life, essentially based on religion, and all engage in the same basic activities—often a matter of subsistence hunting and gathering; even physical differences are at a minimum. The individual is absorbed into the *conscience collective*—one is either 'in' a society or 'outside' it; one cannot be an individual in society and members of the society are not mutually dependent. Strictly speaking 'mechanical solidarity' is not itself a form of social structure but it is the form of solidarity found in 'segmented societies'—societies originally clan (kinship) based but later based on locality.

Societies held together by organic solidarity have a well-developed division of labour. It is apparent on a common-sense level that the division of labour has economic advantages—several hundred workers using specific skills and doing specific tasks can build more jumbo jets than one person working by him- or herself in the back garden. But Durkheim suggests it has another function, beyond increasing economic prosperity. Difference acts to bring people together—whether they be men or women in marriage or friendships based on different qualities; the differences involved in the division of labour also bring people together:

We are therefore led to consider the division of labour in a new light. In this case, indeed, the economic services that it can render are insignificant compared with the moral effect that it produces, and its true function is to create between two or more people a feeling of solidarity.   (Durkheim 1893/1984: 17)

Durkheim makes a particularly important point about his use of the term 'function'—one often forgotten by later sociologists who went under the label of 'functionalism'—that to identify the function of the division of labour does not explain its existence. We need a historical explanation of how something comes into existence; the function of this something might then explain why it continues in existence. The function of the division of labour is not its 'aim' or 'intention'—some modern sociologists might refer to it as an 'unintended consequence'. It remains in existence because it holds society together.

The social structure associated with this type of solidarity is the one we are all used to—highly complex and organized. The *conscience collective* remains but becomes less and less important, covering a smaller proportion of our lives and concentrating on the individual. It is here that the distinction between system integration and social integration becomes important. System integration, the division of labour, is highly organized through markets, the state, and so on; social integration—the shared norms and values of a society—becomes less important. We find ourselves living amongst and working with people with very different sets of beliefs and views. It seems to me that one of the features of our contemporary world is precisely the highly organized social system in which we live—Giddens calls it the 'juggernaut' of late modernity which leaves us dependent on many things beyond our experience—contrasted with the vast space we have in which to be individuals, created by the weakening of social integration through the *conscience collective*. It can come to seem that we have complete control over our lives; that we have a high degree of independence because our dependence on others is so well hidden.

The external manifestation of organic solidarity is restitutive law, which is concerned with the relationships between individuals and groups, aiming less to punish than to restore the *status quo ante*; the situation as it was at the beginning of the relationship. It becomes important to ensure that contracts are kept, that people deal honestly in their relationships with each other, and are compensated for any wrong they might suffer in these relationships. If a builder takes the old roof off my house and then vanishes with my money without putting the new roof on, I might be very angry with him or her but I would not seek through the courts to have the person publicly flogged, sent to jail, or executed. I would concentrate on getting my money back, perhaps with some compensation, so that I can pay somebody else to do the job. Steven Lukes (1973: 158) cites civil, commercial, procedural, administrative, and constitutional law as comprising restitutive law.

The paradox of organic solidarity based on the division of labour is that members of society become both more individuated and more dependent on society at the same time: more individuated because in modern societies people fulfil many different social roles, behave differently in those roles, and work with different, specialized bodies of knowledge. Beliefs and knowledge shared by the whole community are no longer sufficient to enable each individual to fulfil his or her task. We become more dependent on society and more bound into society because we are dependent on everybody else fulfilling their task—vitally dependent. If I were a member of a hunter-gatherer society, I could go off by myself for long periods of time, looking for food, finding my own shelter, and so on. In contemporary society I am dependent on other people—many of whom live on the other side of the world—to grow my food, make my clothes, supply me with warmth and light, print the books I read, service the word processor I write on, and so on. I could have or do none of these things without society.

The *conscience collective* comes to attach, in Lukes's words, 'supreme value to individual dignity, equality of opportunity, work ethic and social justice' (ibid. 158). It is important to remember that the value of individualism is a *collective* value shared by the whole society. One of Durkheim's targets was the utilitarian argument typified by Herbert Spencer, the English sociologist. This is an argument which will be familiar to anyone who has listened to modern right-wing politicians or economists who talk about market forces. If we each pursue our self-interest on the open market, then solidarity will ensue—it will be in each person's self-interest to honour contracts, and so on. Durkheim's point was that there is, in fact, an underlying collective agreement that individuals should pursue their own interest—in fact, individuation and the development of self-interest in the first place depend upon the development of the *conscience collective*. As in the development of the division of labour itself, it is the moral dimension which underpins its continued existence. This is in direct contrast to a Marxist approach, which would see individualism *and* its associated morality as a product rather than a producer of the division of labour.

It is also important to note that these issues, translated into the language of modern politics, are at the very centre of contemporary debates at least in the USA and the UK: arguments about the benefits and the limitations of the free market and its undermining of the stability of social life contend with arguments about the importance of our obligations to society, our sense of community, and so on. One possible Durkheimian interpretation of the contemporary western world might be that the individualism of the *conscience collective* is eating away at its own foundations, the underlying consensus which once supported individualism. Christopher Lasch, for example, has argued that élites no longer identify with the well-being of their society but are concerned *only* with their own well-being (Lasch 1995).

In the term *organic* a whole social theory is hidden: the idea that there is rather more than an analogy between societies and organisms—that societies can actually be considered as living organisms. Rather like the human body, in which the different organs—heart, liver, kidneys, intestines—complement each other and depend upon each other for their continued functioning, while the body as a whole depends upon each and all of them, so society and its separate parts depend upon each other for its continued existence. These ideas recur constantly throughout the history of sociology.

One final point, before moving on from this particular set of issues, has to do with the theoretical usefulness and empirical accuracy of looking at the world in this way. Steven Lukes (1973: 159) makes the point that Durkheim 'vastly understated the degree of interdependence and reciprocity in pre-industrial societies, as well as vastly overstating the role of repressive law' in such societies. Now it seems to me that we do not have to regard these two models of integration as empirically existing realities, but rather as ideal types in the Weberian sense. Perhaps both forms of solidarity are always present, but their comparative weights and relationships differ.

Abnormal forms of the division of labour

The organic analogy implies a high level of system integration and stability and it has always been a criticism of functional theories that they cannot explain, or perhaps even recognize, social conflict. In a society where there is a highly developed division of labour and a balance between system integration and social integration, things would work smoothly. Whether such a state of affairs has ever existed might be debatable, but it certainly did not exist at the time Durkheim was writing and does not exist now. But Durkheim was no fool and could see what was going on around him, as could later functionalists. The accusation that a theory cannot account for something as obvious as a social conflict assumes a stupidity on the part of the theorist which is not credible, and Durkheim's attempt to deal with this came under the heading of 'the abnormal division of labour'. He suggested that there were three forms.

The most obvious form of conflict at the end of the nineteenth century was class conflict. Anthony Giddens (1978) makes the point that we can find in Durkheim's way of dealing with this a division in the history of sociological theory. Whereas, for Marx, class conflict marked the appearance of a new type of society—capitalism—for Durkheim it was a feature of the incomplete development from mechanical to organic solidarity through the development of *industrial* society. It was a product of the *anomic* division of labour. Industrialization had developed too quickly and economic enterprises had not yet developed the values and rules which would enable their smooth functioning; nor had society as a whole yet developed the mechanisms by which competition could be controlled and the markets regulated. Once again we find the arguments of a century ago being rehearsed again in contemporary politics. We also find another dualism at the centre of social theory—that of capitalism/industrialism. I shall refer to this as a secondary dualism—it is not involved directly in the fundamental dilemmas of social theory which we would find in discussing any society, but refers rather to ways of thinking about contemporary society and its comparatively recent history.

The second form of the abnormal division of labour also has echoes in contemporary political arguments. Durkheim called it the *forced* division of labour. The constraint comes from external inequalities which prevent the healthy development of the division of labour. Thus people might be allocated to positions in the division of labour to which they are not suited by their natural talents or their abilities. An example would be somebody who becomes a manager of an enterprise through family connections rather than through managerial ability, or somebody who pursues a menial job because of parental poverty and lack of opportunity to develop talents. A similar misallocation might come through the economic inequality which results from inheritance—if some people start life in a worse economic situation than others, the poorer are necessarily subjected to the rich, and real organic solidarity cannot develop.

Contemporary arguments about equality of opportunity and 'level playing fields' address precisely these issues.

The third abnormal form of the division of labour is a managerial deficiency, where the enterprise is not organized to get the best and most out of its members—the more continuous and coordinated the various functions, the more solidarity grows and the more skilled the worker becomes. Various critics (Friedmann 1961; Lukes 1973) have pointed out that this argument is simply not true—the more developed the division of labour, the less skilled and the less happy the workers. It is as if Durkheim himself was confusing social and system cohesion here, assuming that the latter automatically led to the former rather than undermining it, which I think would be the dominant contemporary view.

This is an appropriate point at which to move on to Durkheim's theory of social cohesion.

The sociology of religion and knowledge

> Before all, [religion] is a system of ideas with which the individuals represent to themselves the society of which they are members, and the obscure but intimate relations which they have with it. This is its primary function; and though metaphorical and symbolic, this representation is not unfaithful.
>
> (Durkheim 1912/1915: 225)

Religion is at the centre of Durkheim's sociology; his major work, *The Elementary Forms of the Religious Life* (1912/1915), was published nearly twenty years after *The Division of Labour*. It is the last of the major texts in the Durkheimian canon.

The nature of religion

In the course of his career Durkheim changed his mind about the defining feature of religion. In *The Elementary Forms* we find him abandoning the obligatory nature of beliefs and settling on the distinction between the sacred and the profane. This text is a 'second-hand' study of the religion of Australian aborigines: Durkheim never went to Australia but uses the studies of those who had investigated these tribes first hand, with some extra evidence from studies of native Americans. He assumed that all the essential aspects of religious life would be visible in the simplest religious forms and the most simple was totemism, found in societies closest to 'the beginning of evolution'. Totemism appears in what I referred to earlier as 'segmented societies', or societies based on kinship and divided into clans; the members of each clan believe they are related to each other, not through any definite blood relationship but through the fact that they share the same name—the name of an object, the *totem*, which has a very special—a sacred—significance. In Australian societies this is often if not always something from the natural world—an animal, a fish, or a tree.

The belief in the power attributed to the totem, or, in more complex societies, to the gods or to God or Allah is neither a mistake nor an illusion, nor is it the truth. If religious beliefs were illusions, they would not have lasted throughout human history—they are not simply errors, as some humanist and rationalist thinkers would have us believe. On the other hand, one does not have to accept that these beliefs are literally true—that the Christian God really exists and is all powerful, or that the tortoise that is the clan totem really has special powers. Rather these figures—whether the tortoise or God—stand for something else which really is immortal and possesses special powers, including immense moral power over the individual, and on which the individual depends for his or her continued protection and survival: *society*. Religious beliefs are representations—*collective* representations—of the power a society has over each of its members. When he moves to talking about *collective representations* rather than the *conscience collective*, Durkheim is shifting his focus away from shared norms and beliefs (although they are still important) to shared ways of thinking.

Before going on to explore this, I want to spend some time comparing Durkheim's theory of religion with that of Marx—for whom the topic is of minor importance. The comparison is nevertheless instructive. In a famous comment Marx called religion the 'opium of the people'; a belief in future happiness in the next world which was deployed in this world to justify an acquiescence in suffering. This was a political judgement which, I fear, was often only too correct. His intellectual understanding of religion took up the arguments of the Hegelian philosopher Ludwig Feuerbach: God was a projection of powers that were really human, and progress would involve humanity taking those powers into itself and exercising them itself. Humanity would, as it were, become God, and would establish a proper control over society as a way of gaining its freedom. It seems to me that there is very little difference and all the difference in the world between this view and Durkheim's views—a paradoxical contrast that we will come across time and time again.

The arguments in *Elementary Forms*

Durkheim's argument is subtle and complex; Steven Lukes (1973) provides the best account I have come across and I shall follow him here for a while. He suggests (p. 462) that Durkheim is presenting three 'hypotheses' about religion: the causal, the interpretive, and the functional.

The *causal* explanation of religion is that it is the result of a collective experience; what he called, in a wonderfully evocative phrase, a 'collective effervescence'. It is a fairly common experience that people change when they are caught up in large group processes—we 'get carried away', there is something exciting going on, and we behave differently from the way we behave when we are alone, and this gives us a sense of the power of the collective. Militant trade unionists were once directly aware of this in their preference for shop-floor votes by a show of hands rather than by secret ballots. On the shop floor, amongst one's co-workers, it is possible to sense power; alone, with a voting paper, one can only feel weak against a powerful and wealthy employer. It is this sense of collective strength and excitement which Durkheim sees as the origin of religion.

Lukes (1973: 465–70) is particularly lucid about what he calls the *interpretive* explanation. It is here that we meet again the significant of the word 'representation'. Religion can be seen as an elementary theory of the way the world and society work. The totem is the personification of the clan and its power. This representation enabled the clan to think about itself as well as its social and natural world—for example, the distinction between body and soul can be seen as matching that between sacred and profane, the soul being the representative of the collective, of the totem or the god in the individual. Religion

seeks to translate these [social] realities into an intelligible language which does not differ in nature from that employed by science: the attempt is made by both to connect things with one another, to establish internal relations among them, to classify and systematize them. (Lukes 1973: 467)

Religion is not only a way of thinking about social realities; it is also a way of dramatizing them. The Christian Mass, particularly in its Roman Catholic or High Anglican manifestations, could be seen as theatre in which the consumption by the congregation of the body and blood of Christ (the bread and wine that some believe are actually transformed into flesh and blood) is a dramatic metaphor of our internalization of society and its rules and prohibitions. We eat our leader, the one who represents us, and we become part of him and of each other: 'We break this bread to share in the body of Christ. Though we are many, we are one body because we all share in one bread' (*The Alternative Service Book* (1980), 142). Those of other denominations or faiths might find it a useful exercise to find equivalent dramatizations from their own experience.

The third hypothesis that Lukes identifies is the *functional* hypothesis—the consequences of religion. This is clearly one of maintaining and reinforcing social cohesion. In the case of totemism, the totem is the permanent reminder to the clan of its unity, and to the individual of his or her membership in the clan; the rituals reinforce this, and in a society where many of its members spend much of the year in small groups foraging for food, the rituals strengthen the individuals who might otherwise feel overpowered by their conditions of life. Durkheim makes much of the way in which the individual feels stronger as a result of the ritual and in fact is stronger.

Durkheim's work has inspired interesting analyses of ritual in modern societies (see especially Lane 1981; Alexander 1988). As a useful exercise it might be worth trying to think about collective effervescences that you might have found yourself involved in—group activities where you became aware of the power of the group—and see if Durkheim offers you any new understanding. In the case of modern societies, however, we can rarely see collective symbols as representing the whole of society. A major danger of Durkheim's thought often pointed out by Marxist and radical critics (e.g. Zeitlin 1968) is that it can hide major divisions in society. They are only to a very limited extent 'wholes' which can be unified around symbols. A Durkheimian analysis of the 1953 British coronation (Shils and Young 1953) offers a rather trite analysis of the symbolism of the service as it illustrates social unity, but I know that there are people to whom that symbolism is powerful. I am a republican, but I found myself—to my surprise—moved almost to tears on the one occasion when I saw the queen. But there were even in the 1950s many people who would not be moved in that way—the amount of petty theft rose dramatically on Coronation Day. And of course in a modern society we cannot assume that participation in ritual celebration is a sign of belief—there are good reasons to go to a street party, even if one is a republican; and even amongst religious believers in the same church there can be huge disagreements on the meaning of the symbols.

The sociology of knowledge

Beyond the analysis of the function of rituals and the relationship between the group and the individual, and whatever faults in his work that have been revealed by later anthropologists, Durkheim's work remains relevant for its contribution to the sociology of knowledge, and it is here that the notion of collective representations really comes into its own. I mentioned earlier that Durkheim thought his theory of religion was able to explain the way in which we perceived the relationship between body and soul, the latter being the internal representation of society. It will become apparent when we come to other substantive areas of Durkheim's sociology that he is concerned with the way in which a potentially vulnerable and dangerous human physical organism is brought into the discipline and power of society—a way of looking at the world which is familiar to us these days through the work of Freud (and latterly Foucault); both Freud and Durkheim are concerned with the way in which humans employ metaphors to think about themselves and their relationships.

Durkheim, however, moved towards philosophy rather than psychology. He thought that sociology could solve the dualism of Kantian thought by rooting it in society—in the social itself. Put as simply as possible, the frameworks which we employ to organize our experience come from experience itself—but from what we might call a different level of experience from that considered by empirical sciences. The experience that we organize is our own day-to-day individual experience of the world; our ability to organize comes from our experience of collective life, the life of our society. Each society, depending on its organization, generates its own conceptions of time and space and of logical connection.

There is a problem here which haunts sociological explanations of our subjective capacities: in order to recognize, for example, the spatial relations suggested to us by our social experience, we must already have a sense of space. Kant's organizing categories belong to the *mind* and without them we would be unable to recognize *any* experience, including social experience. There would also be a problem of relativism: each different society would generate different forms of knowledge, and there would be no basis on which we could choose between them. This would clearly be unacceptable to Durkheim, given the rigour of the scientific method he outlined in *The Rules*, and he got round the problem by placing it in an evolutionary context. Our basic form of thinking is in essence no different from that of Aboriginal societies:

Is not the statement that a man is a kangaroo or the sun a bird, equal to identifying the two with each other? But our manner of thought is not different when we say of heat that it is not a movement, or of light that it is a vibration of the ether etc. Every time that we unite heterogeneous terms by an internal bond, we forcibly identify contraries. Of course the terms we unite are not those which the Australian brings together; we choose them according to different criteria and for different reasons; but the processes by which the mind puts them in connection do not differ essentially.   (Durkheim 1912/1915: 238)

The difference is that we have separated logic and scientific modes of thinking from their original religious basis and they have developed independently. The arguments are now pursued with more precision and rigour. In other words, we are doing the same thing as the aborigines, but better. This argument is pursued in a book written with his nephew, Marcel Mauss, called *Primitive Classification* (1903/1963), and, although I don't think anybody would now accept Durkheim's evolutionary theory, the issues raised in this book were taken up in a rather different way by the French anthropologist Claude Lévi-Strauss, a founder of modern structuralist thought, who argued that totemic classifications can reveal the basic organizing structure of the human mind, something that I think Durkheim was close to saying but managed to lose because, paradoxically, he was concerned with establishing a sociological explanation.

If we take the weak sense of Durkheim's argument, we are on much stronger ground. The weak sense is that of the sociology of knowledge: the idea that the structure of the society in which we live is in one way or another responsible for the structure and the content of our thinking. It is this emphasis on the structure of thinking that is important—if we drop the notion of finding a sociological solution to the problems of western philosophy and think instead simply of the ways in which we think, we can gain interesting insights. We can find in the nineteenth and early twentieth centuries, for example, parallel ways of thinking in the social and the natural sciences which tend towards relativism, and this seems to occur concurrently with changes in class structure that represent not an end to old social divisions but a loosening of them and perhaps an increasing ability to see the world from different points of view. I have put this very simplistically, but I hope the idea gets across.

The strength of Durkheim's link is precisely that it is between the structure of society and the structure of thought—he is not just saying that I learn my ideas from society (although, of course, I do), but I learn how to think about my ideas from society. The form of logic that I use—my understanding of the structure of a rational argument, the process of thinking itself—is a metaphor for the type of society I live in—so that, for example (an oversimplified example), a society based on agriculture and the repetitive cycle of the seasons might understand time as a repetitive movement and see human life as repetition through rebirth, etc., and would perhaps produce self-contained philosophical (religious) images with which to think in a circular fashion, deducing everything from the existence of God in such a way that everything that happens proves

God exists. On the other hand, modern society based on linear processes of production and the development of technology sees time as a linear movement from the past towards the future and thinks employing a linear logic: we start with certain assumptions and a certain amount of knowledge and we can deduce from that starting point; or alternatively we start with our sense of the outside world and we can induce general laws from our knowledge of that world.

The weakest point in Durkheim's sociology of knowledge is again his tendency to talk abut society as a whole when referring to modern complex societies. The sociology of knowledge was not a specifically Durkheimian achievement—Marx before him, and many Marxists after him, as well as Karl Mannheim (1938) grappled with these problems and particularly with the problem of relativism: if all knowledge is produced by specific social circumstances and is relative to those circumstances, then how can we claim that one form of knowledge is better than others? Could we argue that one social position actually grants a particular group of people a privilege in producing knowledge—that from their social position, this group can see more than others? Lukacs (1971a) was to claim that the proletariat, the working class, was such a group, and their advantage came from the structure of thinking to which their class position gave rise. Mannheim (1938) was to argue that intellectuals, because of their 'free-floating' class position, were able to integrate and see beyond more limited points of views. And modern 'feminist-standpoint' epistemology (Harding 1986, 1991) attempts to make a similar claim for women.

Now whether or not these claims work, the point I am making is that Durkheim's theoretical framework tends towards seeing society as essentially unitary, even when organic solidarity predominates. He is therefore blinkered to some of these possibilities. He is also blinkered to the possibility that there might be a sense in which religious belief might be 'the opium of the people'. A religion which, in comparatively undifferentiated societies, can be a metaphor for the whole society might continue to exist as that society becomes more differentiated, but it gets taken up into relations between different groups in society and becomes multi-dimensional, perhaps used as an ideology which can contribute towards maintaining a social order which benefits not the whole of the society but only one part of it. The Marxist theory of ideology suggests that ruling-class ideology masks itself as the way in which everybody looks at the world and Durkheim does rather leave himself open to criticism from this point of view. The important point perhaps is to avoid Durkheim's intoxication and recognize that there is more going on in society than he sometimes recognizes.

It was Durkheim's concern with social cohesion that pushed forward his interests in the sociology of education and morality.

The sociology of morality and education

There are two contrasting sides to Durkheim's work—the arch conservative identified by Zeitlin (1968) and more radical reformer that Pearce (1989) talks about. In his work on morality we see a more conservative Durkheim, whilst in his work on education we come closer to the reformer. His discussions of morality appeared after his death in 1917 (Durkheim 1925/1953, 1926/1962). He agrees with Kant that we cannot call a rule moral without implying some sort of obligation, and by now you should be able to predict that Durkheim saw the obligation as coming from society itself. This idea is reinforced by the argument that we cannot call an action moral if it is in pursuit of individual interests. In public life, for example, a politician who uses his or her political position to pursue his or her own private interests would be open to discipline and eventual punishment in most democratic societies. A *moral* action seeks the common good over and above that of the individual and it is directed towards others in accordance with society's ideals and values. This is another dimension to Durkheim's argument against the utilitarians, and it is an argument against those who in contemporary society argue that a free market eventually brings the common good.

In some of Durkheim's statements about morality and the all-powerfulness of society, we can see the evidence for those who accuse him of conservatism: 'it is never possible to desire a morality other than that required by the social conditions of a given time. To wish for a morality other than that implied in the nature of society is to deny the latter and, consequently, oneself' (Durkheim 1925/1953: 38). Such words would not have sounded strange coming from the mouth of an orthodox communist party hack in Soviet Russia, and perhaps Soviet communism possessed a simplistic notion of society equal to that employed by Durkheim in this quotation. However, he was not always as rigid as this. In his discussion of the abnormal forms of the division of labour, Durkheim talked about the rapid pace of change and the need for business concerns to develop a new morality; he argued that forms of morality could become outdated and new forms might develop as society changed, so that at any one time in modern society the morality implied in the 'nature of society' might be open to debate. The sociologist would be able to demonstrate scientifically which moral rules no longer served society and which ones might replace them. Thus, for example, we can take the law of blasphemy, which in the most straightforward Durkheimian sense is a protection of the sacredness of society itself. In a contemporary multicultural society it could be argued that the essential moral content of the *conscience collective* to which everybody must come to subscribe would be an ethic of mutual tolerance in which all religions or none must be protected by a law of blasphemy. But Durkheim seems to have had a rather touching faith in the ability of sociology to make scientific judgements about morality.

In his work on morality Durkheim returned to the dualism of human nature—its impulsive biologically based side and its 'civilized' socialized side. I have already mentioned the parallel with Freud, but there is a close connection with the work of Talcott Parsons (1951), who dominated mid-century sociology at least in the English-speaking world, and who was accused of working with 'an over-socialised concept of man' (Wrong 1957)—and presumably of woman too. Parsons used a tame version of Freud and the work of G. H. Mead to explain the way in which society moulded the personality to fit in with its requirements. Durkheim's account of socialization is rather more interesting and ambivalent. In contemporary debates about morality, it often seems that there is a desire to return to something that is conceived of as traditional morality—as, for example, in the British prime minister John Major's 'Back to Basics' campaign—but, as he found out when his ministers had to resign over sexual peccadilloes, to demand a return to traditional values is easier said than done. President Clinton learnt the same lesson during the 1996 Democratic Party Conference when his special adviser on family values resigned after a sex scandal. The traditional values that the traditional right seem to desire are usually 'Victorian'—paradoxically, the period during which Durkheim began his work and when he could see perfectly well that traditional morality was already gone for ever.

Durkheim approaches the matter of education through his theory of morality, and his lectures were on the subject of 'moral education' (Durkheim 1979). He saw the education of the young in the widest possible sense as the influence of any adult on children not yet ready to become full members of society, and he also saw education as a lifelong process; it is the means by which we learn how to cope with our physical existence, control our desires and impulses, and adjust to the social environment. The aim of education must be to enable each of us to act willingly in the way that society requires if it is to survive, and not just to conform to what is required. But it must also enable us to make our own decisions within these limits—modern society requires free agents.

He contrasts what he calls 'spontaneous' education with more direct teaching. The former describes a situation in which the child learns simply by being with adults as they go through their normal daily activities. This is the sort of education which has been sufficient for much of human history and it is appropriate to mechanical solidarity. Direct teaching occurs when society becomes too complex for the child to learn essentials in such a way—although spontaneous education continues in the ways that teachers themselves behave. If there is a gap between what they say and what they do, problems occur. Direct teaching is concerned with intellectual concepts and moral ideas. One central aim of education is the formation of character, not in the modern psychological sense but in the sense once used by the English schoolmasters (and it was always a very masculine phenomenon—as was Durkheim's sociology itself, since he had little to say about women) when they said that military discipline, cross-country running, rugby, cold showers, and other deprivations were good for character-building. It meant stability and reliability, an inner consistency, a denial of emotion—at which women were notoriously not very good.

Discipline is central to the teacher's work in two senses; one is the sense of regularity learnt through the school routine, conveying a sense of boundaries and of an authority greater than the child and the teacher. The teacher must teach morality as coming from a powerful source over and above the personalities in the classroom. Now in some respects *these* meanings of discipline are akin to ideas in modern psychoanalytic theories of child-rearing: the need for consistent, routine care which provides a sense of inner security, and the laying-down of boundaries of behaviour enabling the child to gain a firm sense of him- or herself, and his or her limitations. Of course, these boundaries have to be carefully judged so as not to damage the child through being too restrictive or too relaxed. However, there is one very significant difference: for psychoanalysis it is important that the authority in both cases be a personal one (although he/she might represent an impersonal authority) so that the child can introject and use a competent 'internal object'; for Durkheim, the authority is impersonal and external and would, I suspect, seem to modern eyes a distant and hostile authority. Ernest Wallwork takes up this point:

Durkheim denies the widespread assumption in his era, as well as in ours, that discipline is incompatible with self-realization, freedom and happiness. Discipline, by restraining limitless ambitions and by canalizing limited reserves of psychic energy in pursuit of determinate goals, is the indispensable means without which regular realization of human potentialities would be impossible. And, genuine psychological freedom, in Durkheim's view, is only possible though self-mastery of the unlimited power of unrestrained appetites.   (Wallwork 1972: 125)

I think that one of the problems with this sort of issue is that in Durkheim's time it was perhaps a little less difficult than it is now to distinguish between authority and power—in the former case, power is accepted and agreed to; in the latter case, power rests on forcing the other person to do something against his or her will. Durkheim is talking about the use of authority to enable the child to develop his or her own authority. And, on a common-sense level, I imagine that most people are aware of somebody who has limitless ambitions but who can barely organize him- or herself to get up in the morning. As Wallwork also points out, Durkheim was well able to recognize that discipline could turn into oppression and tyranny. Moral rules must be explained so that they become acceptable to the child on rational grounds. A tyrannical teacher would frighten his or her charges into submission. Durkheim opposed corporal punishment: the aim of discipline is to demonstrate to the wrongdoer the error of his or her ways in such a way that the reason behind the rule becomes apparent and is accepted; an essential element of the modern *conscience collective* is a belief in human dignity, and corporal punishment is an offence against human dignity. And human dignity is necessary for the self-determination for which modern society seems to call; we have to bring children to the stage where they do not just simply obey, or just understand the reasoning behind the moral rules that they are taught to follow, but can engage in their own independent moral reasoning. Here we move to the liberal Durkheim.

Moral education also involves the teaching of an attachment to society, and teachers should try to develop the child's nascent ability to empathize with others; there is a conflict within the child between egoism, which for Durkheim is always the enemy of morality, and altruism, which in the child is the weakest side. The purpose of education is not just to develop a child's own natural talents but to try to attach him or her to the social ideal—to create something new that was not there at the beginning.

In one of his more impressive in scope but lesser known works (Durkheim 1938/1977), Durkheim traced the development of French—and European—educational ideals, developing the notion of the whole person and a modern ideal of secular education that combined the natural sciences—which had the moral task of teaching the place of humanity in the world of nature—and the humanities, producing a humanism which would come to replace religion as the way in which society thinks of itself, or perhaps better, thinks itself. The aim of education then should be, in Wallwork's words, 'to honour rules respecting human rights, to appreciate the autonomy that man alone enjoys, and to devote themselves to genuinely humanistic goals' (Wallwork 1972: 145). I think this is the nearest we find in Durkheim to a view of what will or could replace religion at the centre of the *conscience collective* in organic solidarity. God/society is replaced by humanity/society. We also see here Durkheim trying to juggle concepts to arrive at a conception of individualism and autonomy which is not egoistic. He is, I think, trying to describe something much stronger than what proponents of the free market would describe as 'enlightened self-interest', which often amounts to saying: 'be greedy but not so greedy that other people will want to punish you for it' and something much weaker than 'Do as you are told and work for the greater glory of the fatherland (or the revolution or whatever)'. We will see that this is a central issue in contemporary politics and it leads on to Durkheim's political sociology.

The sociology of the law, state, and politics

We have already outlined the basis of Durkheim's sociology of the law in the discussion of *The Division of Labour*—the development from repressive to restitutive law. Connected with this was his work on punishment 'Two Laws of Penal Evolution' (1901/1969). This is particularly interesting because there is an indication that the state plays an independent role. Durkheim argues, first, that the intensity of punishment is greater in less developed societies *and in so far as power is more centralized and absolute*, and, secondly, that with the development of organic solidarity the main form of punishment becomes deprivation of liberty for periods depending on the nature of the crime. I will discuss these two laws briefly before going on to make the connection with the state. Now here Durkheim is talking not about the change from repressive to restitutive law with the increasing division of labour, but about the way repressive law itself changes. The explanation of this change has to do with the change towards humanist ideals that were discussed in relation to education—the focus moves to human dignity and the worth of the individual. This enables us to find a certain pity and fellow-feeling for the perpetrator as well as for the victim. It implies a point which needs to be made as much today as it was in Durkheim's day: that a concern for the *criminal* is a mark of civilization, and, by implication, an exclusive concern for punishment is a mark of less advanced societies. But the decline in the desire for punishment and for the more humane treatment of the criminal is not quite as directly related as that, and it is not simply a matter of growth in human sympathy—that could in some circumstances lead to a desire for greater punishment. It is rather that compassion for the victim is not swamped by anger with the criminal, and the compassion can therefore be spread around more.

Now, to return to the state: a strong central power with no opposition was seen by Durkheim as historically contingent, not as necessarily connected to mechanical solidarity. As Lukes points out in his intelligent discussion of this issue, Durkheim did not take the opportunity to discuss the possibility of authoritarian government in advanced societies, but he suggests that 'The influence of Governmental organisation could neutralise that of social organisation' (Lukes 1973: 258).

Durkheim begins his discussion of the state, *Professional Ethics and Civic Morals* (1957) by saying that the opposition of governing and governed is central in political life. It is likely that in the earliest forms of society such a division did not exist and we can only really talk about politics in a society where it does exist. But the division of a social group into governing and governed does not only exist in states—there is a similar division in the patriarchal *household*, so we need to find something which distinguishes the state from such social organizations. He considers size and control of a determinate territory, but neither is adequate—there are always counter-examples. The crucial feature of a state is that it controls not necessarily large numbers of *people* but a number of different secondary *social groupings*. The state is the organization of officials concerned with governing these secondary groups. It is not an embodiment of society as a whole, as Hegel had argued, but a specialized institution.

Durkheim next takes up the relationship of the state to the individual. This was not an issue in societies where mechanical solidarity dominated—the individual was absorbed into the social whole; however, as organic solidarity develops, so the power of the state develops, together with the rights of the individual. The growth of the state does not threaten but enables the rights of individuals.

Here we find the importance of the distinction between society and the state. 'Every society is despotic, at least if nothing from without supervenes to restrain its despotism' (Durkheim 1957: 61). As societies become more complex, then there is a need for individuals to move from group to group and a need to prevent the secondary groups exercising despotic control over their members; it is the function of the state to provide for this need.

We can identify, through this part of Durkheim's work, some real problems in a clearer way than we can through the other thinkers examined in this book, and there is another link with Freud here which highlights an important dimension to psychoanalytic social criticism. We do not find the distinction between society and state in the work of psychoanalysts, but we do find the argument that the stronger the state control over individual lives, the less strong the individual ego and superego. The state or society can become a sort of external superego which leaves the individual unable to take responsible decisions for him- or herself. Durkheim's argument was that, given that individual members of society felt their commitment to society, the function of the state was to create and protect the space where the individuals could exercise such responsibility:

The planning of the *social milieu* so that the individual may realise himself more fully and the management of the collective apparatus in a way that will bear less hard on the individual; and assure an amicable exchange of goods and services and the co-operation of all men of good will towards an ideal they share without any conflict; in these, surely, we have enough to keep public activity fully employed.   (Durkheim 1957: 71)

I think the problem here *is* Durkheim's tendency to get drunk on the notion of society. Although he presents us with a conceptual framework for looking at one range of contemporary issues, his unitary conception of society still dominates and we get no sense of the possibility central to Marx, for example, that the state may act as an instrument for one section of the population. It is essentially a mediator between secondary groups. These develop as the division of labour becomes more sophisticated, and they mediate between society and the individual just as the state mediates between the individual and the secondary group. The secondary groups develop their own *conscience collective*, as the strength of society itself is reduced by the division of labour. We shall see in Part 2 that the role of such groups is, for Durkheim, central to the development of modern society.

Durkheim made other contributions to social analysis. Wallwork (1972) praises him for the first truly modern sociological study of the family, in which he defined the family not as a group of blood relations nor as a group of people living together but as a group of people united by reciprocal rights and obligations sanctioned by society. This is a model sociological definition different from that offered by biology or psychology. It seems to me that Durkheim's lasting value is that he always points us to society, the force of the social, even if sometimes he goes over the top.

Conclusion

I want to use the conclusions to these chapters in Part 2 to look at the way in which each theorist might approach a cluster of connected contemporary political and social problems. The first involves the changes in the labour markets in the western world, the supposed growth of 'flexibility', and the decline in traditional industrial production which has moved to developing countries; the second is the apparent or alleged decline in morality, and /or traditional values, or community; the third is the development of new forms of political movement that seem to be concerned with identity—ethnic, cultural, or gender—or with the environment. In the conclusion to Part 2, I will compare the different approaches. I must emphasize that there is material here for a couple of dozen books and I will sketch a very general outline; you might think of it as looking at the same landscape through different spectacles—or, perhaps more accurately, through the wrong end of different pairs of binoculars.

The first thing that a Durkheimian sociologist would do would be to establish that these trends are actually happening, that they are not common-sense prenotions, and he or she would certainly find variations from area to area and social class to social class, but I will assume that it would be found that they are happening to some greater or lesser extent in most areas in the western world. The evidence would come from statistics about employment, crime rates, marriage and divorce rates, and so on, and attempts to relate them to political movements. It would be at this point that the real theoretical work would start.

I do not think that there is much doubt that, from a Durkheimian perspective, the change in the labour markets would be seen as a result of the developing division of labour on an international level, between societies; generally the process requires the development of more and better communications and these in turn encourage further changes. Many of the less pleasant effects of these changes in the West—higher levels of unemployment, higher levels of job insecurity, and the decline of traditional forms of industrial employment—might be seen in Durkheimian terms as involving periods of adjustment during which abnormal forms of the division of labour were dealt with and a new, more universal set of values emerge.

All this would be straightforward, but the apparent decline of community indicates that something else is happening—that perhaps the individualizing thrust of the division of labour is undermining even the individualist *conscience collective*, that the progress of system integration is undermining social integration and the modern state has protected the individual from the tyranny of secondary groups by undermining those groups. Durkheim talks about the way in which the development of the state freed the individual from the tyranny of medieval guilds in much the same way that modern free-market right-wing politicians talk about freeing workers from the tyranny of trade unions and breaking the power of professional groups. We are increasingly left with isolated individuals.

It is in this context that we can place the development of 'communitarianism' particularly in the USA, although it is now beginning to cross the Atlantic. The work of Etzioni (1995, 1996) seems to be suggesting that we should try to build up a *conscience collective* on a local level, developing support and control systems out of existing community relations. Interestingly, when he talks about the development of what he terms 'authentic communities', he discusses them in a very Durkheimian way, arguing for the need to develop ways of allowing individual autonomy without undermining the coherence of the community. In situations where the community is becoming too powerful, individual autonomy must be stressed, and where individual autonomy threatens the community, community power must be stressed.

If it is the case that system integration has been undermining social integration, then it is possible to think about the new political movements as spontaneous attempts to find a necessary form of social integration on some other basis than membership of a particular nation state or society. A sense of belonging does not come automatically in modern societies; it might never have come easily in any society, but Durkheim's theory offers good reasons for supposing that in complex modern societies it is especially difficult. These issues will be taken up again in Part 3, when we will look at Durkheim's politics and his vision of the future. They will also be considered in relation to the other three thinkers in the following chapters.

Box 7.1. An elaboration of Durkheim on the individual and society

THE INDIVIDUAL	SOCIETY
Durkheim: the individual is formed and limited by society. He/she becomes more important in complex societies and individualism becomes the focus of the conscience collective, binding people together.	**Durkheim:** society exists over and above the individual, over whom it exercises an immense power, especially in less complex societies.
Marx: the 'individuated' individual is an idea produced as part of the development of capitalism.	**Marx:** society is created by human action but acts back upon individuals as an external power.
Weber: the individual is the only reality and analysis must start from individual rational action.	**Weber:** society is the rather fragile result of human interaction.
Simmel: the individual life is engaged in a constant dialectic with social forms.	**Simmel:** 'society' is an increasingly important form organizing peoples' lives.

It is now possible to elaborate further on what I have called the basic dualisms of social theory, pointing out once again that all theories have to consider both sides and this creates tensions and contradictions at their centre.

In Box 7.1 there is an elaboration of Durkheim's handling of the first basic dualism—that of individual and society; in Box 7.2 an elaboration of his handling of the second basic dualism of action and structure; and in Box 7.3 an elaboration of his handling of the third basic dualism, that of social and system integration.

Box 7.2. **Durkheim on action and structure**

ACTION	STRUCTURE
Durkheim: there is no real theory of social action in Durkheim; the individual action is always conditioned by the group, and collective action is taken to reinforce the strength of the group.	**Durkheim:** in societies dominated by mechanical solidarity, the social structure consists of networks of kin groups (segmented societies); more complex modern societies consist of secondary groups formed by the division of labour and managed by the state.

Box 7.3. **The first basic dualism of social theory**

SOCIAL INTEGRATION	SYSTEM INTEGRATION
Durkheim: in all societies social integration is achieved through the *conscience collective*—shared ways of thinking (logic, conceptions of space and time, shared beliefs, norms, and values). In societies governed by mechanical solidarity, religion is central. In more complex modern societies, the *conscience collective* covers less of our lives but focuses on the ethics of individual freedom—it becomes a religion of humanity.	**Durkheim:** where mechanical solidarity predominates, system integration *is* social integration, guaranteed by the *conscience collective*. Where organic solidarity predominates, system integration is achieved by the division of labour.

Further reading

It is always a good idea to read as many of the original texts as possible; in terms of this chapter, there are two important texts: *The Division of Labour in Society* (1893/1984) especially the Introduction; book 1, chapters 2, 3, and 7; book 2, chapter 2; book 3, chapters 1, 2, and 3; and *The Elementary Forms of the Religious Life* (1912/1915), especially the Introduction; book 1, chapter 1; book 2, chapters 1 and 2; books 3, chapters 4 and 5, and the Conclusion.

There are a number of short introductions to Durkheim, of which the best are Anthony Giddens, *Durkheim* (1978), and Kenneth Thompson, *Emile Durkheim* (1982). By far the best and most thorough secondary source is Steven Lukes: *Emile Durkheim* (1973). P. Hamilton's four-volume *Emile Durkheim: Critical Assessments* (1990) includes the most important modern discussions, whilst Jeffrey C. Alexander's collection *Durkheimian Sociology: Cultural Studies* (1988) shows the modern use of Durkheim and Alexander's four-volume *Theoretical Logic in Sociology* (1982–4) contains a sympathetic discussion of his work.

8 | Was Marx a Marxist?

Introduction

Marxism and popular prejudice and simplistic arguments; relationship between Marx's earlier and later work; his starting point in human action; comparison with Durkheim.

Human powers 1: the theory of alienation

Underlying conception of human nature—distinction from a theory of needs; human nature as a transformative power—humans change themselves through changing their environment. The alienation of the worker from the product, from work, from co-workers, and from his/her own nature. Marxist idealism and its problems; the empirical study of alienation; the distinction between economic analysis and the analysis of ideas and action.

Human powers 2: commodity fetishism

The continuity between Marx's earlier and later work; commodity fetishism as the alienation of human relationships; the 'free' market.

Marxist economics: A brief and simple introduction

Classical and marginalist economics; the labour theory of value; use value and exchange value; labour power as a commodity with a use and exchange value; exploitation; surface appearances and underlying reality; capitalism as a system of regular crises; the central contradiction of capitalism—the forces and relations of production; Marx's sociological economics.

Social class

The place of class in Marxist theory; class-in-itself and class-for-itself. The peasantry and its need for strong leadership. The bourgeoisie and its different fractions. The petty bourgeoisie, traditional and new. The proletariat—working-class identity and shared experience; divisions in the proletariat and contemporary attempts to understand them. The lumpenproletariat and the underclass. The contemporary relevance of social class.

The state

Marx's political and analytic writings; the conspiracy theory of the state; the state as alienated human power and revolutionary democracy; comparison with Durkheim; economic explanations of the state and the possibility of its autonomy; the peaceful or violent transformation of the state; the class nature of the modern state; class and citizenship.

Ideology

Ideology as false consciousness and as non-science; ideology and social integration; ideas and the life process—parallels with modern sociology and psychology; ideology as alienation; economic determinist conceptions of ideology; ideology as illusion; ideology as imagination; ideology as the accurate perception of one level of reality; ideology and commodity fetishism; representation as ideology—the link with postmodernism; conclusion—the difficulties with deterministic notions.

Marxism and the family

Primitive communism; private property and the development of the pairing family; the linking of people and property; the social organization of sexuality and love; assessment of Engel's work.

Conclusion

Comparison with Durkheim; development of the basic dualisms.

Introduction

The collapse of the communist regimes in eastern Europe has perhaps shown that we cannot use a social theory to produce a blueprint for social organization—and it is arguable that these societies were nothing like what Marx imagined a communist or socialist society would be like anyway. Neither of these facts, however, mean that Marxism does not offer an interesting and tenable understanding of how some societies—or some parts of all societies—work. And whatever theory we are looking at, there is always a link between understanding and changing society.

Compared with Durkheim, Marx had a comparatively sophisticated conception of 'society', which he saw as structured in a more complex way. For long periods since Marx wrote, it has been customary to present very simplistic accounts of his work. This has often been the fault of Marx's followers, who have constructed political arguments that explain everything in crude economic terms—to the point where Marx himself is alleged to have said 'I am not a Marxist'. My account here will try to emphasize, on the one hand, the importance that he gave to the economic level of society, and, on the other, the complexity of his model of society.

A central issue in Marxist scholarship has been the relationship between his earlier and later work. Up until the middle of this century, he was known primarily through his later work, in particular the three volumes of *Capital* and the simplistic *Communist Manifesto*. The second half of the century saw the publication of Marx's earlier work, *The Economic and Philosophic Manuscripts of 1844* ('*The 1844 Manuscripts*') which cast a very different light on his ideas. Whereas the later work seemed to be concerned with the ways in which individuals were the product of economic and social structures, the earlier work showed a Marx concerned with human freedom, and the realization of human powers. It is as if he moved from one side of the dualism to the other via an invisible bridge.

The earlier work is an appropriate place to start, not simply because it comes first chronologically and helps us to understand his later work, but because it provides a significant contrast with Durkheim. We have seen that, for the latter, society is always the centre, even in modern societies where individual autonomy is so important. It is as if society determines that self-determination. For Marx, the human ability to be self-determining is the starting point, not as an individual characteristic but as a quality which belongs to humanity as a whole.

Human powers 1: the theory of alienation

I mentioned earlier that Marx saw religion as the projection of human powers on to an imaginary figure that we call God. His theory of alienation is about the loss of human powers in society, the way in which a particular type of social organization *alienates* us from our world. Underlying this idea is a particular philosophical anthropology. By this I do not mean the social science of anthropology—the study of other societies. A philosophical anthropology is a conception of human nature which underlies explanations of human social behaviour. Interest in such an area has all but disappeared from sociology over recent decades, or it has become redefined in terms of a theory of 'human needs'. It is argued that a philosophical anthropology is 'essentialist', that it assumes that human beings are the same throughout history whereas in fact they are historical products. Now there is at least a weak sense in which human beings *are* the same throughout history—they have always, with some exceptions, walked upright with one head, two lungs, one liver, and so on. Marx was, however, trying to suggest that there is a stronger sense in which we can think of human nature, and this stronger sense not only sees certain features of human nature as constant but also explains why human beings change through history. The argument is that it is human nature to transform human life and this transformation establishes the developments that we call history.

One of the things that distinguishes human beings from other animal species is that we do not simply adjust to our environment, but *change* it—in such a way that it then entails changing ourselves in order to adjust to it. Other species change the environment but in a way that does not entail changing themselves: when rabbits dig their burrows, that is all they need to do—they do not have to change themselves to adjust to the burrows they dig. When human beings build cities, they have to change themselves in order to live in them.[1] We change psychologically and develop new skills and abilities. We can see this work from generation to generation—I have all sorts of possibilities that my parents could not dream of, such as using a computer or regularly travelling abroad. The changes over centuries are even greater, but not so great that we cannot understand what has been left us from earlier centuries or millennia. We might not understand them so clearly or deeply as did contemporaries, but we do find a resonance in the work of, say, Homer and Horace, not to mention Shakespeare.

So it is human nature to change through creating our own environment and then adjusting to and recreating it. My understanding of what Marx means by *species being* in the *1844 Manuscripts* is that this constant process of transformation is a collective enterprise; it is something in which we are all involved, and in which we are all connected to each other. *Alienation* is a state in which the environment we create takes on a real solidity, comes to seem unchangeable—when it takes on the sense of what Lukacs called a second nature. The system we create acts back on us to form and control us, and it alienates us from our own collective nature as beings who work together to transform our world and ourselves.

Marx was concerned with the particular form of alienation brought about by capitalism, and the crucial part of the *1844 Manuscripts* is the section on 'Estranged Labour'. Much of the work is a criticism of classical economic theory, equally applicable to contemporary economic theory, arguing that it takes for granted what it ought to be explaining. In particular Marx argues that it took private property as the starting point of explanation, a sort of natural state, rather than as what has to be explained. His own starting point is the power of the market; in an idea which already encapsulates a crucial section in the first volume of *Capital* (1867/1970), he argues that market labour itself becomes a commodity—a thing bought and sold like any other object—and the paradox is that the more the labourer produces, the cheaper his or her labour becomes: 'With the *increasing value* of the world of things proceeds in direct proportion the *devaluation* of the world of men' (Marx 1844/1974: 107).

The worker is, in the first place, alienated from his or her product. If I work in a factory producing cars, I have no control over what I produce, and it is impossible to distinguish the work I have done from what anybody else has done or could do. Again the same paradox is at work: the more I produce, the less control, the less power I have:

The *alienation* of the worker in his product means not only that his labour becomes an object, an *external* existence, but that it exists *outside him*, independently, as something alien to him, and that it becomes a power on its own confronting him. It means that the life which he has conferred on the object confronts him as something hostile and alien. (ibid. 108)

[1] Simmel gives a very clear account of the effects of living in cities; see Chapter 10.

Simply because the worker's labour becomes an external quality, not something which comes from his or her inner life, the worker is alienated from the activity of working itself—it is a matter of fulfilling another's desires. I think you can get an idea of what Marx was talking about by thinking of your own work as a student: if you are interested in a course and you want to learn, writing an essay is work which comes from the inside—you are motivated from the inside; if you are taking a course simply because you have to get the qualification at the end, it is a different matter entirely. There is nothing of yourself in the work. The work becomes a burden. For Marx this is the permanent condition of capitalism:

As a result, therefore, man (the worker) only feels himself freely active in his animal functions—eating, drinking, procreating, or at most in his dwelling and in dressing up etc.; and in his human functions he no longer feels himself to be anything but an animal. What is animal becomes human and what is human becomes animal.   (ibid. 111)

Finally, since labour—work on and transformation of the natural world—is a definitive aspect of our 'species being', we are alienated from the species and from our co-workers. We cannot recognize ourselves in those around us—we do not see fellow humans but people who might be competing with us for jobs and scarce resources, people who are potential threats.

There is much more in Marx's early work than I have covered here, including some interesting comments about the relationship between human beings and the rest of nature (see Benton 1993), and he develops a substantial critique of private property. I have concentrated on this section because it leads us directly into Marx's later work, and the analysis of commodity fetishism at the start of the first volume of *Capital*, but before moving on to that I want to spend some time talking about these ideas.

My first point is that we can find the origins of Marxist idealism in his work—the vision of a free and unalienated world in which people can work together in cooperation to improve their lives and develop their culture; Marx identifies this with the political and economic emancipation of wage labour. Private property and wages go together and a free society entails the abolition of both. We would work together as cooperative equals. Whether such a world is possible is debatable, but for the moment, however, what I want to point out is that in this vision we find possibly the strongest and most effective political ideal of the western world, an idea which finds its origins in the French Revolution, more than half a century before Marx was writing and which continues in various ways until this day. Such utopian visions should not be dismissed easily. They can lay the basis for terroristic regimes, as did the French Revolution and, closer to our own time, the Russian Revolution, but they can also act as guiding principles for social improvement and social justice and resistance to tyrannical systems. As with everything else, ideals are always double-edged but perhaps they are necessary.

Now there are reasons to doubt this particular conception of human nature.

If we take Freud seriously, not to mention Durkheim, it entails accepting that perhaps this defining human feature of working collectively is not simply given but an achievement which always requires some sacrifice and suffering. Our 'natural' state is to seek immediate satisfaction of our desires, but the world is not that kind or generous and we have to give up that desire for immediate and full satisfaction and work to achieve what satisfaction we can. In other words, work is always a burden. This undermines the more utopian versions of Marxist theory, but it does not undermine the subtlety of his conception of it being human nature to change human nature. We can keep hold of the importance of work, even if it is not as fundamental as Marx thought, and Marx's distinction between working for other people and working collectively for ourselves remains important. Work might always be a burden, but it can be heavier or lighter and we have some control over that.

There have been various attempts to 'operationalize' the notion of alienation (see e.g. Blauner 1964) in empirical studies, but these tend to lose the philosophical dimensions of the concept and they turn into studies of work satisfaction—Blauner, for example, suggests the alienation moves through an inverted U-curve, at its lowest in craft industries and highly automated industries but at its highest in factory production. It is this sort of study which is used to criticize Durkheim's suggestion that the division of labour means a general deepening of satisfaction with work, since the division is at its highest in factory production. However, I am not sure that Marx is talking about work satisfaction in that sense; we can find various ways to be satisfied with our work and still not experience it as an expression of ourselves, of our own inner world. I remember in my youth sweeping streets for a while and gaining immense and rather obsessive satisfaction from looking back along a clean gutter, but I could not claim that it had much to do with the meaning of my life. Marx is talking about a more profound and less comfortable satisfaction.

Finally we have in the *1844 Manuscripts* the division that still haunts Marxism between economic analysis and the analysis of human action and ideas. In the early work the latter was clearly more important and in his later work the analysis of economic and social structures predominates. It has always been difficult to keep these two sides together in all of the schools of social theory—not just Marxism—and Jürgen Habermas (1972), the most prominent contemporary thinker in the Marxist tradition, has separated the analysis of economic production and of social interaction as distinct areas of investigation. The social action/social structure distinction seems to be a necessary one; we can try to understand the relationships between the two, but they remain separate objects of study.

Human powers 2: commodity fetishism

I mentioned earlier debates over the differences between Marx's earlier and later work. Some argue that there was a radical break between the *1844 Manuscripts* and *Capital* (see Althusser 1969), whilst others (McLellan 1971) argue that there is a continuity. This too is about the action/structure dualism. It is always rather silly to see these things in terms of either/or arguments. It seems to me that there is both continuity and change. The continuity lies in the connection between the theory of alienation and that of commodity fetishism; the development lies in the way that the latter comes to form the basis for the development of Marx's economic theory and his structural analysis of society. The notion of commodity fetishism is very close to the analysis of the alienation of the product of labour, but Marx is concerned this time less with the alienation of labour into its product than with the alienation of social relationships in the division of labour into market relationships between commodities:

A commodity is therefore a mysterious thing, simply because in it the social character of men's labour appears to them as an objective character stamped upon the product of labour; because the relation of the producers to the sum total of their own labour is presented to them as a social relation, existing not between themselves, but between the products of their labour. This is why the products of labour become commodities, social things whose qualities are at the same time perceptible and imperceptible by the senses. . . . There is a definite social relation between men that assumes, in their eyes, the fantastic form of a relationship between things. . . . This I call the Fetishism which attaches itself to the products of labour, so soon as they are produced as commodities. (Marx 1867/1970: 76)

The division of labour, the way in which society divides up its workforce to produce the necessities and the luxuries of life, creates social relationships between groups of people. If I am producing cars, somebody else is fishing, and somebody else again is making clothes; we are related to each other, in fact dependent upon each other—even if we never set eyes on each other. But we do not experience this relationship as a social relationship, we experience it as a relationship between the commodities that we produce. I am paid money for the work I do on the conveyor belt which turns out cars, and I use that money to buy a suit, and whoever makes my suit might use the payment he or she receives for the labour to buy a car I make. Somehow or the other, cars get equated to suits get equated to fish and so on.

We need only think about how contemporary politicians talk about the 'free market' to get a good idea of what Marx meant by commodity fetishism. The market is endowed with human powers: people will say 'let the market decide' as if it had powers of thought and judgement; sometimes the market will dictate, or it will demand; it will move in different directions, but usually either up or down. We are led to believe that our livelihood depends on this invisible, power-ful, thoughtful entity which nobody has seen but which everybody assumes to be real—we are not even expected to have faith in it; it is simply there and our newspapers write about it every day. The classical economist Adam Smith talks about the 'hidden hand' of the market; it seems to be mystically invested with all the powers of the separate individuals and groups that make it up and at the same time seems to control each of them, each one has to react to the market. To understand this in greater depth we need to look at Marx's economic theory—but don't worry, it won't be at too great a depth.

Marxist economics: a brief and simple introduction

Marxist economic theory is not simply an economic theory. We have already seen that it is in part philosophical and we shall see that it is also a profoundly sociological theory.

Marx belongs to an earlier and different tradition from the marginalist eco-nomics that provides the basis for most of what is taught in schools and univer-sities today. The modern tradition is concerned with price, the classical tradition with *value*: not quite the same thing. It worked with a *labour theory of value*. The idea at its simplest is that the value of a good depends upon the labour expended upon it, but it is not quite so simple as that—to leave it there would mean that, if I took five years to write a book, it would be worth five times a book I took a year to write. Marx talked about *socially necessary labour*—this is the average productivity of labour at one particular time—so if everybody else is producing a book in a year, I will get proportionately less for my five years' work.

The problem faced by the classical economists (Adam Smith, David Ricardo, and others) was to explain the source of profit. If I am, say, working in a shoe factory, and I am paid the value of my labour, and the shoes are sold at the value of the labour expended in their production, there is no space for profit—the two amounts would be the same and value would equal price; profit could occur only through some form of dishonesty or unfair exploitation. The way in which Marx dealt with this problem takes us back to the idea of labour as a commod-ity and a central distinction between *use* value and *exchange* value. The former is the value of a commodity to the person who uses it—the pleasure, say, of drinking a couple of pints of beer. The exchange value is what that beer would exchange for via the medium of money. The definition of a commodity is that it is produced for the purpose of exchange rather than use by the producer and it is the exchange value which is determined by the amount of socially necessary labour expended on the production of the commodity. Only it is a little more complicated than that, because what I sell if I am a worker is my *labour power*, or my ability to work.

Now, labour power is a *commodity*—it has a use value and an exchange value. The exchange value of labour power is what is needed to ensure its reproduction—that is, it must be sufficient to enable workers to feed, clothe, and house themselves and enable the next generation of workers to be raised, educated, and so on. There are two components to this: an absolute minimum needed to keep the worker alive plus something extra depending on what is acceptable to society at large. Thus over the last fifteen years in British society it has become socially acceptable to pay very low wages at the bottom end of the market, perhaps in some cases close to a subsistence wage, and at the other end to pay very high wages, many many times above subsistence level.

Now, if I were an employer, the only point in employing workers would be if their use value to me—the value of what they produce for me—is greater than what I have to pay them, the exchange value of their labour power. The difference between the two is surplus value, which is appropriated by the employer. This is Marx's definition of exploitation, and it is not the result of the actions of unscrupulous employers; it is built into the wage–labour relationship itself, into the buying and selling of labour power. There is no such thing as a 'fair day's pay for a fair day's work'. At the same time as I work for my own wage, I am working for my employer's profit, I am producing surplus value, and I am being exploited. If this were not the case, I would not be employed. This sets the scene for permanent conflict between workers and employers.

We find here an implicit but absolutely fundamental distinction between the level of appearances and that of underlying reality. In the case of commodity fetishism, what we can see on the surface is the relationship between commodities as they are determined by the market; the underlying reality is the social relations that comprise the division of labour. In the case of the wage relationship, what we can see is the labour I sell and the wage I receive for it; the underlying reality is the difference between the use value and the exchange value of my labour and the surplus value taken by my employer—what is hidden is exploitation. We shall see when we discuss Marx's various theories of ideology that this distinction is particularly important.

Contained in these ideas as well is the argument that capitalism is a system of permanent crises; Marx suggests a number of ways in which crises can occur, but I would suggest that the crucial crises arise from exploitation, and what is revealed by the distinction between use value and exchange value. If I am a worker and I produce £50 worth of goods in a day (the use value of my labour to my employer), and I receive £10 a day in wages (the exchange value of my labour power), then I do not receive in wages sufficient to buy back the value of goods I have produced. This applies right across the system, so that if stocks of unsold goods build up, workers have to be laid off, and the economy enters a crisis, a depression, or slump, until the stocks of goods are used up and firms go back into production. There is a cycle of growth and slump, something that capitalist economies have been trying to deal with for over a century and a half. A temporary solution was found by John Maynard Keynes in the 1930s through public expenditure on work that does not produce commodities or which produces commodities that have a market guaranteed by the state, such as the arms industries. This circulates money which can then be used to purchase the surplus commodities. But by the late 1970s this policy was seen as responsible for unacceptably high rates of inflation and it was reversed. The results must be familiar to everyone.

We find here what Ernest Mandel (1962, 1970) calls the central contradiction of capitalism between the forces and relations of production. The forces of production are the abilities we possess to create wealth. Capitalism represents a huge step forward in human productive capacities compared with previous forms of society. The competition between private entrepreneurs constantly drives forward the pace of technological change as each capitalist tries to outstrip his rivals (and, of course, in Marx's day, capitalists were only 'he's'). Yet the full potentiality of the capacities, of the productive forces, cannot be realized precisely because of the private ownership of productive capacity. Private ownership involves wage labour, which in turn involves exploitation, which produces regular crises, which reduce productive capacity. As Mandel puts it:

this socialisation of production which transforms the labour of all mankind into objectively co-operative labour is not regulated, directed, managed to any conscious plan. It is governed by blind forces, the 'laws of the market' in fact by the variations in the rate of profit. . . . This is why the totality of production . . . develops independently of the human needs it has itself aroused, and is urged onwards only by the capitalists' thirst for profit. (Mandel 1962: 171)

This has been a very simplistic account of Marx's economic theory, but I hope I have shown that it is a *sociological* economic theory at the centre of which are the social relations entailed by the division of labour and private property. It is sometimes said that Marx was a technological determinist, arguing that the stage of technological development determined the form of social organization, but in fact the important factor is the *social relations* within which technology develops. The same technology could exist in very different types of society. Secondly, it is also often argued that Marx was an 'economic determinist'. There are two replies to this: the first is a repetition of the argument I have just made— that it is social relations that are important. The second is that there are many and various links to be made between these social relations of production and other aspects of social life—far too many for us to interpret Marx as arguing for some tight causal process.

If we want to move on to Marx's wider social analysis from the point we have reached, then it can most easily be done through a discussion of social class. The economic theory as I have presented it here lays the basis for defining two social classes: the owners and controllers of the means of production and the workers, those who sell their labour power: the bourgeoisie and the proletariat.

Social class

> The history of all hitherto existing society is the history of class struggles. Freeman and slave, patrician and plebeian, lord and serf, guildmaster and journeyman, in a word oppressor and oppressed, stood in constant opposition to one another, carried on an uninterrupted, now hidden, now open fight, a fight that each time ended, either in a revolutionary reconstitution of society at large, or in the common ruin of the contending classes.
>
> (Marx 1848/1968a: 35–6)

One might think, rightly, that social class is a central concept in Marx's work, but he had very little to say about it—a famous forty lines at the end of the third volume of *Capital* and scattered comments elsewhere. It always reminds me of a detective story where the victim dies just before he or she can gasp out the murderer's name. The concept of class has the same status in Marx's theory as the murderer in a detective story; it is class which sets the scene and moves things forward—it is guilty not of murder but of creating history.

Sometimes Marx talks about social groups as being classes in a loose common-sense way, but at others he is being more rigorous; at times he talks as if there are only two social classes—as in the first passages of *The Communist Manifesto* quoted above. At other times and in a more realistic way he talks about a number of different classes. The central defining factor in his more rigorous statements has to do with groups of individuals who are united and defined sometimes in very different ways by their relationships to the means of production. But historically they develop in opposition to one another, building up their own culture and practices. The best account of such development is still to be found in E. P. Thompson's *The Making of the English Working Class* (1965), but here I will be concerned with class on a more theoretical level, looking at the classes that Marx and Marxists have talked about and discussing their characteristics.

It is normal to make a distinction between two components in Marx's conception of class: the class-in-itself, as defined by a particular relationship to the means of production, and the class-for-itself, a class whose members have recognized a shared social position and a common interest and opposition to other classes. We can be a member of a class-in-itself without any awareness of the fact, although it might influence our ideas and actions—it is part of an underlying reality, of which we don't necessarily have any direct experience at all. When we do become aware of this underlying reality we begin to see the world in a different way.

THE PEASANTRY

The small-holding peasants form a vast mass, the members of which live in similar conditions but without entering into manifold relations with one another. Their mode of production isolates them from one another instead of bringing them into mutual intercourse. . . . Their field of production, the small holding, admits of no division of labour in its cultivation, no application of science and therefore no diversity of development, no variety of talent, no wealth of social relationships. Each individual peasant family is almost self-sufficient; it itself directly produces a major part of its consumption and thus acquires its means of life more through exchange with nature than in intercourse with society. A small holding, a peasant and his family; alongside them another small holding, another peasant and another family. A few score of these make up a village, a few score of villages make up a Department. In this way the great mass of the French nation is formed by simple addition of homologous magnitudes, much as potatoes in a sack form a sack of potatoes. In so far as millions of families live under economic conditions of existence that separate their mode of life, their interests and their culture from those of the other classes and put them in hostile opposition to the latter, they form a class. In so far as there is merely a local inter-connection among these small-holding peasants, and the identity of their interests begets no community, no national bond and no political organisation among them, they do not form a class. They are consequently incapable of enforcing their class interests in their own name, whether through a parliament or through a convention. They cannot represent themselves, they must be represented. Their representative must at the same time appear as their master, as an authority over them, as an unlimited governmental power that protects them against other classes and sends them rain and sunshine from above. The political influence of the small-holding peasants, therefore, finds its final expression in the executive power subordinating society to itself'.

(Marx 1852/1968c: 170–1)

I have quoted this passage (from *The Eighteenth Brumaire of Louis Bonaparte*, an analysis of political struggles in France from 1848 to 1851 which ended with Bonaparte seizing power in a *coup*) at length, not only because it tells us what Marx thought of the peasantry but also because it provides an illustration of how he thought about social class in general. We can see not only the simple definition of class according to relationship to the means of production, but also the notion of the development of a class for itself and the way in which the material conditions of life condition the development of such consciousness, and, in the case of the French peasantry, prohibit it. Unable to represent themselves, the peasantry respond to a strong leader who promises to do it for them. They are denied the individual richness and variation which might potentially be derived from the division of labour.

In western Europe the peasantry declined with industrialization. The poorer peasants became agricultural labourers and most were forced off the land into the urban working class. Even when it is large, the strength of the peasantry as an independent social force seems to be limited, although, where there is a form of collective organization of the peasant village life under the feudal system, as in China, they might be a stronger force.

THE BOURGEOISIE

The term 'bourgeoisie' originally referred to the French middle classes; its meaning in contemporary society has two dimensions. The first stems from its use by avant-garde artists, referring to the conventional, respectable, narrow, and boring—the supposed lifestyle of lawyers, priests, business men, civil servants, and so on. It is used as a term of abuse and sometimes has the ring of aristocratic arrogance about it—'you're so bourgeois'. The second dimension comes from Marxist theory and refers to capitalists, the owners of the means of production. During the early years of the industrial revolution (from approximately 1750 onwards), the capitalists were the middle class—the group between peasants and workers, on the one hand, and the traditional landed classes, the aristocracy, on the other. At the end of the third volume of *Capital* Marx talks about there being three great classes in society: workers, capitalists, and landowners.

Landowners as a major class were most significant in the period leading up to and into industrialization. Barrington Moore, Jr. (1966) argues that the future development of democracy depended on whether industrialization came from above, from a section of landowners (as in Germany and Japan), or from below, from a bourgeois revolution, as happened in France. After industrialization, the importance of landowners has decreased and they are best seen as what N. Poulantzas (1976)—a modern French Marxist—would describe as a 'fraction' of the bourgeoisie. Another very important fraction of the modern bourgeoisie would be finance capitalists. These groups can in different situations have coinciding or conflicting interests. In Britain for many years industrial capitalists were the dominant section of the bourgeoisie, having achieved important victories over the landed aristocracy in the middle of the nineteenth century, but that place has been taken over by finance capitalists over the course of this century. David Harvey (1989) traces the development of what we call postmodernism to the increasing power of financial capitalists to use modern information technology to move capital to where it is most profitable at short notice. Marx recognized that there were conflicts between these different sections of the bourgeoisie and he suggested that these conflicting interests were managed through the state as a sort of 'central committee' of the bourgeoisie.

There are certainly many points where Marx seems to think that the two main classes of capitalism, bourgeoisie and proletariat, capitalists and workers, will face each other across the barricades with nothing left in between, all other classes having been absorbed into the major blocs. And the bourgeoisie itself would have a comparatively short life—its historical function was to develop capitalism to the point where the working class was sufficiently well developed to take power for itself. In this he was simply wrong, and if anything the intermediate groups have grown in number. One major intermediate group was the petty bourgeoisie.

THE PETTY BOURGEOISIE

This is much closer to what we would today call the middle classes. It would include small business people, who maybe employ a few workers or none at all, and the professionals who have no particular relationship to the means of production; lawyers, small shop keepers, and so on. David McClellan (1971) points out that, in the second volume of *Theories of Surplus Value* (Marx: 1862/1969), Marx censures Ricardo for not recognizing the importance of the growing middle classes. This, however, is only one reference, and it has been left to later Marxists to make up the deficiency. Poulantzas (1976) suggests a distinction between the traditional petty bourgeoisie and the new petty bourgeoisie, the latter including workers in the state system—civil servants, teachers, and so on. The traditional petty bourgeoisie are usually associated with reactionary politics: they cannot see themselves as part of a class, only as individuals, and they feel threatened by the bourgeoisie above them and the more powerful organized workers' movement below them. They do not develop their own political movements but, like the French peasantry, tend to turn to strong leader figures whom they believe will protect them. Poulantzas's argument about the new petty bourgeoisie was that, at times of crisis, it would tend to split politically along the lines of the class of origin of its members. Teachers from working-class backgrounds would move towards the workers' movement whilst those from middle-class backgrounds might move in the opposite direction. At this point I should say that one of the difficulties of Marxist class theory is that the *a priori* reading of likely political behaviour from class position does not always work.

THE PROLETARIAT

In proportion as the bourgeoisie, i.e. *capital,* is developed, in the same proportion is the proletariat, the modern working class, developed—a class of labourers who live only as long as they find work, and who find work only so long as their labour increases capital. . . . Owing to the extensive use of machinery and to division of labour, the work of the proletarians has lost

all individual character, and consequently all charm for the workman. He
becomes an appendage of the machine ...

(Marx 1848/1968a: 41)

To begin with, the working class is geographically scattered and unorganized
and reacts to industrialization by attacking the machinery—as did the Luddites
in nineteenth-century Britain; but slowly they are brought together into large
factories, where they can recognize their identity with each other and their common interest. Their material conditions of work bring them into social relationships with each other, and if labour is dehumanizing it also enables workers to
understand their mutual dependence. This sense of solidarity would spread
from one factory to a group of factories to the development of nationwide
labour organizations and beyond that to international organizations.

Of course, it has not been as simple as this and contemporary Marxists would
recognize all sorts of complicating factors, not least the way in which the working class can so easily get caught up in nationalist rather than internationalist
movements; but there have also been the major divisions within the working
class itself—between skilled and unskilled, white- and blue-collar, men and
women, black and white, and so on. Marx himself indicated that he could see
such problems, although of course they were different 150 years ago. He talked,
for example, of the way in which workers could end up competing with each
other for jobs, relevant today in arguments about immigration and gender
equality. He also made a distinction in his economic theory between productive
and unproductive labour—productive labour being that which produces commodities for sale on the market and unproductive labour that which does not.

In the twentieth century, discussions about the composition of the working
class have arisen around the proliferation of divisions—the divisions not only
between white- and blue-collar workers but between managers and workers,
different levels of managers and workers, and so on. Erik Olin Wright (1978)
calculated that, if we were to take the proletariat as consisting only of productive
workers in Marx's sense, the working class would comprise a very small part of
the population indeed. Wright tried to deal with these problems by talking
about 'contradictory class locations', suggesting that the same person can
occupy different class positions.

THE LUMPENPROLETARIAT

Here we reach the bottom of the pile. In *The Eighteenth Brumaire* Marx talks
about Louis Bonaparte as himself a member of the lumpenproletariat, a
bohemian adventurer who organized this particular class into a sort of private
militia to back him up in his seizure of power. Marx describes this class vividly:

Alongside decayed roués with dubious means of subsistence and of dubious origins, alongside ruined and adventurous offshoots of the bourgeoisie, were vagabonds, discharged soldiers, discharged jailbirds, escaped galley slaves, swindlers, mountebanks . . . pickpockets, tricksters, gamblers . . . brothel keepers, porters, literati, organ-grinders, rag pickers, knife grinders, tinkers, beggars—in short, the whole indefinite, disintegrated mass, thrown hither and thither, which the French term *la bohème*. (Marx 1852/1968c: 136–7)

Now what are we to make of this class today? The social level that Marx is talking about has always more readily supplied mercenaries for the right than the left, and it is doubtless still there, only now there would be less rag pickers and knife grinders, more permanently unemployed, maybe drug pushers, and so on. In contemporary society there would be some overlap with what has become known as an underclass, but I think there is a difference. The underclass if it exists is a section of the population permanently trapped at or below the poverty line, not necessarily unemployed or beggars but people who are employed in low-wage and/or temporary work.

THE CONTINUED SIGNIFICANCE OF CLASS

The significance of social class is still debated both in sociology and in the world at large (see M. Mann 1995; Lee and Turner 1996) and it is a debate which has continued since Marx himself and one that was stimulated by and drawn into Weberian sociology. It has been clear certainly for the second half of the century that the reality is much more complicated than might be expected from Marx's analysis and that rarely, if at all, do we find social classes walking across the stage of history like giant actors, but this does not mean that social class is not a significant factor that we have to take into account in understanding what is happening in late capitalism. It is sometimes suggested that class has no relevance to everyday life in contemporary society and it has been replaced by ethnicity or gender or other factors, yet this is demonstrably untrue to anybody who listens to political debates or looks at the distribution of wealth and illness or the workings of the education system. On a theoretical level, the postmodernist arguments drag in Marx behind them—they do not offer an alternative theory to Marxism but rather a counter-theory. One suspects that, if Marxism did not exist, neither would postmodernism.

My own view is that it is useful to look at Marx's analyses of class and class structure as representing a sort of underlying skeletal structure, and that he makes a very good case that we should see capitalist society as inherently contradictory. The problem then becomes to understand why conflict does not occur in the way that might be expected from Marxist analysis and why history has not developed in the way that Marx predicted. This has led to the most interesting developments in social theory over the last fifty years. It is difficult to overestimate the contribution of Marxism to modern social thought, and, if Marxism is necessary to understand class formation, it is also necessary to understand class fragmentation (Harvey 1989; Jameson 1991).

Marx's discussion of class, in particular the bourgeoisie, takes us on to the nature of the state.

The state

Each step in the development of the bourgeoisie was accompanied by a corresponding political advance of that class . . . the bourgeoisie has at last, since the establishment of Modern Industry and the world-market, conquered for itself, in the modern representative State, exclusive political sway. The executive of the modern State is but a committee for managing the common affairs of the whole bourgeoisie.

(Marx and Engels 1968a: 37)

legislation, whether political or civil, never does more than proclaim, express in words, the will of economic relations.

(Marx 1847/1976: 147)

Marx cannot be accused of being afraid of making rash statements—although it is also useful to remember that he is writing not only as a social analyst but also as a political polemicist and agitator. As Richard Miller (1991) points out, it would be easy to conclude that Marx believed the state to be a sort of conspiracy against the working class, or that the wealth of the bourgeoisie could be used to ensure that whoever is in power pursues its interests. Given the contemporary mistrust of politicians, perhaps both possibilities might be more acceptable now than they were twenty years ago, and paradoxically they are not too far away from ideas expressed by right-wing militias in the USA.

Again, Marx defined his own position by arguing against Hegel, who saw the state functioning to producing harmony between the different groups which made it up and bringing them together at a higher level, which it did through the monarchy, representative assemblies, and the state bureaucracy. Now, as McLellan (1971: 180) points out, Marx subjected this view to the same argument to which he subjected Hegel's view of religion: the state in reality is the projection of society's powers, the powers of the men and women who make up society, onto an external body. Against this Marx developed a notion of radical democracy. In undemocratic states, the law and the constitution exists over and above people, but in a truly democratic society they would be the result of the collaboration of all citizens in the political processes that produce the law and the constitution. This vision has become a central part of Marxist political idealism and its latest forms can be found in the work of the German social theorist Jürgen Habermas.

Like Durkheim, Marx also traced the development of the state to the division of labour—as societies become more complex, so some central organizing agency is necessary. If you remember, for Durkheim, the function of the state was to mediate between different interests and in particular to protect the individual against the power of smaller groups. For Marx, it was also an organizing agency, but one which was necessarily involved in the domination of one class over others. Capitalism is an inherently expanding system, and the social class at its helm is carried into political power not because of any deliberate or conscious action, but because that is the way that society develops. For Marx, the concern of the state for individual liberty could be seen as an attempt to enforce the rights of the individual property owner against those without property, whose only power lay in their banding together to take collective action. This involves a political struggle for trade-union rights which was fought in the UK through the nineteenth century up to the present time, and in the USA throughout this century.

If the first quotation suggests conspiracy or corruption, then the second suggests a simple economic determinism, and this would be equally misleading. Marx made various modifications of and reservations about these earlier views. For example, he talks about different sections of the bourgeoisie engaging in political struggles through and over the state—for example, the factory acts and the arguments over the corn laws in the UK in the 1840s can be seen as a struggle between the industrial bourgeoisie and the agricultural bourgeoisie. He also talks about the state being controlled by people who do not belong to the dominant class, but nevertheless exercise power in the interests of the dominant class. Thus in the UK by the end of the nineteenth century it can be argued that the holders of office came from the landowning class but exercised power in the interests of the industrial bourgeoisie. Returning to the *Eighteenth Brumaire*, it can also be seen that Bonaparte's seizure of power seemed to give the state some autonomy for a while. Although Bonaparte came to power on the basis of the peasantry and the lumpenproletariat, the state does not represent them—the logic of economic development meant that his regime had to protect the interests of the dominant class if it were going to survive. In capitalist society the state becomes more powerful as the bourgeoisie becomes more dominant.

The traditional debate on the left was about whether the capitalist state could be transformed through a democratic process or whether it had to be overthrown by violent revolution; over recent years this has become obviously irrelevant. However, there is still a question about the extent to which a radical, left-wing government can bring about reforms that favour the subordinated classes. If we take UK politics as the example, then the advent of a socialist government, even a moderate one, is greeted with warnings of a 'run on the pound', of businesses leaving the country, and so on. The fate of the democratically elected socialist government in Chile in the 1970s is a frightening reminder of the international power of the ruling class.

At the same time left-wing governments have been able to achieve important reforms, more so in Europe than in the USA. The existence of the National Health Service is perhaps the most dramatic example in the UK—a system of national insurance which originally promised health care from cradle to grave. How are we to explain such reforms being introduced by the 'executive committee of the bourgeoisie'? There are in fact two ways of approaching it. The first is a sort of conspiracy theory: the ruling class (or classes) can weigh up their long-term interests balanced against what they can get away with in the present. A more interesting and certainly a more respectable theoretical explanation leads us to a Marxist functionalism. The state does not simply protect the individual and balance group interests, as Durkheim argued, nor does it simply enforce the interests of one class in a direct and conscious way. Rather it rises in response to the basic system needs of the economy. This is an argument most clearly articulated by the French Marxist Louis Althusser in the middle of the twentieth century, but he succeeds as well as anybody in elaborating on Marx's own writings in this matter. If capitalism is to survive, it requires a reasonably healthy workforce, educated to a level necessary to operate at the relevant level of technological development, and it needs to ensure that the next generation is raised in a reasonable way to whatever standards are required. The state develops in order to fulfil these needs. Now this is not an especially satisfactory explanation—even if we can talk about an economic system having needs, it does not follow that these needs will be automatically met, or met in any particular way. But it does make sense of Marx's view of the state as working in the interests of the ruling class because it is working to reproduce the sort of economic and social system that that class rules—it becomes the guarantor of system integration rather than the agent of a particular section of the ruling class.

There is also a way that the development of the democratic state can be seen as undermining class struggle. I mentioned earlier that we could see the state's defence of individual rights as an intervention on behalf of the bourgeoisie. One way of putting this in a more interesting, and less crude, light is through thinking about the development of citizenship rights. This, it seems to me, is essentially what Durkheim was talking about when he saw the state as protecting the rights of the individual. The British sociologist T. H. Marshall (1950/1973), writing in the mid-twentieth century, distinguished three dimensions to citizenship. He saw these as developing one after the other, although I think they are best thought of as coexisting side by side, each providing a focus for social conflict.

The first dimension is that of civil rights which guarantee individual freedom—equality before the law, freedom of speech, etc.; the second dimension is political—the right to vote and to engage in political organization; and the third dimension is socio-economic—the right to a certain level of economic and social security. Some of these rights, particularly the civil rights and the right to vote, are often historically involved in the establishment of capitalist society and the overthrow of the traditional order; however, the right to political organization and welfare rights can actually challenge capitalism, as Giddens (1973: 157) points out. But more important perhaps is the fact that civil and political rights are often individualizing rights, undermining a sense of class, and perhaps, as Marshall himself wondered in passing, compensating for and enabling people to accept considerable degrees of class inequality. Perhaps civil justice and political freedom can compensate for economic injustice and unfreedom, undermining the class dynamics that Marx identified. The development of these rights could also be seen as fulfilling a functional need of the system. My argument over these last sections has been that, even though class struggle has not developed in the way that Marx predicted, the class structure has become more, not less, complicated, and even though the state cannot be understood in terms as simple as those which Marx proposed, we can still talk about class and about the state as a site for class conflict and class rule. In many examples, this means talking about an objective or underlying reality which is not necessarily apparent to those people who belong to the class or who are participating in political activities. In the case of the state, I would suggest that its function of administering the division of labour and ensuring individual rights—which are very important and certainly not illusory—contributed to undermining the awareness of class. This takes us on directly to the area where modern Marxism has been most creative and Marx himself perhaps was under-creative—the area of *ideology*.

Ideology

INTRODUCTION

The term ideology has changed its meaning quite radically since it was coined by Antoine Destutt de Tracy, a philosopher engaged in the French Revolution who used the term to refer to a science of ideas. Today it is a term often used critically, if not disparagingly. In British and North American culture there is often a profound mistrust of intellectuals, and 'ideology' is used to condemn any theoretical discussion. At other times it might be used to describe a general world-view. For Marx, however, the term applies to partial, one-sided ideas—ideas that are misleading because they consciously or unconsciously serve the interests of a powerful group—or to ideas that are wrong, in error for the same reason. This last notion of ideology as a false representation of the world leaves it juxtaposed to truth or to science. In this way it draws us to the philosophy of science and in particular to epistemology—the theory of knowledge. This has been most developed in modern Marxism by Louis Althusser (1969), but without doubt it was present in Marx's work.

These two uses come together in Lukacs's Marxism: the position of the working class in the production process in particular and in society in general enables it to develop an ideology which was *also* a science. It is worth pointing out at this point that there is a radical difference between Lukacs's vision and that of Althusser, and that this ambivalence, as we shall see, haunts Marx's work. In Lukacs's vision it is possible for people to come to understand and control the society in which they live; in Althusser's vision only social scientists and Marxist theorists can understand society; for the rest of us an ideology is necessary. I will be pointing to the different roots of these theories at several points in what follows.

It is in the theory of ideology that Marx comes to grips with the problems of social integration. Sometimes he seems to be arguing that social integration is simply the product of system integration; at other times he seems to be moving in the direction of suggesting that ideas and their development can be to some significant degree independent of the economic base. There is, in fact, a number of different conceptions of ideology to be found in Marx's work. There follows a long series of quotations from his work in which we can find some of his most simplistic and his most complex comments on the issue. Children's comics sometimes contain complicated drawings in which other drawings are hidden and the reader is asked to find the hidden drawings. These quotations can be seen as such a drawing. I will identify a number of different theories which I think are present in these quotations and it might be a useful exercise to see if you can identify the relevant quotations or parts of a quotation—I am not going to give answers, since that tends to stop people thinking!

The fact is, therefore, that definite individuals who are productively active in a definite way enter into these definite social and political relations. Empirical observation must in each separate instance bring out empirically, and without any mystification and speculation, the connection with the social and political structure with production. The social structure and the State are continually evolving out of the life-process of definite individuals, but of individuals not as they may appear in their own or other people's imagination, but as they really are, i.e. as they operate, produce materially, and hence as they work under definite material limits, presuppositions and conditions independent of their will.

The production of ideas, of conceptions, of consciousness, is at first directly interwoven with the material activity and the material intercourse of men, the language of real life. Conceiving, thinking, the mental intercourse of men, appear at this stage as the direct efflux of their material behaviour. The same applies to mental production as expressed in the language of politics, laws, morality, reality, metaphysics etc., of a people. Men are the producers of their conceptions, ideas etc.—real, active men, as they are conditioned by a definite development of their productive forces and of the intercourse corresponding to these, up to its furthest forms. Consciousness can never be anything else but conscious existence, and the existence of men is their actual life-process. If in all ideology men and their circumstances appear as upside-down as in a *camera obscura,* this phenomenon arises just as much from their historical life-process as the inversion of objects on the retina does from their physical life-process.

. . . We do not set out from what men say, imagine, conceive, nor from men as narrated, thought of, imagined, conceived, in order to arrive at men in the flesh. We set out from real active men, and on the basis of their real-life-process we demonstrate the development of the ideological reflexes and echoes of this life-process. The phantoms formed in the human brain are also, necessarily, sublimates of their material life process, which is empirically verifiable and bound to material premises. Morality, religion, metaphysics, all the rest of ideology and their corresponding forms of consciousness, thus no longer retain the semblance of independence. They have no history, no development; but men, developing their material production and their material intercourse, alter, along with their real existence, their thinking and the products of their thinking. Life is not determined by consciousness, but consciousness by life.   (Marx 1846/1977a: 164)

. . . the division of labour implies the contradiction between the interest of separate individuals or the individual family and the communal interest of all individuals who have intercourse with one another. And indeed this communal interest does not merely exist in the imagination, as the 'general interest', but first of all in reality, as the mutual interdependence of the individuals among whom the labour is divided. . . .

And out of this very contradiction between the interest of the individual and that of the community the latter takes an independent form as the state, divorced from the real interests of individual and community, and at the same time as an illusory communal life. . . . It follows from this that all struggles within the State, the struggle between democracy, aristocracy and monarchy, the struggle for the franchise, etc., etc., are merely the illusory forms in which the real struggles of the different classes are thought out among one another.   (ibid.)

Everything appears reversed in competition. The final pattern of economic relations as seen on the surface, in their real existence and consequently in the conceptions by which the bearers and agents of these relations seek to understand them, is very much different from, and indeed quite the reverse of, their inner but concealed essential pattern and the conception corresponding to it. (Marx 1865/1972: 209)

This sphere . . . within whose boundaries the sale and purchase of labour power goes on, is in fact a very Eden of the innate rights of man. There alone rule Freedom, Equality, Property, and Bentham. Freedom because both buyer and seller of a commodity, say of labour power, are constrained only by their own free will. They contract as free agents, and the agreement they come to is but the form in which they give legal expression to their common will. Equality, because each enters relation with the other, as with a simple owner of commodities, they exchange equivalent for equivalent. Property because each disposes only of what is his own. And Bentham, because each looks only to himself. The only force that brings them together and puts them in relation with each other is the selfishness, the gain, and the private interests of each. Each looks to himself only, and no one troubles himself about the rest, and just because they do so, do they all, in accordance with the pre-established harmony of things, or under the auspices of an all-shrewd providence, work together to their mutual advantage. For the common weal and in the interest of all.   (Marx 1867/ 1970: 172)

IDEAS AS THE EXPRESSION OF THE LIFE PROCESS

This is not so much a theory of ideology as a theory of thinking: that our ideas do not, as Mao Tse Tung once put it, 'fall from the sky', but that they emerge out of our experience of the world, our relationship to the world and to each other; not in any deterministic way—our ideas are not 'caused' by our daily life and its relationships but are based on it, both as an expression of our experience and an attempt to deal with its problems. This gives a hint of what thinking would be like in a socialist society—a constant flux of ideas and debates centred around our everyday living.

This way of looking at thinking is reflected in contemporary sociology and psychology. In sociology the notion of human interaction as a constant flowing process, giving rise to and constantly redefining ideas, has been at the centre of symbolic interactionism (see Blumer 1969). The notion of ideas being the expression of life experience has moved to the centre of some modern psychoanalysis—but there it is less a matter of ideas emerging from 'material experience'—the experience of production and of daily life—than from earliest physical experience of ourselves and other people (Bion 1976). In fact these two contemporary approaches illustrate both the limitations and the advantages of Marx's position. The first limitation is that Marx and many Marxists pay no attention to childhood, when we learn to think. Jean-Paul Sartre, who became a critical Marxist after the Second World War, talked about Marxists writing as if people were born fully developed onto the factory floor. The second limitation is that work is not the only thing we do in our daily lives: there are the activities of friendship, of family life, play, love, etc., which Marxism often ignores. The great advantage of Marx's position is that it develops an understanding of how these ideas that we build up from our experience can be systematically distorted.

IDEOLOGY AS ALIENATION

I have already mentioned Marx's theory that religion represents a projection of *human* powers into a supernatural being. Similarly, but on a more concrete level, the state is a representation of human communal life—a projection of the real collective powers that belong to our relationships with each other. The end of this sort of alienated ideology comes from practical political action: if we collectively take over the state, 'seize state power', and the state ceases in reality to be an institution counterposed to society, then we have abandoned ideology. McLellan argues that, in his earlier work, Marx 'had set the scene for his conception of ideology. The mistaken conception of religion and politics that he criticized were not merely errors; these inverted conceptions have their basis in a real social world that was so misconstructed as to generate these compensatory illusions' (McLellan 1971: 11). This view of ideology sees it as the alienation of our free and creative thinking.

THE ECONOMIC DETERMINIST CONCEPTION OF IDEOLOGY

Sometimes when Marx is talking about political struggles, he seems to be saying that ideologies are illusory ways of seeing the world that are determined entirely by class position or the economic structure/stage of the development of a society. Thus in *The Eighteenth Brumaire* he argues that the two conflicting monarchist parties represent different sections of the bourgeoisie. It is not a matter of rational justifications of a monarchy and rational and legal argument between the two factions. Rather the whole process is driven by economic interests. But not consciously—each class believes that its own interests are in fact the general interests of the society as a whole.

I want to suggest here that each of Marx's conceptions of ideology is useful and if we play them off against each other we develop a very complex position. Now if we compare the simpler economic-determinist arguments with the theory of alienation and Marx's references to the life process, we can perhaps argue that in trying to make sense of our life processes we transform our own interests into some general belief about the world—in the way my son justifies his demands for pocket money by referring to fairness. A French bourgeois in 1848 would not cynically have chosen one monarchist faction because it would have been to his advantage; rather the arguments of that faction would resonate with him because they shared his life conditions.

IDEOLOGY AS ILLUSION

Next is Marx's frequent insistence on the illusory nature of ideology, ideas as phantoms, inverted impressions of the real world. Many later Marxists talk of false consciousness, although Marx does not usually use the term. It is often attributed to Lukacs, although I am not sure that this is particularly fair either. I think these statements are best read as polemical attacks on more conventional ways of thinking. In particular, Marx is trying to underline that we should not start with ideas since this places us immediately in the world of the imagination, but with the activities out of which ideas are produced. If we start with ideas and simply assume that they are true, then we are likely to be left with illusions. He is also saying that we should not take things at face value. Just as we do not take what an individual might say about him- or herself as necessarily the truth, so we should mistrust the way in which political parties and groups present themselves and the ways in which societies think about themselves.

IDEOLOGY AS IMAGINATION

There is a sense in which, in referring to these ideas as imaginary, Marx is a century ahead of his time; if we can return for a moment to the work of Althusser (1971), part of his rewriting of Marx borrows from contemporary French psychoanalysis (Lacan 1977) to argue that ideology consists not in one particular set of ideas but in a particular imaginary relationship to the world: we *imagine* that we are in charge of ourselves and our lives, that we make free decisions according to rational considerations and open choices. It actually takes very little thought to realize that, however much we might like to hold on to this as an ideal, life is really not like this. We are constantly finding that we are not as aware of ourselves or of what we are doing as we thought we were. Sometimes, in fact, we can find out that what we are doing, especially within the field of political activity, turns out to be the opposite of what we thought we were doing.

To take an example where it seems to me that Marx's analysis is almost precisely right: during the social upheavals of 1960s, the student left developed a slogan 'the personal is political'. At the time it seemed a radical extension of politics to everyday life, and the argument was that political action should not just involve changing governments but should transform the quality of everyday life itself. On the one hand, this can be seen as a radical slogan; it was, for example, important for the genesis of modern feminism. But it seems to me arguable that it also had another effect in opening the way to the political *control* of everyday life, not its political liberation—the opposite of what was intended.

But ideology can never completely be a matter of the imagination. Its imaginary aspect adds another dimension to those I discussed earlier, different from creative thought, thought unconsciously governed by self-interest and the projection of powers involved in alienation. But another thing one learns from modern psychoanalysis is that the imaginary and the real are often mixed together, sometimes inextricably. This moves us on to the core of Marx's later theory of ideology.

IDEOLOGY AS THE ACCURATE PERCEPTION OF ONE LEVEL OF REALITY

If we think about the earlier theories of ideology, there is always some point at which a real perception of the world enters. Marx seemed to assume—even when he was talking about the imagination and phantoms—that there was some real basis for the development of these phantoms, that there is some perception of the reality of the life process, and that it is in fact the nature of the life process which prevents us from grasping the reality of our lives and leads to us creating these phantoms. If we think about the process of alienation, it is a *real* human power that we invest in God, a real communal power that we invest in the state.

We can find in the theory of commodity fetishism the mechanisms that lead to the production of phantoms, and the reality of these phantoms. It is at the level of appearances that ideology is rooted—the appearances that mask the inner reality of the capitalist system and which are built into the system through the sale of labour as a commodity. It is at the level of exchange on the market that the full force of 'bourgeois ideology' lies, because there everything seems to work as the economists and politicians say it works. When I sell work to the university, I get paid for what my work is worth—within limits, and when those limits are breached, it seems the fault of bad management or bad government, or perhaps my own fault for not selling myself sufficiently vigorously. Life seems to be a matter of relationships between individuals, almost always a matter of bargaining and trading. This is not simply true of the world of work; several centuries ago Kant noticed that this way of thinking was penetrating marriage, and that is even clearer today. It is not just that people in the West are beginning to make agreements to protect property before entry into marriage; it is that the market is now providing a model for the emotional connection as well. Anthony Giddens (1991) talks about a process of 'effort-bargaining' between partners which can easily be seen as an economic trade-off, and the American sociologist Arnie Hochschild (1994) has suggested that certain forms of modern feminism have encouraged a commercial model for personal relationships. In the UK it is also easy to see how the market model has eaten away at traditional ideals of public service and a national health service and is also gradually entering the education system, in the development of interchangeable commodities (called modularization) and through the increasing role of student choice and assessment. It has not quite reached the stage where the only courses available are the ones that sell well, but that is the logic of the development.

It is developments such as these which generate the illusions of ideology and the alienated projection of human powers into external structures—and, in the context of what I have just been talking about, the market as an invisible entity is invested with the human power of allocating resources to the best effect and making choices between possible courses of action. We are now back to where started: Marx's economic analysis of capitalism.

REPRESENTATION AS IDEOLOGY

There is one last aspect to Marx's theory of ideology which has emerged only in recent years. It is difficult to explain in simple terms but I will do the best I can. The argument is basically that Marx's analysis of money as the medium of exchanging different goods identifies one stage in a historical development in which signs have become dominant. The sign, in linguistics, can be seen as enabling an exchange between (crudely) concept and reality. The sign 'desk' links my idea of a desk with this wooden construction on which I am writing. In

Marx's economic theory, money is the sign which enables the exchange of two very different objects—for example, £20.00 can equate a hardback book with half a dozen bottles of cheap wine, three haircuts, or half an hour with a psychotherapist. Jean Baudrillard, who has developed this argument furthest, argues that the sign which started full of meaning, as a religious icon, becomes flattened out, losing meaning, and then in contemporary society comes to be able to mean anything and therefore nothing. Contact with 'reality' is lost—we are left only with free-floating signs and signs of signs.

CONCLUSION

If we take ideology to be based on an accurate, but surface, conception of reality, then we can see that the deterministic notions of ideology, the formulations in which it is seen only as epiphenomenal, do not hold water. The liberal ideologies of utilitarianism have been governing economic thought ever since Marx and have developed independently in many different directions. Ideas do seem to have a life of their own; they develop not only as a result of changes at the economic level and developments in the progress of class struggle but also as a result of debate, research, and thought that goes on the basis of those ideas. There is always a degree of original as well as illusory thinking in ideology. What Marx gives us is a number of ways to explore the relationship between our life processes, our everyday activities, and our sensuous experience of the world and each other, which later Marxists have encapsulated under the label *praxis*, and the ways in which systems of ideas grow up and develop is more or less alienated from our *praxis*. And in Marx's work as well we find these ideological forms juxtaposed to a knowledge of the world which can penetrate these surface experiences to underlying structures. Over the last century, these ideas have generated a variety of different critiques of modern society, as well as themselves providing an ongoing and highly relevant critical approach to our own society.

Perhaps it would be more accurate to say that, while Marx has left us with a powerful tool of critical theory, the gaps in his arguments have created even more powerful tools. These gaps have to do with making theoretical sense of the move from the analysis of social structures to the analysis of human experience and action—*praxis*—and then to the analysis of ideas and systems of thought—a set of problems which are still at the centre of social theory.

Marxism and the family

Of the four theorists that I am discussing here only Marx has contributed anything substantial to modern feminism and this owes more to his companion

Friedrich Engels (1968), whose work has inspired a number of analyses of the position of women under capitalism (Zaretsky 1973; Sacks 1984; Hartman 1986).

Engels tries to trace the development of the family from primitive times in an exercise not unlike Durkheim's study of religion, involving the use of ethnographic material provided by others. The basis as always with Marxism is production, a matter of asking who does the work and who owns the tools. He posits a state of primitive communism, in which the tribe collectively owned the resources (although because of this very fact, the question of ownership would have made no sense to them). The tribe only produced what was sufficient for day-to-day life. Engels suggests that sexual relations were promiscuous, and one way of looking at the development of the family is as a process of the steady limitation of those with whom sexual relations are permissible:

the communistic household implies the supremacy of women in the house just as the exclusive recognition of a natural mother, because of the impossibility of determining the natural father with certainty, signifies high esteem for the women, that is for the mothers. That woman was the slave of man at the commencement of society is one of the most absurd notions that have come down to us from the period of Enlightenment in the eighteenth century. Women occupied not only a free but also a highly respected position.   (Engels 1884/1968: 481)

Decision-making in these groups involved everybody.

The development of the pairing family was intimately bound up with the development of private property, which in turn is involved in the production of a surplus—or more than the tribe needs to feed itself on a day-to-day basis. This occurs as nomadic groups settle to raise crops and (especially) animals. These formed the basis of private property although, as Sacks (1984) points out, they are not really private property in the modern sense; rather their owners have more power of disposal than hitherto. Looking after domestic animals and the growing of crops were men's activities, outside the family, and consequently it was men who came to own property. As wealth increased, tribes began producing for exchange purposes, thus producing a surplus.

The result of this was, again in Sacks's words, 'that people and property became entwined, and each became part of the definition of the other'. The property that is passed on becomes important, and it becomes important for the man to ensure that his property is passed on to his own children. The primitive form of group or communist family changed: women's work became clearly different from that of men and subordinated to it—their main function came to be the bearing of children who would inherit their father's property and position. This required not only a pairing marriage but also monogamy—at least for the women—since that was the only way the man could be sure that he was passing on property to his own child.

An important concomitant of this was that the social organization of sexuality changed to a system of 'hetaerism'—the practice of sexual intercourse outside marriage alongside monogamy:

With the rise of property differentiation . . . wage labour appears sporadically alongside of slave labour; and simultaneously, as its necessary correlate, the professional prostitution of free women appears side by side with the forced surrender of the female slave. Thus the heritage bequeathed to civilisation by group marriage is double-sided, just as everything engendered by civilisation is double-sided: on the one hand, monogamy, on the other hetaerism, including its most extreme form, prostitution.   (Engels 1884/1968: 495–6)

The contradiction and conflict between men and women carries in embryonic form the antagonisms which split society into different classes. In modern society, marriage is always to some degree a marriage of convenience, determined by the class position of the participants, effectively often only a form of prostitution for the wife. Rather romantically, and I think mistakenly, Engels argues that sexual love can only become the rule amongst the oppressed classes—it is not often possible where property must be taken into account. Even amongst the oppressed classes, brutality towards women has taken root, although, amongst those without property, the woman has in fact the right to leave. Engels talks about the slow movement towards women's legal equality—which I think has probably been a much slower process than even Engels imagined a century ago. However, at the end of this particular part of his discussion we get an idea of what Engels saw as the real basis on which women can achieve social equality—drawing a parallel with the way in which the democratic state does not abolish the inequality between social classes:

In the industrial world . . . the specific character of the economic oppression that weighs down the proletariat stands out in all its sharpness only after all the special legal privileges of the capitalist class have been set aside and the complete juridical equality of both classes is established. The democratic republic does not abolish the antagonism between the two classes; on the contrary, it provides the field on which it was fought out. And, similarly, the peculiar character of man's domination over woman in the modern family, and the necessity as well as the manner, of establishing real social equality between the two, will be brought out into full relief only when both are completely equal before the law. It will then become evident that the first premise for the emancipation of women is the reintroduction of the entire female sex into public industry; and that this again demands that the quality possessed by the individual family of being the economic unit of society be abolished.   (ibid. 504)

If property is returned to common ownership, then the family would lose its economic function—housekeeping and child-rearing would become a social activity, 'a social industry'. However, we would not return to the promiscuous sexuality of primitive communism. The Middle Ages saw the appearance of what we would now call romantic love and Engels calls sexual love; the development of socialism would enable this to come into its own—there would develop a 'true monogamy' in which couples would come together freely through love. Sexual love is spontaneously, naturally monogamous, but this monogamy will not be accompanied by the dominance of the man, and people will be free to leave each other as well as to come together: 'If only marriages that are based on love are moral, then, also only those are moral in which love continues' (ibid.). The antagonism between men and women, the first form of class struggle, will disappear.

The empirical basis of Engels's work, particularly the evidence on which he claimed that early societies are matriarchal, is now generally accepted as inadequate, but the suggested link between women and private property and inheritance is an interesting one. What has become clear is that the market economy tends towards producing a limited equality between men and women, but it is the equality of the 'abstract individual'—not the collective freedom of men and women working together that Engels envisaged. The evidence from the contemporary world, especially from the eastern European societies that called themselves communist, is, whatever the legal and economic status of women, they are still expected to take responsibility for work *in* the home. Again it has been the failure of more orthodox Marxist approaches to such issues that has stimulated so much modern research and argument. One line of argument has moved through Marx's theories of ideology to psychoanalysis and postmodernism, or to more conventional analyses of mothering; others have tried to develop a concept of patriarchy as a system of oppression interwoven with, but different from class oppression. And these debates have been matched by political debates within the feminist movement between liberal, radical, and socialist feminists (Barrett 1980; Barrett and McIntosh 1982; Walby 1990).

Conclusion

I think that perhaps the crucial difference between Marx and Durkheim is that Marx saw industrial society as essentially divided against itself, whereas Durkheim saw it as possessing an essential unity. For Durkheim, it follows that ideas and belief systems express the whole of a society, whereas for Marx they can mask society and its divisions and prevent the conflict that would emerge if people were to become aware of their real interests.

Turning to the contemporary problems that I am considering at the end of these chapters, it would be true to say that a Marxist sociologist would also look for empirical evidence that these processes are actually occurring, but he or she might be interested in different figures (changes in the relative distribution of wealth, relative profit rates, or numbers of days lost through strikes might, for example, be considered more important than, say, the symptoms of anomic or egoistic states), and the same evidence might be interpreted in different ways.

To begin with, a Marxist might focus on the growth of monopoly capitalism and multinational companies, as the capitalist market seems to have permeated nearly every corner of the world and produced organizations that transcend the boundaries of the nation state. This is a process that sociologists have come to term globalization and it has produced conceptions of a 'world system'—an idea not confined to Marxists (Wallerstein 1974; Giddens 1981). One argument is that this process of globalization creates an international labour market and that factory production, for a good part of this century established in the 'developed' world, moves to the developing world, where labour costs are cheaper. The dominance of finance capital and the growth of information technology— encouraged by the globalization process—means that capital can be moved around the world rapidly to wherever the return in greatest. It is this that produces the emphasis on flexibility and change, a 'short-termism'. The best account of this development can be found in Harvey (1989). The class conflicts which occurred in the UK in the late 1970s and early 1980s, in Germany and France more recently, and to a lesser extent in the USA under Reagan are symptoms of these changes.

Contrasted with a Durkheimian approach which might see the 'natural evolution' of the division of labour, the Marxist account would emphasize the mechanisms of competition and conflict and different class interests which drive the process forward. The apparent loss of a shared morality, shared norms, and community life would be seen as the result of these economic changes. Capitalism has always tended to break down traditional communities and beliefs and then to build up new communities and break them down again— first destroying the traditional rural communities and building up working-class communities around the new heavy industries and now breaking them down again. Whereas a Durkheim might see this change as a result of industrial society *per se*, a Marxist would see it as a result of capitalism—an underlying structure of social relationships.

A Marxist might try to explain the rise of new types of political movement less as a result of a modernizing process which eats away at social cohesion than in terms of the decline in class-based politics in the West which follows on the political and industrial battles of the last twenty years. This in turn would be seen as enabling the fragmenting effects of the competitive market to dominate and people would be seen as trying to create communities on the basis of surface factors such a gender or sexuality. It has become harder to see through these surface appearances to the underlying forces that are at work, and even if we can see through the appearances it is more difficult to know what can be done about it. As far as the West is concerned, capitalism has won for the foreseeable future and perhaps the function of Marxism would be seen as the analytical one of pointing to underlying structures and maintaining a critique of modern ideologies. Postmodernism in particular fits very easily with the individualism and fragmentation created by the market economy; it loses sight of the existence of a global system, emphasizing differences and rejecting causal explanations. Whereas postmodernist theory might see many of these changes as a form of liberation, freeing the individual to create him- or herself at will (see especially

Gergen 1991), Marxism would see them as involving a sophisticated form of enslavement—the more we are dominated by a global system, the more we believe we are free individuals. It might be argued that this is the central feature of modern capitalism.

Boxes 8.1–8.3 show Marx's contributions to the central dualisms.

Box 8.1. An elaboration of Marx on the individual and society

THE INDIVIDUAL

Durkheim: the individual is formed and limited by society. He/she becomes more important in complex societies and individualism becomes the focus of the *conscience collective*, binding people together.

Marx: the 'individuated' individual is an idea produced as part of the development of capitalism. The 'natural' state of the individual is as an integral part of the group.

Weber: the individual is the only reality and analysis must start from individual rational action.

Simmel: the individual life is engaged in a constant dialectic with social forms.

SOCIETY

Durkheim: society exists over and above the individual, over whom it exercises an immense power, especially in less complex societies.

Marx: society is created by human action but acts back upon individuals as an external power—a dominant force in all but the most primitive and most advanced (communist) societies.

Weber: society is the rather fragile result of human interaction.

Simmel: 'society' is an increasingly important form organizing peoples' lives.

Box 8.2. Marx on action and structure

ACTION

Durkheim: there is no real theory of social action in Durkheim; the individual action is always conditioned by the group, and collective action is taken to reinforce the strength of the group.

Marx: in capitalist societies, the major agents are social classes—primarily the bourgeoisie and the proletariat. Some classes—the middle classes and the peasantry—do not share the life conditions which enable them to act as collective agents, and they tend to follow a strong leader.

STRUCTURE

Durkheim: in societies dominated by mechanical solidarity, the social structure consists of networks of kin groups (segmented societies); more complex modern societies consist of secondary groups formed by the division of labour and managed by the state.

Marx: different types of society have different forms of social structure. In capitalist societies the economic structure and resultant class structure are most important, and the state and state institutions are central features of social control.

Box 8.3. **Marx on social integration and system integration**

SOCIAL INTEGRATION	SYSTEM INTEGRATION
Durkheim: in all societies social integration is achieved through the *conscience collective*—shared ways of thinking (logic, conceptions of space and time, shared beliefs, norms, and values). In societies governed by mechanical solidarity, religion is central. In more complex modern societies, the *conscience collective* covers less of our lives but focuses on the ethics of individual freedom—it becomes a religion of humanity.	**Durkheim:** where mechanical solidarity predominates, system integration *is* social integration, guaranteed by the *conscience collective*. Where organic solidarity predominates, system integration is achieved through the division of labour.
Marx: a 'false' and rather tenuous integration is achieved through ideologies, and the development of the market constantly threatens whatever integration is achieved. The major contending classes strive towards achieving their own integration in opposition to the others—the proletariat being the class most likely to achieve this.	**Marx:** system integration in capitalism is constantly threatened by class conflict and is supported by the state and by ruling ideologies.

Further reading

From the original works, the best starting point is *The Economic and Philosophical Manuscripts of 1844* (1974)—as much of it as you can but especially the section on alienated labour; much more difficult but also very important is Volume I of *Capital* (1867/1970)—especially part 1. The best of Marx's own political analyses is to be found in *The Eighteenth Brumaire of Louis Bonaparte* (1852/1968c), but it might be an idea to read it in conjunction with a simple textbook on nineteenth-century French history. On ideology, as well as Volume I, part 1 of *Capital*, see David McLellan's selection from *The German Ideology* (1846/1977a).

You should also read *The Communist Manifesto* (Marx 1848/1968a) and Engels, *The Origin of the Family, Private Property and the State* (1884/1968).

The best secondary source for the beginner is David McLellan, *The Thought of Karl Marx* (1971), and, on Marxist economic theory, Ernest Mandel's excellent little *An Introduction to Marxist Economic Theory* (1970). On the family, see Karen Sacks's article 'Engels Revisited' (1984) and Eli Zaretsky, *Capitalism, The Family and Personal Life* (1973).

For accounts of different forms of Marxism since Marx, see Ted Benton, *The Rise and Fall of Structural Marxism* (1984), and Perry Anderson, *Considerations on Western Marxism* (1976). For a Marxist critique of postmodernism, see Fredric Jameson, *Postmodernism or the Cultural Logic of Late Capitalism* (1991) and for postmodernist discussion of Marxism, see Crook, Pakulski, and Waters, *Postmodernization* (1992).

9 | The liberal Weber

Introduction
Weber's complexity; Weber and Marx.

The fundamental concepts of sociology
Legitimacy; conflict; Weber's cautious evolutionism; communal relations based on identity; associative relations based on interest; corporate groups and different forms of control; the nature of politics and the state; power as an end in itself.

Weber's economic sociology
Weber's concern with the sociological preconditions of the capitalist economy; the advantages of the market; formal and substantive rationality; the stability offered by the market to precarious social and political institutions; free disposal over goods and free labour and other preconditions of the development of formally rational accounting in productive enterprises; different types of capitalism and the peculiarity of western capitalism.

Class, status, and party
Weber and a theory of social structure; comparison of Marx and Weber on social class; class situation as market situation and life chances; the possibility of solidary class relations; the complexity of class structure seen in Weberian terms; the possibility of combining Marxist and Weberian conceptions; status as social esteem and lifestyle and the ambiguity of Weber's concept; the relationship between class and status in Weber's and Marx's sense; status groups in contemporary society; status groups and educational qualifications; professional groups and self-interest—comparison with Durkheim; parties and their ineffectiveness—Weber's determinism.

Power, domination, and authority
Types of domination; charismatic leadership—comparison with Durkheim; the routinization of charisma; traditional patriarchal domination and its development into patrimonialism; feudalism and its development; legal–rational domination and the characteristics of the modern state; the absence of any absolute basis for authority; the basis of legitimacy in legal–rational domination; Weber's ideal type of bureaucracy.

Conclusion
The fragility of the social order.

Introduction

> ... it is, of course, not my aim to substitute for a one-sided materialistic and equally one-sided spiritualistic interpretation of culture and of history. Each is equally possible, but each, if it does not serve as the preparation, but as the conclusion of an investigation, accomplishes equally little in the interest of historic truth.
>
> (Weber 1904–5/1930: 184)

These lines, the conclusion to Weber's famous *Protestant Ethic and the Spirit of Capitalism*, show Weber at his best and perhaps explain why he has been the most popular classical theorist in the development of British sociology, displaying the straightforward common sense for which British intellectuals seem to yearn. But Weber is difficult to pin down. I think it is arguable that there are several Webers, although for the purposes of this book I shall concentrate on two. In this chapter I shall focus on the Weber who put the free market at the centre of his work, arguing that it provided a source of fragile social stability; in Part 3 I shall concentrate on the tragic Weber who saw history taking us into an iron cage. The above quotation is often taken as an example of the dictum that Weber was forever conducting a debate with Marx's ghost, and in his religious studies and in his work on class, status, and party we can perhaps see him as an exceptionally sophisticated Marxist. Bendix (1966) describes Weber as holding to a 'complex . . . position in which ideas must be understood within their social context but also as having a power of their own'. The most important starting point for understanding Weber is that, despite the scope of his theory, it is not totalizing; we saw in Part 1 that he works with a conception of multi-causality, and focuses on meanings.

To begin with I will follow Weber's own outline of his work, on which he was working at his death, and which has been translated as *The Theory of Social and Economic Organization* (1925/1947), the opening sections of which I have already discussed in Chapter 5. It is important to remember that at this stage he is not engaging in substantive sociological analysis; rather he is using rational argument to try to set up a number of distinctions and classifications which can then be used as part of a substantive analysis. At one point he feels it necessary to defend himself against the accusation of the 'apparently gratuitous tediousness involved in the elaborate definition of the above concepts'. I have tried to select the most important distinctions.

The fundamental concepts of sociology

Weber here is concerned with the nature of legitimacy, conflict, organization, and the use of force.

LEGITIMACY

After outlining the forms of social action, Weber goes on to discuss the concept of 'legitimate' order. Action may be oriented to a belief in a legitimate order, and the probability that people will actually act in such a way is called the 'validity' of that order. 'Order' has a number of connotations, and the way in which Weber goes on to elaborate the notion pushes it towards what Durkheim meant by a social fact. It is a rule which has to be followed, not out of habit or self-interest, although these might be involved, but also because of a sense of obligation or duty, and indeed he goes on to talk about the law as an example of such order.

The legitimacy of a particular order may stem from either 'disinterested' motives which may be based on emotional allegiance or a belief in ultimate values (such as are involved in religion). If the validity of a particular order is guaranteed by the disapproval that I would incur by going against it, then Weber says it should be called a convention, and he distinguishes this from the law which entails the presence of a group of people specifically devoted to its enforcement. The most important basis for legitimacy in modern society is legality—reached by agreement and/or imposed by what is generally held to be legitimate authority. An understanding of his meaning can be gained by looking at what happens when an authority oversteps its conventional legitimacy—for example, when the Thatcher government imposed a poll tax which was generally considered to be grossly unfair. In the USA there seems to be a constant debate over the legitimacy of the federal government.

CONFLICT

Conflict is defined as a social relationship in which one person or group of people attempt to achieve their will against the resistance of others; this can range from all-out war to well-regulated competition, but Weber here introduces a very crude Darwinism. Conflict cannot be eliminated, and attempts to do so will always result in its reappearance in some other form; its purpose is to sort out those who are best suited to prevailing conditions and eliminate those who are not. Weber recognized the practical and moral difficulties of establishing this sort of argument:

There is, above all, a danger of being primarily concerned with justifying the success of an individual case. Since individual cases are often dependent on highly exceptional circumstances, they may be in a certain sense 'fortuitous'. In recent years there has been more than enough of this kind of argument. The fact that a given specific social relationship has been eliminated for reasons peculiar to a particular situation proves nothing whatever about its 'fitness to survive' in general terms.   (Weber 1922/1947: 135)

COMMUNAL AND ASSOCIATIVE RELATIONSHIPS

Communal relationships occur when a group of social actors see themselves as belonging together and they act accordingly; associative relationships depend on the mutual adjustments of interest—this may be on the basis of the market, or self-interest, or because of adherence to some ultimate value. Thus my relationship to my family is communal, and that to my trade union, my church, and my local shopkeepers are associative. This echoes a distinction made by Ferdinand Tonnies (1957) between 'community' and 'association', *Gemeinschaft* and *Gesellschaft*, which represented for him a major historical change away from homogenous societies characterized by clear status positions and intimate relationships to societies based on calculated self interest and contacts. This clearly mirrors Durkheim's understanding of the move from organic to mechanical solidarity and it also mirrors contemporary debates about the nature of community.

Weber makes the point that the existence of common biological factors, a common language, or any other common qualities does not imply the existence of communal relationships between the people who share these qualities; he has no conception of people belonging to a 'class-in-itself', independently of their consciousness. He regards market relationships as a most important contemporary form of associative relationship, and we shall see that his conception of market-based classes has been very important in the development of sociology.

CORPORATE GROUPS

Today, a corporate group might be called a 'collective actor'. It is a relatively closed group in which order is enforced by a number of individuals whose specific task it is to do just that. Weber distinguishes between 'power', the probability that one individual will have his or her orders carried out, and 'imperative control', the probability that a specific command will be obeyed. The notion of a corporate group does in the end seem to depend on an individual issuing orders which the group then carries out. As we shall see when we discuss Weber's view of political democracy, this places a limit on democracy—the need for some sort of sovereign who personifies the unity of the group.

Out of this discussion comes an interesting and important point. He argues that we cannot define a *political* corporate group from its purpose. Political groups have all sorts of purposes and there is no one purpose which they would all recognize. Thus we cannot achieve any clarity from such a definition: 'Thus it is possible to define the "political" character of a corporate group only in terms of the *means* peculiar to it, the use of force. This means is, however, in the above sense specific, and is indispensable to its character. It is even, under certain circumstances, elevated into an end in itself' (Weber 1922/1947: 155).

This is interesting because it sees power in a way we have not encountered so far, as an autonomous factor over which struggles can take place. For Durkheim, in so far as power was a problem, the exercise of power was a function of the division of labour. For Marx, power was determined by social class and the state of the class struggle. Weber's conception continues through to Parsons and on to postmodernism via the connection to Nietzschean philosophy, the 'will to power' which replaces notions of morality or justice or equality or freedom. This leads Weber on to the state:

The primary formal characteristics of the modern state are as follows: It possesses an administrative and legal order subject to change by legislation, to which the organized corporate activity of the administrative staff, which is also regulated by legislation, is oriented. This system of order claims binding authority, not only over the members of the state, the citizens, most of whom have obtained membership by birth, but also, to a very large extent, over all action taking place in the area of its jurisdiction. It is thus a compulsory association with a territorial basis. Furthermore, today, the use of force is regarded as legitimate only so far as it is permitted by the state or prescribed by it. (ibid. 156)

This concern with force is unique amongst the founding thinkers of sociology.

Weber's economic sociology

In his introduction to *The Theory of Social and Economic Organization*, T. Parsons makes it clear that Weber is not trying to provide an economic theory but to do something which modern economists generally do not do—that is, offer a theory of the institutions that are involved in the capitalist economy. He points out that Weber assumes first, that social structures are inherently unstable and variable, and, secondly, that the rationalization and the dominance of the 'capitalist spirit' are an ongoing process—crudely, an attitude to life which sees the accumulation of capital *in a rational and systematic way* as the most important value, around which daily life should be systematically organized, at the expense of pleasure and relaxation.

Weber underlines what he saw as the positive aspects of the market economy. The use of money broadens the possibility of exchange and widens the scope for planning, for rational calculation, and for increasing wealth. He makes an important distinction between formal and substantive rationality. Formal rationality points to the extent to which rational calculation is possible—and he seems to be saying that it refers only to calculability. Substantive rationality, however, refers to the extent to which a group is provided with goods which meet its needs, and this is much more difficult, since absolute values enter in. Substantive rationality cannot be understood simply in terms of rational calculation—it concerns the things we value. A high level of formal rationality tends to enter into conflict, or at least tension with a high level of substantive rationality. This is a lesson which contemporary free-market economists are beginning to learn again. Effectively he is pointing out that economic efficiency does not necessarily get us what we want. Weber himself seemed to be doubtful about the possibility of a resolution to this tension. These days one might suggest that a fully developed socialist economy might achieve a high degree of substantive rationality but would be likely to have all sorts of problems in the realm of rational calculability. For a fully developed market economy, the opposite would be the case.

Weber based his arguments on the marginalist economics which replaced classical tradition in which Marx worked and which concentrated on the play of supply and demand, but unlike the economists themselves he was concerned with the social ramifications or preconditions of the processes by which price is determined. He argued that the market had an important stabilizing function in relation to political and social institutions. As one might expect from a theorist whose starting point was a rigorous methodological individualism, he saw such institutions as precarious and inherently unstable, without the power of tradition to anchor them down. They certainly did not have an existence in their own right over and above the individuals who comprised them. In this situation the successful, spontaneous determination of price through the matching of supply and demand provides a fixed point of orientation for a range of activities. If I know what goods and services are available and at what price, and if neither I nor anybody else can influence that price by our individual actions, then the range of rational actions open to me is limited and comparatively stable. In this sense the market can replace tradition as a fixed point in the midst of potential chaos.

There are a number of preconditions for the market to work in such a way: first, the owners of the means of production must have the right to dispose of them as they wish—they must not be bound by laws of inheritance, for example, or, as church-owned land once was, by rules which narrowly stipulate the uses to which it can be put. Political battles over this issue today tend to be fought out in terms of government interference and regulation rather than the abolition of traditional feudal restrictions, with which I think Weber was most often concerned. Secondly, there must be 'formally free' labour—no slavery, no serfdom, only wage labour. Although this enables the development of formal rationality, it is not clear that it enables the development of substantive rationality. Labour has to eat, and this provides the employer with a weapon which perhaps enables him or her to exercise *de facto* appropriation rights over workers—the use of the 'truck' system in nineteenth-century England, where workers were compelled to buy food from their employers' shops, would be an example. Marx made a similar point when he talked about 'wage slaves'. Whether we are talking about land, labour, or capital, however, the modern system of production is, for Weber, inherently unstable. In Weberian terms, value commitments are constantly entering into economic life. Many of his points fit well into contemporary debates about the role of the market, and in this context Weber would most often, I think, be supporting the political right. In the words of Parsons:

Perhaps his most important insight is that there is both a similarity of effect and an intrinsic connection between appropriation of the means of production by workers and appropriation of workers by owners. As to effect, both tend to break down the mobility of economic resources, human and non-human, and to open the door to traditionalistic stereotyping of economic structures.   (Parsons 1947: 64)

This makes sense if we see it in the context of a society emerging from feudalism and where some fall-back into feudal relationships is a major danger; whether it makes sense in a society which has left feudalism well behind is another matter.

Weber's own summary of the necessary preconditions for the full development of the capitalist market is as follows—I have glossed them in square brackets where I think it necessary:

The following are the principle conditions necessary for obtaining a maximum of formal rationality of capital accounting in productive enterprises:

(1) The complete appropriation of all the non-human means of production by owners, and the complete absence of all formal appropriation of opportunities for profit in the market; that is market freedom. [The owners of the means of production should have complete freedom to dispose of their property as they wish and there should be no restriction on who can pursue opportunities for profit.]

(2) Complete autonomy in the selection of management by the owners, thus the complete absence of formal appropriation of rights to managerial functions. [Managers do not own their jobs.]

(3) The complete absence of appropriation of jobs and of opportunities for earning for workers, and, conversely, the absence of appropriation of workers by owners. This involves free labour, freedom of the labour market and freedom in the selection of workers. [The workers don't own their jobs, and employers don't own the workers.]

(4) Complete absence of substantive regulation of consumption, production and prices, or of other forms of regulation which limit freedom of contract or specify conditions of exchange. This may be called substantive freedom of contract. [No government interference.]

(5) The maximum of calculability of the technical conditions of the productive process; that is a mechanically rational technology. [We need to know what things cost.]

(6) Complete calculability of the functioning of public administration and the legal order and a reliable formal guarantee of all contracts by the political. This is formally rational administration and law. [A state apparatus which guarantees the other conditions and the contracts which are agreed within them.]

(7) The most complete separation of the enterprise and its conditions of success and failure, from the household or private budgetary unit and its property interests. It is particularly important that the capital at the disposal of the enterprise should be clearly distinguished from the private wealth of the owners, and should not be subject to division and dispersion through inheritance.　(Weber 1922/1947: 275)

It is only on this last point that Weber perhaps differs from the contemporary political right, who are often to be heard encouraging small family businesses.

Weber makes one more important set of distinctions, this time in connection with types of 'capitalist orientation'; this takes us to the edge of his comparative sociology, which will be considered in greater depth in Chapter 13. He distinguishes between six 'qualitatively different' capitalist orientations to profits, which we can think of as six different types of capitalism. Again I will quote Weber at length and add my own occasional comment in square brackets.

1. Profit-making activity may be oriented to the exploitation of market advantages in a continuous process of purchase and sale on the market where exchange is free; that is, formally not subject to compulsion and materially, at least relatively, free. Or it may be oriented to the maximisation of profit in continuous productive enterprises which make use of capital accounting. [i.e. the system we have just been discussing.]

2. It may be oriented to opportunities for profit by trade and speculation in money, taking over debts of all sorts, and creating means of payment. A closely related type is the professional extension of credit, either for consumption or for profit-making purposes. [Merchant capitalism.]

3. It may be oriented to opportunities for acquiring 'booty' from corporate political groups or persons connected with politics. This includes the financing of wars or revolutions and the financing of party leaders by loans and supplies. [This is the sort of activity that got King John into trouble with the barons in thirteenth-century Britain and led to the Magna Carta.]

4. It may be oriented to opportunities for continuous profit by virtue of domination by force or of a position of power guaranteed by political authority. There are two main sub-types: colonial capitalism, operated through plantations with compulsory payments or compulsory labour and by monopolistic and compulsory trade. On the other hand there is the fiscal type, profit making by farming of taxes and of offices, whether in the home area or in colonies. [I think this is self-explanatory.]

5. The opportunities for orientation to profit opened up by unusual transactions with political bodies. [I think he might mean corruption.]

6. The orientation to opportunities for profit of the following types: (*a*) to purely speculative transactions in standardized commodities or in the securities of an enterprise;

(*b*) by carrying out the continuous financial operations of political bodies; (*c*) by the promotional financing of new enterprises in the form of sale of securities to investors; (*d*) by the speculative financing of capitalist enterprises and of various other types of economic organization with the purpose of a profitable regulation of markets or of attaining power. [Again, the system we have just been talking about.]   (Weber 1922/1947: 276–7)

Weber goes on to point out that types 1 & 6 are peculiar to western Europe whereas the others can usually be found in other places but do not have the same type of consequences that produce modern western societies. The theme of the uniqueness of the West is central to Weber's sociology and his understanding of historical development and we will come across it, in close relationship to his notion of the rationalization of society, time and time again. These issues will be pursued in detail in the Chapter 13 but you should bear them in mind through-out this chapter.

Now, what can we take from Weber's economic sociology. First of all, it is important to note that it is an *economic sociology*—unlike that of Marx, which was a sociological economics. Holton and Turner (1989), who offer an apologia for Weber's work on the economy, argue, I think rightly, that Weber was well aware of the alternatives to capitalism, and Marxist criticisms that he takes the market economy as a natural given (e.g. Clarke 1994) are mistaken. I think the real criticism from a Marxist point of view would be that Weber takes as a basis what is actually the result of complicated underlying processes and structures, and it is in fact his methodological individualism that leads him to do so. For Weber, individuals are taken for granted and come into relation with each other through the market; for Marx, individuals in this sense are a result of the market. For Weber, the free market unifies individuals; for Marx, the free market individualizes social groups.

Turner and Holton look at Weber's conception of the market as a way of over-coming what they call the problem of intersubjectivity—if we start with the individual then how do we explain collectivities, mutual understanding, and so on? In the form known as 'the problem of order', this is sometimes seen as the *raison d'être* of sociology, *the* question that it sets out to solve. However, it is only *the* problem if we start with the individual; if we start—as did Durkheim, and in effect Marx—with society or social facts, then the problem of order arises in a different and much less basic way.

It is probably fairly clear that I am not very enthusiastic about this part of Weber's work. He does seem to me to take too much for granted and he offers us an understanding of the institutions necessary for market capitalism to reach its apogee, but he does not offer more than that. If we read him as giving us a whole truth, I think we are lost; if we look at him as talking about the surface preconditions for a market economy, he becomes interesting.

Class, status, and party

If Weber had a theory of social structure, rather than a theory of individuals act-ing together, then his comparatively short piece on class, status, and party, together with his analysis of the state and bureaucracy, would be at the centre of it. Despite its brevity, it has had a massive influence on American sociology, where status was a concern for structural functionalism, and on British soci-ology, where it has been used to produce a more elaborate analysis of stratification than that offered by Marx.

Each grouping is focused around, or 'oriented towards', power as an independent point of conflict. Each represents an aspect of and a basis for power.

CLASS

There are moments when Weber sounds distinctly Marxist. Class is defined by property. The ownership of property confers a real power on the employer, and lack of ownership of property confers a real powerlessness on the worker—Weber here recognizes that the worker is compelled to work. He does not talk about 'wage slavery' but he does talk about the 'wage whip', but at the same time he did not seem to see the conflict that arose from this, or the worker's lack of property in itself, as having the significance that Marx attached to it. He criti-cized Marx's definition for not being able to take account of divisions, partic-ularly amongst the proletariat—almost anybody who wasn't a property owner could be a worker; as a university teacher I would find myself alongside a coal miner, a computer programmer, and an airline pilot, all of us in the working class, and it is difficult to see how any common interest could result from that. We have already seen that, in fact, Marx's categorization was not quite so simple, but that is by the way.

Weber's definition of class was in terms of a group of people who shared the same 'typical chance for a supply of goods, external living conditions and per-sonal life experiences insofar as this chance is determined by the . . . power to dispose of goods or skill for the sake of income in a given economic order. . . . "Class situation" is, in this sense, ultimately "market situation" ' (Weber 1922/1947: 181–2). One thing that is clear about this definition is that it does not help the basic problem of arriving at a coherent theory of class. Instead of the unlikely collection of people that I listed just now belonging to one class, we would, by Weberian criteria, each belong to separate classes; and it could be argued that there are different classes even within, say, the same occupational group, depending, say, on age or geographical area.

There is one occasion on which Weber tends to move away from this view to a position closer to Marx. In *Economy and Society* (1925/1978) he talks about the classes developing as 'solidary' as opposed to 'associative' organizations, which is closer to the way Marx saw the working class, if not the other classes, as a community. This occurs, he suggests, when a group shares the chances of moving between a limited number of class positions, but moving into a wider range of positions is blocked by power differentials. Thus one might argue that women have a limited number of employment possibilities between which they can move, but major changes are blocked by men and this gives rise to the possibility that women could form themselves into a social class. Perhaps this approximates to what has happened over the last thirty years. The classes defined in this way that Weber saw in the first decades of this century were the working class, the petty bourgeoisie, the intelligentsia and specialists, and classes privileged by property and education.

If Marx leaves us with too simple a model of class structure, then Weber leaves us with a complex and chaotic one. It is a definition of class from surface factors, and that can be useful, but it is not a model of a class *structure*. I think if we return to the notion of there being different levels of reality, then we can make sense of Weber as offering a way of understanding groupings within limits set by an underlying (Marxist) definition and as pointing to the complexity of class groupings. In a classic Weberian text, Rex and Moore (1967) talk about 'housing classes' to refer to empirically defined groupings—council tenants, private tenants, landlords, owner-occupiers, etc.—*within* the major classes, while David Lockwood (1958) used the concept of market position to explain why white-collar workers did not identify with manual workers. These different positions will interrelate with the underlying class position in different ways. Perhaps the right sort of imagery is that Weber offers us a pattern of groups which are always on the edge of collapsing into chaos, whereas, by combining Weber and Marx, the chaos is transformed into a sort of kaleidoscope—changing patterns of groups held in an underlying framework.

An alternative way of thinking about this is that implied by Holton and Turner (1989). They point out that Weber saw the formation of class communities as a contingent, rather than a necessary, feature of capitalism, and one constantly undermined by developments in social mobility. In this context Weber can be seen as describing a stage in the historical disappearance of social class as a significant feature in social life. There are a number of reasons to be careful of such an argument, not least because people have been announcing the disappearance of class for a number of decades and the arguments continue. I think the weightier argument, however, is that, even if social classes do not play the role that Marx thought they would, there is a continuity in the social classes that people identify as important and they seem to coalesce around the underlying framework that Marx identified rather than forming and disappearing purely and simply around market positions.

STATUS

The same sort of ambiguity can be found in the way that Weber deals with status or 'social honour'; on the one hand, he acknowledges that in the long term it goes with the possession of material wealth, but he also wants to maintain that it is an autonomous focus for conflict over power. 'Status situation' refers to that part of a person's life chances which are decided by the social esteem in which he or she is held; such esteem might be positive or negative. An attempt in the UK during the 1970s to form a public-contact group for paedophiles did not do much to improve the life chances of the organizers.

Along with the social esteem, we can often find a specific lifestyle and restrictions on social contact which are not subordinated to economic interest. Thus somebody who joins the Roman Catholic priesthood will wear distinctive clothes, will live according to distinctive rules, and will not marry, however rich his possible bride and however much she might offer to donate her riches to his church. In other status groups marriage might be prescribed within the group—orthodox Jewish communities would be a good example. There is usually a monopoly of ideal or material goods which is part or parcel of stratification by status—thus only the Roman Catholic priesthood can administer the sacraments and once upon a time, when services were in Latin, they might have been the only ones to understand what was happening.

At the time Weber was writing, there was probably a greater distinction—in some respects—between status and class than there is today, especially in Europe. For example, the distinction in British upper-class circles, especially in the nineteenth century, between 'old' and 'new' money meant that the impoverished aristocrat of a renowned and once powerful family might receive much more esteem and respect than the newly rich industrialist; and it is a well-documented fact that the latter would wish their children to marry into the former—although, of course, honour did not rub off as easily as the *nouveau riche* might have hoped.

I have already suggested that we can combine Marx's theory of class with Weber's, and the notion of status groups can add to such a model, as groups within or cutting across several classes. However, Weber's ambivalent relationship to Marxism remains. Bendix points out that:

The distinction between class and status group is directly related to Weber's sociology of religion. On the one hand, he investigated group formation on the basis of shared religious ideas. Here ideas serve as a bulwark of group cohesion, a means of status distinction, and as a basis for monopolizing economic opportunities. On the other hand, he examined given social groups . . . in terms of the religious propensities engendered by their class situation and status interests. Here ideas become a reflection of material interests.   (Bendix 1966: 87)

So status groups of this type are difficult to distinguish from social classes, in Weber's definition at any rate. So far I have talked about Weber defining such groups at the empirical level, rather than in the context of some underlying structure, but another way of putting the same thing is that most of the time class and status are defined by the distribution of goods and services, not (as in Marx) by their production.

There are other types of status group that are perhaps more significant for Marxist theory—these are groups which cut across social-class boundaries but are based on another 'solidary' identity—such as ethnicity or religion. Thus it is arguable the we can understand more about Northern Ireland using the notion of status group than we can using that of social class (although I think both would be necessary), and perhaps the same might be true of the former Yugoslavia; and of course ethnicity has become particularly important, as has gender, in contemporary societies, and it is conflict drawn along these lines as much as class conflicts which divides these societies. Weber thought that status conflict would come to the fore in periods of economic stability, rather than rapid economic change, which would bring class conflict. Frank Parkin, writing in the mid-1980s, shows how oversimple an assumption this is.

This proposition would seem to have a fairly limited historical validity. Class conflict in the nineteenth and early twentieth centuries was no doubt sufficiently acute and absorbing as to force most other social questions into the background. Class action during this period was aimed not merely at a more just distribution of goods and opportunities but at the incorporation of the propertyless masses into civil society. When the conflict between classes revolves upon issues as large as the political transformation of society, it might well be that all status group demands pale into insignificance. But when class conflict becomes domesticated and routinized, there is more social leeway for the furtherance of both class and status ambitions. Under modern capitalism, conflicts on the class and status fronts seem able to co-exist quite happily.   (Parkin 1982: 100)

Weber suggests that ethnic groups in particular offer their members a social esteem that is not available to them in the wider hierarchy—and it is a source of esteem open to everybody in the group; it is worth adding in support of Weber's contention that within the wider social hierarchy it is often amongst the lowest strata of the dominant ethnic group that we can find the most rabid hostility to subordinate groups—here ethnicity becomes the only claim to status and hence vitally important, to be reinforced at every opportunity. Holton and Turner (1989) argue that the notion of status group is particularly important for understanding modern multicultural societies.

The other important criterion for closure of status groups is educational qualification; professional groups such as doctors have a series of educational hurdles to pass, and these arguably become more and more specialized. Groups 'professionalize' by demanding higher qualifications—in the UK over the last decade the professionalisation of psychotherapy has led to increasingly elaborate and strictly governed training and has moved towards insisting on a Master's degree as an entry qualification. This leads to a consistent inflation of qualifications—if everyone has a Master's degree, then advancement will require doctorates.

Here we have a very different conception of the professional group from the one we found in Durkheim. If for Durkheim the professional group was able to develop its own norms and values, its own *conscience collective* which governed the behaviour of its members and provided a source of social solidarity, then for Weber they were groups vigorously pursuing their own self-interest on the market. In reality, both positions have something of the truth and it seems reasonable to suggest that whichever dimension predominates depends upon the state of the wider society: in a free-market economy, which moves closer to Weber's ideal type, the professions will pursue their own interests against others; in a society where the free market is limited, then perhaps the development of a collective morality is more important. But it must not be forgotten that both will go on all the time; human animals are creatures of self-interest *and* they are rule-following, moral beings as well. The difficulty is holding both sides together.

Parkin points out a significant and puzzling lack in Weber's treatment of status groups: the lack of any reference to the state, which can grant legal monopolies. This prevents him, argues Parkin, from developing any analysis of structured inequality. However, I have already suggested it was Weber's overall individualism which tended towards blinding him to the more structured and collective aspects of society, although he did sometimes talk about the state and the state bureaucracy as if it were itself the most important status group. My own point of view is that, if we start from a methodological individualism, then it is very difficult to talk about the state without seeing it as a privileged status group, seeking to pursue its own interests, and we lose sight of notions of the public interest or the common good.

PARTY

With the question of political parties we run into Weber's scepticism about democratic politics and the possibilities of social change. He did not think political parties would be able drastically to effect social reform or bring about greater economic equality. He distinguishes between patronage parties—which were concerned primarily with gaining power and dividing up the goodies between themselves—and parties of principle—which ended up, through a process of bureaucratization, doing much the same thing. Parties, too, become status groups pursuing their own self-interest. Weber was sympathetic to the view of his contemporary, Robert Michels, who argued (1911/1962) that such ideals inevitably become displaced—that, as the political party is organized, so the maintenance of the organization itself takes priority over the original ends, and an inevitable process of bureaucratization takes place.

So here we find a strange determinism in Weber's position—strange at least if we think of Weber as the theorist who contested Marx's determinism; it is not socialism that is inevitable and the mode of production that determines politics; rather it is the process of rationalization that determines everything. We shall see later what he thought of socialism.

Power, domination, and authority

We have already touched briefly on Weber's political sociology, his theory of the state and of authority in imperatively coordinated associations. I want to turn now to the centre of that political sociology, his more developed theories of power, domination, and the state. The starting point for this is his typology of types of domination: charismatic, traditional, and legal-rational. These are *ideal-typical* in the sense discussed in Chapter 5, and they are also related to his typifications of action, particularly in the case of legal-rational and traditional authority. There is also a possible historical order to them as well—most obvious again in the case of traditional and legal-rational domination, but this will be more significant in Chapter 13. In practice, the three types can coexist in any situation, but it is likely that one or the other will be dominant. Groups competing for power are always trying to transform the means at their disposal and so in modern society in particular there is an inherent instability in the form of domination.

I will follow Bendix's (1966) order of exposition of the different types, which is the opposite to that of Weber himself, and for the same reason: that, in Weber's own discussion, the point he is trying to make gets lost. I will begin with the notion of charisma, which has entered everyday language.

CHARISMATIC LEADERSHIP

> The term 'charisma' will be applied to a certain quality of an individual personality by virtue of which he is set apart from ordinary men and treated as endowed with supernatural, superhuman or at least specifically exceptional powers and qualities. These are such as are not accessible to the ordinary person, but are regarded as of divine origin or as exemplary, and on the basis of them the individual concerned is treated as a leader.
>
> (Weber 1922/1947: 358–9)

This type of power should be distinguished from power on the basis of charismatic authority. Thus Jesus possessed charisma and the disciples obeyed him because they knew him and he was (presumably) a remarkable man; the pope possesses an authority based on that charisma, but without the personal aspect;

people obey the pope, if in fact they obey him, without knowing Jesus except in some metaphorical sense. Charismatic leadership can arise at times of trouble when other forms of domination do not seem to be fulfilling their task; it is a product of a collective enthusiasm which sees in this person a solution to the troubles that plague them, and the leader promises such a solution. There is a dramatic opposition between charismatic leadership and everyday life; the leader must seem to be separate from the concerns of everyday life, and the leader's disciples are themselves special, separating themselves from their own past lives. Bendix quotes Luke's gospel (14: 26): 'If any man come to me and hates not his father, and mother, and wife, and children and brethren and sisters, yea, and his own life also, he cannot be my disciple.' This is the call of the millenarian leader—'leave everything behind, follow me and we will save the world'. The pope, of course, is not noted for encouraging people to abandon their families and this marks an important difference.

Charismatic leadership is of the same sociological type, whether the activity of the movement is legal and illegal, morally good or bad: Jesus Christ, Adolf Hitler, Robin Hood, Mahatma Ghandi all fall into the same category. Under such leadership, well-established rules, whether traditional or legal-rational, are abandoned.

We can get an alternative view of charismatic leadership by returning to Marx's analysis of Bonaparte's *coup*. Bonaparte, according to Marx, came to personify the interests of the peasantry, the lumpenproletariat, and others who could not represent themselves; if we combine this with Durkheim's notion of the sacred and of 'collective effervescence', it is possible to see an alternative understanding of charisma: not as a quality of the leader but as a quality projected on to a leader by virtue of situation, opportunity, and events. Thus, for a few years it appeared that the British prime minister Mrs Thatcher was the most remarkable British leader of the century—she certainly possessed charisma. But it came and went: the first few years of her premiership were not at all successful and her charisma seemed to appear with victory in the war over the Malvinas and then was reinforced for some by a victory in an industrial conflict against the coal miners, and then it disappeared very quickly as she lost power in 1990. Her charismatic power was projected upon her and then retracted. Great leaders are created by their followers.

Charismatic leadership exists in its pure form only for a short period and has to adjust to the reassertion of the demands of everyday life—the opposite problem to the other forms of authority, which are adjusted to everyday life but cannot deal with times of trouble. The need to adjust to everyday life involves the 'routinization of charisma'. In the case of Christ, for example, the disciples became apostles and priests, and they travelled around setting up branches of the church in different places; they created an organization. If non-Christians will forgive me, this is a particularly good example to carry through to illustrate Weber's points.

The first major problem comes with the succession and Weber argues here that there is a special relationship between charismatic and tradition authority, since both are invested in a particular person rather than a set of rules. A new leader has to be designated—possibly on the basis of charismatic properties that he or she is thought to possess, or he or she is appointed by the original leader of the disciples. Thus St Peter became the first pope and his successors have been appointed in unbroken line by the College of Cardinals. The further we get away from the original leader, the further we are from the unique qualities of 'pure charisma—as charisma is passed on but becomes second-hand, less powerful.

Charismatic leadership, once it is established, is in a sort of Catch-22 situation; if it is to be preserved, it must transform itself to the demands of everyday life—a society needs stable families rather than people going off to change the world; on the other hand, when it transforms itself, the charisma begins to fade. Another crucial problem is that the disciples themselves wish to ensure their own power and position, which is threatened by the instability of the charismatic leadership of just one person. This pursuit of self-interest becomes easier if the charisma is somehow lifted from its original leader and attached to a position or to a family. This is effectively what has happened in the Roman Catholic Church and it is also a basis for the British monarchy. Charisma can be inherited (the monarchy), or passed on by ceremony (the Roman Catholic Church) and education. Familial charisma ensures only succession, but institutional charisma takes on a lasting power as an organization which can act as a balance to secular power. The routinization of charisma in an institutional form involves the emergence of priests as a distinct status group, making universalistic claims to dominance, over and above the claims of family and, as time goes on, nation as well. A body of knowledge—theology—grows up and is taught to new entrants. Such churches do not exist everywhere (as we shall see in Chapter 13). Where they do exist they are inevitably conservative; the priesthood hold on to their privilege of interpreting the word of God to their followers and new charismatic leaders are resisted. Monastic orders are often a threat to the church because they embody the way of life of the original charismatic leader, renouncing the world. The monk is a 'model' religious person, perhaps the first proper professional of the western world.

Weber spends a lot of time discussing the relationship between the secular and religious power, a competition which continues today in all sorts of interesting ways. In the USA, charismatic religious leaders offer a challenge to the federal government, particularly when that government is dominated by the Democrats; and in the UK the relationship between the Church of England, an 'established' church supported by the state, has moved from a very close connection with the ruling party in the first part of the century (when it was known as 'the conservative party at prayer') to a situation where it was distancing itself from government policy fairly rapidly during the 1980s, and thus coming under attack for ignoring its spiritual duty and inappropriately engaging in politics.

Weber points out, rightly, that for most of the time a compromise is reached. Each power needs the other: the church can supply ideological justification for the state, whilst the state can protect the church.

It is tempting to read a theory of historical development into Weber's work, perhaps that charismatic leadership pushes forward social change, or that it provides a bridge between traditional and rational-legal forms of domination. Bendix (1966) suggests that this would be mistaken. If the social order is inherently unstable, than charismatic leaders can arise at any time. I think both interpretations are tenable—there are different Webers. Frank Parkin seems to think that Weber underestimated the likelihood of charisma transforming a legal-rational society.

Weber would have been unsurprised at the spectacle of the sons and daughters of the modern bourgeoisie held in thrall by chubby mystics from the East. He might, though, have been more surprised, as well as deeply shocked, at the apparent ease with which a charismatic leader on his own doorstep would revolutionize an entire society and its rational structure to the most devastatingly irrational purposes.   (Parkin 1982: 87)

But, of course, Hitler was not just a product of his own charisma or his own powers, or of the disorder of the Weimar Republic. He was much more the product of the belief that the German people placed in Hitler's offer of an easy target to blame for their troubles and their surrender of their own powers to him.

Weber suggests that, in any form of domination, his three types will exist side by side in different relationships to each other. Charismatic leadership can exist in any historical period, but not its more routinized forms—familial charisma, for example, may not exist in rational-legal forms of domination, although even here one might argue that the existence of a constitutional monarchy belies this.

TRADITIONAL DOMINATION

The pure form of traditional domination is 'patriarchalism'—the domination of the father over the household, the members of whom live together and work together. The women of the household are physically and mentally dependent on the master, the children are helpless or have been trained into dutiful obedience, and the servants, as well as being trained, require the master's protection. The master's will is absolute, and not limited by law; only by tradition. It is as if he has a credit of tradition which he can spend by demanding tributes from his household; but if he should overspend, and demand more than is sanctioned by tradition, then his power could be in trouble. Patriarchalism runs into difficulty first when the master's property grows; his initial reaction is to divide his land up between his dependents, but together they then develop an interest in having their rights and duties clarified—they are no longer so amenable to the master's arbitrary authority. But, once these rights are written down, they become more limited than when the master simply had to ensure the goodwill of his dependents. The problems multiply when large areas of land are involved.

The result of this extension is patrimonialism—which existed in the despotic regimes of Asian and European mediaeval society—where the master's household grows to sometimes an immense size over a large area, in which all his subjects owe him the same loyalty as the immediate members of his household. The administration of the society is bound up closely with the administration of the household. The ruler's domination of a large area enables him to carry out his own trade and to control and profit from that of others in order to maintain his extended household. The further extended these regimes become, the more decentralized they tend to become, perhaps with rights and duties to be determined by independent courts. But on the whole power remains personal, and office-holders become office-holders through 'connections, favours, promises and privileges'.

Such regimes are inherently unstable because of the difficulty of keeping the loyalty of widespread forces, and they can suddenly disappear. Patrimonial domination can develop through the use of military force as a personal instrument. If administrators are appointed, they can help extend the dominated area, but they can come to form a status group that can contest power with a central authority—perhaps rather like the barons who forced King John to sign the Magna Carta—or they can be pawns in struggles between central authorities, particularly when the officials are celibate clergymen who do not have a family interest of their own and who can be kept in order by the promise of a pension.

Weber suggests that feudalism is a second variety of patriarchalism. In a feudal system, the nobility are united by a sense of status honour. He suggests that in England the Norman invasion instituted an essentially patrimonial system which was opposed by an entrenched local baron, and the two systems became entwined, often producing conflict between monarchy and nobility. To balance the power of the nobility, the monarchy created local notables—the yeomanry, which developed a strong sense of its own status honour.

It is the development of a distinct status honour that takes us into feudalism. The paternal authority of the master is replaced by a contractual relationship in which the subordinate owes military service—or whatever—in return for the protection of the master. As Bendix points out, this distinction is really useful only if we remain on the level of theory—on the ground, there were a wide mixture of arrangements. Weber is working at a fairly abstract level of ideal types. The existence of a contractual relationship means that rights and duties are more formalized than in patrimonial systems.

The military becomes important when the feudal lord finds it necessary to raise a cavalry equipped with horse and armour like his own. This becomes a military élite in fief to the lord, which, unlike patrimonial authority, can dispense with the goodwill of its subjects. Whereas education in patrimonial regimes tended towards preparation for administrative service, education under feudalism is for martial skills and aristocratic honour and nonchalance. Frank Parkin points out that the peasantry are a silent witness to all the power struggles between the lords and their officials and knights.

When we come to his understanding of legal-rational authority, it is more difficult to deny that there is a theory of history in Weber's work—it all leads to the modern word, and, in addition to his ideal-type methodology, I think that one of the reasons that he draws a distinction between patrimonialism and feudalism is because the latter is a step towards modernity, via the establishment of formal rights and duties.

LEGAL-RATIONAL DOMINATION

There are, according to Weber, four defining characteristics of the modern state. First, it has a legal and administrative order which is subject to change by legislation—not by the whim of a lord or the dictat of a charismatic leader. Secondly, it has an administration which works in accordance with legislation—civil servants and the judiciary do not make up their own rules but implement those formed by the legislature. The state has binding authority of all its members—membership is usually by birth—and over the acts carried out in its territory. Finally, it can use force if that is legally prescribed or permitted. The modern state is legitimate if people believe in its legitimacy—and as with other forms of domination, this argument is circular and illustrates something important about Weber's work. Laws are legitimate if they are enacted according to the law. Each system justifies itself—traditional domination is justified by tradition, charismatic domination by charisma. There is no overall or superior set of values by means of which we choose better or worse systems. We cannot choose between the three on any rational grounds, and each can be justified only on its own grounds. Weber goes on to discuss the 'natural-law' justification which replaces tradition and the routinization of charisma. The basic principle is the individual's right to acquire or dispose of property, and this freedom is limited only by the fact that it must not impose limits on itself—so, for example, trade-union closed shops or legal monopolies do not accord with natural law. He thought that a conception of positivist law might be replacing that of natural law, but what was important was that in practice there was a general recognition of legitimacy of enacted laws. This implied that any norm could be enacted as a law with the expectation that it would be obeyed; government and government apparatuses are bound by the abstract system that these laws comprise, and justice is the application of these laws. People who hold authority do so by virtue of being temporary office-holders rather than from possessing a personal authority, and people obey the laws rather than the office-holders who enforced them. The state could not interfere with individual rights without the consent of the people through their duly elected representatives.

Generations of students have come to know Weber through his idea type of bureaucracy, the features of which have probably been learnt by heart by more students than any other sets of ideas in sociology. Bureaucracy is the most typical organizational form of legal-rational domination. Under the rule of law, a bureaucracy is governed by the following principles. Again my own comments follow in square brackets.

(1) A continuous organization of official functions bound by rules. [not at the whim of a leader, or an official. We expect government departments, for example, to be open five days a week, excluding public holidays, for a fixed and predictable number of hours a day, and to proceed in a predictable way. They should not be closed when the boss wants a day off or open on a Sunday because he or she wants to get away from the family.]

(2) A specified sphere of competence. This involves (a) a sphere of obligation to perform functions which has been marked off as part of a systematic division of labour. (b) The provision of the incumbent with the necessary authority to carry out these functions. (c) That the necessary means of compulsion are clearly defined and their use is subject to definite conditions. [Thus the Inland Revenue will deal only with taxation, and another agency will deal with social security, yet another health, and so on; there is a systematic organization of the different agencies; the official who assesses my taxes is authorized to do so, and we both know what powers the official has to penalize me—he or she cannot fine me because of bad handwriting, but there might be some sanction if I delay returning my forms for too long after the due date. However, I know that I will not face execution. I am using the state bureaucracy as an example, but Weber points out that such organizations—'administrative organs'—can exist in the armed forces, private organizations, and political parties.]

(3) The organization of offices follows the principle of hierarchy; that is, each lower office is under the control and supervision of a higher one. There is a right of appeal and of statement of grievances from the lower to the higher. Hierarchies differ in respect to whether and in what cases complaints can lead to rulings from an authority at various points higher in the scale, and as to whether changes are imposed from higher up or the responsibility for such changes is left to the lower office, the conduct of which was the subject of complaint. [Different organizations will deal with complaints in a different way, but there will be formal procedures. Although currently hierarchies might be being 'flattened out', what seems to be happening is a reduction of levels rather than a fundamental change in organization. And in some areas—the UK National Health Service, for example—levels of management seem to be increasing.]

(4) The rules which regulate the conduct of an office may be technical rules or norms. In both cases, if their application is to be fully rational, specialized training is necessary. It is thus normally true that only a person who has demonstrated an adequate technical training is qualified to be a member of the administrative staff of such an organized group, and hence only such persons are eligible for appointment to official positions. [Again, there is a contemporary deskilling going on, but I am not sure that it dramatically changes the nature of the bureaucratic organization. There is an argument that in contemporary societies the norms which govern public organiza-

tions are changing and that, for example, notions of public service are declining in favour of self-interest.]

(5) In the rational type it is a matter of principle that the members of the administrative staff should be completely separated from ownership of the means of production and administration. Officials, employees and workers attached to the administrative staff do not themselves own the non-human means of production and administration. These are rather provided for their use in kind or in money, and the official is obligated to render an accounting of their use. There exists, furthermore, in principle complete separation of the property belonging to the organization, which is controlled within the sphere of office, and the personal property of the official, which is available for his own private uses. There is a corresponding separation of the place in which official functions are carried, the 'office' in the sense of premises, from living quarters. [This last distinction is now being blurred by the development of computer technology which enables people to work from home for the office, but the distinction between personal and official property is still quite important. I might sometimes use office envelopes for personal purposes, and sometimes use my personal telephone for office purposes. But if this distinction is blurred too far then it opens the door either to exploitation—I have to supply my own notepaper, use my own telephone, buy my own filing cabinets and desk, or I don't get the job—or corruption—I use the university's property and facilities to run, say, a small estate agency; or I use a research grant to pay off the mortgage of my house. The move towards short-term contract-based employment also blurs some of the boundaries—if I did not own my own computer and have an office at home perhaps I would be unable to work at my job.]

(6) In the rational type case, there is also a complete absence of appropriation of his official position by the incumbent. Where 'rights' to an office exist, as in the case of judges, and recently of an increasing proportion of officials and even of workers, they do not normally serve the purpose of appropriation by the official but of securing the purely objective and independent character of the conduct of the office so that it is oriented only to the relevant norms. [Thus I do not own my position in the university—I can't sell it to the highest bidder, or nominate the person who will take over when I retire, or will it to my son when I die; on the other hand, I did once have tenure—it was not possible to fire me if, for example, the university wanted to cut back on its wages bill, and I could not be fired because I was saying things that people didn't like, or investigating something which presented a threat to those in the organization who were higher up in the hierarchy. This acted as a protection for academic freedom, just as a judge's tenure of office acts as a guarantee of his judicial independence—he cannot be sacked for giving a decision that upsets those in political power. The fact that academic tenure has been eaten away in the return to the values of a market economy is perhaps a matter for some reflection.]

(7) Administrative acts, decisions and rules are formulated and recorded in writing, even in cases where oral discussion is the rule or is even mandatory. This applies at least to preliminary discussions and proposals, to final decisions, and to all sorts of orders and rules. The combination of written documents and a continuous organization of official functions constitutes the 'office' which is the central focus of all types of modern corporate action. [Thus all interaction can be traced in written

records which can be used as evidence in complaints that the rules have been broken, and can be used for reference purposes. This consistent recording of decisions and encounters seems to be on the increase, in the case of the UK at least, as a result of ways of attempting to make public services—the health service and education, for example—'accountable'. The way to establish that we are doing our jobs properly is to write down what we do. One might think that there was a conflict between formal and substantive rationality here.]   (Weber 1922/1947: 330–2)

Weber goes on to mention that he has not mentioned the supreme head of a system of legal authority, which, as we shall see, is important for his understanding of democracy. Pursuing his analysis of bureaucracy, he goes on to talk about the employment of the bureaucrat—only the head of the organization can hold a position through 'appropriation, election or [being] designated for the succession' (ibid. 333); but even then the scope of his or her power is legally limited.

The pure type of bureaucratic employment leaves the office-holder personally free outside his or her professional obligations: my job is delineated more or less clearly, and my boss cannot tell me what to do in my free time outside the organization or call on me to wait at table when he or she has a dinner party—as might happen under patrimonial authority. The employee is part of a clearly organized hierarchy—I know who is superior to me and who is below me in the hierarchy—and each position has a clearly defined 'sphere of competence'—i.e. I know what I can and cannot legitimately do. The official holds office through a contractual relationship for which there is an open and free selection, and office-holders are selected on the basis of technical qualifications—rather than, say, personal friendship or wealth or whatever might have been the basis of selection under patrimonial authority. Officials are paid a salary, often with a pension attached; they can be dismissed only in specified circumstances, although they can resign at any time. Salary is usually graded in accordance with position in the organization, although, Weber adds, interestingly, that account might be taken of the requirements of the official's social status. The office is the primary or sole occupation of the official (again unlike patrimonial authority), and the official has a career where promotion comes through seniority and/or achievement, and is decided upon by superiors in the hierarchy. The official does not own his or her office or means of administration, and is subject to systematic discipline in the way he or she carries out the duties of office.

Bureaucratic domination is unstable in the same way as other systems in that it is constantly open to change through the struggle for power between different status groups, but these changes in modern society tend to be changes in control over bureaucratic organization rather than in the organization itself. All these issues will be taken up in Chapter 13, when we look at Weber's conception of social change; there his sociology of law and of religion will become important.

Conclusion

We do not find in Weber references to societies as a whole, whether in terms of modes of production or the Durkheimian 'society' as something which exists over and above individuals; but nor do we find the individual stories that one might expect from Weber's methodology, and, as I have already mentioned, there is an unexpected determinism in his account of modern societies. The key to all of this is his notion of rationality, which brings together the myriad of individual actions into recognizable patterns and also makes sense at least of modern history as a process of rationalization. Thus the changes in the labour market that we have experienced over the last decades can be seen as a result of the development of capitalism as a system embodying rational calculability. One of the clearest accounts of a Weberian approach to these changes can be found in Holton and Turner (1989) and they point to the way in which Weber, like Marx, saw capitalism as bringing about a process of constant revolution. We can see this process at the root of regular changes in values—it seems that at almost any time over the last 250 years at least we can find notable people lamenting a decline in values. The Weberian approach raises the issues of the dominance of instrumental rationality, a favourite topic of modern critical Marxism, and in the Weberian context the relationship between formal and substantive rationality. A common contemporary debate is about how far formally rational activity on the part of enterprises—'downsizing', 'contracting out', etc.—undermines the community or society in which this occurs together with its more tradition values, creating disillusion and possibly unrest; these actions could be seen as substantially irrational.

To begin with, this constant revolution creates social classes, but then, a Marxist would argue, fragments them—a Weberian would argue destroys them. They point to the evidence about the decline of the traditional urban working class that emerged during the 1970s and 1980s and that has clearly accelerated since then. They follow Parkin in making a distinction between status groups that develop *within* social classes, such as skill groups, and the distinctions say between the industrial and financial bourgeoisie, and status blocs which cut across social classes, and they suggest that modern capitalism, as it undermines the traditional proletariat, creates new status blocs, based perhaps on gender or ethnicity or age. In this context the new political movements can be seen as status-group movements battling in the struggle for political power; it might be possible to see established political parties as losing their traditional connections with social classes but establishing new connections with status blocs. In democratic societies, the value of equality tends to inflate expectations and it provides a central issue for competition between status groups.

Thus a modern Weberian would not see capitalism in terms of some central contradiction or of class struggle; Holton and Turner suggest that there is in fact a particular tension between democracy and the requirements of the market economy. If the principle of equality (democracy) is established, those who find themselves belonging to groups that are underprivileged will take action to correct the situation: 'The very success of democracy produces clientelism which requires greater bureaucratic regulation and state intervention, bringing about further social control within the political sphere and a greater tax burden of the economy' (Holton and Turner 1989: 155). The evidence in support of this can be found in all the equal opportunity and affirmative action legislation that has been established in the West over recent decades. This would include not only women and ethnic minorities but also gays and the disabled, those with learning difficulties, and so on. Underneath a lot of the silliness of 'political correctness', there are some serious issues. The contemporary state ends up administering a system of status blocs—Holton and Turner call these modern political systems 'state-administered status bloc politics'. Referring back to Weber's methodology, we see it as the result of the rational pursuit of a value—that of equality/democracy. We can now turn again to the basic dualisms (see Boxes 9.1–9.3).

Box 9.1. An elaboration of Weber on the individual and society

THE INDIVIDUAL	SOCIETY
Durkheim: the individual is formed and limited by society. He/she becomes more important in complex societies and individualism becomes the focus of the *conscience collective*, binding people together.	**Durkheim:** society exists over and above the individual, over whom it exercises an immense power, especially in less complex societies.
Marx: the 'individuated' individual is an idea produced as part of the development of capitalism. The 'natural' state of the individual is as an integral part of the group.	**Marx:** society is created by human action but acts back upon individuals as an external power—a dominant force in all but the most primitive and most advanced (communist) societies.
Weber: the individual is the only reality and analysis must start from individual rational action.	**Weber:** society is the rather fragile result of human interaction and struggles for power between different types of group.
Simmel: the individual life is engaged in a constant dialectic with social forms.	**Simmel:** 'society' is an increasingly important form organizing peoples' lives.

Box 9.2. **Weber on action and structure**

ACTION	STRUCTURE
Durkheim: there is no real theory of social action in Durkheim; the individual action is always conditioned by the group, and collective action is taken to reinforce the strength of the group.	**Durkheim:** in societies dominated by mechanical solidarity, the social structure consists of networks of kin groups (segmented societies); more complex modern societies consist of secondary groups formed by the division of labour and managed by the state.
Marx: in capitalist societies, the major agents are social classes—primarily the bourgeoisie and the proletariat. Some classes—the middle classes and the peasantry—do not share the life conditions which enable them to act as collective agents, and they tend to follow a strong leader.	**Marx:** different types of society have different forms of social structure. In capitalist societies the economic structure and resultant class structure are most important, and the state and state institutions are central features of social control.
Weber: status groups and market-based social classes can become 'collective actors' in the form of communal or more usually associative groups. Such groups exist only if members recognize a common identity or shared interest. The only 'real' actor remains the individual.	**Weber:** social structure is a fragile achievement; in traditional societies it is based on kin and status groups and in modern societies market-based classes enter into play. Bureaucratic organization and the state become more important.

Box 9.3. **Weber on social integration and system integration**

SOCIAL INTEGRATION

Durkheim: in all societies social integration is achieved through the *conscience collective*—shared ways of thinking (logic, conceptions of space and time, shared beliefs, norms, and values). In societies governed by mechanical solidarity, religion is central. In more complex modern societies, the *conscience collective* covers less of our lives but focuses on the ethics of individual freedom—it becomes a religion of humanity.

Marx: a 'false' and rather tenuous integration is achieved through ideologies, and the development of the market constantly threatens whatever integration is achieved. The major contending classes strive towards achieving their own integration in opposition to the others—the proletariat being the class most likely to achieve this.

Weber: at this point there is no real conception of social integration in Weber's work.

SYSTEM INTEGRATION

Durkheim: where mechanical solidarity predominates, system integration *is* social integration, guaranteed by the *conscience collective*. Where organic solidarity predominates, system integration is achieved through the division of labour.

Marx: system integration in capitalism is constantly threatened by class conflict and is supported by the state and by ruling ideologies.

Weber: it is a gross exaggeration to use the word 'system' in connection with the writings we have looked at in Chapter 9. Social structures are held together by different forms of domination and by stability provided by the market.

Further reading

All the relevant original texts for this chapter can be found in Weber, *The Theory of Social and Economic Organisation* (1922/1947), and Parson's introduction is a useful secondary source. Reinhard Bendix, *Max Weber: An Intellectual Portrait* (1966), contains a useful discussion on forms of domination and authority. A liberal interpretation of Weber can be found in R. J. Holton and B. S. Turner, *Max Weber on Economy and Society* (1989). The best brief account of Weber is Frank Parkin, *Max Weber* (1982). For good contemporary discussions, see Bryan S. Turner, *Max Weber: From History to Modernity* (1992), and *For Weber* (1996), and the good, but difficult *Maturity and Modernity: Nietzsche, Weber, Foucault and the Ambivalence of Reason* by David Owen (1994).

10 | Simmel: the social and the personal

Introduction
Simmel's originality; the mutual implications of Simmel and Durkheim.

Society and the individual
The evolution of the individual/group relation from a starting point of near merging; individuation and the development of individual norms; the paradox of the emergence of the individual and the growing power of the group; the development of multiple and conflicting roles; similarities between Simmel and Parsons; Simmel's radical critique of universal institutions; the significance of the size of social groups; the dyad and its internal fragility; the move from the dyad to larger groups.

The Philosophy of money
Value and exchange; human beings as valuing creatures; Simmel and existentialism; the objectification of subjective value; comparison with Marx; the exchange of value and the exchange of representations—Simmel and postmodernism; money as the extension of freedom and its psychological consequences; the growth of objective culture and the decreasing importance of the personality; Simmel's theory of alienation; the ambivalent implications of the division of labour; the decreasing ability to love objects; conclusion—Simmel and Marxism, Simmel and Weber.

Simmel's sociology
Simmel as a sociological impressionist. *Simmel on relationships*: faithfulness in the maintenance of relationships; the renegade; the distinctive nature of Simmel's notion of the life process; Simmel and Freud; gratitude as a cement for and generator of relationships; Simmel and Kleinian psychoanalysis; sociability as a play form and an example of formal sociology; domination as a form of interaction; domination by an individual, by a plurality, and by principle or law; comparison with Weber; conflict as a contribution to integration; the importance of secrecy; the secret society. *Simmel on social types*: the notion of type in literature and social theory; the miser as a seeker of total control; the miser's similarity to the spendthrift; the adventurer as an artist; the stranger as a newcomer and/or outsider; the objectivity of the outsider; objectivity as participation. *Simmel on modernity*: the psychological effects of urban living; the head ruling the heart; the sophistication of the town-dweller; the standardization of social

life; the individual's conflicting needs for identification and separation and fashion as satisfying both; the psychological satisfactions of science; class and status differences in fashion. *Simmel on social groups*: the poor; different obligations and duties; the emergence of the poor as a group in modern societies through state welfare systems; modern developments of Simmel—the social construction of poverty; comparison with Marx; the aristocracy—united by the highest status honour; in-group marriage; the possibility of decadent emptiness; women, love, and sexuality: the masculine nature of objective culture; the psychological differences between men and women and comparison with modern gender theorists; the possibility of gender equality in relation to the objective culture; male and female sexuality; flirtation as a play form; Simmel's essentialism; comparison with Engels.

Conclusion

Simmel's compatibility with other theorists; further development of the basic dualisms.

Introduction

Whilst we might talk about Marxist or Weberian or Durkheimian sociologists, it is difficult to talk about 'Simmelians', although perhaps one might call a particular piece of work 'Simmelesque'. The true Simmelian would not be a Simmelian—he or she would be trying to convey an individual grasp of the world. There have been attempts to trace a phenomenological sociology and symbolic interactionism, and other strands in American sociology, back to his work, but a systematic linking is not possible and his most distinctive contribution is, I think, rightly identified by David Frisby (1981) as the idea that we might look at society as an aesthetic object, a work of art. In a remarkably romantic passage also quoted by Frisby, Simmel writes:

For us the essence of aesthetic observation and interpretation lies in the fact that the typical is to be found in what is unique, the lawlike in what is fortuitous, the essence and significance of things in the superficial and transitory. . . . To the adequately trained eye, the total beauty and total meaning of the world as a whole radiates from every single point.   (Simmel 1968: 71–2)

The whole world can exist in a grain of sand.

This imagery, I think, contradicts a strong contrast that Frisby, in this same text, draws between Durkheim and Simmel:

In contrast to Durkheim, who viewed society as a 'system of active forces' operating *upon* individuals, Simmel . . . sees society as constituted by interactional 'forces' *between* individuals. This enables him to reflect upon our experience of society in every single social interrelation in which we engage.   (Frisby 1992: 14)

The problem with this formulation is that each position implies the other. If we conceive of the social world as a web of relationships between individuals, then we can conceive of a *society* which this web comprises as something more solid than Weber suggests; and if we conceive of a society, then we need to consider the web of interaction which that society contains and, therefore, must determine. There is a difference of emphasis, but, in their unthought-out implications, Simmel and Durkheim can possibly be seen as *closer* to each other than either is to Marx or Weber, concentrating on different sides of the same version of the individual/society dualism.

In what follows I have been selective—there is a fair amount of Simmel's work that I do not cover. My criteria in choosing what to include are first that it conveys the most important aspects of his *œuvre* and his way of working, and, second, that it is relevant to the themes of this book.

Society and the individual

Here I want to concentrate on Simmel's analysis of the different forms of relationship which can exist between the individual and society, as it is set out in his early (1890) untranslated work and outlined by Frisby (1984). He begins with a conception of what we might call 'primitive' society, akin to Durkheim's notion of mechanical solidarity. In such societies there are comparatively few ties binding the individual into the group, but they bind him or her very closely. Simmel uses the analogy of an organism very clearly here (1890) and talks about its 'life forces'—its power to resist, its healing power, and its ability to preserve itself—but he insists, that these powers do not exist independently of the individuals in the society but are the expression of their interaction.

At this level there is a merging of the individual and the group in such a way that it is difficult to punish wrongdoing—there is a collective responsibility for actions. As societies become more differentiated, so individuation becomes possible and important. It also becomes more difficult for the individual to achieve his or her desired ends; we have to bargain with other people and this leads to individuals servicing each other's interests in ongoing bargaining—you scratch my back and I'll scratch yours. This, in turn, produces a collective morality which regulates the pursuit of self-interest. The more the individual comes to the fore, the more universal become the norms which govern behaviour. But at the same time the individual is subjected to a much greater range of stimuli and this reaches a stage where it is difficult to deal with. Frisby produces a quotation which could almost come from Durkheim:

The actions of a society, compared to those of the individual, possess an unswerving accuracy and expediency. The individual is pushed hither and thither by contradictory impressions, impulses and thoughts and his mind offers at each moment a multitude of possibilities for action, between which he not always knows how to choose with objective accuracy or even merely with subjective certainty. In contrast, the social group is indeed clear who it holds to be its friend and who its enemy.   (Simmel, quoted in Frisby 1984: 84)

We can already see a number of tensions present in Simmel's work. The larger and the more variegated the social group, the more developed, but also the more confused the individual becomes. Simmel, going back to the organic analogy, also talks about the principle of energy saving, which encourages individuals and the smaller social group to hand over functions to the wider collective. Thus, as the individual comes to the fore, so the society grows stronger. There is a further tension between the vulnerability of the individual arising from movement through incompatible spheres with conflicting interests—an idea which was tamed by later sociologists as role conflict—and the individual's ability to combine membership of widely different groups where he or she can find the support of a range of sympathetic people. Frisby writes:

Hence in the modern world there are other groups outside the family which may also possess a close-knit structure. How far this is the case can be measured by whether and to what extent they have evolved a particular sense of 'honour' which ensures desirable behaviour on the part of their members. Such groups do not require external compulsion to achieve this aim.   (Frisby 1984: 86)

In the light of a further century, we can perhaps see Simmel's suggestion as optimistic; the power of differentiation eats away at any sense of honour that might be developed. It is arguable that in the contemporary world people turn in on themselves in a fantasy that security can be found internally (Craib 1994).

Part of the paradox of Simmel can be found in two very different ideas that Frisby then takes up from his early work. When he talks about the division of labour, the argument is that, to begin with, it creates separate spheres and these come together on a more abstract level and a new social sphere appears. This is identical with Talcott Parsons's theory of social evolution which he developed half a century later—that there is a constant process of differentiation and reintegration at a higher level involving more universal values. This type of functionalist theory is generally considered to be a very conservative conception of social change and of social cohesion, leaving no space for conflict and assuming an inherent tendency to stability. At the same time, as Frisby points out, Simmel comments that it is a 'peculiar manifestation of social life' that 'meaningful, profoundly significant institutions and modes of life are replaced by others which *per se* appear utterly mechanical, external and mindless' (Frisby 1984: 88). This is a far from conservative view of the development of universal institutions.

SIZE MATTERS

Simmel (1908/1950) pays a great deal of attention to the size of social group and again foreshadows Parsons in working up from an analysis of the dyad, a relationship between two people; typically, however, he starts with the isolated individual, pointing out that isolation is itself a *social* relationship, a relationship to other people. It is not necessarily a matter of being alone—one is never more isolated than when in a crowd of strangers—and it is particularly important in relationships whose purpose is to deny isolation. For example, I might marry or live with another person in order to avoid isolation, but as soon as I am engaged in this relationship, periods in which each of us might be alone could be essential for its survival. In this context, isolation implies freedom which, like most things for Simmel, is double-edged. It can be seen as an attempt to avoid being dominated by my partner (or others in my social group) and it can also be seen as an attempt to dominate, to establish power over my partner or colleagues.

The most important thing about the dyad is that, whilst it might appear to be a cohesive unity to outsiders, it is not so to its members. They do not experience the dyad group as a collectivity over and above themselves; each partner sees only him- or herself confronted by the other. As a result the relationship is haunted by death—only one member has to die for the union to end, and this gives the dyad its particular emotional tone, that of an 'authentic sociological tragedy', but also an elegiac and sentimental quality. The dyad involves an irreplaceable individuality on the part of its members and without that (if, for example, all that matters to me is that my wife does the housework) it can disappear; in any case, it can easily go wrong for the same reason that it can generate intimacy: it doesn't 'result in a structure that goes beyond its elements' (Simmel 1950: 126). Intimacy requires sharing things unique to that relationship and the danger is that the two partners do not share the most important part of their personalities, the objective dimensions that they share with others, such as intellectual interests; if these are excluded from the relationship, they can undermine it. If all this sounds as if Simmel is talking about a friendship or an affair rather than marriage, you might be right. Marriage, he argues, is not a typical dyadic relationship, since both members can feel that they are part of a wider whole—the institution of marriage sanctioned by the wider society.

The dyad is also defined negatively, by the absence of features that are present in larger groups such as the delegation of individual powers to the group organization and the loss of individuality that we experience in a crowd. Things change as soon as a third member is added: one new member brings two new relationships—as well as *A–B*, there is *A–C* and *B–C*. This enables factions to form and the role of mediator to develop to protect the continued existence of the group. A third member can create or exploit conflict between the others in pursuit of his or her own interests. Anybody who has lived in a family of more than two should be able to recognize all this.

We can see in this the beginning of what we would now call a role structure, the beginnings of what Simmel calls 'objective culture', as well as the beginnings of *micro-sociology*. Many modern sociologists try to follow through from the discussion of small-scale interactions to large-scale social analysis. Parsons builds his system on the analysis of the dyad, and the most recent attempt can be found in Anthony Giddens's *The Constitution of Society* (1984). Giddens, however, loses the sophistication that comes with Simmel's acknowledgement of the qualitative changes resulting from increased group size. These take the form of emergent properties of the group process: in a group we find features that do not seem to belong to any one individual and the group is more than the sum of individuals who make it up; it has an existence over and above them.

We get a different sense of relationships between individuals when we turn to Simmel's *Philosophy of Money*.

The Philosophy of Money

> The attempt is made to construct a new story beneath materialism such that the explanatory value of the incorporation of economic life into the causes of intellectual culture is preserved, while these economic forms themselves are recognized as the result of more profound valuations and currents of psychological or even metaphysical preconditions.
>
> (Simmel 1900/1990: 56)

The Philosophy of Money was first published in Germany in 1900 and it develops a number of ideas from the earlier work. The quotation opening this section is an invitation to take a Lukacsian approach to Simmel. If economic forms are a product of human psychology combined with metaphysical causes, then it is unlikely that we can do anything about them—they become a fixed, 'second nature'. However, it is, of course, more complex than this.

VALUE AND EXCHANGE

Simmel begins with a discussion of value, defining it in terms which for Marx would limit it to use value. Value is not some quality of the natural world—the natural world is just there, neither good nor bad, valued nor unvalued. 'Value is an addition to the completely determined objective qualities, like light and shade, which are not inherent in it but come from a different source' (Simmel 1900/1990: 60). It comes from my desire: the valued objects I see around me are those I desire, and I, like all other human beings, am a creature of desire and therefore a valuing creature. It is precisely this conception of human beings as

meaning- and value-choosing beings that characterized Jean-Paul Sartre's existentialism in the mid-twentieth century, but, whereas Simmel uses this as a
starting point for understanding sociation, Sartre (1957) used it as a starting
point to emphasize the loneliness and adrift-ness of human existence. But both
would agree that values do not come from anywhere else but the valuing subject.
Simmel goes on to argue that economic value is the objectification of subjective
value. This occurs through the act of exchange: 'The technical form of economic
transactions produces a realm of values that is more or less completely detached
from the subjective personal substructure' (Simmel 1900/1990: 79). Here
Simmel draws on the theory of marginal utility and opportunity cost. Valued
objects are bought into relation to each other through exchange—if I want to
buy books, then I have to give up something else that I might buy with the
money—say food, or furniture. In this way I equate a sociology textbook with
two McDonald's meals. Other people making their choices at the same time as I
make my own create the objective value relationships between objects. 'The fact
that the object has to be exchanged against another object illustrates that it is not
only valuable for me, but also valuable independently of me; that is to say, for
another person' (ibid. 81).

This is where we move on to sociology. The act of economic exchange is an
act of sacrifice: I give up one good in order to gain another, and Simmel argues
that this is the basic model for all social interaction—every interaction that we
have is an act of exchange, although in most cases without the sacrifice which is
peculiar to economic exchange. Simmel makes no distinction between use value
and exchange value, and exchange value is seen as the same as price, which is not
the case in Marx's theory. And, directly counter to Marx, Simmel is barely interested in production, criticizing the labour theory of value on the ground that
mental effort involves an unpaid contribution to production which cannot be
adequately measured or paid for—and this makes manual labour an inappro-
priate measure for measuring labour.

REPRESENTATIONS

The model of exchange is then transformed into a theory of knowledge. Social
interaction is seen as an exchange of representations (such as money—something which stands for something else), and truth—like value—is to do with a
relation of representations to each other. Society is thus a combination of
exchange relations between individuals, it is in constant movement, and money,
as it emerges from economic exchange, embodies this constant movement. It is
as if money becomes the symbol which represents everything:

The philosophical significance of money is that it represents within the practical world
the most certain image and the clearest embodiment of the formula of all being, accord-

ing to which things receive their meaning through each other, and have their being determined by their mutual relations.   (Simmel 1900/1990: 128–9)

In this sense money is an essential part of and a signifier of progress. It is worth noting here how yet again Simmel foreshadowed contemporary ideas, in this particular case the varieties of postmodernism that talk about the significance of representations and representations of representations. In one respect, perhaps the work of Baudrillard can be regarded as an immensely elaborate philosophy of money: 'The increasingly influential principle of economizing strength and materials leads to more and more extensive experiments with representatives and symbols that have virtually no relation to what they represent' (ibid. 151).

MONEY AS THE EXTENSION OF FREEDOM AND ITS PSYCHOLOGICAL CONSEQUENCES

Large sections of the book unravel the cultural, social, and psychological meanings of money, moving all the time from one level to another and back again. Money takes on an independence: 'The functioning of exchange, as a direct interaction between individuals, becomes crystallized in the form of money as an independent structure' (Simmel 1900/1990: 175) This extends immensely the range of actions open to the individual human:

Primitive man, who has only a limited knowledge of natural causes, is consequently restricted in his purposive action. For him the arc of purposive action will contain as intermediate links little more than his own physical action and the direct effect he can have upon a single object. (ibid. 208)

First of all we develop tools which extend the chain of means and ends and this gives us greater power. I can do more with a hammer than I can with my hand; and I can do more with a wheel, or even better a number of wheels, than I can with a hammer. Money gives me access to an immense number of means—'it is the purest example of the tool'. If I have £10,000 in cash or in the bank, I can do infinitely more than if I have £10,000 worth of coffee beans piled up in the back garden. And money can be used to earn more money through loans and interest. Money becomes an end in itself, particularly for the marginalized, the underprivileged, and the dispossessed. It becomes a means whereby they can work their way back into society.

The move towards money itself as an ultimate end can lead to greed and avarice, or to extravagance, when it is spent on 'non-sensical' goods unsuited to the conditions of the person spending the money; I would be squandering money if I bought a fleet of fast cars if I could not drive and did not want to go anywhere. Simmel also explores ascetic poverty—the positive choice of poverty as a way of life, the right way to live. However, the most important part of this section of the book concerns the subjective underside of the meaning of money—the development of cynicism and a blasé attitude which Simmel describes as 'endemic to the heights of a money culture' (ibid. 255), suggesting that they can be seen as the opposite of avarice and greed.

Whereas the cynics of antiquity pursued strength of mind and indifference as ultimate values, modern cynicism allows no ultimate values, and is concerned with degrading those that others might espouse; it seems to be summed up in the phrase 'everybody has their price'. The blasé attitude involves having no particular reaction to value at all, not even the perverse reaction of the cynic to degrade it. The cure of this is found in the search for excitement. Much later, Simmel suggests that money is the purest example of the tendency in modern culture, particularly in the sciences, to the reduction of the qualitative to the quantitative, almost as if science itself becomes cynical. The concern of many twentieth-century sociologists with small-scale quantitative studies perhaps explains why Simmel has been neglected by later generations of sociologists.

THE GROWTH OF OBJECTIVE CULTURE AND THE STRUCTURE OF SUBJECTIVITY

Simmel engages in a long exploration of the meaning of money for human life in general, developing what might be called a theory of human nature as well as a double-edged approach to modern culture. He constantly reasserts the importance of exchange and its result in creating an objective world. Money extends the range of human freedom, removing personal obligations and duties to others—these can be paid off by money rather than, say, by service. And it enables the production of objective values which can be shared by everybody. This long quotation is typical of his argument:

man has been defined as the political animal, the tool-creating animal, the purposeful animal, the hierarchical animal. . . . Perhaps we might add to this series that man is the exchanging animal, and this is in fact only one side or form of the whole general feature which seems to reflect the specific qualities of man—man is the *objective* animal. Nowhere in the animal world do we find indications of what we call objectivity, of views and treatment of things that lie beyond subjective feeling and volition.

I have already indicated how this reduces the human tragedy of competition . . . more and more contents of life become objectified in supra-individual forms: books, art, ideal concepts, . . . [knowledge] . . . all this may be enjoyed without any one depriving any other.   (Simmel 1900/1990: 290–1)

Some of his most interesting observations concern what happens to the personality in a money economy. Today we are often presented with an argument that the Enlightenment produced a conception of a unified, rational subject which was simply taken for granted by sociology up until the last couple of decades, when poststructuralism and postmodernism showed us how wrong we were. In fact, conceptions of the self have been much more varied, as have, incidentally, conceptions of what rationality might involve. Simmel *starts* from the position (which I would regard as self-evident) that 'Just as the essence of the physical organism lies in the fact that it creates the unity of the life process out of the multitude of material parts, so a man's inner personal unity is based upon the interaction and connection of many elements and determinants' (ibid. 296). He continues a little later in what I regard as a profound passage, which I am therefore quoting at length:

Only the combination and fusion of several traits in one focal point forms a personality which then in its turn imparts to each individual trait a personal-subjective quality. It is not that it is this *or* that trait that makes a unique personality of man, but that he is this *and* that trait. The enigmatic unity of the soul cannot be grasped by the cognitive process directly, but only when it is broken down into a multitude of strands, the resynthesis of which signifies the unique personality.

Such a personality is almost completely destroyed under the conditions of a money economy. The delivery man, the money lender, the worker, upon whom we are dependent, do not operate as personalities because they enter into a relationship only by virtue of a single activity such as the delivery of goods, the lending of money, and because their other qualities, which alone would give them a personality, are missing. . . . The general tendency . . . undoubtedly moves in the direction of making the individual more and more dependent upon the achievements of people, but less and less dependent upon the personalities that lie behind them.   (ibid. 296)

Simmel thinks that socialism is the end state of this process—an interesting comparison with Marx's actual statement of socialist ideals, in which the personalities of people would be more important than ever before. For Simmel, the more people we are dependent upon, the more it seems that personalities are unimportant—any one bus driver is as good as any other and this cultivates 'an inner independence and feeling of individual self-sufficiency'—the qualities now encouraged on an emotional level by contemporary forms of psychotherapy (see Giddens 1991).

Simmel is rightly ambivalent about the increase in human freedom involved in this process. Money adds to the range of possible human relationships, but these relationships do not touch people in any profound way. As well as being freer, we gain what might be called a broader personality, but one which loses its depth—it becomes more fragmented. This process goes hand in hand with a decline in the importance of individual objects and an increasing importance and dependence on classes of objects.

SIMMEL'S THEORY OF ALIENATION

The last chapter of *The Philosophy of Money* brings us close to the theory of alienation in the young Marx and in Lukacs. In fact Simmel's notion of objective culture is similar to Lukacs's notion of a second nature—except that Simmel does not hold out any hope of changing it.

Simmel analyses this in terms of the division between subjective and objective culture—the latter being the objects that a culture produces which are beyond influence by any single person. As society grows larger and objective mind or culture itself grows larger, discrepancies occur between objective and subjective culture. My observations on Simmel will, when they are published, become part of the objective culture. However, they will enter only in a very marginal way to the subjective culture of a few people. A society in which objective and subjective culture coincide—a society in which we all knew as much as it is possible to know—would be a sort of Golden Age.

The growth in objective culture eats away at such a possibility and most important in this process is the division of labour. Simmel argues—referring to Marx—that the product is 'completed at the expense of the development of the producer', recognizing more clearly than Durkheim that the division of labour did not always produce individual satisfaction and contributed to the fragmentation rather than the wholeness of the individual. In this respect, those of us who are engaged in some of the social sciences or the arts are privileged over those studying or practising the natural sciences or a narrower social science such as economics, since our work will tend to flow back into the main purpose, the wholeness of our lives. But, for that to have meaning, the wholeness of the objects on which we work is important. When I discussed Durkheim's conception of the division of labour, I pointed out how many more jumbo jets it enabled us to build, comparing it with each person working away in the back garden on his or her own jet. Simmel's point is that, if it were personal wholeness and satisfaction that we were after, we would choose the back garden every time. The division of labour does not allow us to see our whole selves in what we produce: we are alienated from the product of our labour. The separation of the worker from the means of production works in the same way.

Simmel goes on to look at the implications of this in everyday life. The objectification of culture affects our relationship to objects. In a paragraph which I can imagine will be as resonant to my contemporaries as it might have been to Simmel's, he says:

During the first decades of the nineteenth century, furniture and objects that surrounded us for use and pleasure were of relative simplicity and durability and were in accord with the needs of the lower as well as of the upper strata. This resulted in people's attachment as they grew up to the objects of their surroundings, an attachment that already appears to the younger generation today as an eccentricity on the part of their grandparents.   (Simmel 1900/1990: 459–60)

As classes of objects become more important, it is increasingly difficult to endow one object with a special, personal significance. Simmel suggests that there are three reasons why this has happened: the sheer quantity of objects has meant that it is difficult to form a close personal relationship with them, and the objects which people do love—an old jacket or slippers or whatever—are often occasions for poking fun. This is reinforced by the standardization of objects and rapid changes in fashion, of which more later.

CONCLUSION

Now what are we to make of *The Philosophy of Money*? I have presented Simmel as the unsystematic theorist, but in this work we find a general theory of modern society and history and of the way it works which underlies all his essays, which taken as a whole could just about be interpreted as a systematic social theory. In part we are up against the unavoidable paradox that I spoke about in the introduction: that the denial that there can be any general theory of society is itself a general theory of society; buy Simmel is not as crass as that. He is in fact producing a theory of modern society in a quite self-conscious way, although those who might claim him as forerunner of postmodernism might not like seeing it that way. A sign of this is the way it was taken up by Marxists and in particular by Lukacs. Strictly speaking, Simmel is much closer to Weber and the marginal utility theorists—what Simmel had to say about objective culture can be seen as part of the process that Weber saw as rationalization, and both accept the 'givenness' of the market economy rather than seeing it as a product of underlying relationships. I think that what Simmel held on to that Weber did not manage to hold on to is a sense of human experience and the way in which it was transformed and fragmented by modern society. This enables him to start from a position that was similar to Weber's starting point and to end with a position very close to Marx's starting point.

Simmel's sociology

Frisby (1981) uses the helpful metaphor of impressionism to discuss Simmel's sociology. Impressionism was an artistic movement which developed through the latter half of the nineteenth century, breaking with traditional conventions, moving out of studios into the open air, trying to capture variations in light and shade as they actually appear to the eye. The most famous impressionist was Van Gogh. Frisby (1981) points to Lukacs's comment that Simmel's sociology was the 'conceptual formulation of the impressionist world view'. Lukacs goes on to argue that, though the impressionists rejected traditional forms because they inhibited or stultified or trapped the multidimensional flux of life, they had themselves to develop a new classical form more appropriate to the complexities of modern life.

The same is true of Simmel and explains his ambivalence about form and the social world that I discussed in Chapter 6. As Lukacs noted, his work contains a real commitment to the individual and the unique—the individual's experience of the play of social light and shade; at the same time, he has a conception of the totality and history which emerges in *The Philosophy of Money,* but he is interested only in particular aspects of that totality. And, just as the impressionists were portraying the same external world as the classicists, so Simmel is portraying the same social world as that described by the other classical theorists. Each of Simmel's sociological essays explores a particular topic from different points of view. I have divided his essays into four groups: first, those where the dominant theme is relationships and the maintenance of relationships in everyday interaction—his *micro*-sociology; secondly, those that deal with a social type which illustrates something important about the social whole—the miser, the spendthrift, the adventurer, etc.; thirdly, the essays which have been most influential on modern sociology and deal with his analysis of what we would now call modernity; and, finally, his discussion of different social groups—including his essays on women, sexuality, and femininity.

Simmel on relationships

FAITHFULNESS AND GRATITUDE

> Without the phenomenon we call faithfulness, society could simply not exist, as it does, for any length of time. The elements which keep it alive—the self-interest of its members, suggestion, coercion, idealism, mechanical habit, sense of duty, love, inertia—could not save it from breaking apart if they were not supported by this factor.
>
> (Simmel 1908/1950: 379)

Here Simmel seems to start from an extreme individualist position as opposed to his earlier evolutionary viewpoint. If we start from individuals, we have to explain why they maintain consistent relationships; if we start from society, this is not a problem.

Faithfulness cannot be measured, it is a quality that keeps a relationship in existence beyond the disappearance of the conditions that originally brought it about. 'Faithfulness might be called the inertia of the soul.' We can go on loving our partner as he or she, in Simmel's straightforward terms, becomes ugly, even if it was beauty which first attracted us. Faithfulness is a psychic state, not a feeling: I can be faithful to my friends or to my country, whatever I feel about them. We become habituated to a relationship, and its mere existence over time produces faithfulness. Faithfulness must exist for society to exist.

This leads Simmel to note that faithfulness can develop where relationships start for non-emotional reasons and it can generate affection and love—

although affection is not necessary for faithfulness, nor *necessarily* entailed by it. A special instance of this occurs with the figure of the *renegade*, the person who changes sides: the convert is characteristically more enthusiastic about and committed to his or her new faith or country or political party than established members. Most members of the Roman Catholic Church will recognize this phenomenon—those born into the church will find all sorts of ways around the pope's ruling on birth control, whereas converts will follow it enthusiastically.

If the original motive remains, then faithfulness itself takes on a more energetic form—this again is often the case with the renegade, who cannot go back. Faithfulness is unlike feelings towards other people, such as love, since it is concerned with maintaining a relationship more than with self-satisfaction:

This specific sociological character is connected with the fact that faithfulness, more than other feelings, is accessible to our moral intentions. Other feelings overcome us like sunshine or rain, and their coming and going cannot be controlled by our will. But *un*faithfulness entails a more severe reproach than does absence of love or social responsibility, beyond their merely obligatory manifestations.   (ibid. 385)

In this essay I think Simmel is embarking on a project which has largely been lost to modern sociology. He talks about habit, but he also talks about many other things, the intra-personal and interpersonal shifting sands of emotional life. He calls this the life process, a constant flux which contrasts with the rigidity of social forms. The forms, the relations we are engaged upon, never bend to fit the flux of our life process—it is as if we are wearing shoes that are just too small for us. Now modern sociologists have reduced this life process to habit, the routine and taken-for-granted *forms* of interaction (see e.g. Giddens 1976, 1984), with no sense of the underlying flux. Simmel in this essay shows a very sophisticated conception of the inner life. He points that this external contrast between life process and form is reproduced internally as we produce formulae and directions of how to live. This is not too far away from the functions which Freud attributes to the ego and superego, different levels of internal control over our drives. Whether internal or external, forms can move either slightly ahead of or slightly behind the life process, rather like children's clothes: they can become clearly too tight and small as the child grows quickly, and the new ones will be too large—deliberately so—in order that the child can grow into them. Faithfulness crosses the boundary between form and life process; it brings some firmness of form to the life process.

Turning to gratitude, Simmel comments that its sociological significance is more obscure than that of faithfulness but is very important. It is obscure because its external manifestations appear insignificant. All contracts rest on the exchange of equivalents, and this is enforced by law; however, there are many other interactions which involve exchange which are not backed up by law, and here gratitude is an important supplement. In another version of a theme from *The Philosophy of Money*, Simmel talks about the objectification of human relationships in the exchange of objects; as this develops, the exchange of objects becomes more important than human interaction. Gratitude also emerges from interaction and Simmel seems to think of it as the internal equivalent of the external process of objectification and it can on its own generate new interactions. Gratitude, like faithfulness, survives the beginning of the interaction: it is one of the feelings that keeps relationships going:

It is an ideal living-on of a relation which may have ended long ago. . . . Although it is a purely personal affect . . . its thousandfold ramifications throughout society make it one of the most powerful means of social cohesion. It is a fertile emotional soil which grows concrete actions among particular individuals . . . although it is interwoven with innumerable other motivations . . . it gives human actions a unique modification or intensity: it connects them with what has gone before, it enriches them with the element of personality, it gives them the continuity of interactional life. If every grateful action, which lingers on from good turns received in the past, were suddenly eliminated, society (at least as we know it) would break apart.   (ibid. 388–9)

Here Simmel describes in a very common-sense way an aspect of human relationships which was developed as basic to psychoanalytic theory several decades later by Melanie Klein (1957). Klein developed her ideas in a dialectical form which would have delighted Simmel, derived from an account of human drives in which gratitude and reparation are seen as a balance to and development from human destructiveness, usually in a process of unconscious conflict. In this context, gratitude is basic to all human relationships, not just those with the exchange of objects as their base. Simmel's comments about the 'dark' side point out that gratitude can also be experienced as an obligation, a duty, and a lack of freedom.

SOCIABILITY

Simmel (1917/1950) calls his essay on sociability an example of pure or formal sociology. Some forms become removed from what we might call the 'serious' contents of everyday life and become ends in themselves. If *sociation* refers to the way in which we come into contact with each other in the pursuit of our everyday lives, *sociability* is the play form of such activity. Because it lacks the seriousness of everyday life, many people regard it as unimportant—'small talk'—but this is not Simmel's view. Its relationship to the serious world is rather like that of art to reality. When we are not pursuing our own interests, we are governed by *tact*, and this involves suppressing our most personal characteristics. He talks of upper and lower 'sociability thresholds': the upper point is where serious personal interests intrude in a situation (talking social theory at a cocktail party) and the lower point is where personality features intrude (making a pass at the host or hostess). In between, sociability is a sort of sociological art form creating an artificial world, where at the same time everybody is equal and everybody is special; it is done for its own sake, and it is only false if it is a mask for personal interests—if my cocktail sociability is a way of impressing my boss. My talk should be for its own sake, a matter of give and take for mutual pleasure. But, of course, if I could not engage sociably, it might work against my interests. It is not quite as easy to avoid instrumentality as Simmel seems to think.

DOMINATION

As might be expected, Simmel offers a more psychologically sophisticated conception of domination than did Weber. Even the most tyrannical domination is a form of interaction: I impose my will on you so that you give me what I want. My authority might come through my institutional position (I am senior to you, so you should do what you are told), or it might come through the convincing power of my action or ideas. This is different from prestige, which comes simply from the power of my personality, not through the identification of my personality with any objective feature such as knowledge or position.

Simmel distinguishes three types of domination:

(a) Domination by the individual, which might be accepted or opposed by the group. It may have a levelling effect (we're all equal in the face of the leader), or it may be hierarchical. Simmel believes this is the primary form of domination.

(b) Domination by a plurality, as in the British rule of India. The rights of individuals in the dominant group are not necessarily extended to those in the subordinate group. Simmel suggests that Britain has throughout its history been characterized by high standards of justice for individuals and high levels of injustice towards groups. Relationships between groups are characterized by greater objectivity—they are more distant from each other than individuals and therefore fellow feeling does not develop. He also explores different forms of group domination—are the dominant groups opposed to each other, for example, or hierarchically ordered.

(c) Finally there is domination by a principle or law. This is compared at length to individual domination and to the different situations in which one or the other might be preferable to the subordinate, with the interesting conclusion that, in the last analysis, which is preferable 'depends upon decisions of ultimate, indiscussable feelings concerning sociological values' (Simmel 1908/1950).

Simmel makes many more points in this particular essay, which includes a long discussion of subordination, but very little of what he says has much relevance for contemporary sociology. I think we can see why if we compare this discussion to Weber's analysis of domination.

Weber's analysis is profoundly historical, and his characterization of forms of domination comes from historical analysis whereas Simmel confines himself to the formal—logical and therefore abstract—analysis of the individual–group relationship. The historical background is hidden in Simmel—there is just the link between objective culture and the rule of law (or, in Weber's terms, legal-rational authority).

THE SOCIOLOGY OF CONFLICT

Simmel's essay (1908/1971) on conflict was still important in the mid-century dominance of English-speaking sociology by functionalism and the work of Talcott Parsons. Coser's book *The Functions of Social Conflict* (1956) in many ways answers the criticism that functionalism cannot deal with social conflict, and a great deal of the argument is developed from Simmel.

Simmel argues that conflict must be a form of sociation, since it links at least two people; it results from 'dissociating factors' such as hatred and envy and it is an attempt to resolve the resulting divergences and restore unity, even if it is through the elimination of one of the parties. Both divergence (conflict) and convergence (peace) are forms of sociation, the opposite of both being indifference. Conflict itself combines both positive and negative aspects, and society is necessarily a product of convergent and divergent forces, harmony and disharmony. Unity in the widest sense includes conflict, and, whilst conflict might be destructive on an individual level, it is not necessarily so on a social level.

Conflict contributes towards the integration of a social unit. If I regard one of my colleagues as unbearable, awful in every conceivable way, our conflict can be something which enables us to work together. If I could not fight such a person, if I had to suppress my hostility rather than sublimate it, perhaps through competition, then I could find life so difficult I would want to leave. The relationship would be ended. It is a matter of attaining an inner balance; my hostility need not have any external effect at all—it leaves me feeling better, feeling that I am not trapped. We will see later how Simmel sees our hostility to others as one of the ways in which we keep our sanity and our relationships in the flux of urban life. He also talks about limiting cases of conflict where it does not act as a form of sociation—where conflict is desired for its own sake or there is a desire to kill the other person.

SECRECY AND THE SECRET SOCIETY

If two people interact, then they will have a picture of each other; it won't be a complete picture—it will be what is necessary for the interaction to succeed. A complete knowledge of the other person is impossible; we cannot enter each other's heads, and each of us will have a different picture of a friend or acquaintance from everybody else. I see my newsagent when I pay his weekly bill; a regular customer who chats to him every day will know a different character, and his wife will know yet another. To know another person is to know somebody who is capable of hiding his or her inner truth; in fact, since our inner life is such a complex and jumbled flow, it is impossible to present it fully anyway:

With an instinct automatically preventing us from doing otherwise, we show nobody the course of psychic processes in their purely causal reality and—from the standpoints of logic, objectivity and meaningfulness—complete incoherence and rationality. Always, we show only a section of them, stylized by selection and arrangement. We simply cannot mention any interactions or social relations or society which are *not* based on the teleologically determined non-knowledge of one another.   (Simmel 1908/1971: 312)

One might add to this non-knowledge of ourselves, because we cannot be aware of the constant and multifaceted flow of thoughts when we give priority to our immediate practical purposes. It would not be very far from here to a theory of the unconscious, but that is not the route that Simmel decides to take. Instead he goes on to discuss the sociological significance of lying, which, as always, is double-edged. If I am attracted to another and lie to my wife when she challenges me about it, I might be contributing to keeping the marriage together; on the other hand, if I have a secret affair with that woman and I am discovered, my deceit can break the marriage. If I divulged every passing thought, I doubt if I would keep my friends for very long; by keeping parts of myself secret, I maintain relationships.

The closer one is to a person, the more likely one is to be hurt by that person's lying or secrecy. Simmel suggests that, in more 'primitive' groups, lying is comparatively unimportant, since individuals are leading more or less self-sufficient lives in the group and mutual dependence is at a minimum. Modern societies, in contrast, are 'credit' societies; we are dependent upon large numbers of people to tell the truth about what they are doing, and we can suffer considerably if they let us down—he suggests that in modern societies the lie is the intellectual equivalent of the footpad's club.

Simmel relates secrecy to what he regards as the basic dimensions of human relationships—cooperation and harmony, on the one hand, and distance and competition, on the other—looking at a range of relationships according to the degree of knowledge that participants might have of each other. In a simple interest group—for example, a trade-union branch—all one needs to know is that the others share the same interest. The more we move towards relationships rooted in the total personality, the more we want to know about the other person, and in between my fellow trade unionist and my wife there are any number of possibilities. Simmel places particular social value on acquaintanceship and discretion, and on differentiated friendship, where I look to one friend for intellectual qualities, another for emotional understanding, and so on; these are the relationships that are necessary in a complex society, and they all involve respect for intentional and unintentional secrets. Compared with the childish desire to reveal everything, the ability to hide realities 'is one of man's greatest achievements'. As civilization grows, what was once open becomes secret and what was once secret comes into the open. Public affairs are opened up and individual lives become private.

Secrecy holds a certain fascination: to have a secret marks one off and gives one a special sense of possession; people become jealous if they know you have a secret, and this leads to a great temptation to betray. If I were the only person who knew that my boss was having an affair, the temptation to betray would be immense. The importance of secrecy grows with and reinforces the process of individuation; the possessor of a secret increases his or her social distance from others and comes to rely on that distance. The growth of the money economy enables secrecy to reach new heights—bribery can be hidden indefinitely.

Finally, Simmel turns to the secret society, producing a set of ideas that has recently been used in a discussion of the British Institute of Psychoanalysis (Rustin 1991). The first characteristic of secret society is reciprocal protection and confidence—which Simmel regards as a particularly intense relationship of high moral value. To have a real sociological value, such a society must be an organ of transition, enabling the development of a new sort of life content. Thus the closedness of the Psychoanalytic Institutes perhaps allowed the protection of clients during the treatment and is still necessary for that reason. On the other hand, it protects practitioners when perhaps they should not be protected—as the recent conflict about the training of homosexuals illustrates.

Beyond this the secret society uses ritual to create what Simmel calls a 'life totality', confirming the centrality of the group when separation and fragmentation threaten as people leave to pursue their individual lives (a very Durkheimian insight this). Through its hierarchy it becomes the mirror image of the wider society against which it sets itself, perhaps offering a greater degree of freedom. Paradoxically, the more free the wider society, the more authoritarian the secret society—Simmel quotes as an example the American freemasons. Secret societies are more self-conscious and lay greater claim to self sufficiency than other groups; they rely on secret signs by which members can recognize each other (the notorious masonic handshake). They can emphasize social exclusiveness and superiority, and they can pursue their interests at the expense of other groups. Within the secret society there is a process of deindividuation to protect the group and it is likely to be centrally organized. Because of its secrecy, the central government nearly always sees the society as a threat.

Simmel on social types

I will now turn to the essays on social types. In these essays Simmel outlines a particular type of personality which he regards as embodying something particularly important about modern societies. When Georg Lukacs (1972) developed his literary criticism, he argued that the best form of modern realism is peopled by characters who typify important and conflicting underlying social processes—as in Thomas Mann's *The Magic Mountain* (1961) or Solzhenitsyn's *Cancer Ward* (1968). Simmel's portrayal of social types can be seen as a sociological version of literary realism. His clearest statement of his method comes not in one of his social-type essays but at the end of his discussion of the nobility, which I discuss below. We see here his distinctive ability to combine comparatively abstract analysis with an awareness of individuality and the life process:

Every human being emerges as a combination of predetermination and accident; of received material for, and unique formation of, his life; of social inheritance and the individual administration of it. In each person, we see the stereotypings of his race, his stratum, his traditions, his family, in brief, of everything that makes him a bearer of pre-existing contents and norms; we see these combined with the incalculable and the personal, with free autonomy.   (Simmel 1908/1971: 213)

This is extraordinarily like Jean-Paul Sartre's (1963) description of the 'project' in his attempt to bring together Marxism and his existential philosophy. The 'project' is something we have, whether we like it or not: it is what we do with what we have been given, with the materials with which we are provided at the start of our lives, and which we turn into something else in the course of our lives. For Sartre, the important issue is whether we can go beyond what we are given to start with, and produce something new.

THE MISER AND THE SPENDTHRIFT

Each segment of our conduct and experience bears a twofold meaning: it revolves about its own centre, contains as much breadth and depth, joy and suffering, as the immediate experiencing gives it, and at the same time it is a segment of a course of life—not only a circumscribed entity, but also a component of an organism. Both aspects, in various configurations, characterize everything that occurs in a life. Events which might be widely divergent in their bearing on life as a whole may none the less be quite similar to one another; or they may be incommensurate in their intrinsic meanings but so similar in respect to the roles they play in our total existence as to be interchangeable.

(Simmel 1907/1971: 187)

The miser is the person who hoards money for its own sake and who illustrates in an archetypal way the power of money. The miser enjoys the contemplation of what he or she can do with money:

satisfaction in the complete possession of a potentiality with no thought whatsoever about its realization. At the same time, it exemplifies an attraction akin to the aesthetic, the mastery of both the pure form and the ideal of objects or of behaviour, in respect of which every step towards reality—with its unavoidable obstacles, setbacks and frustrations—could only be a deterioration, and would necessarily constrain the feeling that objects are potentially absolutely to be mastered.   (ibid. 180)

It is as if Simmel is here picking up the earlier signs of cultural narcissism (Lasch 1980), the fear of being found wanting or lacking in some way which would be experienced as the destruction of the personality rather than as a practical problem which could be solved, and which inhibits attempts to come to grips with reality.

The spendthrift might at first sight seem to be the opposite to the miser, yet the spendthrift too has problems with coming to terms with the effects of external reality—he or she is attracted by the instant pleasure of spending, which outweighs the pleasure of hoarding money or of possessing the object. Again it is as if Simmel were identifying what we recognize today as the pleasure of shopping, less for what is bought than for the activity itself, a narcissistic pleasure because it doesn't involve commitment or human contact—perhaps better even than promiscuous sex, because it does not involve even the momentary annoyance of adjusting to another person. Simmel goes on:

At this point, the position of the spendthrift in the instrumental nexus becomes clear. The goal of enjoying the possession of an object is preceded by two steps—first, the possession of money and second, the expenditure of money for the desired object. For the miser, the first of these grows to be a pleasurable end in itself; for the spendthrift, the second.   (ibid. 183)

The lack of concern with money—an indifference towards it—is itself a sign of the dominance of the money economy: it is only because money is valued by everybody that its profligate rejection can be so effective. Money encourages immoderation.

THE ADVENTURER

The adventurer is the person who breaks the continuity of everyday life, 'a foreign body' in our existence which is somehow yet connected to the centre. The adventure has a beginning and an end and it is often difficult to remember the details of an adventure precisely because it is not part of everyday life; it fades as a dream might fade for the same reason—its strangeness. In its separation from everyday life, it is also like a work of art. It is separate from but part of life and consequently it seems that it somehow contains the whole of life within it—there is something special about its meaning. The adventurer thus becomes an eternal figure, someone who has broken free of the past and has no future.

It might be a sign of the times that what Simmel called an adventure might sometimes today be called a trauma. Many traumas have the same features as adventures; they are cut out of everyday life yet they seem to contain special meaning. If we momentarily face death and come away unscathed, for example, we are likely to see something significant in the event, however accidental it might have been: 'There is in us an eternal process playing back and forth between chance and necessity, between the fragmentary materials given us from the outside and the consistent meaning of the life developed from within' (Simmel 1911/1971: 191). It is the combination of these two, the external accident and the internal meaning, which makes the adventure so important.

Simmel goes on to connect these ideas to a metaphysical level, suggesting that, if we believe, for example, in the timeless existence of the soul, then the whole of life can seem like an adventure. The adventure is one of the fundamental categories of life:

A fragmentary incident, it is yet, like a work of art, enclosed by a beginning and an end. Like a dream, it gathers all passions into itself and yet, like a dream, it is destined to be forgotten, like gaming, it contrasts with seriousness, yet like the *va banque* of the gambler, it involves the alternative between the highest gain and destruction.   (ibid. 192)

It combines, as well, activity and passivity, certainty and uncertainty—the adventurer treats the uncertain as if it were certain, involving a form of fatalism. After drawing parallels between love and the adventure, Simmel concludes the adventure is not suited to old age—the old person is less able to be overwhelmed by the force of life.

THE STRANGER

In the case of the stranger, the union of closeness and remoteness involved in every human relationship is patterned in a way that may be succinctly formulated as follows: the distance within this relation indicates that one who is close by is remote, but his strangeness indicates that one who is remote is near.

(Simmel 1908/1971: 143)

Simmel's essay on the stranger is the most well known of his essays on social types and takes us into the analysis of modernity. His concern with space is echoed by many contemporary sociologists, and the notion of the stranger is often taken as a metaphor for Simmel himself and his own career. The stranger is in a paradoxical position: he or she is geographically near to the group but psychologically and culturally distant, near and far at the same time, and this puts the person in what we might call a privileged position. McLemore (1991) argues that we can find two research traditions that have developed from Simmel's essay. The first comes from his comments on the stranger as trader and is really the sociology of the newcomer. The second refers to the marginal person and can involve the idea that at some point in our existence we are all marginalized, by others or ourselves. Levine (1991) argues that the emphasis on the marginal character is the less faithful to Simmel's essay. In the sense that historically the stranger has usually been a trader, I suspect he is right. However, I also suspect that a reason for the continued popularity of the essay comes, first, from the theme of marginality and its affinity to the Romantic reaction to the Enlightenment, where we find a belief that people on the edge of society have some special insight not available to the rest of us—whether it be Shelley's country dweller or William Burrough's junkie—and, secondly, from the sense in which contemporary society can be said to leave us all in the position of the marginal, the stranger, given the break-up of traditional communities and increasing geographical and social mobility.

The stranger is considered objective: Simmel refers to Italian cities which used to call in their judges from outside because a native would be too entangled with the litigants. The stranger is free with no commitments to local interests and this enables a commitment to objectivity, and the stranger who passes through is often a receptacle of secrets which cannot be shared with the people to whom we are closest. The stranger can see things that the insider cannot see because he or she is too close, and perhaps say things that the insider cannot say because it would be too damaging. In the introductory chapters I talked about the objective existence of social structures—in the sense of their object—such as qualities which remain the same whatever we think about them. We might call this the 'objective sense of objectivity'. I contrasted it with the more common-sense use of the term as denoting a particular attitude—what we might call the *subjective* sense of objectivity. Simmel offers an excellent criticism of this second sense of the term that also redefines it: 'Objectivity is by no means nonparticipation, a condition that is altogether outside the distinction between subjective and objective orientations. It is rather a positive and definite kind of participation' (ibid. 144). It can be defined, he suggests, as freedom, a position which perhaps should belong to the sociologist.

Our relationship with the stranger is through sharing the most abstract human qualities, and perhaps the stranger is more readily seen as the representative of a particular type or group than as an individual. What Simmel does not deal with is the way in which such groups—Jews, blacks, gays—can become scapegoats which serve to generate a sense of community amongst the home culture.

Simmel on modernity

Now we move on to another issue—Simmel's conception of modernity, which, perhaps more than other issues, is beyond his time.

THE METROPOLIS

> The deeper problems of modern life derive from the claim of the individual to preserve the autonomy and individuality of his existence in the face of overwhelming social forces, of historical heritage, of external culture and of the technique of life. The fight with nature that primitive man has to wage for his *bodily* existence attains in this modern form its latest transformation.
>
> (Simmel 1902/1950: 409)

The essay on the metropolis is one of Simmel's best-known pieces, often cited as a foundation of urban sociology. The big urban centres of the modern world bring about a change in human life, requiring different capacities from those required by the country and the small town. In the latter, life is comparatively slow, and it is possible to build up deep emotional connections with others on an unconscious level. In the big city we are constantly bombarded with changing sense impressions, myriads of fast-moving people, heavy traffic, countless activities, shop displays, advertising, all calling on our attention. It is not possible to survive this world without developing the intellect. The city-dweller reacts with the head—'that organ which is least sensitive and quite remote from the depth of the personality'—rather than with the heart, distancing him- or herself from the shocks and changes that urban life brings.

The metropolis and the urban mind are intimately bound up with the money economy. The complexity of urban life forces us into punctuality, calculability, and exactness and transforms the world into an arithmetic problem. The city-dweller becomes a sophisticate, blasé, and protects him- or herself from being overwhelmed with sensations, on the one hand, or with indifference, on the other, by adopting a reserved, even an antipathetic attitude towards others. Fights break out easily in the city.

Whilst physically closer to other people, the individual is psychologically separated from and independent of them. This gives him or her immense freedom, the reverse side of which is loneliness and an increasing sense of meaninglessness: 'The atrophy of individual culture through the hypertrophy of objective culture is one reason for the bitter hatred which the preachers of the most extreme individualism, above all Nietzsche, harbour against the metropolis' (ibid. 422). Charles H. Powers argues that this essay 'heralds the spread of distinctly modern social roles. Narrow, specialized, standardized, interchangeable

roles are the defining form and are an inherent feature of modern urban life'
(Powers 1991: 354).

It is not simply that Simmel identifies modern role structures; he identifies
processes that have been taken up by contemporary thinkers as essential aspects
of late modernity or postmodernity (Weinstein and Weinstein 1993). Thinkers
as far apart as David Harvey (1989) and Anthony Giddens (1990b) point out
that cities are becoming more and more standardized: shopping centres in
Europe and North America look increasingly similar—often the shops are the
same. The difference between Simmel and the contemporary thinkers is that
Simmel was critical. Weinstein and Weinstein comment mildly on the danger of
metropolitan life generating a 'mild schizophrenia' but on the whole see it as
increasing individual freedom. Simmel's language indicates that he was more
aware of the dangers, and, as Fredric Jameson, a Marxist critic of postmodernist
thought, points out (1991), 'schizophrenia' has become a defining metaphor for
contemporary human life.

FASHION

Simmel (1904/1971) begins by pointing to the contradictory tendency to identify with and separate oneself from society. This contradiction is reflected on different levels—at the biological level it is between heredity and variation. There
is no way of living and no form of society which can satisfy urges. In psychological terms, the side of social adjustment is reinforced by the tendency to imitation, which has the advantage of avoiding both the demands of creativity and
the responsibility for action, which is passed on to another.

Social institutions such as fashion can be seen as the compromise between the
desire for stasis and the desire for change: fashion allows one both to follow
others and to mark oneself off from them as a member of a particular class or
group. The items that become fashionable have very little or no instrumental use
(baseball caps worn backwards in mild weather), and they often come from a
distance (the popularity of kaftans in the 1960s, or, again, in Britain, of baseball
caps in the 1990s). If fashion fails to supply either the need for union with
others, or the need for separation, it disappears. In societies or social classes
where there is little differentiation, fashions change slowly; in modern societies,
where there is a danger of obliteration of the individual, fashion becomes much
more important. The further fashion spreads within a group, the more it heads
towards its end—it is necessarily transitory and carries with it a strong feeling of
the present. The very fact that we know it will come to an end makes it all the
more attractive. It is particularly attractive for dependent individuals, and the
fashionable person is both envied and approved of. The person who follows
fashion can identify with the group and assert his or her individuality. The dude
does this to perfection, always slightly exaggerating the dominant fashion, wear-

ing the baggiest trousers, the shortest skirt, or whatever—employing the fashion in the most individualistic way. This is one of the peculiar paradoxes of fashion—the person who appears to be leading the group is in fact most dominated by it. Simmel sees this as one of the distinctive features of a democratic society.

If following or apparently even leading fashion is a sign of subordination to the group, the explicit and self-conscious rejection of fashion is equally a sign of subordination—the first subordination has a positive sign in front of it, and the second a negative sign. Neither the following nor the rejection of fashion is necessarily an indicator of a strong sense of individuality. Simmel argues that, in the adoption of a fashion, the individual can avoid a feeling of shame that might otherwise attach to his or her action; it is also a means by which we can preserve an inner freedom by following the crowd in matters of external display. Another form of fashion is linguistic—when certain words are applied to all sorts of experiences or objects: 'cool' and 'wicked' seem to be popular now amongst my son's friends—although this can change very quickly, and might be cyclical—I can remember using 'cool' thirty years ago. This sort of fashion treats objects and experiences in a cavalier way, denying their individuality and establishing the control of the individual over the surrounding world. In this sense, it is ego-reinforcing and perhaps exactly what is needed amongst adolescents; in adults, however, I suspect that it is more a matter of avoidance—a way of not thinking about the world.

Simmel goes on to argue that rapid changes in fashion are not likely to be found in the highest classes, since they will be consciously conservative, or in the lowest classes, 'with their dull unconscious conservatism'—a phrase which unfortunately says much about Simmel's own prejudices but very little about the working class, who, as the last century has shown, have developed their own fashions as they have moved above subsistence level and as clothing, in particular, has become mass produced and relatively cheaper. It is a sign of social mobility:

Classes and individuals who demand constant change, because the rapidity of their development gives them the advantage over others, find in fashion something that keeps pace with their own rapid soul-movements. Social advance above all is favourable to the rapid change of fashion, for it capacitates the lower classes so much for imitation of upper ones, and thus the process . . . according to which every higher set throws aside a fashion the moment a lower set adopts it, has acquired a breadth and activity never dreamed of before.   (Simmel 1904/1971: 318)

The development of late modernity has, I think, 'flattened' the sort of status struggles to which Simmel was referring and enabled an even more rapid change in fashions.

Simmel also notes that the spread of changing fashions encourages the production of cheaper goods, and that fashion tends to move in cycles—as soon as an old fashion becomes at least partially forgotten, it can be resurrected.

Simmel on social groups

Finally there is Simmel's discussion of different forms of social groups.

THE POOR

Simmel begins his discussion of the poor by talking about the reciprocities of obligation and duties; if the poor are considered and consider themselves to have a right to sustenance from those better off than themselves either because they are poor or because they belong to the same community as those who are better off, they and society are in a better position than either the situation in which the poor believe that poverty is a cosmic injustice, when they will attack the better-off, or the situation where giving to the poor is motivated by its consequences to the giver. If I give my money to charity because it might enable me to get to heaven, a completely new situation is created—a situation which Simmel clearly thinks is not a good one since it brings about 'the senseless distribution of alms, the demoralization of the proletariat through arbitrary donations which tend to undermine all creative work' (Simmel 1908/1971: 154).

When the welfare of society requires assistance to the poor, either to ward off social disruption or to increase productivity, attention turns away from both the giver and the recipient. This type of help seeks to alleviate individual needs, not the needs of all citizens. Its aim is to mitigate inequalities that would otherwise challenge the society—to reinforce rather than transform the existing society through creating overall equality. It is a process which subordinates the needs of the individual to those of the wider society: 'Within the modern, relatively democratic State public assistance is perhaps the *only* branch of the administration in which the interested parties have no participation whatsoever' (ibid. 157). In this sense, the poor have the same status as a road that the government might decide to build; on the other hand, they are also citizens. Their position is rather like the stranger, outside society and at the same time incorporated into it as part of a larger whole.

Simmel suggests that there is another reciprocal right and duty between the wealthy and the community as a whole, on the one hand, and the poor, on the other, to relieve suffering. In this relationship, the poor are an end in themselves: 'The State assists poverty; private assistance assists the poor' (ibid. 169). In modern societies where the state assists poverty, we can talk about the poor as a group; otherwise we can talk only about poor individuals: this person is poor and unemployed, this one a poor farmer, this one a poor single mother—they become part of *the* poor only when they receive state assistance; the poor, in modern terminology, are socially constructed. This might have a distinctly modern ring to it for some readers, and they would be right in the sense that it has been taken up by the New Right and by centre–left parties as they move to the right.

Lewis Coser (1991*b*), developing Simmel's argument, illustrates the general tendency. There are no absolute measures of poverty; definitions are always relative. This is fair enough: poverty in London or Paris or New York might be very unpleasant but it would often not be regarded as poverty in Rwanda or Somalia or some areas of India. Returning to Simmel's point about the state classification of the poor, Coser goes on to argue that, although the fact that the state takes a measure of responsibility for the poor and recognizes that they are members of society, it also degrades them, assigning them to a stigmatized role—this is perhaps particularly true of the American system even at the time Coser was writing (1965) but the European systems also tend towards degradation—constant checking, surveillance, steady withdrawal of benefit over time, and so on. Not only does the provision of assistance degrade; it also keeps the poor dependent. Coser then makes a leap:

I showed earlier how the core category of the poor arises only when they come to be defined as recipients of assistance. We now see that correlatively the poor will be with us as long as we provide assistance so that the problem of poverty can be solved only through the abolition of unilateral relationship of dependence.   (Coser 1991*b*: 238)

This view produces various schemes intended to push the poor into looking after themselves and thus no longer being poor.

It might be useful to think about this argument in contrast to a Marxist approach. It seems to me that it is possible to accept the argument about the state defining 'the poor' through fixing minimum standards of living and providing assistance to those who fall below it—this is a surface analysis which would involve writing a history of the development of the welfare state. However, this works only on one level. There is a process of the social construction of poverty on another, prior level. The mechanisms of economic competition and the overproduction/underconsumption crises produce systematic social inequalities which leave some people at the bottom of the pile and some people at the top, with those at the bottom suffering distinct physical and environmental disadvantages—higher infant mortality rates, higher levels of disease, lower life expectancy, and so on, as well as the day to day absence of many of the goods necessary to become good citizens. The social definition that Simmel and Coser are talking about, then, occurs on the basis of this primary inequality and involves a selection of the point in the hierarchy where we begin using the *word* poor. This defines the poor, but does not create them. This is an example which would support the need for theoretical pluralism, using the different approaches at the same time, and I will return to the relationships between the theoretical approaches in the conclusion to Part 2.

THE NOBILITY

Simmel begins his essay on the nobility by arguing that, like the middle classes, the nobility are between the highest and the lowest classes, but, unlike the middle classes, they are relatively bounded both above and below, and this produces the particular nature of the aristocracy. We expect them to be privileged in respect of people below them, but Simmel points out that historically they have had special responsibilities in relation to those below them. Whilst the lower classes, for example, could be expected to steal and would be subjected to routine punishments, the aristocracy were not expected to engage in such behaviour and would be more severely punished. The invariant social position of the nobility produces a homogeneity: they can make many assumptions in their interactions and can get down to personal details much more quickly than other members of other classes.

In other social strata it is usually the case that what is shared by all members is a sort of lowest common denominator; in the case of the nobility, the opposite is the case—members share in the glory attained by the highest members, not through the possession of externals such as power and property but through internal qualities preserved through the tendency to marry within the class. A person born into the aristocracy automatically shares in its glory:

> This recruiting from within conveys the unique insularity and self-sufficiency of this status group which, so to speak, can and may need nothing that lies outside itself; the nobility is, thereby like an island in the world. It is comparable to a work of art, within which each part also takes its meaning from the whole, and which shows through its frame that the world cannot enter, that it is absolutely sufficient unto itself.   (Simmel 1908/1971: 208)

This socially transmitted honour can, however, lead to what Simmel calls a 'decadent emptiness'. Socially transmitted features have to be combined with an inner creativeness on the part of the individual; at its best this can create ideal examples of independence and responsibility, but where that individual component is not there, decay sets in. The aristocrat does not work: the 'substance' of nobility comes from inside the person, and it is not to be transmitted to an object—although Simmel acknowledges that this may be changing. The ideal aristocratic pursuits are warfare and hunting—the subjective factor has importance over the objective factor, and, in this, there is an analogy to the work of the artist.

WOMEN, LOVE, AND SEXUALITY

> The man externalizes himself. His energy is discharged into his performance. Thus he 'signifies' something that is in some sense independent of him, either dynamically or ideally, in a creative or a representative fashion.

The constitutive idea of the woman, on the other hand, is the unbroken character of her periphery, the organic finality in the harmony of the aspects of her nature, both in their relationship to one another and in the symmetry of their relationship to their centre. This is precisely what epitomizes the beautiful. In the symbolism of metaphysical concepts, the woman represents being and man represents becoming. This is why the man must establish his significance in a particular substantive area or in an idea, in a historical or cognitive world. However, a woman should be beautiful in the sense that this represents 'bliss in itself'.

(Simmel 1911/1984: 88–9)

In arguments that with a little translation will be very familiar to those who have followed contemporary feminist debates, Simmel (1911/1984) begins by suggesting that the modern women's movement poses two 'value questions'. The first is the access of women to already established 'objective culture'—the sort of issues that would now be seen in terms of equality of access and opportunity; the second is whether the movement can add anything new to the objective culture, qualitatively different from what has gone before. Now objective culture is not asexual; it is masculine, at least in the sense that men have produced it—the artists and scientists and philosophers who have contributed to it have all been men. However, Simmel wants to go beyond this, to establish that there is something about objective culture that is specifically associated with the male personality. In his useful introduction to Simmel's essays on these issues, Guy Oakes (1984) lists a number of basic differences between men and women that Simmel sees as important.

To begin with—and Oakes rightly calls Simmel's reasoning here 'banal and hardly persuasive'—is the fact that the division of labour, as it has developed since the industrial revolution, has moved men out of the home into a separate specialized economic role; women's activity in the home has remained unspecialized. Simmel's conclusion is that men are able to engage in specialized activities without a threat to their sense of self or identity, whereas women cannot be so incorporated. Following on from this, man is able to engage in actions that are *detached* from the centre of his being, whilst woman is only able to engage in actions which are integrated with her self. Men are more able to deal with other people in a depersonalized way, whereas women become more wholly involved in their relationships and so are more vulnerable. They are unable to objectify and free their action from its personal and subjective roots. Women have to express their emotions directly whereas men can express theirs through the mediation of objective culture.

These ideas might sound quaint to modern ears but they are not so different from the more contemporary arguments of Parsons (1951) or Chodorow (1978), except that Simmel is concerned to establish that being male and being female are two irreducible forms of being. For Parsons there is a functional division of labour in which men are assigned to work and women to the home, and for Chodorow the difference has to do with women's mothering role and is passed on by the psychological differences in mother–daughter and mother–son relationships. The characteristics which each thinker assigns to men and women are not the same as those discussed by Simmel, but they belong recognizably to the same families.

Simmel is ambivalent about the possibility of women contributing anything to objective culture. On the one hand, the two forms of being are important and should be maintained as such; if a woman were to try to take on and contribute to objective culture, she would no longer be feminine—feminine culture is entirely subjective. On the other hand, he suggests that there *might* be a feminine objective culture which has not yet been discovered, presumably because of male domination. He hints at a specifically feminine art—rather as, several decades later, Virginia Woolf talked about the feminine sentence that had yet to be written, and several decades after that Carol Gilligan (1982) was to write of women having different conceptions of morality and justice compared with men.

Postmodern feminists would accuse Simmel of reproducing a traditional 'essentialism'—the idea that men and women have essential, different characters, independent of context. A modern form of this sort of argument can be found over whether there is a specifically feminist epistemology (Harding 1986, 1991), which suggests that women have something very important to add to objective culture, at least so far as the philosophy of science is concerned, and this has to do with the subjective side of existence. The paradox is that in these terms Simmel's concern with the subjectivity and relationships can be seen as putting him in the feminine position in relation to the other classical sociological thinkers.

I think that it is probably the case that Simmel was simply reproducing common prejudices. This becomes clearer in his discussion of female sexuality; it follows from the above that sexuality for the man is something that he does, whereas for the woman it is something that she *is*. Her femininity is independent of her relationship to the man—as is evidenced by pregnancy, where the woman is at her most feminine and has no further need of the man: 'she is *intrinsically* sexual. . . . It is as if she has a secret sense of self-possession and a self-contained completeness' (Simmel 1911/1984: 108). Man is always drawn in two directions—towards the sensual and the transcendentally spiritual, on the one hand, and, on the other, towards recognizing autonomy and the desire to control and change. A woman, according to Simmel, stands 'beyond' this dualism; if she does not feel that she is connected with anything, then it does not concern her.

When he discusses flirtation, Simmel seems at first to be saying something different: that in flirting the woman is saying yes and no at the same time, departing from the unitary, 'centralized' nature that he attributes to her; however, he argues that these two apparently contradictory messages actually unite the whole of a woman's relationship to a man—following the biological imperative of nature, the woman chooses the man. Flirtation is the play form of a sexual relationship, in which we can, as it were, all be promiscuous:

flirtation ensures that in definitive not-having, there is still a sense in which we can have. . . . With the advance of culture . . . increased sensitivity, on the one hand, and the equally large increase in the number of provocative phenomena, on the other, have produced an erotic repression in men. It is simply not possible to possess all the attractive women— whereas in primitive times, such an abundance of attractive phenomena just did not exist. Flirtation is a remedy for this condition. By this means the woman could give herself—potentially, symbolically or by approximation—to a large number of men, and in the same sense, the individual man could possess a large number of women.   (ibid. 150)

In his writings on femininity Simmel is one of the few sociologists who can really be regarded as essentialist, and he seems to be talking about a very mysterious essence, a form of pure self-identity. Men are defined in relation to women but not vice versa, yet the two are also spoken of as comprising two elements of a dichotomy and we would expect each to be defined in terms of the other. Compared with Engels on the family, we could say that Simmel has little contact with mundane reality, although he occasionally notes the similarity between marriage and prostitution and he is perhaps closer to some forms of the subjective experience of sex and gender differences. However, neither Simmel nor Engels is really able to cross the barrier between seeing the relationships between the sexes in social-structural terms and seeing them in experiential terms. Before turning to these issues, I want to bring the discussion of Simmel to an end.

Conclusion

It is perhaps a tribute to the breadth of Simmel's sociological vision that there have been regular attempts to integrate him into widely different sociological traditions. Thus Jonathan H. Turner (1991) argues that if we take Marx and Simmel together we can begin to build a proper conflict theory; in the same volume Jim Faught (1991) argues that there are significant convergences between Weber and Simmel in their discussion of politics and rationalization, and Lawrence Scaff (1991) emphasizes their joint concern with the development of modern culture. In the course of this chapter I have drawn parallels between Simmel and Durkheim, and finally there is Weinstein and Weinstein's (1993) recent attempt to claim Simmel for postmodernism. I think that the reason for this is Simmel's concentration on the individual/society dualism—he is closer to social psychology than sociology, and that is a gap in the other approaches which can be plugged with some of his ideas. Turning to the issues at stake in these conclusions, I think that perhaps a true 'Simmelian', if there could be such a thing, might have given up sociology altogether, seeing it as having become irretrievably part of the objective culture. Paradoxically, I suspect that some of the contemporary ideas that owe most to Simmel would be what would drive him into retirement. In any case, he or she would not be interested in systematizing a method or a theory.

I do not think that Simmel would have a lot to say about the changes in the labour market; the only account of social change that he offers is a comparatively simple, neo-Durkheimian notion of organic evolution in which the individual emerges from the group. His version of globalization would, I think, be in terms of the increasing universalization of objective culture, and this would carry with it the decline in significance of local communities. This was a decline that Simmel had begun to chart in his essay on the metropolis and which he, I think unconsciously, senses when he talks about the stranger, but he is less interested in communities than in the psychological consequences for individuals. The conflict between what I have called the life process and objective culture is at the centre of his work; it is the fact that he sees this as a dialectic rather than a process of socialization or the social construction of subjectivity that makes him more interesting than postmodernism, whilst in other ways he might be taken as a precursor of some postmodernist ideas (Weinstein and Weinstein 1993). I think the important point in this respect is that noted by Powers in the earlier quotation: that Simmel was the one of the first to note the development of a multiplicity of standardized and specialized roles; we can move from there to talking about a multiplicity of techniques for socializing people into these roles—or what Nikolas Rose, developing Foucault, calls the government of conduct (Hall and du Gay 1996). What is lost in all this is precisely the notion of a life process, an individuality which can transform and resist such governance.

It is difficult to think of what a Simmelian would make of the new political movements. Given Simmel's work on poverty, such a sociologist might well follow Holton and Turner and talk about 'state-administered status blocs', and he or she would, I think, certainly be interested in the processes of identification and separation that go in relation to such movements. The basic model for this process could be the church or the traditional far left, which have produced regular splits throughout their existence. What characterizes such movements is that they believe they have answers which draw the individual into identifying with them and push him or her into separating from them. Thus we can find divisions within feminism, within the gay movement, within the green movement, in a constant process of formation and reformation. These political movements are not fashions but they behave like Simmel's description of fashions.

A Simmelian sociologist might alternatively be interested in psychoanalytic social criticism along the lines of Christopher Lasch's (1980) argument about the way in which modern society undermines the possibility of coherence within the individual personality and inhibits the development of individual maturity. One of the results of this is the loss of play forms—such an individual cannot engage in sociable conversation, in flirtation, or in play at sport. Everything is very serious. We can now elaborate on Simmel's views of the basic dualism (see Boxes 10.1–10.3).

Box 10.1. **An elaboration of Simmel on the individual and society**

THE INDIVIDUAL

Durkheim: the individual is formed and limited by society. He/she becomes more important in complex societies and individualism becomes the focus of the *conscience collective*, binding people together.

Marx: the 'individuated' individual is an idea produced as part of the development of capitalism. The 'natural' state of the individual is as an integral part of the group.

Weber: the individual is the only reality and analysis must start from individual rational action.

Simmel: the individual life is engaged in a constant dialectic with social forms and the objective culture. In modern societies, the individual is engaged in a struggle to maintain his or her integrity against the objective culture.

SOCIETY

Durkheim: society exists over and above the individual, over whom it exercises an immense power, especially in less complex societies.

Marx: society is created by human action but acts back upon individuals as an external power—a dominant force in all but the most primitive and most advanced (communist) societies.

Weber: society is the rather fragile result of human interaction and struggles for power between different types of group.

Simmel: 'society' is an increasingly important form organizing peoples' lives. It can be understood as 'objective culture'—increasingly universal shared symbols and beliefs which form our lives.

Box 10.2. **Simmel on action and structure**

ACTION	STRUCTURE
Durkheim: there is no real theory of social action in Durkheim; the individual action is always conditioned by the group, and collective action is taken to reinforce the strength of the group.	**Durkheim:** in societies dominated by mechanical solidarity, the social structure consists of networks of kin groups (segmented societies); more complex modern societies consist of secondary groups formed by the division of labour and managed by the state.
Marx: in capitalist societies, the major agents are social classes—primarily the bourgeoisie and the proletariat. Some classes—the middle classes and the peasantry—do not share the life conditions which enable them to act as collective agents, and they tend to follow a strong leader.	**Marx:** different types of society have different forms of social structure. In capitalist societies the economic structure and resultant class structure are most important, and the state and state institutions are central features of social control.
Weber: status groups and market-based social classes can become 'collective actors' in the form of communal or more usually associative groups. Such groups exist only if members recognize a common identity or shared interest. The only 'real' actor remains the individual.	**Weber:** social structure is a fragile achievement; in traditional societies it is based on kin and status groups and in modern societies market-based classes enter into play. Bureaucratic organization and the state become more important.
Simmel: concerned primarily with individual interactions and their relationship to the wider culture; no concept of collective action.	**Simmel:** no real concept of social structure, except perhaps as relations entailed by economic exchange. Instead of a concept of social structure, he employs a notion of 'objective culture'.

Further reading

It is difficult to pick essays that are central to or typical of Simmel's work; my personal favourites, which include the best-known and most influential are 'The Secret and the Secret Society', especially parts 1, 2, and 3, 'Faithfulness and Gratitude', 'The Stranger', and 'The Metropolis and Mental Life', all of which are in *The Sociology of Georg Simmel*, ed. Kurt H. Wolff (1950), and the essay on 'Conflict' in *Georg Simmel on Individuality and Social Forms*, ed. D. Levine (1971). If I had to select one part of *The Philosophy of Money* (1900/1990), it would be chapter 6, where the theory of alienation is developed.

Amongst the secondary works the most straightforward is David Frisby, *Georg Simmel* (1984), but his *Sociological Impressionism* (1981) and *Simmel and Since* (1992) are also important. For a recent application of Simmel, see Michael Rustin's essay on psychoanalytic institutions in *The Good Society and the Inner World* (1991). Larry Ray (ed.), *Formal Sociology* (1991), is an excellent collection which gives a good sense of Simmel's reception in the USA, and the Weinsteins's *Postmodern(ized) Simmel* (1993) brings Simmel into the centre of contemporary debates.

Box 10.3. **Simmel on social integration and system integration**

SOCIAL INTEGRATION

Durkheim: in all societies social integration is achieved through the *conscience collective*—shared ways of thinking (logic, conceptions of space and time, shared beliefs, norms, and values). In societies governed by mechanical solidarity, religion is central. In more complex modern societies, the *conscience collective* covers less of our lives but focuses on the ethics of individual freedom—it becomes a religion of humanity.

Marx: a 'false' and rather tenuous integration is achieved through ideologies, and the development of the market constantly threatens whatever integration is achieved. The major contending classes strive towards achieving their own integration in opposition to the others—the proletariat being the class most likely to achieve this.

Weber: at this point there is no real conception of social integration in Weber's work.

Simmel: social integration is achieved through objective culture—the development of universal symbols and meanings that begins with economic exchange. The growth of such a culture extends human freedom but constricts the integrity and depth of the individual life.

SYSTEM INTEGRATION

Durkheim: where mechanical solidarity predominates, system integration *is* social integration, guaranteed by the *conscience collective*. Where organic solidarity predominates, system integration is achieved through the division of labour.

Marx: system integration in capitalism is constantly threatened by class conflict and is supported by the state and by ruling ideologies.

Weber: it is a gross exaggeration to use the word 'system' in connection with the writings we have looked at in Chapter 9. Social structures are held together by different forms of domination and by stability provided by the market.

Simmel: no real concept of system integration, except perhaps through economic exchange.

Conclusion to Part 2: the theorists contrasted

It is difficult to sum up the information contained in the last four chapters and I think the most useful thing at this point is to try and situate the different theoretical approaches in relation to each other. My first point is the obvious one: they are different from each other but they also overlap—by this, I mean that we are not looking at alternative candidates for a total explanation of social reality as a whole—it is not a matter of saying that one theory is better than another overall; we can, in certain circumstances, say that one or the other of the approaches is better for looking at a particular aspect of social reality; we can talk about what a particular social theory does not or cannot see and what it sees more clearly. The notion of basic dualisms that I have developed stems from the idea that social reality is made up of a number of different aspects which are very different from each other but all of which must be taken into account, and each theory will assign one side of the dualism a more important place than the other. In what follows I will try to relate the different theoretical contributions to understanding the issues that I have discussed in the conclusions to the previous four chapters.

When we think about the worldwide changes in the labour market, it is probably Marxism which can give us the clearest conception of a world-system with its own underlying dynamic and underlying structure, and which would explain developments in the division of labour in terms of this underlying structure. The effects of this would be mediated by the class structure of western society and this in turn would explain some of the industrial and political changes in recent decades and the conflicts that they have generated. But I think Marxism is best at the broad picture—it misses the detailed complexities.

Durkheim's contribution to this would be twofold: first he points to the importance of the division of labour in separating and relating people in different ways and he gives us a number of indices through which we can try to examine the form of social cohesion and community life—crime rates, suicide rates, marriage and divorce rates, and so on. Secondly, he directs us towards an understanding of how a society thinks itself—its collective representations—and through these we can also gain an understanding of the form and depth of social cohesion. It can do these tasks rather better than Marxism, but a Durkheimian approach tends to miss or underestimate the divisions of interest which separate social classes.

Through Weber we can make better sense of the complexity of social conflict and the forms of social and political conflict that Marxism has a difficulty in apprehending—this is especially so given that Weber sees the state not just as an instrument of class rule but as the focus of a power struggle between many different groups. In this sense Weber offers probably offers the best available analytic route into understanding the new social movements. A Weberian analysis also adds to our understanding of changes in the way modern society sees itself—especially through his analysis of rationality and rationalization. Weber's idea is quite compatible with the utilitarianism that Durkheim criticized. Remember that Durkheim's point was that the pursuit of self-interest rested on an underlying *collective* value agreement about the boundaries of the pursuit—an agreement, say, that contracts should be honoured. Although I think he was right about this, his emphasis hid from him the power of rationalization and the instrumental advantages bought about by the division of labour—just as, arguably, Weber (or at least the Weber discussed in Chapter 9) might have some difficulty in seeing how a *conscience collective* could mediate the power of rationalization—why, for example, some colonized nations rejected the rationality of colonization.

What all three miss, and what Simmel above all grasps, is the way these various processes affect and transform individual and group psychology, the forms and depth of relationship that are possible between individuals and groups. I think it is probably fair to say that Simmel is the only one of the four who values the individual in a concrete sense. For Marx, the notion of the individual in a modern sense is a product of capitalism, and I think this is true if we are talking about a view which sees the individual as free and self-creating, but often he seemed to see real people only as examples of human nature and of alienated human nature and as members of a social class. They might be all of these, but they are also living beings with difficult internal struggles and Simmel is the one sociologist who offers a possibility of understanding. Durkheim overemphasizes socialization, and sees individuality as possible only through the modern *conscience collective*—what Simmel would regard as the very objective culture which would deny individuality. And Weber seems only to see the individual as already colonized by rationality.

Earlier I commented that a Marxist would be interested in different evidence from a Durkheimian; it should be clear why this is the case, not only for these two approaches but for all four: they are talking about related but different aspects of the social world. It is a matter of finding not the evidence that will enable us to choose between the approaches but the evidence that will enable us to extend the depth of the understanding offered by each theory.

Part 3

History and social change

Introduction to Part 3

I want to turn now to issues that have been implicitly or explicitly present throughout, but have only now come to the fore. My focus now moves to history and social change, and the direction in which that change might be moving. It is as if so far I have described the machinery of society as each thinker sees it, and it is now time to look at that machinery in motion—only here we are dealing with a strange machine that changes its nature as it progresses: it might start off as a crude wheelbarrow, but will develop into a horse-drawn chariot, a wagon, and a model T Ford, and then at some point it will take off and develop jet propulsion.

I am using the word 'history' to indicate a long process stretching back into the mists of time up to the present day. We cannot think about society without in some way or another implying a theory of history. Even if we claim that we have no theory and that history is this vast sense is not amenable to 'a theory', some sort of theory is implicit. We cannot escape a theory of history just as we cannot escape a general theory.

The late nineteenth century was dominated by theories of evolution and on into the mid-twentieth century it was almost automatic to apply some sort of evolutionary framework. Even Weber implies a theory of social evolution. The late twentieth century has seen the development of relativist rather than evolutionary visions of the world, with an emphasis on value choices and chance. The difference is one between a view that the primitive wheelbarrow has some internal quality which will lead to its eventual transformation into a space rocket and a view that it is only through the ingenuity of some character who could easily not have been born that humanity got as far as hitching animals to cart-like structures. My own view here, which will inform the following discussions, is that there is no evidence for a 'hard' evolutionary theory in social science, but there does seem to be some mileage in a looser theory which perhaps sees evolution as a movement from the comparatively small and simple to the comparatively large and complex. Even those theorists such as Anthony Giddens who dismiss evolutionary theory tend to produce classificatory theories that have evolutionary implications (see Wright 1989; Bottomore 1990; Craib 1992a).

By social change I mean less the broad sweep of history than the nature of change in the modern world since the industrial revolution up to the present time and into the foreseeable future. Here the question of whether the modern world is best characterized by what has become known as 'modernity' or 'capitalism' comes to the fore, as well as the significance of imperialism (Marx) and the significance of the history of western Europe (Weber). Both writers seem to imply—for different reasons—that the history of modern society necessarily draws the rest of the world into its orbit. This happens either through the expansionist dynamic of capitalism, which continually seeks new markets, and sources of cheaper raw materials and cheaper labour, or through the dominance of western rationality, which is more practically efficient and pulls everything along behind it. It also raises again the problem of the relationship between the individual and society. One might think, at least in modern society, that the scope of individual freedom is becoming wider and wider, but there are arguments to suggest that this apparent freedom is coupled with an increasing control over our internal psychological processes. As the forces of tradition decline, we are changed internally by the conditions of modern life. We can already see this argument developing in the work of Simmel and Weber, and it is one of the options open in Marx's view of history.

I have already suggested that perhaps we are in a situation where structural cohesion is becoming firmer and beyond the perception and often the understanding of most—if not all—people and this generates a situation in which social cohesion begins to fragment. Each theoretical tradition has different and perhaps contradictory ways of saying the same thing. For Durkheim, it would be the abnormal division of labour eating away at the power of the *conscience collective*; for Marx, it would be the increasing dominance of the capitalist system over those groups which might oppose it; for Weber, it might be the iron cage of rational calculability; for Simmel, the increasing dominance of objective culture. This raises the question of how far modern social structures are open to conscious political change; whereas socialist and communist parties once promised revolutionary change, they now seem to offer only a counter-balance to the more extreme manifestations of the free market. The classical thinkers still set the limits of our thinking around all these issues: it is as if the picture they painted in broad outline has become more and more detailed and less and less clear, but no new outlines have emerged: we are still caught in the same picture.

Now each of these theorists, as well as suggesting what can happen, also explicitly or implicitly says what *should* happen—what the world should be like: they each imply a set of values which can be realized in our social organization and in our individual and collective behaviour. They imply what we might call social moralities and these will turn out to be connected with the dualisms that I have tried to use as a guiding framework for talking about the classical theorists. I think in this respect I would argue a position that is close to Charles Taylor's (1989) in his remarkable study of the development of our moral conceptions of the self. The values which these imply are usually all desirable, but contradictory. This means that, if we choose one value then we have to sacrifice another—that, for example, there might be a choice, in degree, between social cohesion and individual freedom; between freedom and stability in personal relationships; between freedom and equality; between personal autonomy and a welfare state. Part of the social function of social theory should be to explore these alternatives and clarify what would be entailed by different intentions.

11 | Durkheim's organic analogy

Introduction

Durkheim on history and politics.

The organic analogy and Durkheim's theory of history

The explanation of change in the *Division of Labour*; change through population growth; primary and secondary factors in the division of labour; increasing universality of the *conscience collective* and the growing freedom of the individual; the importance of organic and psychological factors in the division of labour; Durkheim's materialism and his increasing concern with cultural patterns. The explanation of change in *The Rules of Sociological Method*; the classification of social types; the primitive horde and more complex combinations; societies as species; the distinction between society and civilization; critique of the species analogy; Durkheim and modern evolutionary theory.

Durkheim's conservatism and Durkheim's socialism

The debate about Durkheim's politics; the importance of placing limits on human nature; his critique of modernity and his critique of socialism as an ideological reaction to industrialization compared to sociology as a scientific reaction—comparison with Engels. Durkheim's liberal/left sympathies; the emphasis on the importance of professional groupings which would control the state (his syndicalism); his support for the Dreyfusards and his individualism—the sacredness of the individual in general; the importance of freedom of thought and the cognitive role of the state; the problem of politics and analysis in Durkheim; his conservative views on divorce and women.

Conclusion

The continuing importance of Durkheim as a theorist of society and social cohesion; the *conscience collective* in the modern world; the importance of his conception of the state as protector of the individual and civil society; his lack of a theory of action; criticism of his theory of history.

Introduction

> The division of labour varies in direct proportion to the volume and density of societies and if it progresses in a continuous manner over the course of social development it is because more societies become regularly more dense and generally more voluminous.
>
> (Durkheim 1893/1984: 205)

This quotation conveys the sense of Durkheim's theory of history as a steady process; generally it seems to me that this is less interesting than what he has to say about modern societies but we cannot fully understand the latter without the former.

The organic analogy and Durkheim's theory of history

Durkheim's use of the organic analogy is at its clearest in his writing on social evolution, particularly in the development from the *Division of Labour* to *The Rules of Sociological Method*.

THE DIVISION OF LABOUR

Durkheim does not present a very elaborate theory of social change in *The Division of Labour*. The basis for the development from mechanical to organic solidarity is mainly a matter of population growth, of social density. In segmented, tribal societies, clans live at a distance from each other and do not necessarily come into much contact; as they grow in numbers and contact between them becomes easier, higher levels of social interaction give rise to competition and conflict for resources. This in turn provides the basis for the differentiation of functions which is the organic division of labour. The development begins with the settlement of nomadic groups into agricultural communities, creating centres of population which can then grow by attracting others to a more settled existence. This leads on to the development of the towns. It is wrong to associate urban growth with decline and decadence; in fact, it is a product of societies of the higher type—France, for example, was never an agricultural society in its pure type. Durkheim predicts, rightly, that the process of urban growth will continue, and Anthony Giddens (1981) argues that the city is now the dominant form of life, so that even comparatively remote country areas are under its sway.

Finally, the improvement of transport and communication brings the settlements closer together.

Darwin's theory placed a lot of emphasis on random variations which might not survive in the struggle for life; Durkheim chooses the struggle for survival as an important impetus for social development, emerging from the competition for scarce resources. The more alike these social groupings are, the fiercer the conflict. On the other hand, if the neighbouring societies belong to different types with different needs, the necessity for conflict abates—this is as true for humans as it is for plants and animals. Within societies, particularly with an urban environment:

different occupations can coexist within being forced into a position where they harm one another, for they are pursuing different objectives. The soldier seeks military glory, the priest moral authority, the statesman power, the industrialist wealth, the scientist professional fame. Each one of these can therefore reach his goal without preventing others from reaching theirs. This is the case even where the functions are less remote from one another. The medical eye specialist does not compete with the one who cares for the mentally ill, the shoe maker does not compete with the hatter, the mason with the cabinet maker, the physician with the chemist etc. As they perform different services they can perform them in harmony.   (Durkheim 1893/1984: 209–10)

Where conflict does result, the loser can deal with it only by going off and doing something else and hence the division of labour progresses. We have seen that, as this process develops, organic solidarity becomes the dominant form of social cohesion and the *conscience collective* both changes in importance—it becomes less important—and moves towards a more individualistic base. The material basis for the increasing division of labour, the growth in population and density, is aided by what Durkheim calls 'secondary factors', what Marxists would refer to as ideological factors, and Weberians perhaps refer to as value choices.

The pressure towards individuation and the division of labour is in fact countered by the strength of the *conscience collective*; for the division of labour to take place and for the external pressure to have its effect, the individual must be free to move in whatever direction is appropriate. The first secondary factor is the autonomy of the individual. On the face of it, this seems to be a tautology: in order for the individual to gain autonomy, the individual must possess autonomy. Durkheim draws on the biological analogy, talking about 'the law of the independence of anatomical elements'. By this I take him to mean that, for example, the hearts and the lungs and the liver do not merge into each other but remain identifiably separate, each carrying out its specific function for the body. In organisms this independence is a primative fact—it just *is*; there never was a stage where hearts, lung, and liver were merged. In societies, it has to be achieved.

As societies grow larger, the experiences of its members begin to vary. The *conscience collective*, if it is going to symbolize all the experiences of all the members of society, must become more inclusive—as Durkheim puts it, 'rising above' local variations and therefore becoming more abstract. This is seen most clearly in the way in which divinity is abstracted from specific objects in particular places to become more and more abstract, until eventually we reach notions of 'the one', God, or Allah who is no longer anywhere specific in this world. The more abstract our symbols become, the more rational they become—universality and rationality necessarily imply each other. And the more universal the *conscience collective* becomes, the more the individual variations it can allow.

There are other factors at work in all this. It takes a long time for the *conscience collective* to change, not least because it comes to us with all the weight of the past behind it. This is especially powerful where segmented societies exist—if I can only live and work in my own particular family, or geographical area, then the power which the group has over me is very strong; when this type of society begins to break down, so that I can move from group to group and area to area, the power of the dead generations fades. I move away from my father, and my father's generation, who taught me their ways, and he cannot keep his power over me on a day-to-day basis. I use the word father deliberately as we are dealing with patriarchal societies, but in modern societies the same goes for the relationship between mother and daughter. With the growth of towns and then large cities, the power of the older generation reaches its lowest point.

It is easy to see the way in which we can be more free in large towns and cities. We become anonymous and can carry on our various sexual, intellectual, and work activities without our families and neighbours knowing anything about them. This also sets up a nostalgia and a conflict—a desire for a return to community life and family values. If Durkheim shows anything, it is that societies and individuals have to face these choices, and, in so far as they have any power over events, make decisions about them.

Mechanical causes ensure the domination of the individual by the collective. Segmentary society exercises a tight grip over its members, limiting their horizons and tying them into tradition; but the same mechanical causes begin to enable the individual to begin to gain some independence. This is part of Durkheim's ongoing argument against the utilitarians—the division of labour does not occur because it is useful (which it is) or because it makes people happy (which it might do) but because it is the natural result of the growth of population and consequent decline of segmented societies. It is the social result of a social process. Professional societies and classes develop to fill the space left by the disappearance of segments (the clan groupings), but their regulations do not restrict the individual in the same way. First they limit only professional life—I might have a code of ethics to follow at work, but at home I can do what I like, within reason of course. The new rules never attain the far-ranging authority of the original *conscience collective* and the same general process of abstraction goes on within the professional groups.

Durkheim goes on to argue that the division of labour is produced by organic and psychological as well as social factors. For example, we each possess at birth natural talents and aptitudes which push us in one direction or another. In very simple societies heredity seems to play no role at all, but with some development it becomes more important. But the power of heredity lessens as the division of labour grows and new modes of activity appear. The things we inherit are static—for example, we inherit our racial characteristics but it is an extraordinarily long time since any new races have arisen; simple and general psychological states may be passed on, but not complex states and specific abilities which are highly individual. The division of labour produces precisely such specific skills, and the place of society, of socialization, becomes much more important than heredity, as do the specific talents of the individual. As we saw in the discussion of the abnormal forms of the division of labour, there is then a question of whether a society can enable individuals to realize these talents.

Perhaps the most interesting feature of the account of social change in *The Division of Labour* is that it is almost a materialist account—it is the material growth of the population and the increased production which comes with settled agricultural communities which pushes the process forward, not via class struggle, as it does in Marxist theories of history, but directly through increasing competition and complexity. This is worth remarking because Durkheim is so often thought of as the theorist of social cohesion through shared norms and ideas. Yet here he is producing an explanation which would differ from but not be foreign to Marxism, as we have seen in Engels's account of the origins of the family. The point to be taken from this—and it is well worth repeating—is that, although the thinkers we are studying are different from each other, what they offer is less a matter of mutually exclusive alternatives than differences of emphasis.

Having said this, it is also true that, as his work progressed, Durkheim was increasingly concerned with the processes by which and forms in which human beings symbolize their lives; nevertheless it must be remembered that they have material lives and an experience of the material world which have to be symbolized. These symbolic systems come to mediate the effect of changes in the external environment. Kenneth Thompson (1982: 97) argues that this ambiguity in his work, the failure to distinguish properly between what Gouldner (1958) calls social structure and cultural patterns of moral beliefs, is responsible for contradictory labels being attached to his position; I would argue that this ambiguity is one of Durkheim's strengths: he raises problems about the relationship which clearly need to be thought about and both the older Marxist crude materialist position and the newer postmodern crude idealist position manage to avoid thinking about such things.

SOCIAL SPECIES

The other work in which Durkheim elaborates his evolutionary theory is *The Rules of Sociological Method*. We saw earlier that for Durkheim it was important to arrive at a classification of social types. He argued that this classification should come through a study of the way in which the different parts of society are bound together:

We know that societies are composed of various parts in combination. Since the nature of the aggregate depends necessarily on the nature and number of the component elements and their mode of combination, these characteristics are evidently what we must take as our basis. (Durkheim 1895/1964: 81–2)

Most conceptions of evolution, strong or weak, see social development as moving from the simple to the complex, and a problem is always the definition of the simple society—what we think of as simple societies have a habit of turning out to be sufficiently complex to be quite different from each other. This was one of Durkheim's criticisms of Herbert Spencer, the British sociologist who is perhaps the major evolutionary sociologist of the nineteenth century. Just to talk about 'simple' societies lumped together very different types of society.

Durkheim's definition of a simple society was one that showed no previous sign of segmentation—an absence of parts: the 'horde'—'the protoplasm of the social realm and consequently, the natural basis of classification' (ibid. 83). Whether such types for society ever existed is, for Durkheim, not very important; what is important is that they provide a basis for classification. Here again there is a theme shared with Freud, who also worked with a notion of a primitive horde, a more or less undifferentiated group under the dominance of the strongest male, who had exclusive access to the women of the group. For Freud, differentiation begins when the younger males in the group overthrow the father and share the women out amongst themselves. Freud called his account a 'scientific myth': its purpose was as a sort of speculative hypothesis which enabled us to think about certain problems (the universality of the incest taboo) connected with human evolution which otherwise we would not be able to think about. Perhaps we can think about Durkheim's idea in the same way—in his case it enables us to develop a way of classifying societies as equivalent to animal species.

We can move from the simple horde to 'simple polysegmental societies'—societies with a number of segments or clans—and then on to polysegmental societies simply compounded—which, as I understand it, is a combination of simple polysegmental societies—and polysegmental societies doubly compounded, compounds of compounds. Durkheim here was holding fast to his biological analogy: animal species do not change very much even over very long periods, and therefore we cannot expect social species to change. If we try to classify societies by historical periodization, it would mean that species were changing all the time:

Since its origin, France has passed through very different forms of civilization; it begins by being agricultural, passed to craft industry and to small commerce then to manufacturing, and finally to large-scale industry. Now it is impossible to admit that the same collective individuality can change its species three or four times. A species must define itself by more constant characteristics. . . . The economic state, technological state etc., present phenomena too unstable and complex to furnish the basis of a classification. It is even very probable that the same industrial, scientific and artistic civilization can be found in societies whose heredity constitution is very different. Japan may in the future borrow our arts, our industry, even our political organization; it will not cease to belong to a different social species from France and Germany.   (ibid. 88)

It is a rather odd view, if you think about it, that France is still essentially the same as it was a number of centuries ago under a feudal regime, and changes such as industrialization are only surface changes. It is a view which one might find among the traditional conservative right: that there is an essential Frenchness or English-ness or, presumably, an American way of life that has existed for centuries and must be defended against dilution and domination by other nations. In British politics, such ideas could be found in the speeches of Enoch Powell and it sometimes emerges in opposition to British involvement in the European Union. For German historians of Durkheim's time and later it would be argued that the 'race' or 'national spirit' remained constant through these changes. The dangers of such positions must be self-evident. However Thompson (1982) does try to save something from these rather odd ideas, suggesting that a cultural inheritance can be inherited across such changes as industrialization.

In fact this is probably as good an example as you are likely to find of an analogy being pushed too far: types of society are *not* animal species, even if the organic analogy is sometimes useful. Durkheim did not try to classify actual societies in the way he proposed and it is difficult to see how useful it could be in this form—as Thompson points out, unless France, Japan, and Germany had surprisingly similar histories, Durkheim would be compelled to think of them as belonging to different species. On the other hand, Durkheim's ideas were developed much later in a different way by Parsons (1966). Instead of conceiving of change as coming from combinations of simple societies, he suggested that societies evolved through their own internal divisions and subdivisions, rather as a cell divides and subdivides (Craib 1992b). As Pearce (1989) points out, the earlier book, *The Division of Labour,* enables us to see modern societies in such a way. Once started along the road, the division of labour generates the division of labour.

If, then, we think about Durkheim as offering a theory of history, we do not get that far if we stick to *The Rules of Sociological Method. The Division of Labour* is more helpful and can take us to the comparatively rapid developments of late modernity.

Durkheim's conservatism and Durkheim's socialism

There has been a debate in sociology of recent decades about Durkheim's conservatism. Some of my critical comments have pointed to his conservatism—for example, his difficulty in understanding inbuilt social conflict, as opposed to social conflict which is a result of functional imbalance. Steven Lukes (1973) points to another conservative aspect of Durkheim's thought—his view that human nature is in need of limitation and moral guidance, although why this should necessarily be conservative is not clear. It is perhaps more of a commentary on political change over recent decades than an accurate interpretation of Durkheim. If human nature needs limitation and morality, then that is what it needs, and what makes it conservative or otherwise depends on the morality itself. That Lukes should see this as necessarily conservative seems to be a result of his writing at a time when long-established restrictions on individual morality, particularly sexual morality, had been lifted. What is clear twenty years later is that the values of the market economy seem to have eaten away at many forms of morality and it is the conservative parties which have supported the freeing of the market. To talk of morality now is no longer conservative. It is, as ever, a matter of finding a middle way between the individual freedom and the authority of social morality.

The changes of the last thirty years have also changed the way in which we can read another aspect of Durkheim's work. In *Suicide* Durkheim talks about the threat to society that comes from unrestrained individuality, less from egoism—which, as we saw, can be regarded as a form of social integration—than from anomie. If there are no limits to our ambitions, then we constantly try to outstrip ourselves, building up a constant nervous tension:

Since imagination is hungry for novelty, and ungoverned, it gropes at random. Setbacks necessarily increase with risk and thus crises multiply, just when they are becoming more destructive. Yet these dispositions are so inbred that society has grown to accept them and is accustomed to think them normal. It is everlastingly repeated that it is man's nature to be eternally dissatisfied, constantly to advance, without relief or rest, toward an indefinite goal. The longing for infinity is daily represented as a mark of moral distinction whereas it can only appear within unregulated consciences which elevate to a rule the lack of rule from which they suffer.　(Durkheim 1897/1952: 257)

This is as damning a psychological critique of modern societies as any, again not far from Christopher Lasch's conception of narcissism, against which Lasch (1980) poses not the professional group but more of a populist conception of a community of solid, honest people. John Horton (1990) calls anomie a utopian concept of the radical right, and it is easy to see how it could have seemed so when his article was first published, in 1964, but again, as with Steven Lukes' comments about Durkheim's conception of moral authority, such talk now does not seem necessarily to belong to the right.

For all four classical thinkers socialism is at the centre of the political agenda in the modern world. Although Durkheim's study *Socialism and Saint-Simon* was not published until 1928, it was based on lectures delivered in the mid-1890s. His approach to the subject was based on the sociology of knowledge, the way in which particular social conditions generate particular ideas; it is a pity that Durkheim never got as far as taking on Marx head-on, dealing only with the beginnings of socialism and the ideas of Saint-Simon, a French utopian socialist. Durkheim was never to match his own scientific sociology to Marx's scientific socialism.

Durkheim's definition of socialism, according to K. Thompson (1982: 156), made it an 'inevitable development in social evolution': We denote as socialist every doctrine which demands the connection of all economic functions, or of certain among them, which are at the present time diffuse, to the directing and conscious centres of society' (Durkheim 1962: 54). He writes 'the centre of society' rather than the state because he recognized Marx's hope that the state would vanish once a classless society was established. Durkheim distinguished this version of socialism from utopian versions—just as Engels (1967) had distinguished Marx's scientific socialism from the utopian socialists. For both, utopian ideas are individual inventions, not based on a scientific understanding of social development. But, of course, each has a different conception of social science. Durkheim dismissed what he called communist utopianism, which he saw as opposed to wealth *per se*, whereas he argued that the socialist opposition to private property, as expressed by Saint-Simon in France and Robert Owen in Britain, was based on the modern developments of social structures. For Marx and Engels, both Owen and Saint-Simon were utopians.

Durkheim suggested that there had been three reactions to industrialization at the beginning of the nineteenth century: the first was socialism; the second was an attempt to establish a quasi-religious basis for a new morality, and, finally, there was sociology itself as the new science of society. All three had their origins in the work of Saint-Simon and can still be distinguished in Comte. He argued that the time had come to separate them, and his concern was to protect the growth of a scientific sociology. His central criticism of socialism was its concentration upon economic arguments and answers when moral arguments and answers were also necessary, and he was of course critical of the way socialism claimed to be scientific, on a par with sociology when it was an ideology and a social movement. In this respect Durkheim thought that socialism had in fact contributed more to sociology than vice versa—it had stimulated argument and reflection and research, but it also made claims about areas which went well beyond research and beyond any claims that science could make:

The only attitude that science permits in the face of these problems is reservation and circumspection, and socialism can hardly maintain this without lying to itself. . . . Not even the strongest work—the most systematic, the richest in ideas—that this school has produced: Marx's *Capital*. What statistical data, what historical comparisons and studies would be indispensable to solve any one of the innumerable questions which are dealt with there . . . Socialism is not a science . . . it is a cry of grief, sometimes anger. (Durkheim 1958: 40–1)

Durkheim argues that the same goes for the opponents of socialism—*laissez-faire* economics makes equally vast but unsubstantiated claims. Socialism offers a cry of pain but not a diagnosis of the illness.

His own sympathies were to the left, a liberal socialism, and, although he was not especially active politically, he did show his sympathy with the Dreyfusards—those who opposed what would now be known as the French Establishment when Alfred Dreyfus, a Jewish army officer, was scapegoated for crimes committed by his superiors, and he did develop a number of political ideas from his analysis of modernity. For example, he argued that territorial constituencies for elections were a throwback to the days of mechanical solidarity and that the 'natural' constituencies should be functional groups—especially the professional groups. We have seen earlier that Durkheim saw the state as protecting the individual against such groups, but these groups would also protect the individual against oppression by the state, and the state against individualist egoism. J. E. S. Hayward (1990) called this a 'reformist syndicalism'—a system of self-government by groups of workers. Industries and factories and the professions would be run by those who work in them (rather than by the state, as happened with the state socialist societies of eastern Europe), and the state, in so far as it existed, would be governed by the representatives of these groups. However, Durkheim saw this developing through a process of evolution rather than violent revolution—the tendency with which the name is most usually associated. Each group would determine wages and working conditions, pensions and social benefits—modern industrial society was too large and complex for all this to be determined by one central power.

The conservative interpretation of Durkheim is based on his insistence on the need for moral control, as a restriction on the individual, yet in the essay 'Individualism and the Intellectuals' (Durkheim 1898/1990) we find an elaboration of the liberal principles behind the *Dreyfusard* campaign, which he supported. He points out that the intellectuals' support of Dreyfus (particularly the novelist Émile Zola, who produced the famous letter *J'accuse*) had been met by the government and the military with a campaign against individualism. He makes the point that he would agree with the condemnation of egotistical individualism—the sort of self-interest that is seen as a basic motivation by the utilitarians to whom Durkheim was so consistently opposed: 'it is only too clear that all social life would be impossible if there did not exist interests superior to the interests of individuals' (Durkheim 1898/1990: 172).

There is, however, another sort of individualism which Durkheim puts at the centre of European philosophy and politics which has its roots in the work of Kant and Rousseau. Beginning with Kant's moral philosophy, this alternative sees in personal motives the 'very source of evil'. The good is universal, or part of the general will. Moral action involves looking at what we have in common with our fellow human beings. This, in turn, rests on the assumption that it is in relation to the human person that we can distinguish good and evil; the human person is in this sense sacred:

[it] is conceived as being invested with that mysterious property which creates an empty space around holy objects, which keeps them away from profane contacts and which draws them away from ordinary life. And it is exactly this feature which induces the respect of which it is the object. Whoever makes an attempt on a man's life, on a man's liberty, on a man's honour inspires us with a feeling of horror, in every way analogous to that which the believer experiences when he sees his idol profaned. Such a morality is therefore not simply a hygienic discipline or a wise principle of economy. It is a religion of which man is, at the same time, both believer and God.   (ibid. 173)

This religion is an individualistic religion and the philosophers who have developed these ideas are also aware of the rights of the collectivity. This type of individualism involves 'the glorification not of the self but of the individual in general'. It leads on to ideals such as the autonomy of reason and freedom of thought, and here, according to Durkheim, we come across the major conservative objection to individualism: if people think freely and make up their own minds, what is to stop anarchy? This is a reaction not unknown in our own times, particularly when it is a matter of sexual morality. Durkheim's response is that freedom of thought actually carries with it the recognition of the expertise of others: I might at first glance decide that the earth is flat, but if geographers who have greater knowledge of these things tell me it is round, I am, within reason, willing to accept that. But there are also issues which concern people in general which are not matters for experts alone but upon which everyone can express an opinion and this includes the most important political issues. If a doctor diagnoses cancer, I must bow to his opinion; if he argues that everybody with cancer should be painlessly killed, I have something to say about it. The intellectuals who protested against Dreyfus's conviction were not claiming special expertise but were commenting on a matter of common concern. Conservative arguments that what is needed is a return to traditional religion are pointless—the social conditions that produced traditional religion are no longer in existence. The new religion is the religion of humanity.

Giddens (1990a) points out that Durkheim saw the state as having a cognitive as much as an active role in the development of this new way of thinking. It should elaborate on the content of the modern *conscience collective*, and define and implement the principles of moral individualism. It is only through membership of a collective and through recognizing a moral authority that the individual can actually realize him- or herself. Again we find here a parallel with Freud's psychoanalysis where it is only through the discipline imposed by the ego and superego that creativity becomes possible.

Giddens goes on to argue that Durkheim never really tackled the problem of the relationship between sociology and politics; he had a personal disdain for political squabbles, and his concern with the scientific status of sociology left sociology itself aloof from politics. But it also meant that his analytic and prescriptive work tended to blur into each other, since he had no conceptual tools to separate them. The distinction between the normal and the pathological is both analytic and descriptive at the same time. It is certainly true that Durkheim envisaged a classless society, but it would not be classless in Marx's terms; for Durkheim inheritance was the problem, for Marx it was ownership. Nevertheless it is arguable that Durkheim also had what Pearce (1989) calls a radical socialist vision. He points to Durkheim's critique of *laissez-faire* economics in *Professional Ethics and Civil Morals* (1957). Whereas economists argue that the state has no productive function, and in effect only the negative function of protecting individual liberty, Durkheim argues that the state had a positive function. It is, in Pearce's words, 'socially productive'. Pearce uses the following quotation from Durkheim to illustrate that vision. In a complex society, the state must govern economic transactions:

by rules that are more just; it is not simply that everyone should have more access to rich supplies of food and drink. Rather it is that each one should be treated as he deserves, each be freed from an unjust and humiliating tutelage, and that, in holding to his fellows and his group, a man should not sacrifice his individuality. And the agency on which this special responsibility lies is the State. So the State does not inevitably become either simply a spectator of social life (as the economists would have it), in which it intervenes only in a negative way, or (as the socialists would have it) simply a cog in the economic machine. It is above all, supremely the organ of moral discipline.   (ibid. 72)

The basis of Pearce's argument is that if we shed some of Durkheim's assumptions, we can find a picture of a feasible democratic socialist society. He argues that a class society inhibits the development of a truly organic solidarity and Marxism can identify a number of economic and social structural factors that interfere with the development that Durkheim foresaw or desired. At the same time Durkheim can contribute new dimensions to Marxism, eventually replacing a Marxist utopianism with a more realistic sense of what is possible.

Durkheim held what would today be considered some rather conservative ideas about marriage and sexuality, but he does raise some interesting issues. In *Suicide* he points out that, where rules governing divorce are strict there are higher rates of suicide amongst women, where they are easier (conjugal anomie) there is a higher rate amongst men, and generally suicide rates vary directly with divorce. This is a form of anomic suicide.

In the same discussion, he argues that the function of marriage is not simply to control physical desires; in humans the sexual urge has become complicated by moral and aesthetic feelings and social regulation thus becomes necessary— Durkheim is on firm ground here and is explaining an often forgotten reason why we need a sociology of sexuality:

just because these various inclinations . . . do not directly depend upon organic necessities, social regulation becomes necessary. They must be restrained by society since the organism has no means of restraining them. This is the function of marriage. It completely regulates the life of passion, and monogamic marriage more strictly than any other. For by forcing a man to attach himself forever to the same woman it assigns a strictly definite object the need for love, and closes the horizon.   (Durkheim 1897/1952: 270)

Thus it is desire, not the sexual drive itself, which has to be restrained (and I think anyone who has fallen in love has some intimation that the desire for love can be powerful, even addictive). And, if the desire is not controlled, then ambitions rocket and the impact of disappointment grows correspondingly. According to Durkheim, this is true even for the 'humdrum existence of the ordinary bachelor':

New hopes constantly awake only to be deceived, leaving a trail of weariness and disillusionment behind them. How can desire, then, become fixed, being uncertain that it can retain what it attracts; for the anomie is twofold. Just as the person makes no definitive gift of himself, he has definitive title to nothing. The uncertainty of the future plus his own indeterminateness therefore condemns him to constant change. The result of it all is a state of disturbance, agitation and discontent which inevitably increases the possibilities of suicide.   (ibid. 271)

Now for the crunch: women have less need for such regulation because their mental life is less developed; they are more tied to and led by bodily needs and instincts, and have only to follow these to achieve 'calmness and peace'. Marriage for the woman closes off realistic hopes and narrows her horizons, whereas she is protected by divorce—it is a relief for her. One might think it is a relief for her for other reasons that those suggested by Durkheim, but that is for the reader to decide. At any rate, marriage cannot be simultaneously agreeable 'to two persons, one of whom is almost entirely a product of society, while the other has remained to a far greater extent the product of nature' (ibid. 385). But, according to Durkheim, we can imagine a position where women can play a more important social role—although, of course, it would never equal that of men. Women would be given their own specific role in the social division of labour—perhaps, for example, taking a more active role in the aesthetic sphere. Many contemporary readers will, I suspect, read that, with some justification, as saying the women will come to do what we would call 'women's work' and go on to talk about discrimination on the labour market.

But it is worth pointing out that even here there is a radical edge to Durkheim, and, if we allow him to be a (male) child of his time, it is possible to take his ideas as leading somewhere else. He *is* talking about the possibility of increased equality in marriage, even if he does not go as far as talking of a marriage between equals. The course of the division of labour has certainly taken women closer to equality than at Durkheim's time, but the result has been the opposite of stabilizing marriage, which as an institution seems to have been steadily weakened not only by increasingly high divorce rates but by the reluctance of couples to marry in the first place. I think this says something important about Durkheim's political naïvity—at least it is possible to call it naïvity with hindsight. The continued development of the division of labour has not led to the 'religion of humanity' that he thought would be at the centre of the modern *conscience collective*, but to something closer to the unlimited egoism that he feared. The capitalist market which has been the main agent of individualization (as opposed to an organically developing division of labour) reduces people to an abstract individuality and leaves them face to face less with a society than with a global system which has no *conscience collective*.

Conclusion

I want now to try to sum up some of the points I have made about Durkheim in the book as a whole as well as in this chapter. My first point is that Durkheim's value lies most clearly in the fact that, first, he is the theorist of *society* as something which exists over and above individuals, and, secondly, he is the theorist of *social cohesion*, of the way in which a society holds together through shared logics, shared symbolic systems, and shared norms and values. Sometimes he tends towards identifying *society* with the *conscience collective*, when in fact within his framework it would be more accurate to see society as comprising both the *conscience collective* and the division labour and the group relations produced by the division of labour. Another way of putting this in terms of the dualisms I set out at the beginning is that Durkheim tends to merge social cohesion with structural cohesion, rather than examine the possibility that, as the division of labour develops, there might be a conflict, even a contradiction, between the two—that the division of labour might undermine the *conscience collective*.

Yet, even though this might be happening, it is still happening within the framework of something we call society—even if we have to think of that society as existing on a global rather than a national or regional level. It is a society in which individuals are subjected less to collective ideas and more to structural processes. However, the *conscience collective* remains. First, it remains on the deeper level that I discussed earlier—the level of the logical forms (our language, the way in which we conceive of causality, time, and space) are imposed upon us from without, and without them there would be no possibility of communication. Indeed the standardization and universalization of time and space mean that, at this level, we *are* effectively talking about a global *conscience collective*. However, at the levels of norms and values we seem to be looking at a world of infinite variety, a world where the notion of value itself is often challenged, and this provides a focus for political arguments throughout western Europe and North America. We can witness our modern version of the very arguments that Durkheim was discussing in his justification of the Dreyfusard position and his justification of individualism. On the one hand, we find demands for a return to traditional values, against which the forces of chaos and anarchy are ranged, and, on the other, we find demands for individual liberty, minority rights, sexual equality (which perhaps combines both of the foregoing), and a multicultural pluralism.

And again, rather as Durkheim constructed an argument in favour of the *value* of the individual as the centre of the modern *conscience collective*, so we can find arguments in favour of a modern ethic of tolerance. Indeed, some forms of postmodernism seem to elevate tolerance almost to the point of chaos, but that is another matter; certainly this aspect of postmodernism could be regarded as pointing perhaps to a postmodern *conscience collective* of as wide a variety of meanings, ethics, and narratives as possible. From this point of view, it is less the individual *per se* that should be valued, less a religion of humanity, than the multiplicity of internal narratives—not so much the 'me' but the many 'mes' that I am in different situations (see Gergen 1991).

A second alternative focus for the centre of the modern *conscience collective*, arrived at in a very different way, is Habermas's notion of a 'procedural ethics'. Put simply—not to say crudely—the central proposition is that it is not so much the substantive content of a morality that matters; that will vary from culture to culture and even sub-culture to subsubculture; rather it is the way in which decisions about morality are arrived at; our nature as human beings involves us each in rationality and we can set up a social ideal in which we all, by virtue of our rational capacity, participate in decision-making. In other words, it is the democratic nature of decision-making that matters rather than the decision itself. Now, put this simply, there are all sorts of problems with the idea, but I think the basic idea is clear. The 'sacred' element becomes neither individualism, nor tolerance or variety as such, but the democratic process in which everybody is involved in the decisions which affect them.

The important point is that it seems that we cannot think about social life without referring to or implying or arguing for some central 'sacred' value or set of values which comprise a *conscience collective*; even if we are attacking the very idea of a *conscience collective* we are employing some set of values which must stand in its place—just as modern individualism opposing traditional religious forms can be seen as a religion of individualism. It is also the case that these putative contents of the *conscience collective* become more and more abstract— the sort of procedural ethic proposed by Habermas would include cultures with very different moral systems and the movement from content to form is possibly as abstract as one can become where morality is concerned.

Paradoxically, although Durkheim is the theorist of society, he is the only one to talk in any depth about individualism and the difficulties of a society based on individualism. In modern societies the individual is neither a simple product of his or her society nor one of signifying systems—rather he or she is the *user* of signifying systems, of the norms and beliefs of the society, who can argue and judge, accept or reject, what he or she is offered. Durkheim warns us of the importance of preserving the space for these judgements through the setting of moral boundaries, limiting the powers of groups, and encouraging the formation of responsible associations. He offers a conception of civil society which limits both the power of the state and egoism. It seems to me arguable that it is precisely this level of social organization which has diminished in importance with the development of market capitalism—opening the door to the sort of narcissistic and egoistic individualism that contemporary society seems to encourage. He speaks for the middle ground between the free-market individualism of the New Right and the rigid state control of the Old Left. And he leaves us with a greater understanding of the continual and unavoidable dilemma between individual freedom, and on the one hand, and social control, on the other.

It is when we come to look at the modernity/capitalism—socialism dualism that we begin to find the limitation of Durkheim's thought and aspects of what we might regard as a structural determinism. Individual freedom and the development of occupational groups are both the result of the division of labour; they do not themselves bring about any sort of change. There is not a theory of individual or collective action in Durkheim, even though he is not a sociological determinist. This represents a gap, a sort of silence—he does not have much to say about political action, and in particular about class and class conflict. Yet, if we want to explain why the division of labor has not developed in the way that Durkheim thought it would, it is to the theory of capitalism that we must turn; to the development of the free market and of state power. We can perhaps read Durkheim as offering an 'acceptable face' of modernity—a form of socialism that is neither centralized nor simply a matter of limited controls on the free market.

Returning now to the theory of history in the wider sense with which I started this chapter, we can see that, once society develops away from the state of mechanical solidarity, it is not simply a matter of developments in the division of labour but also developments of ownership and the appearance of class divisions which complicate matters. The evolutionary conception of social development is too simple, yet, as we shall see when we turn to Marx, it is not irrelevant to understanding the contemporary world. If Durkheim has difficulty in grasping the importance of the effects of capitalism, then perhaps Marx has difficulty grasping the effects of modernity *per se*.

We can now move to summarizing the different positions around the secondary dualism of modernity and capitalism which I begin in Box 11.1.

Box 11.1. Durkheim on modernity and capitalism/socialism

MODERNITY	CAPITALISM/SOCIALISM
Durkheim: a movement towards a balanced society of occupational groups held together by the state and a new humanist 'religion' which emphasized the value of the individual.	**Durkheim:** Durkheim's concept of socialism was based on his conception of the development of modernity; although problems arise in the abnormal forms of the division of labour, these would be ironed out in continued historical development. He does not seem to see capitalism as a specific form of modern society responsible for either its problems or its benefits.

Further reading

From Durkheim's own work, see *The Division of Labour in Society* (1893/1984), book 1, chapters 5 and 6; book 2, and book 3, for his account of the development of the division of labour and its abnormal forms in modern society; see also *The Rules of Sociological Method* (1895/1964), chapter 4. For his discussion of socialism, see his *Socialism and Saint-Simon* (1928/1959). His discussion of Dreyfus and individualism can be found in Volume IV of *Emile Durkheim: Critical Assessments*, edited by Peter Hamilton (1990), 62–73.

For more modern discussions of Durkheim's politics, see Steven Lukes, *Emile Durkheim* (1973)—check the index references. Zeitlin, *Ideology and the Development of Sociological Theory* (1968), damns Durkheim for his conservatism, but more recently Frank Pearce, *The Radical Durkheim* (1989), gives a very different point of view. More recent discussions of Durkheim include M. S. Gladis, *A Communitarian Defence of Liberalism* (1992), and W. F. Pickering and H. Martins, *Debating Durkheim* (1994).

12 | Marx and the meaning of history

Introduction

Marx's conception of history; Marx and Hegel; dialectical materialism and historical inevitability.

Historical laws and laws of history

Historical laws; Marx's originality; Marx's suggestions as explanation sketches.

Types of society/modes of production

Primitive communism: possible paths of social development starting from the priority of the community over the individual; forms of distributing the surplus; Marx's theoretical ordering of levels of development in terms of the development of individuality. *The Asiatic mode of production*: dominance of communal property and the despot; important role of the state and religion. *The Germanic mode of production*: the inevitable production of traditional relations. *The ancient mode of production*: dominated by the city; development of individual proprietorship; the emergence of the state; transformation brought about by the reproduction of the system. *Feudalism and the development of capitalism*: the ancient and the feudal modes; the town/country division and the division of labour; the development of the towns—the craft guilds—the merchant class—the bourgeoisie; machine production; the money economy; international markets. *Evolution from feudalism to capitalism*: a theoretical understanding of the development; comparison with Durkheim. *The complexities of class analysis of history*: the English Civil War as an example.

Theory and history

Theoretical and empirical distinctions: modern elaborations of the concept of mode of production. *Contemporary notions of evolution*: the nature of historical progress; open-ended conceptions of evolution.

The dynamics of capitalism

The tendency of the rate of profit to fall: living and dead labour and the increasing importance of the latter; countervailing tendencies; the increasing rate of technological change; the expansionist dynamic of capitalism. *Changes at other levels: transformations of the crisis*: Habermas on the evolution of modern capitalism; economic crisis—rationality crisis—legitimation crisis—motivation crisis.

Communism

The importance of the French Revolution; the proletariat as a revolutionary class; violence and revolution; the concept of overdetermination; the state and revolution; earlier and later phases of communism; the importance of utopian ideas; comparison with reality.

Conclusion

Introduction

If Durkheim's conception of history amounts to a smooth evolutionary process from mechanical to organic solidarity, then Marx's conception, whilst evolutionary in the sense of movement from one stage to another, also involves a conception of conflict and revolutionary transformation, at least at the later stages. Perhaps the most useful interpretation of Marx is as offering a conception of history moving on a number of different levels, not necessarily in conjunction with each other. This is not the case if one starts and ends with Marx the economic determinist, but if we allow his theory to open up a little, a number of interesting possibilities arise.

The term 'history' has a particular importance for Marxism both analytically—it is an important concept—and motivationally—several generations of Marxists have seen themselves as on the side of history, even as agents of a history which, in the none-too-pleasant jargon of some Marxist groups, possesses a dustbin into which their opponents will be thrown. Some forms of Marxism have worked with an overarching theory of history developing according to a particular logic—an inheritance from Hegel. The Marxist 'science of history', *dialectical materialism*, is Marx's inversion of Hegel's conception of history, which he sees as a moving force not of ideas but of material practices—the production of goods.

Engels (1940) attempted to formulate universal laws of the dialectic, arguing that everything in society and nature develops in the same way, through a process of conflicting opposites. As Ted Benton (1977) points out in an intelligent discussion, this claim is rather too vast for comfort. It is not as if natural scientists have themselves developed the idea of the dialectic or its laws out of their work; rather Engels has reinterpreted their results and theories and imposed a dialectical logic upon them. There are two classic examples of eminent men making fools of themselves by insisting that there is a dialectic of nature: the first is Hegel himself, who used the dialectic to predict that there would be a star in a certain place where none was ever found; the second was more serious: in the 1930s the Russian biologist Lysenko developed a 'dialectical method' of growing wheat which led to disastrous crop failures.

However, when we come to human thought and human action, it is perhaps a different matter and we can talk about a dialectical logic. But human action, at least when we think about history, is caught up with the natural world in a complex way, so again even when we talk about history, things are not so simple as we would like them to be. Just how complex they are can be discovered through a brief perusal of Sartre's *Critique of Dialectical Reason*—perhaps *the* major attempt to establish a foundation for a non-determinist dialectical thought and a dialectical philosophy of history.

The simplified version of the dialectic of history—that history progresses through the conflict between opposing forces—works best for capitalism. The growth of the capitalist system itself produces the proletariat, the opposing force which will eventually destroy it and establish a socialist system. But the problem of how capitalism, for example, grows out of the feudal system that preceded it is another matter—it is not the case that it emerges through some central contradiction, nor is it the case that the class conflict between peasants and landlords somehow produces capitalism. I don't think that there is anybody who would propose such an overarching theory of history these days—certainly not a Marxist theory, although occasionally people will play about with Hegelian ideas: Francis Fukuyama (1992), for example, goes back to Hegel to argue that history has come to an end with modern liberalism.

Before outlining a more modest version of Marxist evolutionary theory, I want to look in a little more detail, first, at the notion of historical laws and laws of history, and, secondly, at the variety of modes of production that we can find discussed in the work of Marx and Engels and the work of later Marxists. I will answer negatively the question of whether we can really find a tenable overall theory of history in them. However, I shall argue that, when we get to the modern world, it is another matter—we can find a number of complex but none the less clear ideas about the way in which modern society is developing. I will then go on to talk about Marx's conception of socialism and communism.

Historical laws and laws of history

Nicholas Lobkowicz (1978) draws a number of very useful distinctions around the ideas that are often found in Marx or Marxist writings about 'historical laws' or 'laws of history'. Whilst we might think of laws of nature as eternal, unchanging or at least lasting for very long periods—so that, for example, it is likely to be a long time before the laws of gravity cease to apply—this is not quite the way in which we can think of laws which might apply to social life. Lobkowicz comes to the following conclusions about historical laws. I have broken down the quotation into separate propositions. My explanatory comments are in square brackets. By 'historical laws' Marxists mean:

- first of all that specific empirical social laws are historically limited. [For example, a law might apply to capitalist societies only during certain periods of its development.]
- secondly that general social laws which constitute the framework of social science are historically varying. [i.e. general laws vary in the way in which they work from historical period to historical period—so that, if the law is that the economic level of society is determinant in the last instance, the way it is determinant varies from type of society to type of society—see below, for example, for the difference between feudalism and capitalism.]
- thirdly that some historically limited social laws are tendential. [Under capitalist conditions, the law of the falling rate of profit describes a tendency which can, in certain circumstances, be reversed.]
- fourthly that laws that are neither historically limited nor historically varying nor tendential are of no use in social science. [This has resonances of Weber's argument that general laws are not much use—the only sort of laws that would fall into this fourth category would be along the lines of] 'All societies are made up of people, animals and objects'.   (Lobkowicz 1978: 120)

Lobkowicz points out that various thinkers have suggested that there are laws of history, but only in Marxism do we find the idea of *historical* laws of history. He makes the important point that Marx made very limited claims for his laws—that, for example, when he talked about 'historical inevitability' he is only talking about western Europe. At another time:

in a letter to a Russian newspaper, written in 1877 and first published in Russia in 1886, he explicitly says that he did not intend to advance 'historic-philosophic theory of the general course of development every people is fated to tread' but only the 'inexorable laws' of the capitalist system. And he adds: 'Events strikingly analogous but taking place in different historical surroundings lead to totally different results. By studying each of these developments by itself and then comparing them one can find the clue to the phenomenon, but one will never arrive there by using as one's master key a general historico-philosophical theory, the supreme virtue of which consists in being supra-historical'.   (ibid. 122)

These reservations should be borne in mind whenever you come across claims about Marxist determinism and historical inevitability. As Lobkowicz goes on to argue, there is a sense here in which Marx's claims can be empirically tested and the fact that his predictions have not come true is not so much because the notion of a historical law is misguided *per se* but because this aspect of Marxism produces what the positivist philosopher Carl Hempel calls 'explanation sketches'—outlines of explanations which require filling in. Lobkowicz continues:

Hempel puts great emphasis upon the distinction between explanation sketches, on the one hand, and what he calls psuedo-explanations, on the other. While a scientifically

acceptable explanation sketch is incomplete in that it needs to be filled out by more specific statements but at the same time clearly points in the direction where these statements are to be found, a psuedo-explanation subsumes the phenomena under some
general idea which in principle is not amenable to empirical test and therefore cannot
indicate in which direction concrete research should turn. It has often been suggested
that the Marxist-historicist theory of society is such a psuedo-explanation rather than an
explanation proper. I do not believe that this is the case. Concrete research may not, and
in fact did not, corroborate many of the laws by which Marx was trying to explain capitalist development; but the fact that research is at all relevant to the Marxist theory indicates that the latter in not a psuedo-question.   (ibid. 230)

Lobkowicz goes on to suggest that the reason for maintaining Marx's developmental theory, despite the fact that his predictions have not come true, is that
there is no serious alternative; and I have pointed out elsewhere (Craib 1992*a*)
that attempts such as Giddens's to suggest a non-evolutionary theory of the
development of capitalism is remarkably similar to Marx's own account.

Lobkowicz's argument is a more conventional and orthodox philosophical
version of Lukacs's Hegelian argument that the fact that Marx's predictions
were wrong does not disprove his method—in the same way, perhaps, that a
wrong weather forecast does not undermine either the attempt to forecast the
weather or necessarily the means used to produce that particular forecast;
rather like weather forecasting, social prediction is a matter of informed hit-
and-miss.

Types of society/modes of production

Marx refers to a number of different types of society. A type of society is not
quite a mode of production: the latter refers to relationships of ownership and
control of productive goods, whereas a society includes the various classes and
institutional forms which develop on the basis of these relationships. The relationships to the means of production form the base, the society includes both
base and superstructure.

Primitive communism

It would be wrong to see the pre-capitalist formations as a chain in which each
develops out of the other; rather Marx suggests a number of different ways in
which societies can change from primitive communism, and it is clear that he
does not think that all changes constitute progress. Rather like Durkheim, Marx
sees history as beginning with the horde, or the tribal group, the stage of primitive communism. The individual is only an individual and only possesses prop-

erty by virtue of his or her membership of the community—the community is the precondition of everything.

We have already seen Engels's account of the development from primitive communism. One of the problems with his account is that there are always non-labourers, young children, the old, and the sick, so it would be wrong to say that there is no surplus produced. In a book which in many ways represents the worst type of Marxist a priori argument (i.e. forcing the world into a general schema), but which nevertheless does make some useful points, Barry Hindess and Paul Hirst (1975) suggest that primitive communism can be seen as a mode of production with only two levels: the economic and the ideological (where decisions about distribution are made). Drawing on the work of the Marxist anthropologist Claude Meillasoux (1972), they suggest a distinction between those societies—mainly hunting societies—which employ a process of simple redistribution through a network of relations which are temporary, which might last only long enough for the immediate distribution of the kill, and societies with a more complex redistribution system. Complex redistribution involves a permanent network of relationships and this tends to happen in agricultural societies. Kinship units become more important here, and, with the importance of kinship units, so marriage rules have to be developed. It is very dubious whether there is a direct line from this sort of development to capitalism; rather it is a description after the event of a process of social change which might lead to the development of class societies.

We can find in Marx mention of other modes of production which do not seem to follow each other either theoretically or in reality. The ancient mode of production and the Asiatic mode of production are the best known, although he also talks about a Germanic mode of production (which is not confined to Germanic people) and he mentions in passing a Slavic mode. Then we come to feudalism and the transition to capitalism. But perhaps here, before we move on from primitive communism, it is worth raising the possibility that we are not talking about one *world* history but about several histories, perhaps as many histories as there are different modes of production or types of society.

The analysis I am following here is broadly similar to that suggested by Eric Hobsbawm (1964) in his introduction to Marx's *Pre-Capitalist Economic Formations*. In the first place he points out that the different modes of production do not follow each other in chronological order, nor, with the exception of feudalism and capitalism, do they develop out of each other. On the other hand, Marx does talk about historical stages in the evolution of individuality—the division of labour in Durkheim's framework—which, for Marx, are stages in the evolution of private property. But again these are not chronological stages, they are analytic: by this he means that Marx did not see these stages as necessarily following each other in time. Rather there is a logical order to them which perhaps allows us to arrange societies separated, possibly radically separated, by time and space, in relation to each other.

After the general communal ownership of primitive communism we move to a more developed form of direct communal property (the oriental and perhaps Slavic mode of production) where there is still no development of class societies; at the second level there is communal property coexisting with class societies (the ancient and Germanic modes of production). The third level involves the growth of craft manufacture—the independent craftsman (it was at this stage usually men) who exercised personal control over the means of production: the spinner, for example, would own the loom; the blacksmith would own and control his anvil and hammer. Then finally there is class society proper, where we move from the appropriation of people—slaves—to the appropriation of labour as I described earlier. We can regard these as four paths from primitive communism, not all of which lead to capitalism, but all of which involve some change from simple communal property.

The Asiatic mode of production—oriental despotism

In the Asiatic mode of production, communal property is still dominant; there would be a number of small groups, family based, within the society, and Marx suggests that the inhabitants of these societies feel the power of the collective, which gives them their rights over their land, and they project this power into a single source—the despot from whom the land seems held in trust:

The despot here appears as the father of all the numerous lesser communities thus realising the common unity of all. It therefore follows that the surplus product . . . belongs to this highest unity. Oriental despotism, therefore, appears to lead to a legal absence of property. in fact, however, its foundation is tribal or common property . . .   (Marx 1964: 69–70)

Property is created through agriculture and manufacturing, both of which are carried on in small self-sufficient communities, containing within themselves 'all conditions of production and surplus production'—the surplus being handed over to the despot as a form of tribute and a form of celebration of the group's unity. Where large-scale irrigation systems are required for the continuation of agriculture, together with communication networks over long distances—particularly important in Asian societies—these are provided by the 'higher unity', the despotic government. There is, as yet, no clear division between town and country. There is little or no 'push' towards change in such systems. They remain the same until they are broken down from the outside by the expansion of capitalism.

There have been many debates about the existence of oriental despotism, both on empirical and theoretical grounds. Hindess and Hirst (1975) argue that the concept is incoherent, but that is a negative version of Hegel's claim about a star: instead of theoretically deriving a type of society which does not exist, they are arguing that theoretically such a society cannot exist when in fact it might do so. In either case the argument is not very helpful. More interesting is Karl Wittfogel's (1963) development of the notion. He offers a functional analysis of such societies where the despotism arises less from an alienating projection of communal power, the way that Marx describes it, than from the necessity of large-scale irrigation which only the state is able to undertake. This occurs only in very specific conditions—it is not simply a matter of too little water plus state water control. The society must be above the simpler forms of subsistence economy—there must be a surplus, outside the geographical areas where there is heavy rainfall, but without any significant development of private property.

Under these circumstances, only a bureaucratically organized state system can provide water and maintain the means by which it is provided—it is a managerial enterprise. The state maintains order through its control of the irrigation system—it can bring dissident communities into line by threatening not to maintain water supplies—as well as through a large standing army and a highly organized intelligence network. The ideological cement for such a system tends to be religious. Wittfogel set up a gradation of hydraulic societies according to the density of the population, and he was able to include in the category ancient Egypt and Mesopotamia, Rome and Byzantium, the Ottoman Empire, India and China, Muslim Spain, and others. Wittfogel was an early member of the Frankfurt School of Social Research—the group that in the late 1920s and early 1930s began to develop a Marxism which was critical of the Soviet Union. His contribution to this was to suggest that the Stalinist regime grew out of a preceding 'semi-Asiatic' regime—and there are certainly similarities between the pre-revolutionary Tsarist regime and aspects of oriental despotism. Anne Bailey (1981) suggests that post-Wittfogel research has tended towards the argument that the Asiatic mode of production and tribal societies are not as classless as once thought and they are also systems in which exploitation takes place—again, the general drift has been away from unilinear, fixed conceptions of evolution.

The Germanic mode of production

Marx does not say a lot about the Germanic mode of production, and even less about the Slavic mode. The former represents a slightly more developed form of property than, although of course it does not emerge from, the Asiatic mode. According to Hobsbawm, 'the "Germanic system" as such does not form a special socio-economic formation. It forms the socio-economic formation of feudalism in conjunction with the mediaeval town (the locus of the emergence of the autonomous craft production)' (Hobsbawm 1964: 38). Marx says of these earlier modes:

In all these forms the basis of evolution is the *reproduction* of relations between individual and community *assumed as given*—they may be more or less primitive, more or less the result of history, but fixed into tradition—and a *definite, predetermined objective* existence, both as regards the relation to the condition of labour, and the relation between one man and his co-workers, fellow tribesmen, etc. Such evolution is therefore from the outset *limited*, but once the limits are transcended, decay and disintegration sets in.   (Marx 1964: 83)

In other words, these societies are comparatively static, and if for some reason change does set in, they can disintegrate.

The ancient mode of production

When we turn to the ancient mode of production, Marx argues: 'The *community* is here the precondition, but unlike (the Asiatic mode) it is not here the substance of which the individuals are mere accidents or of which they form mere spontaneously natural parts' (Marx 1964: 71). The basis of the ancient mode is the city as the centre of the landowners—the cultivated area belongs to the city, as opposed to the village being an appendage to the land, as it was in the Asiatic mode.

The relationship between the community and the land can be broken only from the outside, by being conquered, and therefore being prepared for war is central to the society's life, 'the all-embracing task, the great communal labour'. The community of kinship systems must be ordered as a military force. Unlike the Asiatic mode, the individual peasant is not required to contribute communal labour to keep the land productive and is in this sense not directly dependent on the community except in so far as it is a protection against external enemies. The more this occurs the more the tribe becomes united against the outside world. This makes it safe for individual members and their families to cultivate their own particular plots. The peasant is both an individual proprietor *and* a member of the community. Ancient modes of production include the city states:

There is concentration in the city, with the land as its territory; small scale agriculture producing for immediate consumption; manufacture as the domestic subsidiary, labour of wives and daughters (spinning and weaving) or achieving independent existence in a few craft occupations. . . . The precondition for the continued existence of the community is the maintenance of equality among its free self-sustaining peasants, and their individual labour as the condition of the continued existence of their property. Their relation to the natural conditions of labour are those of proprietors; but personal labour must continually establish these conditions as real conditions and objective elements of the personality of the individual, of his personal labour.   (ibid. 73)

Rome is probably the best example of such a society: 'Property formally belongs to the Roman citizen, the private owner of land is such only by virtue of being Roman, but any Roman is also a private landowner.' Marx opposes this to the Germanic mode where the peasant is only the possessor of land. In the ancient mode, the community has its existence through the city—it is a form of independent organism; in the Germanic mode there is no such organism. Marx seems to suggest that it is with the development of the city that we can begin to think of the state with its officials. There exist side by side both state and private landed property. He draws (ibid. 88) a very modern parallel with language: just as the individual can only speak his or her own mind by virtue of belonging to the community that shares the language, so he can own property only by virtue of belonging to the state, the community which also owns property.

In Rome wealth was not the main purpose of production—this tended to be confined to trading groups; the argument was not about what property earned the most but about what sort of property enabled people to become citizens; humanity was the purpose of production and Marx did not lose the opportunity to point to the contrast between Rome and his and our society: 'The child-like world of the ancients appears to be superior.'

Having said this, however, Marx turns to a less attractive aspect of ancient societies. He goes on to argue that, despite appearances, the ancient mode of production, based on slavery and serfdom, is not an alienated system; people are not separated from the world on which they work, rather the slave is regarded as an inorganic part of the world—like the soil or the cattle.

In Rome, as in other city states, the very process of reproduction changed things—this seems to be something new that did not happen in the other modes. Once Rome was built and the land around it settled, the conditions of the society were different from what they had been before. Reproduction becomes a change in, a destruction of, the old form. The increase in population alone changes the situation. Conquest and colonization become important and lead to slavery. Hence we come back to the understanding that human beings change themselves by changing their situation. And it is here that we find the contradiction that leads to the collapse of the ancient mode of production. Originally every citizen is equal; as the land is used up and the population grows, conquest is necessary; conquest leads to slavery and the original democratic city state disappears. Hobsbawm (1964) points out that there is no reason why the breakdown of the ancient modes should lead to feudalism, and it certainly does not lead to capitalism.

Feudalism and the development of capitalism

It is only with the transition from feudalism to capitalism that we find an evolutionary and revolutionary conception of history, which takes us right through to socialism and communism. Feudalism developed not through any evolutionary course from the ancient mode, but out of the ruins of the ancient mode, in Europe out of the decay of Roman Empire. There had been a decline in the population and therefore in agricultural activity with minimal markets leading to a decline in industry and trade. Marx argues that feudalism started from the country. Ownership remained based on the community, but the producers were not slaves but the small peasantry, the serfs. The nobility exercised their power through a hierarchy of landownership and their armed retainers, their private armies.

This form of agricultural production had its equivalent in the town:

in the feudal organisation of the trades. Here property consisted chiefly in the labour of each individual person. The necessity for organisation against the organised robber-nobility, the need for communal covered markets in an age when the individualist was at the same time a merchant; the growing competition of the escaped serfs swarming into the rising towns, the feudal structure of the whole country: these combined to bring about the gilds. Further, the gradually accumulated capital of individual craftsmen and their stable numbers, as against the growing population, evolved the relation of jour-neyman and apprentice, which bought into being in the towns a hierarchy similar to that in the country.   (Marx 1964: 126)

There was little division of labour. In the towns the central social divisions were between masters, journeymen, apprentices, and, as time passed, the rabble, and in the country there were distinctions between princes, nobility, clergy, and peasants. There was little division of labour within or between trades.

Marx then moves on to the growth of capitalism. The division between mental and manual labour is most clear in the division between town and country: 'The existence of the town implies, at the same time, the necessity of administration, police, taxes, etc., in short, of the municipality and thus of politics in general' (ibid. 127). The town represents the concentration of population, the country represents isolation; antagonism between the two grows on the basis of private property and the abolition of the conflict between town and country will be one of the first conditions of communist life. The separation between the two marks the beginning of the conflict between landed property and industrial capital.

The serfs, escaping from the land and entering or establishing the towns, had only their labour and the minimal tools of their trade as property; this required the establishment of a police, but it also needed the construction of markets and other material preconditions of trading, and there was also a need to protect skills. All of these contributed to the development of craft guilds. New arrivals had to subject themselves to the guilds if they possessed a skill; if not they became day labourers, part of the urban rabble, unorganized and without power, watched over by an armed force. The journeymen and apprentices were tried to their masters through powerful obligations and possessed an interest in the system in that they could become masters themselves. There was no basis for effective uprisings in the towns, and the great class conflicts of the Middle Ages were peasant rebellions, but the peasantry were isolated and so unsophisticated and ineffective.

Marx's discussion of the craftsman's relationship to his work in the towns is interesting: on the one hand, he describes a situation that on the face of it might seem desirable. There is a minimal division of labour within the guild, so each craftsman must be an expert at every aspect of his work; we can often find in such craftsmen an interest and proficiency which might reach 'narrow' artistic heights. At the same time, however:

every mediaeval craftsman was completely absorbed in his work, to which he had a contented, slavish relationship, and to which he was subjected to a far greater extent than the modern worker, whose work is a matter of indifference to him.   (ibid. 130)

Marx describes capital in the town as 'natural', by which he means the basic necessities of work, the house, the tools, and traditional customers—all of which passed from father to son. Unlike modern capital, it was connected to specific persons and things.

The division of labour then evolves through a separating-out of a specific merchant class. This created the possibility of communication and trade beyond the immediate area of the town, but whether this occurred depended upon the state of roads, public safety, and so on, which in turn depended upon political conditions. So to the next stage, and here Marx is reminiscent of Durkheim:

with the extension of trade . . . there immediately appears a reciprocal action between production and commerce. The towns enter into relations *with one another*, new tools are brought from one town into the other, and the separation between production and commerce soon calls forth a new division of production between the individual towns, each of which is soon exploiting a dominant branch of industry.   (ibid. 131)

Out of the growth and interaction of the towns and conflict with the landed nobility there gradually arose the new 'burgher class'—the bourgeoisie. By freeing themselves from feudal restraints, they came to share common work conditions and a common enemy, and these called forth similar customs, similar ways of behaving and thinking. The class develops slowly and splits according to the development of the division of labour, absorbing previous ruling groups into itself and eventually turning the non-possessors of property, as well as some sections of the old possessing classes, into the proletariat—this happens as all property is transformed into industrial and commercial capital. In a clear account of class formation, Marx writes of the bourgeoisie:

The separate individuals form a class only in so far as they have to carry on a common battle against another class; otherwise they are on hostile terms with each other as competitors. On the other hand, the class in its turn achieves an independent existence over against the individuals, so that the latter find their conditions of existence predestined, and hence have their position in life and their personal development assigned to them by their class, become subsumed under it. This is the same phenomenon as the subjection of the separate individuals to the division of labour and can only be removed by the abolition of private property and of labour itself. We have already indicated several times how this subsuming of individuals under the class brings with it their subjection to all kinds of ideas etc.   (ibid. 132)

In terms of the development of manufacture, the process can be slow and unsteady and it can go into reverse—a development in an isolated town can be lost through war with nobody else knowing about it.

With the development of the division of labour between towns, manufacture began to outgrow the guild system and, through a sort of natural selection, the work which from the beginning involved machinery—weaving—had the advantage. A new class of weavers arose who worked not only to supply the home market well beyond the immediate locality but also overseas markets. Weaving demanded little skill, and soon divided into many branches, breaking free of the guilds, and the areas where 'guild-free' weaving developed soon grew faster than the traditional towns dominated by the guilds. Merchant capital began to develop, more mobile, more like modern capital, which in turn enabled the peasantry to enter into production without the interference of the guilds. Manufacture also absorbed those who had steadily been driven off the land by the enclosures, as the landed nobility turned to sheep for profit (through the wool trade) and shed their agricultural workers (you need very few people to look after sheep). This process went on for several centuries, as did the change in the nature of international trade. From 'inoffensive exchange', it developed to trade wars and physical wars, a matter of intense competition. The whole process got an immense boost from the discovery of America and the sea route to the East Indies.

In manufacture, money replaced the patriarchal relationship of the guild, and manufacture itself replaced the guild. International markets expanded rapidly and the impetus built up to the industrial revolution in the middle of the eighteenth century. The movement from cottage manufacture to capitalism proper involved the moving of machines which had hitherto been in the home into one location, where economies of scale were rapidly developed. Work and home became separate and we arrive at the fundamental movement of modernity.

Evolution from feudalism to capitalism?

I want now to look back over this last section, the one true evolutionary account of Marx, and ask about its theoretical content. I have presented it, as does Marx himself, as a real historical process, a story in which one thing leads to another. If we work this way, how does theory inform our history? In the first place, it tells us what to look for: Marx's account is in terms of the changes at the economic level of social organization and how these affect other levels, ranging from the individual's experience of work to international relations. There are, of course, other ways in which we could write a history of the same period—in terms, for example, of the actions of kings and major political figures, and how we decide between such explanations is itself a theoretical question, albeit a fairly simple one in these circumstances. Did the economic changes occur because great men took decisions about what they wanted the world to be like, or were the decisions of great men hemmed in and pushed in one direction or another by economic developments over which they had no control? Nobody and no group decided that the guild system should develop or that it should decline, or that the bourgeoisie should become a class; some sociologists would argue that these things happen as the unintentional consequences of human action, and that, of course, is true; but these actions were taken under a range of pressures pushing in a particular direction, and it is these pressures that Marx is talking about.

Comparing Marx's account with Durkheim's, we can see that both are concerned with the progress of the division of labour. Marx is probably superior, because he does not assume that it is an automatic process, whereas for Durkheim that does seem to be the case. For Marx, more is going on than the straightforward division of labour—class formation, for example—and it is in many ways a hit-and-miss process, one not of organic evolution but of chance, though not necessarily on a grand scale; it seems to me likely that something like capitalism would have developed, but there were very wide possibilities as to when, where, and how. However, where the two thinkers are furthest apart, in Durkheim's concentration on the *conscience collective*, it seems Durkheim has more to offer. Marx's analysis works on the level of system integration and has a more sophisticated grasp of the process, whereas Durkheim has a more sophisticated grasp of the process of social integration.

The complexities of the class analysis of history

Perhaps one example of the complexities of this come from debates about the nature of the class conflict that was fought out in the context of the English Civil War. The simple Marxist account would see this as a conflict between the rising bourgeoisie, both industrial and financial, on the parliamentarian side, and the old landed aristocracy on the side of the monarchy. The problem with this is that, at an abstract level, it is probably right—the policies desired by each side would probably have benefited the classes that were supposed to support them. But when we get down to looking at which real persons supported which side, it becomes much more difficult. The wrong people crop up in the wrong place all the time. The way in which we can understand this more concrete level of analysis, why people would fight for the side against their own class interest, is to look more closely at what Marxists would call ideological factors. In this case the important point is the religious divisions that were beginning to appear and the way they become subordinated to sectional interests. These beliefs, as do all symbolic systems, have a dynamic of their own and can carry people in unexpected directions.

Theory and history

Theoretical and empirical distinctions

Theory can do more than simply guide us to look at certain things first and other things later; at a theoretical level we can make much clearer distinctions between modes of productions then we can get through the historical account. If we stick to the latter, it is difficult to say when feudalism ends and capitalism begins, and it is difficult to know what to make of cottage industry—is it a separate mode of production, a transitional stage, or something else. On a theoretical level, we can make finer and firmer distinctions. I will try to show this first and then I will return to the relationship between the theory and the reality.

The theoretical distinctions can be found in the work of Althusser and Balibar (1970), who offer a highly abstract but none the less useful definition of modes of production. A mode of production is defined in terms of a combination of relations and elements. The elements are the means of production—the machines and tools employed in the production process—and the labourers and the non-labourers. The relationships between them are (crudely) those of control and ownership. As we shall see, the elements themselves vary between modes of production, but the relationships are constant.

I will begin with the relationships—of ownership and control of the means of production. Ownership might appear self-evident, but its nature can vary from society to society. It does not necessarily mean modern legal ownership in the Weberian sense, where the owner has complete disposal of his or her property. In the feudal system, for example, the king held land in fief from God, the lords in fief from the king and the peasants in fief from the lord. None had the freedom to dispose of land as he thought fit. Yet, in terms of this model of the mode of production, the lords owned the land and were the non-labourers. Control of the means of production means the ability to decide when the tools are put to work, and in what context. Thus, in feudalism, if ownership was in the hands of the non-labourers, the lords, control was in the hands of the peasants. This was not necessarily any big deal: there was not much choice—to work most daylight hours growing a limited range of crops.

The 'transitional mode' reverses these relationships. The transitional mode is cottage industry. The labourer owns the means of production, the spinning jenny, the loom; but he or she was dependent for the ability to put the machines into operation on the non-labourer, the merchant who supplied raw materials and ordered finished products, deciding when the machines would be used and what was to be produced.

The capitalist mode produces the concentration of both relationships in the hands of the non-labourer. The capitalist, whether an individual or a corporate body, owns the machinery and the factory, and decides what will be produced, the hours that the worker will work, and so on. The non-labourer neither owns nor controls the means of production. The socialist mode of production reverses these relationships: the labourer both owns and controls the means of production.

In logical terms we cannot derive much more than the four modes of production from this schema and it is quite possible that Marxism perhaps does not have much more to say about other types of societies. However, this approach does succeed in clarifying sharply between types of society and enabling us to understand them in terms of the different dynamics of each, the ways in which they are reproduced. For example, in the feudal system the dues, perhaps a proportion of the harvest, which are to be paid to the lord do not automatically reach him—they have to be given or taken. The peasant, bluntly, has to be fooled or beaten into giving the lord his due. In terms of the different levels of society, this means that the ideological level (religion) or the political level, or both together, play an important part in determining what happens. In capitalist systems, as we saw, the surplus is extracted at the same time as the worker works for his or her own living. Consequently the economic level is dominant—at least in early capitalism—determining the major lines of development. These differences are the result of the different relations of control—the peasant controls the means of production, the industrial worker does not. But if we expect these types to exist in pure form, we will be mistaken: the theory enables us to make sense of a complex reality and one might surmise that it underlay Marx's organization of his account of history, but it was not imposed upon it.

Contemporary notions of evolution

Before going on to talk about the development of capitalism through to the contemporary world, I want to elaborate on some modern conceptions of evolution that I began discussing in relation to Durkheim. I said then that evolutionary theories of history were not the most popular amongst contemporary sociologists and I want now to look at some contemporary versions of this process that perhaps capture the central aspects of Marx's arguments. Erik Wright (1989) makes a distinction between 'organic growth models' and evolutionary development, both of which can be found in biology. The first is genetically determined and involves a more or less inevitable process of growth, which in the social sciences would be a deterministic theory, and it seems to me the critics of evolutionary theory in the social sciences direct their fire against such a version. There is also the proper evolutionary model—in which there are random variations, some of which survive for environmental factors white others die out. This is a much more precarious process—societies can move in either direction and go off at different angels and this is much more appropriate to the social sciences. And it is much more in accordance with the sort of process that Marx is portraying in his account of pre-capitalist economic formations: the Asiatic mode does not develop, but awaits transformation from the outside; the ancient mode does develop, but not very far before it falls into decay and the growth of feudalism from that disintegration is not an inevitable process. In feudal societies, progress can be made and lost according to local conditions. Capitalism seems to develop only where machine production can be maintained and where local conditions allow a sufficient volume of trade to develop. And the development of such conditions themselves, of course, must be a matter of a number of other chances; a proper evolutionary conception allows for contingency and random variation.

In a recent paper W. G. Runciman (1995) takes up a defence of evolutionary theory which I think owes much to Marx though disagreeing with him—particularly about the claim that class and class conflict are the 'bearers' of evolutionary development. He suggests it is 'social practices' that matter, and capitalism is defined in Weberian terms as the employment of free labour by competing enterprises. He argues that there are many varieties of capitalism; the nature of the employing agency can vary and the economic system can coexist with a range of different political and ideological systems, and each development requires its own specific explanation. He goes on to distinguish between endogenous and exogenous evolution—the former developing from some internal feature of the society, the latter developing from some external development. What we cannot say is that evolution moves in one direction or that it is necessarily progressive. He is arguing against the idea that capitalism has necessarily triumphed over other forms of production—a view which seems particularly easy to hold since the collapse of the communist regimes in eastern Europe. He argues that these regimes collapsed not because of the failure of their economic practices but because of the collapse of the mode of coercion—the political regime which surrounded the economic practices. He concludes:

The proposition is that social, like natural, evolution proceeds not from stage to stage but from byway to byway. To borrow a metaphor used by Stephen Jay Gould for biological evolution, it must be seen not as a ladder but as a branching bush. It is true that there is a sequence of distinguishable modes of production, persuasion and coercion, but it is not true that the sequence is in any sense progressive. Likewise, it is true that history never repeats itself, but it is not true that social evolution only goes in one direction. The process of social selection not only permits but requires that modes of production, persuasion and coercion will not succeed each other in a uniform manner across the globe. (Runciman 1995: 46)

This is a Weberianized, open-ended Marxism which seems to me fully in the spirit of Marx's explorations of history. Yet, even allowing for Runciman's argument, it seems to me that we can still give a little more than he does to an evolutionary process which on certain levels has a progressive dimension. Erik Wright suggests that, when societies have made advances in knowledge or in their productive forces, they are unlikely to give them up easily. They might be bombed

back into the stone age or collapse into the sea but they will not voluntarily gi$\lor$
up what they consider as advances. They will not, of course, necessarily be successful in this enterprise but it is this which provides the evolutionary push.

The dynamics of capitalism

If Marx's conception of the development of capitalism from feudalism can be
called evolutionary, his conception of the development from capitalism to
socialism can be called revolutionary. Socialism does not emerge from the normal development of capitalism, but more from the failure of capitalism to
develop. The capitalist system is driven by contradictions which put it in a permanent crisis, and it comes to an end when these contradictions reach breaking
point. There are a number of different dynamics at different levels of society that
we can identify and pull out of Marx's work, not all of which push towards
revolution. What is clear is that the simple model of *The Communist Manifesto*,
of capitalism dividing into two huge opposing armies of bourgeoisie and proletariat, with the latter getting stronger and eventually overwhelming the bourgeoisie—this simple model was not really tenable even in Marx's lifetime. Other
aspects are, however, much more tenable. I will begin with changes at the
economic level, changes which are framed within what Marx saw as the basic
contradiction between the forces and relations of production, and I will then
move on to developments which occur at other levels. Some of these ideas come
from Marx himself and some from later developments—I will be concentrating
on the usefulness of these ideas for our understanding of contemporary society.

The tendency of the rate of profit to fall

I tried earlier to show how there are regular cycles of crises—overproduction or
under-consumption—which leave stocks of goods building up, workers being
laid off, surplus productive capacity (empty factories, etc.) increasing. The
forces of production, the capacity to produce, are increasing: the competitive
dynamic of capitalism forces enterprises to seek constant changes in production
techniques to allow cheaper production, to find new markets, and so on. But
these capabilities would periodically outstrip the relations of production, the
private ownership of the means of production.

All the classical economists had noticed a tendency of the rate of profit to fall,
but they disagreed on its causes. Marx's explanation had to do with the accumulation of capital, of 'dead labour'. Profit could be made only from living
labour; it comes from the difference between the exchange value of labour
power—what I pay my workers, what is necessary for them to maintain a life

which enables them to keep working for me—and its use value, what I can get them to produce for me. As productive capacity increases through the growth of capital goods, I need less labour and I pay out more on machines—'dead labour'—and consequently I make proportionately less surplus value. This is not necessarily less 'profit' in absolute terms but less profit as a proportion of outlay.[1] Critics have argued that there are three counteracting tendencies. First, the growth in the mass of 'dead' or constant capital reduces its value and might counteract the tendency (i.e. proportionately I pay out less on it); secondly, the rate of exploitation can be increased to the point where it counteracts the tendency of the rate of profit to fall (i.e. I cut wages and/or insist on longer hours); and, thirdly, to quote Simon Clarke:

Marx ignores the fact that the capitalist will only introduce a new method of production if it provides an increased rate of profit, so that faced with the prospect of such a fall capitalists will continue to use the old method of production and earn the old rate of profit, at least until such a time as shortage of labour leads to a fall in the rate of profit as a result of rising wages, at which point labour-saving methods might become profitable. (Clarke 1994: 212)

I think it is possible to draw from this a number of themes in our understanding of the development of contemporary society. The first is that the cycle of crises has continued and, as Ernest Mandel notes, the period of the cycle has lessened from round about ten years at the beginning of the century to four or five years now. His explanation of this is that the renewal period for constant capital has become shorter and shorter, not least because of the spin-off of the vast expenditure on arms during the cold war. This was part and parcel of the long-term expansion of capitalism since the end of the Second World War, and Mandel (1970: 57) refers to it as 'a permanent technological revolution'. This is clearly continuing, and the sort of contemporary economic developments that David Harvey (1989) analyses within a Marxist framework are a continuation of such developments—the growth of information technology, the movement of industrial production to low-wage economies, the increasing emphasis on short-term production cycles, and so on.

It is worth underlining the expansionist dynamic of capitalism. I find this a difficult issue; on the one hand, it seems to me that the Runciman argument that I discussed earlier is basically right—there is no necessary development towards the triumph of capitalism, nor, by implication, socialism. And, of course, capitalist relations can exist with very different political and ideological systems. On the other hand, the development of imperialism—the tendency of capitalism to export itself and subordinate if not actually replace other modes of production—is important. And the continuation of this process leads on to the 'world-

---

[1] I am using 'profit' and 'surplus value' here as equivalent, although they are not—one should remember that Marx's economics can become very complex! For a good discussion, see Clarke (1994).

system' analysis of modern sociology, the greater and more consistent degree of system cohesion that seems to exist in contemporary society. Interestingly, Immanual Wallerstein's response (Runciman 1995: 46), as a leading world-system theorist, to Runciman's argument is that capitalism is best defined not by free labour but by the accumulation of capital, and in fact it is not free labour which pushes capitalism to expand but the necessity of accumulation in the competitive market. However, if we take them on their relevant levels, I do not think the arguments are contradictory. We can talk about a capitalist world system which includes within itself different forms of capitalism in relation to other modes of production; or, if we prefer, we could talk about capitalism as being defined by both the accumulation of capital and free labour, and in fact for Marx the two depend on each other: capital can be accumulated only through the exploitation of free labour. This definition takes account of Runciman's objection to Wallerstein—that, if we employ the accumulation of capital as a defining feature, then we would have to take the Roman Empire and the Soviet Union as capitalist; on the other hand, it allows us to recognize the sort of differences between societies that Runciman refers to. However, it would be within the context of an overall capitalist system to which other forms of production could exist in a subordinate position. None of this helps us understand any development towards socialism.

Changes at other levels: transformations of the crisis

The economic dynamics of capitalism—regular crises, the accumulation of capital, an expansionary process, and increasingly rapid transformations in technology—are not, of course, the only ones. The various Marxist attempts to understand the development of capitalism without revolution have, as I remarked earlier, concentrated on ideology. I indicated then the various ways in which the other levels of society were related to the economic level. Habermas (1972, 1974, 1976, 1979) presents an evolutionary model of human society of which the period of early capitalism is only one stage. It is not my intention here to give a full account of Habermas's work, but I do want to look at his attempt to develop an evolutionary theory of modern capitalism which takes us in a rather different direction. He talks about an 'evolutionary learning curve' along which different societies might move in different ways. His model of social evolution is the individual's cognitive evolution—from the perception and grasp of specifics to the perception and grasp of universals: from recognizing that thing in the garden as our tree, to recognizing it as one of a general category of tree. Societies also develop towards universal values and universal standards of rationality, morality, and law, towards the growing independence of the individual, growing ability to make moral decisions, but it is not a simple process of development and in that process economic development is very important.

The stages that interest us here are those that come through the sort of developments in capitalism that we have been discussing. The crises of early capitalism are economic crises—crises in system cohesion. To deal with these, the state intervenes to boost demand in what are seen as under-consumption crises; the state becomes involved in economic regulation and welfare provision. This shifts the crisis to another level: the state has to borrow to fund its activities and this fuels high inflation and a financial crisis. The state becomes unable to reconcile the demands of industrial and financial capitalism, hence Habermas calls it a *rationality* crisis. This is a crisis at the level of system integration, but it also has effects on the level of social integration, where it is a 'legitimation' crisis—the state loses its popular justification. This should be a familiar story to anybody with a knowledge of western politics of the last few decades, and perhaps its latest and most dramatic manifestation is the militant opposition to the federal government in the USA.

If the political system can manage the rationality crisis, it moves on to what traditional Marxists would call the ideological level, but Habermas calls social integration. The new crisis is a *motivation* crisis. This brings us back to a regular thesis of this book: the increase in state power and control needed to deal with the earlier crises undermines motivations for participating in the system. Politics become more centralized, the profit motive is less important, and the work ethic declines in significance. We can see all these issues arising in contemporary political arguments: do welfare payments keep people idle or encourage them to work? Are taxation levels too high to encourage initiative? Why don't politicians take any notice of what people say?

The main point of my argument at this stage has been to suggest that we can identify an evolutionary process—towards the 'world system' and/or universal systems of justice and morality of which Habermas speaks, but there are many ways of getting there and a range of possibilities within the system, not least perhaps that of moving backwards. The next question is what this has to do with socialism.

Communism

Communism (is) the *positive* transcendence of *private property*, as *human self-estrangement*, and therefore as the real *appropriation of the human* essence by and for man; communism therefore (is) the complete return of man to himself as a *social* (i.e. human) being—a return become conscious, and accomplished within the entire wealth of previous development. This communism, as fully developed naturalism, equals humanism, and as fully developed humanism, equals naturalism; it is the *genuine* resolution of the conflict between man and nature and between man and man—the true resolution of the strife between existence and essence, between objectification and self-confirmation, between freedom and necessity, between the individual and the species. Communism is the riddle of history solved, and it knows itself to be this solution.

(Marx 1844/1974: 135)

There are a number of different ways in which we can think about socialism and the way in which it might be achieved. The Marxist social vision is very different from that of Durkheim, who sees it as a matter of evolution into an organic whole, a balance of individualism and collectivism, the state guaranteeing the balance between the two. For Marx, the emphasis is less on balance than on control—not the individual's control over his or her life which has become the centre of so much contemporary concern, but the collective control of our living conditions and activities. Unlike Durkheim, Marx raises questions of radical democracy, of the organization of social life on a collective basis not through professional associations but through an understanding of a shared human condition.

It is 'common-sense' knowledge that Marx saw socialism as coming about through revolution—a seizure of political power which would transform the economic, social, and political conditions of life; less well known is the fact that he thought this would realize once and for all the ideals of the French Revolution: liberty, equality, and fraternity. Popular prejudice would often maintain that socialism or communism is about dictatorial power, the violent seizure of power and wealth by a minority, and it is arguable that this is what eventually happened in the Soviet Union and eastern Europe. However, it is not what Marx had in mind. David McLellan (1971) comments on how Marx was preoccupied for many years with the failure of the French Revolution, and the possible realization of its ideals. Marx argued that the distinctive feature of the proletariat as a revolutionary class was that its particular interests coincided with the interests of society as a whole, and this explained the failure of the French Revolution, a 'partial, purely political revolution' in the interests of one class:

What is the basis of a partial, purely political revolution? It is that a part of civil society emancipates itself and attains to universal domination, that a particular class undertakes the general emancipation of society from its particular situation. This class frees the whole of society, but only under the presupposition that the whole of society is in the same situation as this class, that it possesses, or can easily acquire for example, money and education.   (Marx 1971: 125)

Now in one sense the French bourgeoisie who carried out the revolution liberated the whole of society, breaking the traditional feudal ties and granting each man a right to citizenship. However, this is only a formal political right; it does not affect the material conditions of the citizen's life. The bourgeoisie cannot grant a real equality and a real liberty, since that would involve the abolition of private property; it can grant only an individual—not a collective—freedom, and, of course, the individual by him- or herself is powerless.

The proletariat is in a very different position. It is the *universal* class:

Of all the classes that stand face to face with the bourgeoisie today, the proletariat alone is a really revolutionary class. . . . In the conditions of the proletariat, those of old society at large are already virtually swamped. The proletarian is without property; his relation to his wife and children has no longer anything in common with the bourgeois family relations; modern industrial labour, modern subjection to capital, the same in England as in France, in America as in Germany, has stripped him of every trace of national character. Law, morality, religion, are to him so many bourgeois prejudices, behind which lurk in ambush just as many bourgeois interests.

All the preceding classes that got the upper hand sought to fortify their already acquired status by subjecting society at large to their conditions of appropriation. The proletarians cannot become masters of the productive forces of society, except by abolishing their own previous mode of appropriation. They have nothing of their own to secure and to fortify; their mission is to destroy all previous securities for, and insurances of, individual property.

All previous historical movements were movements of minorities, or in the interests of minorities. The proletarian movement is the self-conscious, independent movement of the immense majority, in the interests of the immense majority. The proletariat, the lowest stratum of our present society, cannot stir, cannot raise itself up without the whole, superincumbent strata of official society being sprung into the air.' (Marx 1848/1968a: 44–45)

McLellan (1971) points out that, when Marx talks of violence as part of the revolution, he sees it primarily in terms of a response to the violence of the ruling classes, who will not always be willing to give up their privileges without a physical fight; in some countries it might be possible to win power through the ballot box, and he never expressed any approval of the sort of revolutionary terror that followed the French Revolution. If that were to happen after the socialist revolution, it would mean that the time for the revolution had not come—that the society had not yet reached the stage of development or the intensity of contradiction that would lead to the establishment of socialism without oppression. Marx also commented that, whilst Russia wasn't fully industrialized—and therefore did not have a fully developed industrial proletariat—communism could take a root there because of the communal nature of the Russian peasant village. Paradoxically, it was precisely this structure that Stalin destroyed during forced collectivization of agriculture.

The simple model of a victorious proletariat taking power when its time comes with the support of other classes and with minimal opposition has faded, although more sophisticated conceptions have developed on the basis of the experience of the Russian Revolution. Both Lenin and Trotsky developed analyses which Althusser pursued in a theory of what he called 'overdetermination' (Althusser 1969). The revolution is seen as a result of the conjunction of a number of contradictions, not just that resulting from the contradiction between the forces and relations of production and the consequent conflict between bourgeoisie and proletariat. In Russia in 1917 there were conflicts between native

Russian capitalists and entrepreneurs from western Europe, between both of these and the landed aristocracy, between proletariat and bourgeoisie, peasantry and landlords, financial and industrial bourgeoisie, and so on (see Trotsky 1967). In such a situation, it is not just the strength of the revolutionary forces that matter but the inability of the ruling classes to act against them because of internal divisions. When Althusser develops this sort of analysis he suggests that contradictions can also come together to produce a stalemate. What is clear is that revolutions are more complex and dangerous than Marx imagined in his theory, and that revolutionary parties have not been the democratic creations of the working class that he expected them to be.

McLellan also points out that Marx was wary about making predictions— that was the work of the utopian socialists. In practical terms he seemed to be caught between two stools. On the one hand, he foresaw the disappearance of the state; for Marx, it is not a mediator but an instrument of class oppression, and if social classes disappeared then there would be no need for the state: 'for Marx the abolition of a state based on class distinction involved the abolition of an independent state apparatus in which an irresponsible executive and judiciary insured the invulnerability of the bureaucracy' (McLellan 1971: 213). However, one of the aims of the revolutionary movement was to push towards the centralization of power, so that it would be that much easier to take over the state; but once class society is abolished, the question arises about what functions the state would then have. In the 'Critique of the Gotha Programme' Marx (1875/1977b) says as much as he says anywhere about the future communist society. The Gotha programme was a compromise between two wings of German socialism drawn up in the spring of 1875. Marx argues that the state is always a product of bourgeois society, and it is not, as the Gotha programme assumes, an entity which continues to exist in all forms of society. But the state will not immediately disappear after the socialist revolution—there will be a period of transition:

What we have to deal with here is a communist society, not as it has developed on its own foundations, but, on the contrary, just as it emerges from capitalist society; which is thus in every respect, economically, morally and intellectually, still stamped with the birth marks of the old society from whose womb it emerges.   (ibid. 568)

For example, the worker still has to work and he or she will be paid according to how much time is worked and this will be an act of exchange with 'society', presumably the state, which would supply the worker with a certificate which he or she would then use to withdraw what goods he or she needs from the common stock; so in the period after the revolution there would still be the exchange of commodities. As a consequence of this—one amount of labour exchanged for what has been produced by another equal amount of labour—this transitional society will still maintain the notion of equality basic to bourgeois society. One of the defects of this arrangement is that people are in fact unequal—in terms of strength and stamina and ability to work, or in terms of knowledge or family size—so this system will produce necessary inequalities during the transitional period. The Gotha programme places too much emphasis on equal distribution, when in fact it is production that is important. The notion of equal rights and equality of distribution will steadily disappear as the society moves forward:

In a higher phase of Communist society, after the enslaving and subordination of the individual to the division of labour, and therewith also the antithesis between mental and physical labour, has vanished; after labour has become not only a means to life but one of life's prime wants; after the productive forces have also increased with the all-round development of the individual, and all the springs of co-operative wealth flow more abundantly—only then can the narrow horizon of bourgeois right be crossed in its entirety and society inscribe on its banners: from each according to his ability, to each according to his needs.   (ibid. 569)

Marx goes on to emphasize the primacy of production, and argue in effect that the distribution of wealth and goods is a red herring—or rather an anti-red herring. The distribution of wealth reflects and depends upon the production of wealth.

It is reasonable to ask questions about the possibility of achieving this democratically ordered, stateless society. McLellan points out that when Marx was writing the state was a much less formidable institution than it is now in Europe and North America; it had not yet, for example, taken on any of the welfare functions that we normally associate with it, nor had it taken on many of its contemporary economic functions. It is now unlikely that it would simply wither away, especially if we add to this the fact that a communist party would come to power in times of civil unrest, or that its coming to power, even through elections, might actually *create* civil unrest (as, for example, it did when the Chilean socialist party won power through the ballot box in the early 1970s). In fact, it was already difficult to imagine when Lenin wrote *State and Revolution* (1972), and even in theory the eventual disappearance of the state receded further and further.

The utopia at the end of the process would not necessarily be one in which there is plenty for everybody; the argument is that human beings themselves would change during this period. They would become free, able to cooperate and argue with each other as the occasion demanded and organize their lives in collectively satisfying ways. They would lose the acquisitiveness, the selfishness, and the mutual mistrust engendered by capitalism, and the need for state-administered social control would disappear. The oft-heard right-wing argument that human beings are selfish is clearly not true—not all societies have been based on acquisitive and self drives, although such drives exist in all societies. This should already be clear from Weber's account of traditional attitudes to work and of other forms of capitalism.

However, it is debatable how far personalities can be transformed, and how quickly, and during the last part of the twentieth century the movement has been away from emphasizing collective responsibility towards a steadily greater individualism. This utopian aspect of Marxism is perhaps the best way into the conclusion.

Conclusion

It is perhaps difficult to think of the sort of radical transformation that Marx desired as a real possibility and I suggested earlier that, if we take Freud seriously, we would have to say that human beings would not spontaneously choose to work, however ideal the conditions. Work always involves an internal repression, and human relations are always to some extent hostile and envious. However, it is possible to use psychoanalytic ideas to maintain the importance of these ideals: Freudians often talk about a superego—an internalized social control which can become punitive if we do not do what we think we should do—and an ego-ideal, an idea of the sort of person we would really like to be. The two are closely related: if I do not live up to my ego-ideal, then my superego springs into critical action. They are also different: the ego-ideal carries hope, and the superego has irrational aspects. We have to live with both.

The political utopia offered by Marxism can combine both. Marxist parties and Marxist states have too easily taken over the destructive superego side, whereas the utopia has also acted as an ego-ideal, inspiring those who want to build a better, more equal and humane society. I think it is the universalism of this idea that is important and it is an ideal which comprises a central root of sociology, and which tends still to be carried by modern elaborations of Marxism. In that sense the best parts of Marxism can still contribute hope to sociology.

If Durkheim is primarily the theorist of society, then Marx is the theorist of social structure. I did not make any big deal out of the base/superstructure distinction when I mentioned it before because it can easily become a cliché, but if we can think about a multi-story building with different activities developing on different floors, each depending upon and affecting the others without determining them, its usefulness becomes clearer. In the first place we can see 'society' as a complex *structure*—not a jumble of activities (Weber) or an organism (Durkheim). Some levels of this structure are more important than others and that depends upon the various stages of development of the activities that go on at each level. There are also different rates of development at each level—one could think of the activities as Runciman's evolving bush, but it is an indoor plant, contained within the structure.

Marxism is also the central realist theory of classical sociology—parts of the social structure are not available to our perception, and these are usually the most important parts (perhaps the basement levels of the building). They have to be theorized and understood in order for us to grasp what is going on at a surface level (or the levels about the surface). And, because of this distinction between underlying and surface levels of reality, Marx is also the theorist of *ideology*, the theorist most able to take a critical approach to systems of ideas and beliefs about the social world. From a Marxist point of view, there is always the space to be wrong about what is happening in the world, the space between what we see and what causes what we see. The building is designed to hide its structure—there are no obvious signs, for example, of a basement, no steps leading down from the outside, no lighted windows below ground level, and inside there are multiple split-level floors and unexpected connections. It is by no means always clear how the activities carried on inside are connected.

There are various ways in which the critical role of Marxism can be described: it points to ideas that are caught up only in surface appearances, or it places such ideas in relation to the totality—to other levels of social organization, other developmental processes; it is always the ideas of totality and/or underlying structure and/or process that are important. It is this critical impetus that Marxism has always tended to reflect back upon itself. Whereas the other approaches have developed primarily in relation to external stimuli, Marxism seems to have generated and regenerated its own self-criticism so that, in the mid- and late twentieth century, there have been multiple strands of Marxist thought and it is still at the centre of arguments in social theory. Even the most renowned of the postmodernist philosophers, Jacques Derrida (1995), has recently found it necessary to return to trace a debt to Marx. A much more conventional social theorist, Nicos Mouzelis (1990), has suggested that, rather than Marxism being used as a totalizing theory, it can provide frameworks for analysing specific 'institutional spheres'. Whatever institution we look at—from the economic to the religious—he argues that we always identify technological, political, and ideological levels and we can investigate their interrelationships. And I would repeat again that the best accounts of postmodernism—David Harvey's *The Condition of Postmodernity* (1989) and Fredric Jameson's *Postmodernism or the Cultural Logic of Late Capitalism* (1991)—are both Marxist analyses of the contemporary world. We can now summarize Marx's views on the secondary dualism (see Box 12.1).

Box 12.1. **Marx on modernity and capitalism/socialism**

MODERNITY	CAPITALISM/SOCIALISM
Durkheim: a movement towards a balanced society of occupational groups held together by the state and a new humanist 'religion' which emphasized the value of the individual.	**Durkheim:** Durkheim's concept of socialism was based on his conception of the development of modernity; although problems arise in the abnormal forms of the division of labour, these would be ironed out in continued historical development. He does not seem to see capitalism as a specific form of modern society responsible for either its problems or its benefits.
Marx: the modern world was moving towards the realization of the values of the French Revolution—liberty, equality, and fraternity. This was not an inevitable or smooth process and entails conflict and revolution.	**Marx:** capitalism represented immense progress over previous types of society in terms of the ability to produce wealth, although it is driven by contradictions which do not allow it to realize this ability. The competitive market system produces rapid change and fragmentation—seen by many as defining features of modernity; a socialist revolution would create a collectively organized democratic and more stable society which would realize the ideals of the French Revolution.

Further reading

Marx's own work on pre-capitalist societies can be found in *Pre-Capitalist Economic Formations* (1964); if you read this, together with Eric Hobsbawm's commentary, and then compare them to Barry Hindess and Paul Hirst, *Pre-Capitalist Modes of Production* (1975), you will get a good idea of Marxism at its best and worst. My account of the theory of modes of production comes from Louis Althusser and Étienne Balibar, *Reading Capital* (1970). This is very difficult and it is also the source for Hindess and Hirst—you should read it for ideas and not take it as gospel truth.

In the next chapter you will find Weberian accounts of historical development with which this chapter can be compared; it might be worth looking as well at Giddens's two-volume *Contemporary Critique of Historical Materialism* (1981, 1985) and the discussion of evolutionary theory in T. Bottomore, 'Giddens's View of Historical Materialism' (1990), and E. O. Wright, 'Models of Historical Trajectory' (1989); also look at W. G. Runciman, 'The "Triumph" of Capitalism as a Topic in the Theory of Social Selection' (1995).

For Marx on the revolution and communism, see McLellan, *The Thought of Karl Marx* (1971), and Marx's own 'Critique of the Gotha Programme' (1875/1977b).

13 | Weber as a tragic liberal: the rise of the West

Introduction
Weber's ghostly evolutionism.

The sociology of religion
Choices between tradition and progress/differentiation; prophecy and the growth of universality; a class analysis of religion; humans as seekers of meaning; the tension between immanent and transcendent religions, the latter producing action to change the world.

Chinese religion: Confucianism and Taoism
The power of the family giving power to the countryside over the town; the power of the central government; conflict between central government, its local officials, and local kin groups; the growth of capitalism restricted by the power of the family and the Confucian ethic which devalued economic activity; Taoism as a mystical alternative; comparison of Confucianism and Puritanism.

Indian religion: Hinduism and Buddhism
The caste system; distinction between sects and churches in relation to Hinduism; the Brahmins; the absence of a universal ethic, and of the possibility of social criticism in an eternal order; status conflict in the wider social order; the Brahmin ascetic ideal; the absence of a rationalized pursuit of wealth.

Palestine: ancient Judaism
The importance of positive ethical action and unintended consequences; the history of Israel and its special relationship to Jahwe; the emergence of new ideas on the edge of centres of civilization; prophecy and the prophets; Jahwe as a universal God.

The Protestant ethic and the spirit of capitalism
Introduction: the descriptive and analytic in Weber's work; the 'elective affinity' as an explanation; the work ethic in Weber's history. *The spirit of capitalism*: capitalism based on rational accounting; Protestantism not originally associated with the accumulation of wealth association; Benjamin Franklin as the source of the ideal type of the spirit of capitalism;

accumulation as the supreme good; the notion of a calling; moralized money-making versus traditionalism. *The Protestant ethic*: Protestantism as the origin of the rationality of European capitalism; Luther's notion of a calling; different forms of ascetic Protestantism; Calvin and predestination; worldly success as a sign of salvation; Calvinism as an ideal type; capitalism as an unintended consequence.

Conclusion

Weber's importance to modern sociology; Weber as a theorist of modernity; his view of socialism; the contribution of his religious studies to the basic dualisms; his theoretical ambivalence; his views on German politics.

Introduction

For Weber, history was the product of individual actions, open-ended, and, like social structures, precarious. History, on this view, would be the telling of stories. Yet the stories which he tells, especially in his studies of the world religions, contain a sort of 'ghost' evolutionary theory, one which owes little to Darwin or organic analogies. We have already met it in his discussion of forms of domination; there seems to be steady development of western rationality, from Judaism onwards, which eventually comes to dominate everything. It is this which gives rise to the view of Weber as a tragic liberal—the individualist who ends up by describing the iron cage of modern society. This chapter will concentrate on Weber's sociology of religion—first of all his theoretical framework and then his studies of the major world religions, Confucianism, Hinduism and Buddhism, and Judaism, culminating with his *Protestant Ethic and the Spirit of Capitalism*.

The sociology of religion

Weber starts with the universality of belief in the supernatural and turns his attention to the ways in which this develops, the breakthrough which moves a society beyond a primitive belief. There are important historical points where a society makes choices and he sees these choices in dichotomous terms, between a course of action which will further the differentiation of spheres of life and a course of action which would continue traditional ways of acting.

The first important distinction is between the magician and the priest, or between magic and religion as systems of beliefs. Both mediate between the human and the supernatural, but they do so in different ways. Magic is involved with the demands of everyday life and involves the use of spells or some equivalent to force the supernatural into acting in a particular way on behalf of the magician and/or his or her client. If I am having arguments with my boss, the magical answer is to go and collect some of his or her nail clippings or hair, go home, put these items into a wax model, and stick pins in it in the knowledge that he or she will suffer acute physical pain. Religion, on the other hand, does not work in such an *ad hoc*, immediate way; it is systematically organized and God (or the Gods) cannot be forced into action. The most I can do if I am a Christian is pray to God to give me the patience to deal with my tyrannical boss; there is no guarantee that God will do this, and I might have to wait until the next Sunday before I even get a chance to pray in what I would consider a proper context. Magical forces are not worshipped.

As conceptions of the supernatural order develop, religion gains an autonomy which influences the social order. The importance of the magic/religion appears when he distinguishes between societies based on what he calls 'taboo' and those based on religious ethics. The first are concerned with specific acts: perhaps prohibiting incest or compelling marriages outside the individual's clan. Taboos are not confined to magic but are certainly more primitive than religious ethics, which move away from the specific towards the universal; they work at a higher level of generality and a higher level of personal responsibility, not least because people are no longer subject to magical retribution. The realm of the supernatural always combines both but to different degrees.

The evolutionary process is that of rationalization—increasingly universal and elaborate belief and value systems. This movement to a higher level comes through the appearance of the *prophet*. As far as sociology is concerned, the prophet is the bearer of charisma—he or she might be the founder of a new religion, or somebody breathing new life into the old religion, and, Weber adds, it doesn't matter whether people are more attracted by the person or the doctrine, the sociological point is that the prophet announces a personal revelation. For this reason prophets rarely come from the organized and routinized priesthood. The priest has influence through office, the prophet through 'personal gifts'; unlike the magician, the prophet is concerned with specific revelations and with doctrines, but, like the magician, he is likely to perform some miraculous acts—turning water into wine, raising from the dead, etc. The prophet is also different from the legislator—although the prophets of Israel, unlike those of Buddhism and Hinduism, were concerned with social reform and this might sometimes blur the difference. However, the more concerned they were with social reform, the less prophet-like they were. Ezekiel, 'the real theoretician of social reform . . . was a priestly theorist who can scarcely be categorized as a prophet at all . . . Jesus was not at all interested in social reform as such' (Weber 1922/1965: 51). The messages of Zoroaster, and of Buddha, were also essentially religious. It is worth remembering that there are still debates, at least in the Christian churches, about the relationship between the social and religious duties of the church; interestingly, people who might be considered latter-day prophets, the media evangelists, particularly in the USA, are interested in right-wing social reform.

The founders of schools of philosophy cannot be considered as prophets; they do not usually engage in 'vital emotional preaching', whereas the prophet is closer to the 'popular orator'. There are various other related roles which Weber goes on to separate from the prophet proper, who can be either an 'ethical prophet', preaching God's word as an ethical duty (Muhammad) or an 'exemplary prophet', who shows the way to salvation by personal example (Buddha).

The exemplary prophet tends towards the conception of a God who is somehow present everywhere in this world and the concern is with how to experience the deity, to achieve personal enlightenment, an experiential state very different from the meaning of enlightenment in western philosophy. The ethical God, on the other hand, is transcendent—he, she, or it stands outside the world and demands obedience. Christianity is clearly an ethical religion but the contrast is not an absolute one; there is, for example, a long tradition of Christian mysticism which at times does not seem too far away from Buddhism (see, e.g., *The Cloud of Unknowing* (anon. 1960)).

Weber goes on to suggest that there is a connection between types of religious organization and forms of domination in the wider society; one of the things that makes prophecy important is that it breaks from the established order and the prophet and followers stand in a special relationship to those who do not follow the prophet as a subgroup in the wider society whose special concern is religion. Whereas exemplary prophets tend to generate an élite of the enlightened and a rather indistinct mass of followers, ethical prophets tend to generate a more firmly organized church. The latter favours the development of rationalization—especially if a written tradition is established.

There then follow two chapters which show Weber at his best, in his sophisticated Marxist guise—he presents what can be seen as a class analysis of religion, a way in which different sorts of religion may be carried by different classes. He begins with the peasantry, who, he argues, are dependent on nature and natural cycles; they have little interest in rational systematization and will turn to religion only when they are threatened—either by an external army or by enslavement or by proletarianization—and when such a threat appears, prophetic cults rise in opposition to the established church. Here it is a matter of war or class struggle pushing the development forward. Most of the time, however, the peasantry stay with their magic. The idea of the peasant as the main support of traditional organized religion is, with few exceptions, a modern phenomenon. In early times, urban centres were also centres of religion—from early Christianity right through to the Middle Ages.

The feudal ruling classes were not bearers of religion—the life of the warrior noble had little to do with religious ethics and it would run counter to their honour to submit to the authority of a prophet or a priest. The noble might be drawn in for a while on the upsurge of a prophetic movement—which at the beginning might draw supporters from all classes—but he is likely to drop out, particularly as routinization sets in. The exception is when the religion gives a purpose to the warrior—for example, in the Crusades (on both sides). Religion, he suggests, has more appeal to professional, standing armies with a bureaucratic command structure. It also appealed to some urban officials who were involved in bureaucratic administration. Such social groups will occasionally be attracted to prophetic movements, but usually they carry 'a comprehensive sober rationalism' and an 'ideal of disciplined order'. Irrational religion does not appeal to them. Confucianism represents the distinctive bureaucratic attitude to religion, the absence of emotional needs, and the absence of any transcendental root or justification for an ethics.

The most privileged social strata produce striking contrasts in their attitudes to religion. Prophetic movements have been movements not of the dispossessed, but of the middle classes, who have made economic sacrifices in the process. There are two factors which seem important in determining whether a group is likely to be a 'carrier' of a rationalizing religion: the first is whether that group in its normal life involves generalized rational and responsible procedures, and the second is whether the group is separated in their lives from the traditional order of religion. Amongst the first group, merchants and artisans could be included; amongst the second, subordinate groups of artisans, apprentices, and journeymen.

Next Weber turns to intellectuals as a social group. One might expect them to be at the centre of the process of rationalization but this can be counteracted by their identification with traditional ruling groups—for example, when the intellectuals are priests in an established church. If these groups move towards 'salvation religion', it is often via mysticism, the movement being created by inner rather than social tensions. To seek enlightenment in this way takes one above any concern with social status; this was particularly important in the development of Indian religion. He argues that the intellectualism of relatively deprived groups is particularly important. The notion of relative deprivation has been important in modern sociology (Runciman 1966); the *relative* part is more important than the *deprivation*—it allows comparisons to be made with those in a better and/or worse position and this raises the possibility of change. Where deprivation approaches the absolute, change is inconceivable. The particular groups that Weber thinks were important in this respect were the Jews, the early Christians, and the Puritans.

The process of rationalization within which all this takes place is a process of finding meaning in the world. Human beings for Weber in this context are essentially meaning-finding or rather meaning-hunting beings, and this brings people up against the understanding of the apparently meaningless: of suffering, of death, or whatever—particularly when they afflict those who do not deserve it. There is a discrepancy between what we expect from leading the good life—rewards, justice, success—and what we get—pain, mistreatment, and suffering. This sort of problem seems to me not only still a matter of religion in the contemporary world but one at the centre of every aspect of our lives—it is extraordinarily difficult to accept the contingency and meaningless dimension of the things that happen to us. Whether we are dealing with accidents, natural disasters, death, or illness, we look for somebody to blame.

Attempts to explain such things become ever more abstract and generalized from everyday life. In immanent religions (where God is seen everywhere in this world) we find more radical discountings of the world, whereas in transcendent religions (where God is outside the world) we find the attempt to make the world closer to what is expected or hoped for. Weber calls this the problem of salvation, the area of tension between the real and the ideal, worldly compromise and perfection. There are some who cannot accept compromise and seek salvation according to standards of perfection, and this is at the root of social change:

Our concern is essentially with the quest for salvation, whatever its form, insofar as it produced certain consequences for practical behaviour in the world. It is most likely to acquire such a positive orientation to mundane affairs as the result of a pattern of life which is distinctively determined by religion and given coherence by some central meaning or positive goal . . . a quest for salvation in any religious group has the strongest chance of exerting practical influences when there has arisen, out of religious motivation, a systematization of practical conduct resulting from an orientation to certain integral values.   (Weber 1922/1965: 149)

This systematization can be inhibited by magical features of the search for salvation—the sacramental system of the Roman Catholic Church is offered as an example of this. If the tensions of the world are dealt with by withdrawal, then the process of rationalization, of social evolution, is not helped. If there is an attempt to solve the worldly tension, then the evolutionary process is pushed forward. We do not have to look far back into the history of religion to find examples of this, they are there in the secular and political history of the last three decades. The period of social turmoil that developed to differing degrees across western Europe and in the USA in the 1960s and 1970s, which might have been student-led in some countries but also involved ethnic minorities, women, and workers, shows, at least as far as the student and youth dimensions are concerned, a similar division. There were those who sought an inner enlightenment and retired from the world, and there were those who rejected compromise and sort to change the world to something closer to their ideals, which were often seen in terms of individual freedom, individual rights to self-expression, and so on. It is arguable that the tensions that Weber found are still present, not only in religious life but also in radical political life. The current form on inner resolution is perhaps being sought by those around 'New Age' groups and the this-worldly solutions being sought by the green movement, some forms of feminism, and some ethnic movements, but with a lot of over-lap.

Chinese religion: Confucianism and Taoism

One of the common criticisms of Weber's (1915/1951) study of Chinese religion is that he cited material from the very earliest period up to the beginning of the twentieth century as if he were talking about the same society; Reinhard Bendix (1966) (whose account of Weber's religious studies I would recommend highly) argues that this can be justified—there had, in fact, been comparatively little change in some aspects of Chinese society, Weber was concerned with showing the potentialities of this society, and such an analysis could be developed from different periods of its history.

Weber's prime concern, however, was with the early stages of Chinese history. One feature of Chinese society is that cities, whilst recognizably centres of population, craft, and trade as they were in the West, never developed the same autonomy—they did not receive charters or obtain political independence and did not function as corporate bodies. The residents of the towns remained tied to their villages through kinship relations, in which the practice of ancestor worship was particularly important. Relationships to the supernatural were not a direct individual matter as they became in the West, but were mediated through the family. The towns remained subordinate to the countryside, and to the central authority. Here we find Weber's version of oriental despotism. The central government needs to defend large and open boundaries and defend against flooding as well as regulate irrigation to supply the cities.

However, central power was not absolute and local groups were strong, but they could not organize opposition to the central power. Local rulers derived their power from their ancestral inheritance, but, according to Weber, this also inhibited them coming together in a unified status group to oppose the emperor. Because of the early centralization of power and development of an administrative body, power struggles were about office rather than land. Office-holders could be freely removed from office (whereas in the West they were inherited positions), and any movement towards a more rational form of organization was automatically inhibited by the power of the emperor, who was also the chief priest in the state religion, which had no prophetic tradition.

The emperor kept a fairly strict control over his regional officials; appointment was by educational qualification, not birth, for comparatively short periods and away from the area where the official was born; they were subjected to regular assessments, the results of which were made public. In this way, they were kept on a tight rein. This is a lesson which has been learnt by the contemporary British government and management—regular audits, 'quality assessments', the publication of league tables for hospitals and schools, all establish a very high level of central control.

In China, however, these regional officials were dependent on local translators and officials and this masked the power of the central government—central decrees did not take on the aura of orders from above. The tax system did not boost the central government either. At each stage in the process, an official would have to extract his own salary and expenses and that of his staff, and this encouraged immense pressure on the peasant who actually paid the taxes, but the amount of money paid upwards at each stage becomes less and less. This sets the scene for a three-way struggle between status groups: the central government, its appointees, and the local kinship networks, which were very powerful and organized along a mixture of democratic and what Weber calls 'hereditary charismatic' principles. These networks involved all male members of the family and provided the basis for regular ancestor ceremonies.

Here we come to the central issue for Weber: why did capitalism not develop in China. In terms of the social structure, the strength of the kinship network was important—preventing the development of legal-rational authority necessary for the growth of capitalism. By definition the family is a bastion of traditionalism, especially where ancestors are religiously important; the centrally appointed officials remained dependent on their families' support, and, importantly, no separate class of lawyers developed. The family group was responsible for the law.

This enabled the development of a limited form of commercial capitalism run by 'purveyors to the state and tax farmers'. But it did not enable the development of rational industrial capitalism, which needs the stability of conditions in which rational accounting can develop, and the dominance of the family network does not allow this. Moreover, the 'feud' element of feudalism—struggles between local rulers—did not develop into rational warfare as it did in the West. On the other hand, there was a period of increasing agricultural production and population increase, and considerable personal fortunes were amassed and personal freedom of movement was increasing—all conditions which would favour capitalism. These forces were in turn negated by the absence of a rationally administered and formally guaranteed legal system and by the 'ethos peculiar to a stratum of officials and aspirants to office' (Weber 1915/1951: 104). This was the Confucian ethic by which officials led their lives.

The Chinese official was educated in literature, in proper ways of behaving, in writing instead of speaking; his charisma derived from this and was proved by his 'harmonious' administration. Confucianism is the religion of intellectuals: education can remove human faults and lead to the dominance of the 'heavenly' aspects of human nature over its demonic aspects—the 'gentleman ideal' was that of all-round perfection, 'who had become a "work of art" in the sense of a classical, eternally valid, canon of psychical beauty, which literary tradition implemented in the souls of disciples' (ibid. 131).

It was not appropriate for such a man to engage in economic activity—except insofar as he was concerned with the proper level of consumption, neither too little nor too much. The pursuit of wealth for its own sake was disapproved of because it would involve an imbalance in the development of the self:

> Confucian virtue, based upon universality or self-perfection, was greater than the riches to be gained by one-sided thoroughness. Not even in the most influential position could one achieve anything in the world without the virtue derived from education. And vice versa, one could achieve nothing, no matter what one's virtue, without influential position. Hence the 'superior' man coveted such a position, not profit.   (ibid. 161)

This was directly opposed to the western feudal ethic of accumulation for lavish expenditure. However, if the Confucian ethic did not encourage economic activity and rational calculation, what about the more popular religions: Taoism and Buddhism?

Taoism was developed from the same sources as Confucianism. It rejected

Table 13.1 Contrasting Confucianism and Puritanism

Confucianism	Puritanism
Belief in impersonal, cosmic order; tolerance of magic.	Belief in supramundane God; rejection of magic.
Adjustment to the world to maintain harmony of heaven and earth; the ideal of order.	Mastery over the world in unceasing quest for virtue in the eyes of God; the ideal of progressive change.
Vigilant self-control for the sake of dignity and self-perfection.	Vigilant self-control for the sake of controlling man's wicked nature and doing God's will.
Absence of prophecy related to inviolability of tradition; man can avoid the wrath of the spirits and be 'good' if he acts properly.	Prophecy makes tradition and the world as it is appear wicked; man cannot attain goodness by his own efforts.
Familial piety as the principal governing all human relations.	Subordination of all human relations to the service of God.
Kinship relations as the basis for commercial transactions, voluntary associations, law, and public administration.	Rational law and agreement as the basis for commercial transactions, voluntary associations, law, and public administration.
Distrust of all persons outside the extended family.	Trust of all persons who are 'brothers in faith'.
Wealth as the basis for dignity and self-perfection.	Wealth as a temptation and unintended by-product of a virtuous life.

worldly concerns and encouraged the use of magic. Both Taoism and Confucianism, but particularly the latter, were important inhibitions on economic activity in China. Confucianism was able to use Taoism to defend its own interests, although both Taoism and Buddhism were persecuted if they presented a threat; but for most of the time they did not—they emphasized withdrawal from the world and contemplation in the search for salvation, and as part of this a submissive obedience to the external order. Clearly neither could provide the basis for a rational capitalism.

Weber ends his study with a comparison of Confucianism with the Puritanism which he saw as primarily responsible for the growth of capitalism in the West. As we have seen, his analysis of Chinese society is concerned with the economic level and the way in which different status groups form on the basis of economic organization, political and administrative organization, and religious beliefs. There were elements in economic organization which favoured the growth of capitalism as well as inhibited it; the main political inhibition came from the strength of the family and the importance of ancestor worship—a religious belief. But it was the wider religious ethic that was perhaps crucial and here we must begin to look at Puritanism. Bendix (1966: 140–41) produces an excellent table of the differences that Weber identifies when he is comparing the two (see Table 13.1).

Indian religion: Hinduism and Buddhism

Weber's study of Indian religion begins with the caste system, the role of which is as central to the development of Indian society as the relationship between the family and the bureaucracy was to Chinese society. In China the effect of religion on the social structure was indirect—the beliefs of Confucianism had the effect of inhibiting capitalist development, but did not prescribe a particular type of social structure. In India, however, the caste system *was* Indian social structure and was intimately bound up with Hinduism.

He distinguishes first between different sorts of religious groupings: sects (which in the modern West include such groups as the Plymouth Brethren, Jehovah's Witnesses, and so on) and churches (the Anglican Church, the Roman Catholic Church, or the Greek or Russian Orthodox Churches):

A 'sect' in the sociological sense of the word is an exclusive association of religious virtuosos or especially qualified religious persons, recruited through individual admission after establishment of qualification. By contrast a 'church' as a universalistic establishment for the salvation of the masses raises the claim, like the 'state', that everyone, at least each child of a member, must belong by birth. It demands sacramental acts and, possibly, proof of acquaintance with its holy learning as a precondition of its membership rights, but establishes as a duty the observance of the sacraments and the discharge of those obligations which are a condition of its membership rights. The consequence of this is that when the church reaches its full development and has power, it coerces opponents to conform. . . . The individual is normally 'born' into the church, single conversions and admissions occurring only until the time the church has attained its principal goal—the unification of all men in the universal church.   (Weber 1921/1958: 6)

Hinduism possesses properties of both sect and church; membership is by birth to Hindu parents, but it has the sect's exclusiveness; no one can enter from the outside and it has no aspiration to universalism, to convert the whole of humanity. Each caste is recruited from only one social group, who share the same status by virtue of their rituals, and movement between castes is not allowed. They are an exceptionally rigid form of status group—although there is some variation in rigidity brought about through social aspirations and status consciousness.

The family is particularly important. In the West we are familiar with the notion of the 'divine right of kings'—or for that matter queens—which involves a familial charisma which is passed on from generation to generation, even if some generations don't appear to possess as much of it as others. For Weber, Indian society was dependent upon familial charisma, which bound kin groups together into castes, giving religious significance to all sorts of status distinctions. The caste system developed partly due to military conquest, with the invading groups refusing any intermixing with the conquered but claiming the land and a proportion of its product. The subordinate group owed obligatory service to the ruling group as a whole, not to its individual members. This led to a division of labour between rather than within groups.

This was reinforced by the conversion of tribes (already economic units with their internal division of labour) to Hinduism; sometimes this happened because the ruling groups of these tribes saw the chance of gaining a religious justification for their position, or perhaps because a tribe or specialist group had lost its territory, so it took on the status of a pariah group and they formed the lowest castes. Castes would also subdivide—new practices might appear because environmental conditions change. As ever, Weber offers a multi-causal analysis for the predominance of the caste system.

Rather like the Confucian literati, the highest caste—the Brahmins—gained charisma from their knowledge of literature; but, whereas the former were officials, such careers were rare amongst the Brahmins, who comprised 'princely chaplains . . . counselors, theological teachers and jurists, priests and pastors' (ibid. 140). For the Brahmin, the pursuit of a career, the highest Confucian ideal, meant very little. And, in contrast to China, there was a separation between church and state: the kings were not priests, and in fact they were subordinated to priests. Whereas the Confucian officials were concerned with written literature, and relegated magic to the people, the Brahmins cultivated and protected an oral tradition and relied on magic for the maintenance of their position. There was no universal ethic, but different ethics for each caste within an overarching world-view which saw the rank order of castes as a matter of retribution

for misdeeds in a previous life. There was no idea of natural right or of fundamental human equality as appeared in the West and there could be no basis for
social criticism. Everyone existed in a pluralistic, eternal order. In the wider
social structure, patrimonial and feudal organization existed; in the struggle
between various groups, no one was able to establish overall power, and there
was a fluctuation between the appearance of centrally governed patrimonial
empires and fragmentation into small areas of control.

There was a period of competition for popular support between Hinduism
and Buddhism, but the latter's concern for contemplation did not encourage
conflict and Buddhism fragmented and declined. Weber identifies two important Hindu beliefs. The first is a belief in the transmigration of the soul: the belief
that the soul moves into another world on death, and sacrifice and prayer in this
world ensure it a peaceful life until eventually it undergoes another death and
rebirth into another existence in this world. The second is a belief in *karma*: that
retribution for misdeeds in this life involves being born into a lower caste, and
proper ritual observances in this life lead to being born into a higher caste. There
can be no concept of the 'accident of birth' which lies behind western ideas such
as equality of opportunity despite the social class into which people are born.
We deserve what we get and, if we conscientiously observe the prescribed rituals, we can do better next time. These are not beliefs likely to fuel criticism,
protest, or rebellion.

To buttress their position at the top of the caste system the Brahmins
developed an ascetic ideal—an ideal of self denial, in dietary and sexual and
other matters—which distinguished them as truly holy men. Here Weber seems
to be close to a crude Marxism, an argument that these ideas developed to
justify and protect a particular class position. A form of apathetic austerity
became the highest ideal of Hindu life. On the birth of the first grandson, the
Brahmin should withdraw from everyday life, and seek internal emancipation,
a 'blissful state'. When the Brahmins seek emancipation, it is not just from the
concerns of this world but from the everlasting cycle of death and rebirth. Yoga
is one intellectual method of achieving this special state. Originally, Weber suggests, such ascetics became teachers (gurus) and formed the nucleus of monas-
teries.

On occasion it seemed that the ideal of the holy man took him well away from
the world of religious observance as well, beyond the claims of rituals and of ethical systems—he should aim at a state of indifference as to whether his actions
were good or evil, and this brought into question the possibility of salvation for
the ordinary person. It also meant that the holy man could be engaged in action
and at the same time indifferent to it. Bendix sums up the dominant theme of
Brahmin wisdom which:

achieves an image of the world in which not only each man's daily duties but also each
man's goal of salvation has become relative to his position in the caste order. Whatever
they might be, each man's actions and devotions are valuable *in their own terms*; in a

world that has been devalued few men can have more than relative merit.   (Bendix 1966: 182)

The Brahmins managed to hold on to their position despite various challenges and, like the Chinese literati, they tolerated magic and popular religion for the lower orders, which allowed a number of sectarian doctrines to develop. However, the guru was given a new and powerful position with absolute power in the matter of salvation. Under Islamic and later British rule, the Brahmins became ever more important figures.

   The overall effect of this on economic activity should be fairly evident. Wealth and professional and economic success could never be seen as a sign of salvation. At the same time, Hindu adherents amongst the masses were involved in every-day economic activities and enthusiastically accumulated wealth, but this was not carried out in the rational, calculative way in which it was pursued in the West. It was, rather, intimately bound up with magic and magical practices. Weber refers to it as a 'magical garden' from which rationality could not develop. The acquisitive drive has to be incorporated into the inner worldly life ethic before it can contribute towards the development of capitalism, and the force of tradition in the caste system as well as the beliefs of Hinduism did not allow this.

Palestine: ancient Judaism

In his study of Judaism, Weber focuses on what differentiates western from east-ern religion. The crucial factor is the notion of positive ethical action—of changing the world for the better under God's guidance. But in the end it is the *unintentional effects* of religious belief that are most important.

   There are important suggestions in both Judaism and Christianity that people should make themselves the tools of God, the means by which God pur-sues his ends in this world. The world is a constant temptation, threatening to take people away from God's purposes; and a particular danger lies in sitting back and simply fulfilling ritual expectations. This latter course was represented by medieval mystical Christianity. This is important for Weber, because for him the uniqueness of the West lay in the Judaic tradition of prophecy. The Jewish experience of religion was radically different from the Indian. It was a matter not of ritual observance but of seeking a radical change. The tribes of Israel were the chosen people, the children of God who had lost their privileges, and that priv-ileged position had to be restored. In a very real sense the world had to be turned upside-down—it was not a matter of eternal cycles of the same thing but of a long, changing process. Judaism was soaked in what we would now call history:

The whole attitude toward life of ancient Jewry was determined by this conception of a future God-guided political and social revolution. This revolution was to take a special direction. Ritual correctitude and the segregation from the social environment imposed by it was but one aspect of the commands upon Jewry. There existed in addition a highly rational religious ethic of social conduct; it was free of magic and all forms of irrational quest for salvation. To a large extent this ethic still underlies contemporary Mid-Eastern and European ethics. World-historical interest in Jewry rests upon this fact.   (Weber 1921/1952: 5)

The development of ancient Palestine was rarely a peaceful one—the history of conquest and war runs through the Old Testament. Weber argues that this was in part the result of contrasting ways of life in the region. Settlement and cultivation were possible in the north, whereas, to the south and the east, some settlement was possible but it usually involved seasonal migration, or there was the possibility of a permanent nomadic existence. There was regular conflict between nomads, herdsmen, peasants, and city-dwellers. Under the reign of Solomon, Israel was a major power, developing from the confederacy of tribes that followed the Exodus from Egypt. This period was in turn followed by decline and Babylonian captivity. The basic tenets of Judaism were developed through the period leading up to the monarchy, and, after its fall, they became the basis for the prophetic movement to which we owe the development of the modern world.

The time of 'confederacy' saw no permanent institutions; social cohesion was provided by common religious beliefs which united disparate extended families. The tribes came together as a political unity mainly in times of war. There were a number of specific features of Judaism and its belief in Jahwe (or Jehovah), who was to become the Christian God. 'Everywhere', Weber argues, 'deities are the guardian of the social order. They sanction its violation, reward conformity to it' (ibid. 120). But Israel had a special agreement with God set out in Moses' tablets of stone. God would be Israel's God and no other nation's. And, in return, the Israelites promised obedience to Jahwe and no other God. Originally Jahwe was a God of war and natural catastrophes such as plagues of locusts and snakes and famines and floods; there is perhaps an ironic memory of this in the way the term 'Act of God' is used by modern insurance companies. On occasion he could be angry at being slighted and bring about dramatic punishment to remind people of his power. He was a fierce God, fiercer than the Christian God, but we still have a sense that there might be this fierce absolute power some-where. Jehovah did not sanction a permanent order. He had an agreement with His people which could change if He so desired. He could direct events according to His will, to reward or punish His people. The notion of a special covenant with God was unique in the Middle East. There were long battles with different beliefs within and outside Judaism; the important internal divisions were between priests (the Levites) and various mystic or orgiastic tendencies.

Whereas the Gods of other tribes would respond to sacrifices, Jehovah expected obedience, and this was the only way to seek his favour. This under-mined the power of both magicians and priests; when things went wrong, it generated relatively rational argument about which commandment had been broken and how and why.

It was this tradition which developed when Israel went into Babylonian captivity. Israel was not one of the three great Middle Eastern centres of civilization—rather it was at the crossroads between such societies, and this enabled creative interaction of intellectuals and socially declassed citizens to produce new religious ideas. Weber points out that it is on the margin of great empires or centres of civilization that new religious ideas emerge. He might have added that it was not only religious ideas that emerged in such situations. Marx had also pointed out that new ideas in general come from the edges of the great centres of social change rather than from within them. For Weber, life at the centre of the great civilization is caught up unreflectively in the existence and beliefs of that society, whereas on the edges, where the effects of that life are felt, albeit at a distance, people begin to ask their own questions and learn to develop their own way of dealing with life. There is space and a necessity to reflect on these issues. We find the same happening in modern Europe: it was the German philosopher Hegel who was the first to try to systematize an understanding of the French Revolution—something that could be done only from a distance but not too far a distance. And it is was the thinkers of the Scottish Enlightenment—the philosopher David Hume, the economist Adam Smith—who began thinking through the implications of the industrial revolution in England. As Bendix (1966: 233) puts it: 'The possibility of questioning the meaning of the world presupposes the capacity to be astonished about the course of events, and surprise is not always possible when one is in the midst of events.'

Returning to ancient Palestine, the monarchy developed into an autocratic state of the Egyptian model. This provoked a rebellion and a split into two, Israel and Judah, which survived because of a lull in the expansionary ambitions of the surrounding empires of Egypt and Mesopotamia. Once these started their wars of conquest, the region witnessed scenes that Weber says reached a frightfulness and magnitude never seen before:

Blood fairly drips from the cuneiform[1] inscriptions. The king, in the tone of dry protocol, reports that he covered the walls of conquered cities with human skins. The Israelite literature preserved from the period, above all the oracles of classical prophecy, express the mad terror caused by these merciless conquerors. As impending gloom beclouded the political horizon, classical prophecy acquired its characteristic form. (Weber 1921/1952: 267)

The form taken by that prophecy is perhaps not surprising and Weber argues that it could develop only under external threat and against the king and his prophets, who were seen as of declining importance:

usually the prophet spoke on his own, i.e. under the influence of spontaneous inspiration, to the public in the market place or to the elders at the city gate. The prophet also

[1] The name given to the characters of Assyrian script.

interpreted the fates of individuals, though as a rule only those of politically important persons. The predominant concern of the prophet was the destiny of the state and the people. This concern always assumed the form of emotional invectives against the overlords. It is here that 'the demagogue' appeared for the first time in the records of history. (ibid. 269)

Old Testament prophecy was authoritarian in character and gained power from the fact that it was uttered by a private citizen; the rulers reacted with fear, wrath, or indifference as the occasion demanded. During this period we find the first examples of political pamphleteering. But it would be wrong to draw too close a parallel with modern politics and political situations. These prophets were asserting absolute ethical positions and had little contact with the political realities of their situations. In fact, their prestige depended in part on their separation from the nation's politics. We can get a hint of what this might have been like when political outsiders take up moral positions in contemporary political debates—Ross Perot in the 1994 American presidential election comes to mind. But their prestige also depended on their high social status. However, they cursed both the great and the uneducated masses, and—perhaps not surprisingly—they gained little public support.

Their most distinctive feature as a status group, Weber argued, was the gratuitous nature of their prophecies: they were free and spontaneous, very different from the official prophets and the 'industry of prophecy'. As Weber puts it: 'One does not pay for evil omens.' What he calls their inner independence was, he argues, not a result of their activities but a cause of it. This is an interesting way of seeing it and it takes us back to my earlier comments about charisma. I suggested that Weber did not see charisma as a social product, but as a sort of independent psychological variable. Here he is talking not about charisma but about an inner independence, which he seems to see too as an independent psychological variable. But I think we are entitled to ask whether this inner independence would have arisen without the security of a high-status background—only Amos of the prophets came from a shepherd background.

This type of prophecy was a sign of the weakness of the priesthood—and here Weber acknowledges that their family background was important and kept the enmity of the priests at bay. The prophets saw themselves as tools of God, but not as specially privileged humans in the sense that they did not claim to be free from sin. The prophet delivered his own personal message from God, but did not offer any magical solution or sign to prove his communication with Jehovah. The populace at large seemed to assume that the prophetic message was validated by the fact that nobody in his right senses would risk incurring the wrath of the powers that be without some special reason, and hearing the voice of God would be such a reason. The insistence of the moral law against all earthly powers that tried to persecute them was the achievement of these prophets—it made the *morally correct actions of everyday life into the special duty of a people chosen by the mightiest God* (Bendix 1966: 247; emphasis in original). And the will of this God was open to understanding—not a matter of obtaining a mystical state and not requiring metaphysical speculation. If misfortune befell the people, then it was because of God's will, and if God willed them misfortune, then it was because of disobedience. Weber makes much of the fact that they could have constructed alternative explanations, but that would have moved towards irrationality. Disobedience lay in oppressing the poor, idol worship, neglect of rituals, and—surprise, surprise—suppression of prophecy. But redemption was always possible and the pious would be rewarded. This explanation enabled the transformation of Jehovah into a Universal God, not one among many in competition with the others. He alone was responsible for the fortune and misfortune of his special people. The worse things became, the more the prophecies were fulfilled, the greater the Israelites' devotion to God. And these beliefs prepared the way for the emergence, many centuries later, of the Saviour.

The Protestant ethic and the spirit of capitalism

Introduction

So we come at last to Weber's much heralded classic work on the Protestant ethic. As you might expect if you have read the previous sections, the rise of Puritanism crowns and hastens the process of rationalization that originated with the pact between Jehovah and Israel and was developed by the Old Testament prophets and the arrival of Christianity. This, in turn, led to the development of western capitalism.

The three books that have just been discussed are what we might call sociological histories of religion, looking at the relationship between religious beliefs, economic situations, and social structures and the way in which they interlock in social development. They are *stories*, tales of development. There is a similar element to the Protestant ethic, but that is perhaps less important than the *analytic* aspect. Weber is not simply telling a story but he is suggesting a causal connection between what he calls the spirit of capitalism and the Protestant ethic. The connection is an 'elective affinity'—it is as if one way of thinking about the world seeks out and encourages another. But this affinity is not necessarily a conscious one, working itself out directly through people's thinking and action. It is more indirect. The Puritans do not decide singly or collectively to set out to develop an economic system called capitalism; rather they faithfully follow their beliefs and the growth of capitalism is what some contemporary sociologists would call an 'unintended consequence'.

Bendix (1966) talks about Weber's own work ethic, the punishing demands he made upon himself at the outset of his career which eventually led to his breakdown, and suggests that he took on this attitude to his work from his entrepreneur uncle, who worked hard and lived frugally, in a way Weber thought typical of the great entrepreneurs of early capitalism. Modern psycho-analysis would see this tendency in terms of a strict, if not punitive superego, a strict, internalized authority figure which constantly demands more and more in the way of effort and will allow little relaxation and enjoyment. A very differ-ent thinker, the twentieth-century Marxist philosopher Herbert Marcuse (1969), has employed psychoanalytic ideas to argue that capitalism establishes itself on the basis of an immense internal repression that pushed people into the sacrifice of pleasure. We have seen that Freud's argument was that some repres-sion was necessary to make civilization possible at all; Marcuse's point was that capitalism made very special demands in this respect—rather than consuming wealth for enjoyment, it must be reinvested for the accumulation of capital.

I hope this is not so much of a diversion as it might appear; Weber's thesis in *The Protestant Ethic* is very similar but does not draw on notions of the uncon-scious. It is concerned with conscious beliefs and ideas, which he sees as moti-vating action in a comparatively unproblematic way, and he goes on to the way in which these actions have, for the actors, unintended consequences. I will look first at what Weber has to say about capitalism, and then at his discussion of Protestantism, following the order of his argument.

The spirit of capitalism

Capitalism, 'the most fateful force in our modern life', is defined as entailing a particular sort of action which:

rests on the expectation of profit by the utilization of opportunities for exchange, that is on ... peaceful chances for profit. . . . Where capitalist acquisition is rationally pursued, the corresponding action is adjusted to calculations in terms of capital. This means that the action is adapted to a systematic utilization of goods or personal services as a means of acquisition in such a way that at the end of a business period, the balance of the enter-prise in money assets ... exceeds the capital, i.e. the estimated value of material means of production used for acquisition in exchange.   (1904/5/1930: 17–18)

More simply, capitalist economic action aims to make a calculable profit. Such capitalism has existed at all times in most places, but in the West it has taken on a new form, involving the capitalist organization of free labour, the separation of business from home, and the development of rational bookkeeping. He notes the importance of technology and the systematic and rational application of technology to capitalist production, which owed much to the pre-existing 'rational structures of law and of administration' (ibid. 25). At this point Weber seems to be compiling a list of contributing factors rather than ordering them into some tentative causal explanation, although he does emphasize the import-ance of free labour. However, the crucial factor is the peculiar rationalism general to western culture and a general willingness to accept rational techniques. In other cultures religious beliefs and practices have inhibited such activities.

Weber points out that Protestant areas seem to favour the growth of capitalism. This revolt against traditional religion was not against religion as such but the replacement of a very relaxed religious control by a very strict and all pervasive religious control. At Weber's time it was possible to argue that Protestants were much more acquisitive than Roman Catholics, but in the past the opposite had been the case; the original Protestants were Puritans, not concerned with the 'joy of living', with personal pleasure, or consumption.

To build up his conception of the spirit of capitalism, Weber draws on the writings of Benjamin Franklin, an eighteenth-century American who might now be called a 'management' or 'business' consultant and who wrote popular books on how to get rich. The two from which Weber takes his model go under the titles of *Necessary Hints to Those that Would Be Rich* and *Advice to a Young Tradesman*, written in 1736 and 1748 respectively. Franklin sets out what Weber regards as the spirit of capitalism in its pure type. Here I will simply summarize his points with the odd quotation. Many of them take the form of sayings which have entered into common usage:

1. Time is money.
2. Credit is money.
3. 'Remember that money is of the prolific, generating nature. Money can beget money, and its offspring can beget more, and so on. . . . He that kills a breeding-sow destroys all her offspring to the thousandth generation. He that murders a crown, destroys all that it might have produced, even scores of pounds.'
4. 'The good paymaster is lord of another man's purse'—i.e. if I pay my debts when they are due I will always be able to borrow as much as I can. 'The most trifling actions that affect a man's credit are to be regarded. The sound of your hammer at five in the morning, or eight at night, heard by a creditor, makes him easy six months longer.'
5. Keep careful accounts of income and expenditure—basically look after the pennies and the pounds will look after themselves.
6. Always be known for prudence and industry, don't spend time idly; all money that is spent idling loses not only its own value, but the money that it might have been turned in to.

Weber points out that the implication of this is that increasing capital is a duty, not simply a matter of 'business astuteness'. However, the virtues that Franklin proposes are strictly utilitarian; they serve an end and need be espoused only at the level of appearance. It is important that I appear to be honest and hard-working, so that people will trust me and bring me business. Weber argues that it is not quite so simple as this. For Franklin there is something more profound—a real religious conviction and search for salvation:

the *summum bonum* [greatest good] of this ethic, the earning of more and more money, combined with the strict avoidance of all spontaneous enjoyment of life, is above all completely devoid of any . . . hedonistic admixture. It is thought of so purely as an end in itself, that from the point of view of the happiness of, or utility to, the single individual, it appears entirely transcendental and absolutely irrational. Man is dominated by the making of money, by acquisition as the ultimate purpose of his life. Economic acquisition is no longer subordinated to man as the means for the satisfaction of his material needs. This reversal of what we should call the natural relationship, so irrational from a naive point of view is evidently as definitely a leading principle of capitalism as it is foreign to all peoples not under capitalist influence.   (Weber 1904/5/1930: 53)

This is the same phenomenon that Marx understood in terms of the subordination of use value to exchange value and the accumulation of capital. But, whereas for Marx it was the result of a change in the relations of production, for Weber it is the result of a change in ethical orientation towards the world. For both, however, once capitalism is established, it has an almost unstoppable expansionary dynamic.

Returning to Franklin and the spirit of capitalism, Weber argues that the making of money as an end in itself is not quite that but a sign of something else—of 'virtue and proficiency in a calling'. When Weber was writing, the notion of a 'calling' was more familiar that I suspect it is today. It involves the idea that we might be 'called upon' to do something in our lives, called upon by God and perhaps society as well, to pursue a particular employment, a particular line of business, and this must be done to the best of one's ability.

Weber himself makes the sensible reservation that an established capitalism does not depend on such a notion of a calling—it has become an 'immense cosmos' which presents itself to the individual as an unalterable situation to which he or she must adjust; in a statement which would not shame a Marxist, Weber writes:

It forces the individual, in so far as he is involved in the system of market relationships, to conform to capitalistic rules of action. The manufacturer who in the long run acts counter to these norms, will just as inevitably be eliminated from the economic scene as the worker who cannot or will not adapt himself to them will be thrown into the streets without a job. Thus the capitalism of today, which has come to dominate economic life, educates and selects the economic subjects which it needs through a process of economic survival of the fittest.   (ibid. 54–5)

But the system had to originate somewhere in the activities of a group of people who acted in the same way. At many other periods of history the sentiments expressed by Franklin would not have met universal acclaim; and the areas where unscrupulous money-making was acceptable were not the areas in which capitalism developed. Capitalism is characterized by a moralized money-making and its main enemy is characterized by Weber as 'traditionalism'.

Where the worker is concerned, the traditionalist attitude is one that I find I have myself possessed for a large part of my working life: what is important is the preservation of a way of life, and I have been content with earning enough to enable me to live in the way that I desire. If I were imbued with the capitalist spirit, I would be seeking to maximize my earnings even if it meant living in a different way that I did not find attractive. The example that Weber uses is of agricultural workers paid piece-rates (i.e. according to the amount of work they do) at harvest time. He claims that, in situations where the piece-rate has been raised, the workers have produced less—they do not aim to maximize their income, simply to maintain it, and if they can do so by doing less work, all well and good. The obvious solution (to the employer) of increasing work by paying less has its limits—low wages do not keep workers in good health, or attract workers with the necessary skills.

Capitalism cannot, or at least at its beginning could not, rely on workers to adopt the attitude that labour was an end in itself, not simply a means to enjoyment, a comfortable life, and so on. Workers who did adopt such an attitude—such as Methodist workers in Britain—often incurred the hostility of their workmates, who would go as far as destroying their tools. If one or two workers in the group work harder than their colleagues, then everybody will be expected to work harder.

Just as workers can maintain traditionalist attitudes to work, so can employers. Many large enterprises can be content to make 'enough' profit without setting about it in a systematically rational way. Weber's example is of the 'putter-out' in the textile industry in the nineteenth century. Peasants would bring their product to the putter-out, who would buy it and then sell to customers who came to him. He rarely sought customers personally, relying on letters and samples; working hours were moderate, enough to maintain a respectable life. He would have a good relationship with competitors and devote part of the day to socializing. The ease of such a life was changed when some ambitious youngster would start organizing himself more efficiently, personally soliciting customers, supervising his workers more closely, thereby changing them from peasants to labourers, and reinvesting profits in the business. Weber argues that it was not the sudden investment of new money which brought about this transformation but a change in attitude, the appearance of a new spirit.

It is worth going off on a detour here, because this argument seems on the face of it to be very close to contemporary right-wing rhetoric about the way in which the poor should be treated. It is argued that, if social security payments are too high, then the recipients develop a dependent culture, and lose the desire to work—in Weber's terms, they develop a traditionalist attitude, which, so the argument goes, must be changed. However, Weber's point is that such an attitude cannot be changed by varying financial rewards, or the absence of financial rewards, or financial punishments. It is a value choice motivated by something unconnected with finance of any sort, and part of a changing collective consciousness— or even *conscience collective*—which is not brought about by an act of will.

One might think that the moral qualities of sober hard work involve a rational, enlightened attitude that modern sensibilities might regard as the opposite of religious belief. If entrepreneurs were asked why their lives were dedicated to work rather than the other way round, why they were so constantly restless, seeking new achievements, they would produce all sorts of subjective reasons, such as providing for their children, which would have operated equally strongly in traditional societies. Power might be a motive, but the true capitalist seems little interested in its trappings:

The ideal type of the capitalist entrepreneur . . . avoids ostentation and unnecessary expenditure, as well as conscious enjoyment of his power, and is embarrassed by the outward signs of the social recognition which he receives. His manner of life is distinguished by a certain ascetic tendency . . . a sort of modesty which is essentially more modest than the reserve which Franklin so shrewdly recommends. He gets nothing out of his wealth for himself, except the irrational sense of having done his job well.   (ibid. 71)

This attitude would be incomprehensible to the traditionalist, as would the obligation felt by many entrepreneurs to provide for their fellow human beings. Weber here cites Benjamin Franklin's attempts to bring about civic improvements in Philadelphia.

The Protestant ethic

The emergence of capitalism cannot be seen as part of a slow and universal process of rationalization which was uneven, and Enlightenment rationality did not find its adherents primarily in the countries where capitalism was most advanced. Legal rationalization did not proceed hand in hand with the development of capitalism either—in Britain, for example, the legal system went into reverse, and law was always at its most rational in Roman Catholic countries. So where did the peculiar rationality of European capitalism come from? It originates in Protestantism, more specifically in the writings of Martin Luther after he became a reformer. Most importantly, we find there the notion of a 'calling': 'the valuation of the fulfilment of duty in worldly affairs as the highest form which the moral activity of the individual could assume' (Weber 1904–5/1930: 80). All callings had the same value in the eyes of God. At the beginning, the search for material rewards beyond one's personal needs was seen as a sign of a lack of grace, especially since it could be achieved only at the expense of others. Moreover, as Luther developed and emphasized the notion, he came to place a faith in Providence. It is, for example, God's will that I should clean streets; it is 'meant' and my duty is to do it as well as I can. In this sense, Luther's conception of a calling is traditionalist—I have to adapt to God's will. There is no direct relationship with the idea of the calling as we find it in the spirit of capitalism. To get a clearer idea of the connection, Weber turns to the doctrines of the Scottish Protestant John Calvin, which, he suggests, have always been seen as the real enemy by the Roman Catholic Church and even drew the disapproval of the Lutherans. In moving over to the study of Calvinism, Weber presents a statement of his method and of what he is trying to do which clearly represents the complexity of his analysis and its movement to and from causal explanations:

we are merely attempting to clarify the part which religious forces have played in forming the developing web of our specifically worldly modern culture, in the complex action of innumerable different historical factors. We are thus enquiring only to what extent certain characteristic features of this culture can be imputed to the influence of the Reformation. At the same time we must free ourselves from the idea that it is possible to deduce the Reformation, as a historically necessary result, from certain economic changes. Countless historical circumstances, which cannot be reduced to any economic law . . . especially purely political processes, had to concur in order that the newly created Churches should survive at all.

On the other hand, however, we have no intention of maintaining such a foolish and doctrinaire thesis as that the spirit of capitalism . . . could only have arisen as a result of certain effects of the Reformation, or even that capitalism as an economic system is a creation of the Reformation . . . we only wish to ascertain whether and to what extent religious forces have taken part in the quantitative formation and quantitative expansion of that spirit over the world.   (ibid. 91)

Weber suggests that there are four main forms of ascetic (i.e. self-denying) Protestantism: Calvinism, Pietism, Methodism, and the Baptist sects. These groups engaged in all sorts of struggles with each other and with established churches over doctrine, but Weber is less interested in the details of dogma than in what he calls the 'psychological sanctions' which direct peoples' actions. The essential element of Calvinist belief was predestination: the idea that we are already chosen for eternal life or eternal damnation, and we cannot do anything about it. Salvation is a gift of God, not my own achievement. We can find the same idea in Luther, but it is not central. For Calvin, we could not know God's choice. We might get glimpses of it, but basically it was just like that—not a matter of justice or personal worth: 'for the damned to complain of their lot would be much the same as for animals to bemoan the fact that they were not born as men' (ibid. 103). The psychological effect of this must have been to produce an 'unprecedented inner loneliness'—I am damned or I am saved, I cannot know which and I cannot change matters through my own actions, nor can I find anybody—a priest, for example—who might offer forgiveness and consolation. This is the state of existential loneliness *par excellence*. At the same time, worldly goods and pleasures are denied me—they are signs of corruption and would confirm that I am one of the damned. All this comes across in John Bunyan's *Pilgrim's Progress* (1928), the classical Puritan story. Even religious ceremony is rejected.

For the Puritan, there was no problem about the meaning of life; God had ordered the cosmos to serve the utility of the human race and humans were meant to work out God's purpose on earth; the Puritans were lonely but in a situation where they did not have to search for meaning. Yet there was a search for some confirmation that the individual was one of the saved. Calvin personally had no problem with this: the lucky man was sure that he was one of the elect. However, this would not work for the mass of his followers. The advice given to the faithful was to reach a psychological certainty of their own election, of their own salvation, through the daily struggle of work. Instead of a collection of humble and repenting sinners, Puritans offered an army of self-confident saints. Perhaps the public figure who comes nearest to this model in contemporary British public life is the Reverend Ian Paisley, the Northern Irish Protestant leader. Such people are, of course, completely unbearable if one is not a believer.

Anyway, the Calvinists recommended hard work as a way of achieving the certainty of one's own salvation and dispelling doubts. This is a long way from the mystical communication with God which the Lutherans aimed to achieve. The Calvinist becomes convinced of his salvation (there seems to be little reference to women in all this) through systematic self-control and good works; it is this systematicity, a sense of a planned life, that was missing for the Roman Catholic lay person. Weber points to the relevance of the name 'Methodist' given to those who participated in the eighteenth-century Protestant revival. The aim was to control and suppress spontaneity and impulse enjoyment and bring order into every aspect of life.

Calvinism for Weber was the pure type of Protestant asceticism and the other Puritan sects moved away from it in one way or another. Pietism placed too much emphasis on emotional experiences which undermined the rational orientation of everyday life. Even so there were two important elements of Pietism which he thinks outweighed its emotionalist tendency—the beliefs.

(1) that the methodical development of one's own state of grace to a higher and higher degree of certainty and perfection in terms of the law was a sign of grace; and (2) that 'God's Providence works through those in such a state of perfection', i.e., in that He gives them His signs if they wait patiently and deliberate methodically.   (ibid. 133)

Despite this the Pietists encouraged humility rather than self-confidence and there was a distinct Lutheran tendency.

Methodism was also an ascetic form of Protestantism, but had a strong emotional base and rejected many of the beliefs of Calvinism. It held that the emotional certainty of forgiveness was the only sure sign of salvation, but added nothing new to the notion of a calling. The Baptists also placed an emphasis on emotionality, but here Weber suggested another way in which Protestantism influenced everyday life: 'But in so far as Baptism affected the normal workaday world, the idea that God only speaks when the flesh is silent evidently means an incentive to the deliberate weighing of courses of action and their careful justification in terms of the individual conscience' (ibid. 149). The decisive point for all these forms of Protestantism, however, is the belief in a state of grace which marks its possessor off from worldly degradation, and it is this which leads us to the link between protestantism and capitalism. It should be evident to you, if you think back to Benjamin Franklin's maxims, that the systematic and rational pursuit of profit is clearly similar to the systematic and rational pursuit of one's everyday duties. In the modern development of the Protestant ethic, wealth is disapproved of in so far as it is an incentive to idleness and enjoyment—'But as a performance of duty in a calling it is not only morally permissible, but actually enjoined' (ibid. 163). One's calling is a moral duty for the benefit of the community, but it is more than that. If God shows the chance of a profit, He has His reasons and the chance must be taken to enable His purpose on earth to proceed. And so business success became a sign to reassure the uncertain and lonely believer that he was in fact one of the chosen; it offered psychological comfort; in economic terms, the impetus to make money without spending it on personal consumption and enjoyment led to the accumulation of capital.

It is not a matter of Protestants deciding that they wanted to be capitalists, but of their following the teaching of their prophets, which led them into systematic rationally organized day-to-day life, carrying out God's purpose on earth. Their belief in predestination meant that they experienced an inner loneliness, for nothing they or anyone else could do could effect their salvation. Success in day-to-day business activities came to be taken as a sign of salvation. Since the beliefs forbade their personal pleasure and aggrandisement, profits were reinvested into the business, and business success bred business success.

Conclusion

I have set out Weber's arguments at some length, first because it is an example of historical and comparative sociology which people are still producing today. In fact there has been a rebirth of this type of work (see Giddens 1981, 1985; Runciman 1983, 1989; M. Mann 1986; Anderson 1990), and I think Weber offers a particularly clear example of the genre. More importantly, however, Weber offers a fundamentally important analysis of the growth of capitalism and of modernity that provides dimensions not touched upon by any of the other thinkers discussed in this book. Weber is the theorist of instrumental rationality. The moral philosopher Charles Taylor calls the problem presented by instrumental rationality a 'massively important phenomenon of the modern age':

No doubt sweeping away the old orders has immensely widened the scope of instrumental reason. Once society no longer has a sacred structure, once social arrangements and modes of action are no longer grounded in the order of things or the will of God, they are in a sense up for grabs. They can be redesigned with their consequences for the happiness and well-being of individuals as our goal. The yardstick that henceforth applies is that of instrumental reasons. Similarly, once the creatures that surround us lose the significance that accrued to their place in the chain of being, they are open to being treated as raw materials or instruments for our projects.

In one way this change has been liberating. But there is also a widespread unease that instrumental reason has not only enlarged its scope but also threatens to take over our lives. The fear is that things that ought to be determined by other criteria will be decided in terms of efficiency or 'cost benefit' analysis, that the independent ends that ought to be guiding out lives will be eclipsed be demands to maximise output.   (Taylor 1991: 5)

The other thinkers added to our comprehension of it, Marx through examining its economic roots and its philosophical and psychological results in the theory of alienation, Durkheim by offering us an analysis of the same situation through the way in which the division of labour replaces and revises the *conscience collective*, and Simmel by examining the more intricate psychological effects of the money economy. Despite his explicit statements, we can find in Weber the conception of *society* as something existing over and above the individuals who make it up. He is not happy about the disenchantment that comes with modern rationality, nor is he happy with the iron cage it produces. This is his tragedy.

In terms of the secondary dualism which is central to this part of the book, Weber is the theorist of modernity as opposed to Marx as the theorist of capitalism. Weber had a lot to say about capitalism, but he did not see any desirable alternative. Socialism would simply be more bureaucratic than capitalism, and perhaps continue the process of disenchantment further than it would go even under capitalism. By emphasizing his view of the free market, John Horton and Bryan Turner try to reject the notion of Weber as a tragic liberal, but it is difficult to see how this position can be maintained in the face of the arguments in *The Protestant Ethic and the Spirit of Capitalism*. The iron cage is a liberal nightmare, not a liberal vision.

Weber's historical work shows how he moved towards a clearer conception of social cohesion: the power conflicts which both push a society forward and threaten its stability take place within and between wider frameworks of belief, and those beliefs which push towards practical action to reorganize the world (and therefore eventually to practices governed by rational calculability) have the advantage. And, once established, such practices seem unchangeable. It is as if we have developed an instrumentally rational *conscience collective* which holds us together with our compliance or perhaps against our will. We have been separated from our traditional communities and can find alliances only through common instrumental interest. Although the capitalist spirit provided a motivation and a way of looking at the world which might become generally shared, it also encourages both an individuation—a separation from traditional bonds—and an individualism—a concern with personal ends and ambitions which loses overarching commitments to God or community. When this state of affairs is reached, there is only a social system and a fragmentation of social life. With this last point, I don't think we can do better than quote Derek Sayer's comparison of Marx and Weber on modernity. Sayer takes up the way in which instrumental reason manifests itself through science, rather than through the capitalist spirit:

An elective affinity, then, for the modern age: between those qualities we most prize in scientific discourse—objectivity, universality, logic, consistency, simplicity, systematicity, quantifiability, precision unambiguity and a certain aesthetic elegance—and the principles upon which Weber's machines of modernity operate. In neither is there room for the concrete, the particular and the personal. They are banished to the 'irrational' realm of private life. The modern era, as Marx said, is ruled by abstractions. It may be that capitalism is the foundation upon which this rule is first erected; Marx and Weber provide compelling reason for thinking it is. But it may also be that today, this abstraction has gone very far beyond capitalism itself and we will not be rid of it just by changing the title deeds on property (or still less by 'capturing' 'state power'). This is the enduring importance of Weber's analysis of rationalization and bureaucratization, which is its ubiquitous concomitant. Disembodied, the very form of our sociality turns against us, and within them there is no place for humane values. The soulful corporation or the compassionate state are, by virtue of the very constitution of these soulful forms, contradictions in terms. . . . Insubstantial as modern bourgeois liberties may be—and Weber had few illusions on the matter—they are preferable to none at all.   (Sayer 1991: 153–4)

Weber emerges from all this as the ambivalent theorist—ambivalent in his attitude to modernity and the process of disenchantment that it involved, ambivalent in his attitude towards Marx, ambivalent in his personal life as well. We can find the same ambivalence in his political alignments. Apparently he thought often of joining the German socialist party, but we also find some particularly right-wing positions. To begin with he adopted what one might call a 'hard-realist' position, arguing that there can be no 'ethical' politics and the economic struggle for existence never abates—we do not do future generations any good by suggesting that this should be changed. A strong Germany should be ready to exercise its power in international affairs, but Weber did not think that the ruling class that had united Germany—the old aristocracy—were strong enough to do this, but neither were the new bourgeoisie or the proletariat. Giddens suggests that from this point Weber's main concern was to encourage the development of a liberal political culture in Germany. However, social inequalities and domination will not be removed by democracy and there was a continual conflict between democracy and bureaucracy. Whilst the growth of democracy actually entails an expansion of bureaucracy, the expansion of bureaucracy does not entail the extension of democracy. This is why an elected leadership is important—the worst possible outcome would be unlimited domination by bureaucracy. In his own alignments Weber had to juggle his support for German nationalism with his aim of representative democracy to balance the growth of bureaucracy, but, as Sayer suggests, he was well aware of its limitations.

Perhaps the firmest thing that could be said about Weber is that he was true to his depressive tendency: a carefully protected liberal democracy based on the market is the best we could hope for; socialism would take us in the direction which threatened us most—the triumph of bureaucracy. The trouble is that capitalism

---

Box 13.1. An elaboration of Weber on social integration and system integration

SOCIAL INTEGRATION

Durkheim: in all societies social integration is achieved through the *conscience collective*—shared ways of thinking (logic, conceptions of space and time, shared beliefs, norms, and values. In societies governed by mechanical solidarity, religion is central. In more complex modern societies, the *conscience collective* covers less of our lives but focuses on the ethics of individual freedom—it becomes a religion of humanity.

Marx: a 'false' and rather tenuous integration is achieved through ideologies, and the development of the market constantly threatens whatever integration is achieved. The major contending classes strive towards achieving their own integration in opposition to the others—the proletariat being the class most likely to achieve this.

Weber: at this point there is no real conception of social integration in Weber's work. In his work on religion however, it is arguable that he sees social cohesion as developing through the dominance of rational calculation.

Simmel: social integration is achieved through objective culture—the development of universal symbols and meanings that begins with economic exchange. The growth of such a culture extends human freedom but constricts the integrity and depth of the individual life.

SYSTEM INTEGRATION

Durkheim: where mechanical solidarity predominates, system integration *is* social integration guaranteed by the *conscience collective*. Where organic solidarity predominates, system integration is achieved through the division of labour.

Marx: system integration in capitalism is constantly threatened by class conflict and is supported by the state and by ruling ideologies.

Weber: it is a gross exaggeration to use the word 'system' in connection with the writings we have looked at in Chapter 9. Social structures are held together by different forms of domination and by stability provided by the market. In his work on the world religions, however, there are indications that the growing dominance of instrumental rationality creates a system which can work by itself.

Simmel: no real concept of system integration, except perhaps through economic exchange.

would take us there as well. This second Weber allows us to elaborate on his conception of social integration as well as his views on the secondary dualism.

Box 13.2. Weber on modernity and capitalism/socialism

MODERNITY

Durkheim: a movement towards a balanced society of occupational groups held together by the state and a new humanist 'religion' which emphasized the value of the individual.

Marx: the modern world was moving towards the realization of the values of the French Revolution—liberty, equality, and fraternity. This was not an inevitable or smooth process and entails conflict and revolution.

Weber: modernity is the process of the increasing dominance of rational calculability and the greatest threat is domination by large bureaucratic organizations. A free market economy in the liberal democratic state is the best protection against this.

CAPITALISM/SOCIALISM

Durkheim: Durkheim's concept of socialism was based on his conception of the development of modernity; although problems arise in the abnormal forms of the division of labour, these would be ironed out in continued historical development. He does not seem to see capitalism as a specific form of modern society responsible for either its problems or its benefits.

Marx: capitalism represented immense progress over previous types of society in terms of the ability to produce wealth, although it is driven by contradictions which do not allow it to realize this ability. The competitive market system produces rapid change and fragmentation—seen by many as defining features of modernity; a socialist revolution would create a collectively organized democratic and more stable society which would realize the ideals of the French Revolution.

Weber: socialism and communism would lead to the more rapid development of bureaucratic domination.

Further reading

Everybody should read Weber's *Protestant Ethic and the Spirit of Capitalism* (1904–5/1930). Bendix, *Max Weber: An Intellectual Portrait* (1966) offers good, clear accounts of his religious studies. Weber's *Sociology of Religion* (1922/1965) is also worth reading. For an example of modern sociological history, see W. G. Runciman's two-volume *A Treatise on Sociological Theory* (1983, 1989). On Weber's politics, see Giddens, *Politics and Sociology in the Work of Max Weber* (1972).

For contemporary work on Protestantism and Capitalism, see Gordon Marshall, *Presbyteries and Profits: Calvinism and the Development of Capitalism in Scotland, 1560–1707* (1980) and *In Search of the Spirit of Capitalism* (1982). For an excellent and sympathetic collection on Weber and modernity, see Bryan Turner, *For Weber* (1996).

14 | Simmel: countering an overdose of history?

We do not find in Simmel anything like the careful sociological analysis of other societies that we can find in Durkheim's work on religion, Weber's analysis of the world religions, or even Marx's comparatively sketchy works on pre-capitalist societies. He does not write the history of societies, and in some fundamental sense I would suggest that he actually stands *against* history in so far as it is a manifestation of objective culture which threatens to engulf subjective culture.

Simmel's *Philosophy of Money* contains as much as he offers of a theory of history and here he charts the rise and effects of what he calls objective culture. The individual emerges from the primitive group and develops an individuality through exchange relationships. These relationships create an objective culture against which the individual has to struggle to maintain his or her integrity. We are caught in a trap of our own making. When I discussed this in Part 2, I suggested that this part of his work was closest to that of Georg Lukacs and the early Marx—that he can be seen as giving a more elaborated and intricate exploration of some of the subjective consequences of alienation. However, as time went on this historical dimension was left behind, and he seemed to think of the opposition of these two culture types as a sort of metaphysical state to which all societies, all cultures, are subject. It is part of the existential condition of humankind. In 'The Concept and Tragedy of Culture' he wrote:

The 'fetishism' which Marx assigned to economic commodities represents only a special case of this general fate of contents of culture. With the increase in culture these centres more and more stand under a paradox. They were originally created by subjects for subjects, but in their immediate forms of objectivity . . . they follow an immanent logic of development. . . . They are impelled not by physical necessities but by truly cultural ones. (quoted in Frisby 1981)

If this is the case, it is just part of the nature of the social world and nothing to do with capitalism. At this point it is worth looking at the relationship between

Simmel and Nietzsche, who is generally regarded as being at the root of post-modern theory. The argument is put well, if not always clearly, by Weinstein and Weinstein (1993). In *The Use and Abuse of History* (1957) Nietzsche argued for what amounts to a rejection of history, of the idea that we are somehow or other determined by our past. We suffer from an 'excess of history', which weakens the inner life. The grand historical theories of the nineteenth century—those of Marx and Hegel most obviously but one might add Comte and many others—invade our inner selves and make it difficult for us to find an authentic voice. We are not puppets of history but come to believe that we are; we can see no point in seeking an authentic voice, since we will be swallowed up by history. In Simmel's terms, objective culture eliminates subjective culture; the personality becomes completely socialized and we descend into cynicism; nothing we can do has any real importance for us.

Weinstein and Weinstein argue that by the first years of the century Simmel, 'whether or not he was aware of doing so', had adopted Nietzsche's way of look- ing at history, talking about it as an 'idol'. It becomes a 'central idea' in terms of which we make moral and cognitive judgements, just as the Marxist militant might have put him- or herself at the service of the movement of history as rep- resented by the communist party, surrendering any independent moral or polit- ical judgement. The party central committee makes 'scientific' judgements about the course of history and the 'correct' policy to be followed.

Weinstein and Weinstein argue, rightly I think, that Simmel's target is rather different from that of Nietzsche—not so much history as *historicism*—the explanation of everything in terms of history. They go on to argue—and I am not so sure about this—that Simmel's solution is one of play: the historian's job is to tell stories on the basis of historical facts, which we cannot do anything to change. This view, as stated by the Weinsteins, is certainly a form of contempo- rary postmodern 'theory':

The freedom of the historian is to construct narratives, that is, to link events or forms of culture into dated temporal sequences according to standards of significance under the control of fact. In this view of history, which is at the antipodes of a 'scientific' history in quest of causes, there are as many histories as there are interests of historians and relev- ant facts for them to weave into narratives . . . there is no 'history' to engulf us and pro- duce us here—history is a *genre*. (Weinstein and Weinstein 1993: 181–2)

We have detective stories, westerns, romantic novels, and histories. It seems to me that this rather misses the point as far as Simmel is concerned. He was not concerned with arguing for a banal relativism, which it seems to me to be what Weinstein and Weinstein turn it into, but with asserting one value over another—the value of subjective authenticity over objective culture as mani- fested in grand theories of history; this is not a matter of equal values but of one being preferable to, better than, another. It is this stance which puts Simmel in the existentialist tradition from Kierkegaard through Nietzsche to Heidegger and Sartre and Maurice Merleau-Ponty. There is a religious/psychological wing to this movement which begins with Kierkegaard and is alive today in the form of existentialist psychotherapy. There is also a philosophical wing which splits into a leftist and a rightist version. The latter includes Nietzsche, who is often linked indirectly with Nazi philosophy, and Heidegger, who continued to teach throughout the period of Nazi rule. For both, history and society were consigned to the realm of the inauthentic. In this respect the later Simmel belongs to this tradition.

The left-wing tradition through to Sartre and Merleau-Ponty was more concerned, after the end of the Second World War, with the opposition of the individual and society and the relationship between existentialist and Marxist philosophy. The Simmel of *The Philosophy of Money* is closer to this tradition. In his personal politics he remained a liberal reformer throughout his life, taking as his focus not the struggle for power (as did Nietzsche and Weber), but the aesthetics of social life, a much more gentle concern. At times he writes as if any freezing of the life process into concepts is impermissable. It should not or cannot be analysed; we can, however, transform our understanding into an aesthetic appreciation: 'Simmel clearly conceives of the relationship of the sociologist and society as if it were that of the art critic observing a work of art' (Frisby 1981: 153). It is the money economy which first produces this distance between observer and observed, but the aesthetic perspective is privileged because it rescues us from some of the worst excesses of the money economy and modernity. Even here, as Frisby points out, he tends towards a relativism, I suspect because even an aesthetic perspective freezes the life process (just as impressionism became a new form rather than the end of forms) and in the end 'the inward retreat becomes his final political perspective' (ibid. 156).

This is perhaps the final word on Simmel. Returning to the dualisms, Simmel sees society, system cohesion, and social cohesion as objective culture, a process which increases the choices open to the individual whilst at the same time freezing and colonizing the internal life process. We cannot analyse the life process without turning it into its opposite, and in the end there is only the integrity of the individual perspective. This represents a retreat from politics which we can find in much postmodernist thought. The crucial link between Simmel and postmodernism is, I think, via Foucault, who is above all the philosopher who shows how the individual is colonized—but without the sense of the vitality of the life process that Simmel offers us.

Simmel presents an essentially pessimistic view of the secondary dualism (see Box 14.1), and it is appropriate perhaps that this chapter should end suddenly.

Box 14.1. **Simmel on modernity and capitalism/socialism**

MODERNITY

CAPITALISM/SOCIALISM

Durkheim: a movement towards a balanced society of occupational groups held together by the state and a new humanist 'religion' which emphasized the value of the individual.

Durkheim: Durkheim's concept of socialism was based on his conception of the development of modernity; although problems arise in the abnormal forms of the division of labour, these would be ironed out in continued historical development. He does not seem to see capitalism as a specific form of modern society responsible for either its problems or its benefits.

Marx: the modern world was moving towards the realization of the values of the French Revolution—liberty, equality, and fraternity. This was not an inevitable or smooth process and entails conflict and revolution.

Marx: capitalism represented immense progress over previous types of society in terms of the ability to produce wealth, although it is driven by contradictions which do not allow it to realize this ability. The competitive market system produces rapid change and fragmentation—seen by many as defining features of modernity; a socialist revolution would create a collectively organized democratic and more stable society which would realize the ideals of the French Revolution.

Weber: modernity is the process of the increasing dominance of rational calculability and the greatest threat is domination by large bureaucratic organizations. A free market economy in the liberal democratic state is the best protection against this.

Weber: socialism and communism would lead to the more rapid development of bureaucratic domination.

Simmel: modernity is the steady growth of objective culture, dominating the individual life process.

Simmel: there is no historical or sociological alternative to modernity; there is an individual alternative in that it is possible to transform both disciplines into art forms.

Further reading

Weinstein and Weinstein's *Postmodern(ized) Simmel* (1993) provides the best account of these issues, but see also Frisby's *Sociological Impressionism* (1981).

15 | Conclusion: the framework of social theory

A discussion of the dualisms of social theory and what happens when they are ignored or when theorists attempt to transcend them; the necessary problems of social theory.

The dualisms that I have referred to in the course of this book set problems for theory but they are not *theoretical* problems, they cannot be worked through and solved by theory or theorists. The same dualisms exist in the real world and they set problems not just for sociologists but for everybody, and not only problems in understanding what is going on in the world, but practical problems in our everyday lives. There are real individuals, real societies, real social structures, real actions, real relationships between real social institutions, and real relationships between real individuals. If am made redundant, then I am one of a number of individuals who lose their jobs through the workings of the society, or a failure in system integration, or contradiction in the social structure. If I join a trade union or a political party or a new political movement, then I am engaging in social action aimed at changing social structure. If my neighbours are constantly hostile, if I feel unsafe walking the streets at night, if people seem to subscribe to alien moral codes or to act without moral judgement, I am dealing with a problem of social integration.

The classical theorists did not formulate these dualisms, but that is basically what they were working with. I have tried to show how they have framed the way in which we think about contemporary society, not only in social theory, but also in terms of contemporary political debates. We *have* to see the world in these terms. If we do not, then we create blind spots of various kinds.

If we take the individual/society dualism as a first example in relation to crime, we open up a prominent contemporary debate in the Western world. If we start from the side of society, we have to say that there is something about a society that produces crime—high levels of unemployment, for example, or lack of moral regulation—and the solution would lie in bringing about some sort of social change. If, on the other hand, we start from the side of the individual, the issue is seen from the point of view of individual morality and the focus moves from social change to issues of punishment or the possibility of reforming criminals.

We might expect a sociologist to start from the side of society and it is from this side that he or she might have most to offer the public debate, since the common-sense perception of crime tends to blame the individual criminal rather than look for underlying causes. However, this sort of sociological understanding does not produce a full understanding of crime or the criminal. Not every unemployed person turns to crime, and not everybody living in a society where morality is subject to argument commits a crime. Sociology can tell us what social conditions make crime more or less likely but not who will commit a crime or what to do about criminals as individuals.

An alternative sociological approach might look at the interaction between individuals and the conditions and mechanisms of the growth of criminal subcultures. This would help us understand a further element in the production of crime, but, in the first place, like the approach from the point of view of society as a whole, it would not tell us why particular individuals are recruited to criminal subcultures. Not everyone who comes into contact with such a subculture becomes a member. It might be that to understand such issues we have to step outside sociology altogether. But we cannot ignore the individual, especially if we adopt an interactionist approach. In the second place such an approach will not lead us on automatically to looking at the wider social dynamics we find if we start at the society end of the dualism.

In fact, neither side leads automatically to the other; one side is blind to the mechanisms of interaction and the other to structural mechanisms—at some point we have to jump. I think that most sociologists would recognize that we have to look at both sides but would tend to gloss the jump—the move to a different *type* of object—when they cross from one to the other.

The same sort of argument can be made in relation to the social action/social structure dualism. Individuals and societies are different forms of being and one does not produce the other, although each depends upon the existence of the other. Similarly, social structures and social action are different forms of being; one does not determine or explain the other, although each depends upon the other. There has to be a jump between two different levels of analysis, and if we start one and do not move beyond it we end up either by ignoring important parts of social reality or by offering an inadequate understanding of them. Elsewhere (Craib 1992b) I have argued that the different twentieth-century schools of social theory all have trouble with this divide. If they start with an understanding of social structure (structuralism, structural Marxism), then, when they move on to understanding social action, the theory begins to have conceptual problems and fragments as people try to produce different solutions. On the other hand, those theories which start with social action either turn into theories of social structure (Parsons's structural functionalism) or have great difficulty (or even find it impossible) in understanding the structural features of social life (symbolic interactionism, ethnomethodology, phenomenological sociology).

We have seen the difficulty of moving from structure to action with Marxism; the move from the analysis of the relations of production to class structure to class actions doesn't work—the wrong people turn up in the wrong places doing the wrong things. We need to look at least at processes of class formation around political and ideological issues at levels closer to the surface, and this involves in turn looking at social action—a switch in object—an understanding of individual and collective interpretations of the world. Structural factors do not account for this interpretive process.

On the other hand, if we try to move from action to structure—the Weberian rather than the Marxist direction—we lose sight of underlying causes and mechanisms and have to resort to 'unintended consequences' to explain the occurrences that are not directly intended by somebody's actions. The surface effects of social structure tend to be systematic and patterned—for Durkheim, this was a central way in which we could identify the effects of 'society'. During an economic depression industries do not decline at random: certain types of industry decline, certain others remain steady, and some even grow, and I do not think it is adequate to see these effects as somehow accidental—which is what explanation by unintended consequences amounts to. People's individual and collective actions are transformed by the underlying structures of relationships in systematic ways—paradoxically it was such a process that produced Weber's iron cage.

If we turn to the distinction between social integration and system integration we find a similar situation: the two do not determine each other. I have suggested that our contemporary situation is one in which there is a high level of system integration, which could be understood in part as produced by the process of globalization, but this has been accompanied by a fragmenting of social integration: it is as if the universalization of norms and values does not pull everybody along behind it and people seek an identity through returning to more local and traditional values or by surrendering attempts to construct values altogether or inventing their own value collages. Similarly, it is possible to envisage a high degree of social integration with a low level of system integration. There are two levels at work, two distinct objects, which require two different forms of understanding.

Perhaps the best illustration of the dangers of running the two together can be found in Parsons's structural functionalism, developed through the middle of this century (Parsons 1951). What I am going to say now is an oversimplification, but I think the point should be clear. As his theory developed, he became more and more interested in systems theory—an approach which its more enthusiastic proponents thought could be applied at almost any level of analysis to almost any object. Parsons developed elaborate models of the social system, the personality system, the economic system, and the cultural system. For systems theorists, the elements which controlled a complex system were high on information and low on energy—just as a washing machine is controlled by the programme rather than the electric motor which drives the drum. In Parsons's theory, this was the cultural system, the universal values of modern society; this was the programmer and the systems and subsystems all fitted together comparatively neatly. It was, in fact, this theoretical system which led to the development of Lockwood's distinction between social and system integration (Lockwood 1964)—societies do not develop in quite as coherent a way as Parsons suggests. Since the Second World War there have been a number of economic crises in the western world, all of which could be seen as crises in system integration but none of which seems to have produced major crises in social integration in the sense of a breakdown of social order and demands for a transformation of the system. Further, I have argued in the course of this book, particularly when discussing Durkheim, that, if there is a contemporary crisis in social cohesion, in the sense of a fragmentation of morality and beliefs, it is due to an increasing level of system cohesion.

Parsons's framework is also a good illustration of the problems that occur when there are attempts to synthesize the dualisms—to find theoretical solutions to real problems: in simple terms, his system began to fall apart. Lockwood's arguments represent one aspect of this; another aspect is represented by Dennis Wrong's paper 'The Oversocialised Conception of Man in Modern Sociology' (1967), which I mentioned earlier. It was Parsons's emphasis on society as opposed to the individual which encouraged, in the 1960s, the popularity of symbolic interactionism and other forms of sociology that seemed to give space not just to individuals but also to the experience of everyday life.

Perhaps the most interesting point about Parsons's synthesis, however, is that in the course of its development he crosses from one side of the action/structure dualism to the other. He begins with an elaborate theory of social action, beginning, as did Simmel, with the dyad, but ends with a highly developed analysis of the structure or system which seemed to obliterate or determine action. In fact, any attempt to bring about a synthesis of different approaches or transcend the dualisms tends to end by giving dominance to one side or another and often implicitly if not explicitly reintroduce the dualisms.

Continuing my policy of oversimplifying, the most recent attempt at synthesis/transcendence is Anthony Giddens's structuration theory (see especially Giddens 1984). Giddens ends up giving action the dominant place. He achieves this by first of all subjecting various structural theories to a criticism which strips them of any determining features and redefines structure in terms of the rules that govern action. Structure, therefore, becomes a property of action. Giddens takes up what he calls the 'linguistic turn' in twentieth-century philosophy and theory, which in sociology has manifested itself in the tendency towards seeing language as actually constituting social reality, and effectively Giddens is saying that action is structured in the same way that language is structured. But structure is dissolved into action; there is no possibility of talking about underlying structures or even surface structures which are not produced by or part of action. He sets up a picture of the social as consisting in and produced and reproduced by rule-governed action, and this 'proper object' of sociology he calls 'social practices'. He then says that these practices can be analysed from two points of view: from the point of view of strategic action and from the point of view of institutional analysis. This seems to me close to reintroducing the action/structure dualism under another name.

So this takes me back to where I began this chapter, and perhaps I can make the same point in yet another way. There is no *one* object of sociology. The three basic dualisms around which I have tried to organize the ideas in this book identify six different objects of sociology and to concentrate on any one takes us away from all the others, yet for any social phenomenon to be understood properly we have to take account at least of the opposing object in a particular dualism, if not all the others. Social theory, then, is engaged in a number of different investigations into different realms of social reality, and, although there must be dialogues between the different approaches, there can be no unified social theory, because the social world itself is not unified.

I have not yet said anything by way of conclusion about the secondary dualism—modernity as opposed to capitalism/socialism; I described this as a secondary dualism because it is not built into social theory as such, as the others are, but represents a focus on one particular historical period and it has to do with the possibilities for change in the modern world. It should be apparent by now that, whichever theorist we choose, we find a more or less ambivalent attitude to the modern world; it represents progress but it also represents a danger. For Durkheim, it establishes the possibility of individual freedom within a comparatively harmonious society, but also runs the risk of increasing anomie and egoism. For Marx, capitalism frees immense productive forces, but it is a system based on exploitation and oppression which offers a future which he posed in the dramatic terms of a choice between socialism and barbarism. For Weber, modernity provides comparative stability at the risk of bureaucratization, the domination of instrumental rationality, and disenchantment; for Simmel, the modern world frees the individual from domination by the primitive group but then subjects him or her to domination by the objective culture against which the individual has to struggle to preserve his or her integrity.

These are issues at the centre of contemporary political debate. There are issues of equality, of the range of differences in wealth that we think is permissible in our society and whether these differences should be linked to differences in power: should the very rich be allowed to build up huge media empires, for example? Should we be concerned with restricting the market economy and to what extent should the state intervene in social and economic affairs? To what extent should we value our individual freedom over and above the demands of society and the local community? To what extent is bureaucracy desirable or undesirable? To what extent do we tolerate those who are different from us or do we try to change them? And, although the classic theorists have comparatively little to say about racism and sexism and the environment, these issues can be understood in terms of the wider debates with which the classical theorists are concerned.

Each of these theorists' conceptions of the modern world is profoundly historical; this is true even of Simmel, who has the thinnest historical analysis of the four—objective culture does not simply arrive but develops over a long time. Their theories of history may vary from the solid evolutionism of Durkheim through to the tentative and reversible process described by Weber, but they all involve some sense of progress towards the contemporary world and the assumption that this contemporary world cannot be understood unless we understand how it has developed. It seems to me that we should always be wary of claims that the world has changed dramatically. I would suggest that there are no radical breaks from what has gone before; we do not wake up suddenly to find ourselves in a different world; perhaps what changes is the range of available ways of living with our problems.

It follows from this that the political choices that were relevant to the classical theorists have been modified but not profoundly changed. The final dualism is essentially about the possibilities of change open to contemporary society. If we stick to the side of modernity, the implications are that the most significant changes that we experience are part of the modern world, whether we like it or not—we might be able to modify their effects but we cannot envisage any more profound change. If we concern ourselves with the capitalism/socialism side of the dualism, then it opens up the possibility that there are other ways of organizing society which perhaps will change our lives in a way we find desirable.

At the time of writing the former point of view seems to have become the dominant view of western social theorists; whereas in the 1970s the terms 'capitalism', 'late capitalism', 'monopoly capitalism', and 'state capitalism' could be found in most sociology books, by the late 1990s 'modernity', 'late modernity', and 'postmodernity' seem to be everywhere. It is paradoxical that, at the very moment when capitalism has reasserted itself on the world stage with many of the ill effects that it has always had, producing regular crises and high levels of unemployment, widening gaps between rich and poor both within and between nation states, and constantly transforming our living and working conditions— melting, as Marx put it, everything that is solid into air—sociologists should give up the sustained critique of modern capitalism that was produced in the 1960s and 1970s.

It might be that sociologists follow the crowd like everybody else and, when radical left-wing politics come to the fore, they produce works of Marxist theory and analysis, and when the right is in dominance, they turn in other directions. However, I think there might be a sociological explanation of this change: that, as technological change has speeded up, particularly with the revolutions in information technology, and as finance capital has used these revolutions to become more and more powerful, it has become easier to be caught up in the surface appearances of the system, and to believe that the surface appearances are all that exist. I think that this is particularly true in the case of Anthony Giddens's work.

What I want to do here by way of a final conclusion is to make a plea for recognizing the importance of the last dualism. One of the implications of talking about necessary dualisms is that sociology is an open-ended pluralist discipline, generating a range of different theories and methods and a range of debates. Attempts to produce syntheses of the different theories are attempts to close down these debates. If sociology reflects the structure of the real social world and the plurality of different 'objects' that make it up, then the 'real-world' equivalent of trying to find a theoretical synthesis is to try to impose a totalitarian social order and I do not think that either of these attempts are desirable.

If the family of concepts around the idea of modernity dominate, then I think this has the same effect—it reduces the range of possibilities open to us; the arguments about socialism and capitalism open them up. It seems to me that the most important contribution of the founders of sociology was to produce a notion of 'society' as a significant force in our lives—Marx and Durkheim do so explicitly and happily, Weber almost despite himself, and Simmel with great reluctance—and, even if society turns out to be complex and multidimensional, we still need to hold on to the idea.

Once we have the idea of 'society', there is the possibility of asking what sorts of changes are possible, or desirable, and questioning the range of control that we have over the world we live in. The arguments about socialism and capitalism that we find in the classic thinkers raise these questions and it is no accident that the two theorists who have the clearest conceptions of society as a whole raise them most explicitly in ways that are still relevant. Even if it is difficult to imagine the socialist revolution in the way that Marx and Lenin imagined it, we should not lose the sight of the possibility that there are other ways of living and other ways of organizing ourselves.

Dramatis personae

In addition to the four major figures—Marx, Durkheim, Weber, and Simmel—I have mentioned a number of other thinkers of whom students might not be aware. What follows are brief details of philosophers, social theorists, and other major thinkers who were: (*a*) predecessors who had a major influence on one or other of the four, (*b*) approximate contemporaries who have made a lasting contribution to the field, and (*c*) significant mid-twentieth-century figures, now dead, who have contributed to the development of modern social theory. I have suggested further reading only in the case of the main social theorists.

Adorno, T. W. (1903–69) A major figure in twentieth-century Marxism, an original member of the Frankfurt School of Social Research, developing the critical Hegelian tradition of Marxism into a powerful critique of modern culture, demonstrating the way in which independent thinking is stifled and people are drawn into the system. See Adorno and Horkheimer (1972).

Althusser, Louis (1918–90) A French Marxist philosopher of science, and a central figure in the development of social thought in the second half of the twentieth century, developing a realist, structural conception of social science through a reinterpretation of Marx's work. His career came to a tragic end—he had always suffered from depression, and during a particularly bad bout in 1980 he killed his wife. He spent the rest of his life in a Paris mental hospital.

Bergson, Henri (1859–1941) A French philosopher whose name is often associated with Simmel. He thought the intellect was incapable of grasping experience and he posited a vital life-force which he thought was responsible for evolution.

Comte, Auguste (1798–1857) A French philosopher, regarded as the founder of positivism, and the first to coin the term 'sociology'. He saw society as moving through three stages—from understanding the world in supernatural terms, to understanding it in metaphysical philosophical terms, to understanding it through the systematic collection of facts and their correlation. He thought that the laws of society that could be derived from this would put an end to political arguments caused by the French Revolution.

Darwin, Charles (1809–82) Darwin's theory of evolution revolutionized thought in the mid-nineteenth century, first by removing humanity from the centre of creation and seeing it as just another species, and secondly by explaining the biological development of human beings as a process of natural selection depending upon adjustment to the environment. It became very difficult to avoid evolutionary thought—it is central to Marx and Durkheim and haunts Weber and Simmel. See Darwin (1859/1970).

Engels, Friedrich (1820–95) A friend and collaborator of Karl Marx, with whom he founded the Communist Party and contributed to the development and popularization of Marxist thought. He ran his father's business in Manchester and saved Marx from dire poverty—an irony that is often pointed out. He was one of the first male writers to make a significant contribution to understanding the position of women in society. See Engels (1884/1968).

Feuerbach, Ludwig (1804–72) A philosopher who critically developed Hegel's thought, particularly in relation to Christianity; his view that religion involved a projection of human powers onto an abstract idea was important in the development of Marx's theory of alienation.

Foucault, Michel (1926–84) French philosopher usually labelled 'poststructuralist' and the author of a very difficult body of work concerned with tracing shifts in the development of western thought and, in the later part of his career, with the development of the human sciences and social control; the development of medicine and the sciences concerned with sexuality and psychology can be seen as means by which, in modern societies, our subjectivity is constituted and controlled. See Foucault (1973, 1977).

Freud, Sigmund (1856–1939) Born about the same time as Durkheim, Simmel but outliving them by over two decades, Freud is the founder of psychoanalysis and throughout the history of sociology there have been regular attempts to integrate psychoanalysis and social theory. Freud's conception of the individual/society relationship is not dissimilar to that of Durkheim (or later, Parsons): the individual must be regulated and directed by the wider social group. For Freud this involves the repression of sexual drives and the development of ego and superego as internal social controls. Civilization goes hand in hand with misery—the more developed society becomes, the more pleasure we have to sacrifice. See Freud (1985*a*).

Hegel, Georg Wilhelm Friedrich (1770–1831) A major European philosopher, perhaps the last of the great system builders. He saw history as a long process via a series of contradictions through which Reason works itself out. Reason, rational thought, is what motivates historical development and it works towards Truth—the most general level of knowledge. Truth can exist only in the context of a totality of knowledge, not as isolated propositions. Marx was seeped in Hegelian thought which he famously 'stood on its head'—seeing the development of thought, and of societies, as a result of human productive activity.

Kant, Immanuel (1724–1804) A a major European philosopher who, like many since, attempted to reconcile empiricist (starting from external reality) and idealist (starting from thought) traditions. He saw the world as divided into things in themselves—objects out there in the world which could not be known in any essential sense—and consciousness, which possessed certain a priori properties, which can best be seen as, for example, a sense of time and space, the basic categories by which we organize the world. Durkheim claimed to find the basis for these categories of thought in social organization, and they can be seen as the intellectual basis for Simmel's 'forms'. Kant's influence can be traced through most types of sociology that begin with the individual or with consciousness.

Kierkegaard, Soren (1815–55) A religious philosopher who emphasized the importance of the experience of the existing individual over and against philosophical systems, particularly that of Hegel. The first of the existentialists.

Lenin, Vladimir Ilyich (1870–1924) Leader of the Russian Revolution and a brilliant political organizer and strategist. He produced a number of political, historical, and philosophical contributions to Marxism, the most important political contribution being the development of a theory of a political party which would lead the working class

to victory (as opposed to other Marxists, who thought the working class would spontaneously rise up and win power). The most relevant sociological contribution was *The
State and Revolution*, which discussed the withering-away of the state after the socialist
revolution.

Lukacs, Georg (1885–1971) Hungarian philosopher whose personal intellectual history
follows the intellectual history of Europe. It has been argued that he wrote the existential work of the century (Lukacs 1971*b*) on the way from passing from Kant to Marx to
Hegel, but his main fame is for developing the Hegelian strand of Marxism. He argued
that Marx's dialectical method, in which each single proposition only made sense in the
context of the whole, and was open to constant revision, guaranteed its adequacy; he
argued that Marx had finally resolved the subject/object dualism in western thought, and
the experience of the proletariat in the production process enabled this resolution and
gave the class a privileged position in understanding the workings of capitalist society.
See Lukacs (1971*a*).

Mannheim, Karl (1893–1947) Perhaps best seen as a non-Marxist version of Lukacs, he
was one of a circle including Lukacs and Weber who at one period used to meet regularly. He is best known for his development of the sociology of knowledge—the theory
that all knowledge depends upon the social and existential position of the thinker. This
leads to relativism; different points of view are simply different, not better than one
another. Mannheim tried to escape this by suggesting that the more inclusive view was
best and that free-floating intellectuals were in the best position to produce such a view
because they had no special interest or axe to grind. See Mannheim (1938).

Marcuse, Herbert (1898–1979) A German, founder member of the Frankfurt School,
who fled to America when Hitler came to power and did not return. As well as developing the critical Hegelian side of Marxism, he wrote a number of works critical of the 'one-
dimensional' culture of late capitalism, and a particularly important attempt to combine
Marxist and Freudian thought. See Marcuse (1969).

Mead, George Herbert (1863–1931) An American philosopher and one of the founders
of the social of sociology known as symbolic interactionism, which concentrates on face-
to-face interaction and the social development of the self. Often considered one of the
indirect heirs of Simmel's thought. See Mead (1938).

Merleau-Ponty, Maurice (1905–61) A French phenomenological philosopher associated with Sartre and existentialism; he was concerned with exploring the relationship
between the body, consciousness, and the outside world.

Michels, Robert (1876–1936) A German sociologist who argued that there is an 'iron
law of oligarchy' by which democratic radical political parties develop large bureaucracies and come to be dominated by officials who are more concerned with the organization than with its aims. These ideas fit neatly with Weber's ideas on rationalization. See
Michels (1911/1962).

Mill, John Stuart (1806–61) A utilitarian philosopher who introduced Comte's work
into Britain and is best known for his work on scientific method. Durkheim was especially critical of the individualism of his social theory.

Nietzsche, Friedrich (1844–1900) A German philosopher, one of the most important of
the modern period; he offered a radical critique of Enlightenment rationality and

inverted the relationship that the Enlightenment philosophers assumed to exist between knowledge and power—knowledge is seen as a form of domination rather than liberation. He was an important influence on Weber and on the development of postmodernism, particularly Foucault's work.

Parsons, Talcott (1902–79) The most important American sociologist of the second half of the twentieth century, he attempted a massive and systematic synthesis of the classical sociologists—excluding Marx and including Mead rather than Simmel. See Parsons (1951).

Ricardo, David (1772–1823) An economist inspired by Adam Smith who attempted to develop a labour theory of value; Marx developed his theory through a critique of Smith and Ricardo.

Rickert, Heinrich (1863–1936) A German neo-Kantian philosopher, a contemporary of and major influence on Max Weber. His criticism of positivism was important for Weber's methodological writings.

Saint-Simon, Claude-Henri de Rouvroy, Comte de (1760–1825) Ironically, an aristocrat was the founder of French socialism and French sociology. He was imprisoned during the French Revolution but his liberal sympathies saved his life. Many of his ideas were developed by Comte and later by Durkheim—the notion that society moves through three stages, that we can find general laws of society, which should be run by scientists, and that humanity needed to develop a new religion based on positivism.

Sartre, Jean-Paul (1905–80) French existentialist philosopher, novelist, playwright, and political activist and later a Marxist who made a sophisticated attempt to combine the two philosophies. See Sartre (1963).

Smith, Adam (1723–90) Scottish philosopher, economist, and social theorist, a major figure for modern right-wing politicians, who believed in the power of the free market, although Smith himself was able to envisage the state playing a wide social role. He talked about the 'hidden hand' of the market bringing order and stability in a way that Weber assumed, and he developed the labour theory of value that Marx criticized and developed.

Spencer, Herbert (1820–1903) A railway engineer turned journalist turned major English nineteenth-century sociologist. He swallowed evolutionary theory whole, seeing history as an evolutionary process of improvement, pushed forward by the struggle for scarce resources and involving the survival of the fittest. See Spencer (1971).

Tonnies, Ferdinand (1855–1936) A German sociologist who made an important distinction between, 'community' and 'association'. This is echoed in different ways by Durkheim, Simmel, and Weber. The difference is between the deeper and more stable relationships which are reputed to occur in traditional societies and the more fragmented, interest-based relationships more common in modern societies.

Trotsky, Leon (1879–1949) A leader, with Lenin, of the Russian Revolution. He disagreed with and went into exile under Stalin and was eventually murdered by one of Stalin's agents. Wrote widely on politics and the arts as well as developing his own analysis of Russian 'state capitalism'. See Trotsky (1967).

Wittfogel, Karl (1896–?) A founder member, with Adorno, Marcuse, and others, of the Frankfurt School of Social Research. Unlike the others, he was less concerned with the higher reaches of western philosophy, and his major work (Wittfogel 1963) was a development of Marx's comments about eastern empires being seen as a specific mode of production—oriental despotism.

Glossary

action/structure dualism this refers to a major division and necessary division within sociology between approaches which focus primarily on social structure (e.g. Marx, the early Durkheim) and those that focus primarily on individual and social action (e.g. Weber, Simmel)

alienation (Marx) a process in which people become separated from their fellows, the products of their work, and their own life processes

anomie (Durkheim) a state in which there are no clear shared rules or norms of behaviour

ancient mode of production (Marx) a society (such as ancient Rome) in which the city dominates the countryside, and which changes as it reproduces itself

associative relationships (Weber) relationships which depend upon a common, usually material, interest

asiatic mode of production (Marx) a society (e.g. China) in which local communities are dependent upon a strong state, for e.g. constructing irrigation systems

bourgeoisie (Marx) the capitalist ruling class, owners of the means of production

bureaucracy (Weber) the rational form of organization which dominates the modern world

causal adequacy (Weber) an explanation is adequate on the level of cause if, given the same conditions, the same result would follow

charisma, charismatic domination (Weber) special qualities of the personality which enable the person possessing them to exercise power over others (e.g. Christ, Hitler)

citizenship (T. H. Marshall) the status enjoyed by the full members of a community; citizenship rights might undermine class formation especially among the proletariat

class-in-itself (Marx) a group of people defined by a common relationship to the means of production

class-for-itself (Marx) a group of people sharing the same relationship to the means of production, who see themselves as sharing a common interest and act together to achieve it

class, social class (Weber) a group of people who share the same market position

collective representations (Durkheim) shared symbolic systems (such as religious beliefs) through which members of a society represent their organization.

commodity fetishism (Marx) the way in which capitalism transforms, via the market, social relationships into relationships between things

communal relationships (Weber) relationships between people based on common identification (e.g. the family)

conscience collective (Durkheim) refers to the norms and values shared by members of a society and/or the underlying logic and forms of thought shared by a society

determinism, economic determinism (Marx, or attributed to Marx) an explanation in which the result is seen as the inevitable and necessary outcome of a causal process; thus political events and ideas are determined by the relations and forces of production

dialectics, dialectical materialism (Marx) as an argument, dialectics is a debate between opposing positions; as an explanation, dialectical materialism sees society developing through structural contradictions

division of labour (everybody, but especially Durkheim) the way in which different tasks are allocated to different people; Durkheim saw this as a major source of social cohesion

dyad (Simmel) two people, the smallest social group and a starting point for analysis.

egoism (Durkheim) a form of social integration which rests on individual responsibility; not to be confused with selfishness

elective affinity (Weber) refers to the resonance between the Protestant ethic and the spirit of capitalism; not *quite* a causal relationship

emergent properties new elements which emerge from the combination of other elements—e.g. the group can have different properties from the individuals who comprise it

Enlightenment the period beginning in France in the eighteenth century which saw the foundation of modern science and philosophy

epistemology the theory of knowledge and how we come by it

evolution In the social sciences, a notion of steady social development through determinate stages

exchange value (Marx) the value at which a commodity sells on the market; *see also* **use value**

existentialism a philosophical approach which gives priority to our immediate individual experience of the world

false consciousness (various Marxists) a wrong or mistaken view of the world, held by virtue of one's class position

feudalism, feudal mode of production for Weber, feudalism was a form of patrimony—a form of authority resting on personal and bureaucratic power appearing through the routinization of charisma in a traditional setting; for Marx, it was a social order in which the lord 'owned' the means of production, but the peasant controlled; the surplus thus had to be extracted through various forms of rent

forces of production (Marx) the raw materials, tools, and human capacities that are required to produce goods

formal sociology, social forms (Simmel) the organization of social life at various levels in ways that remain the same, whatever the setting; e.g. conflict can be seen as a form of relationship whether it is a matter of two children rowing or a world war

functionalism (attributed to Durkheim) the explanation of the continued existence of a phenomenon in relation to the function it fulfils in the larger whole

Gemeinschaft (Tonnies) close, face-to-face relationships in a stable community, as opposed to *Gesellschaft*

Gesellschaft (Tonnies) relationships based on rational calculation and self-interest in a rapidly changing community

ideal type (Weber) a purely rational construct of a social phenomenon or process, which can then be compared with the real world; a rational 'puppet theatre' (Schutz)

ideology (Marx) a view of the world which is distorted through the self-interest of a social class, or a non-scientific view of the world

individual/society dualism a necessary opposition in social theory which must say something about individuals *and* society, but cannot explain one in terms of the other

instrumental rationality a term used critically by twentieth-century Marxists to refer to a rational organization of activity directed towards practical ends and involving domination over and manipulation of objects and people; Weber develops this conception of rationality but with little critical comment

labour theory of value a theory developed by the classical economists, including Marx, which tries to show that the value of a commodity depends upon the amount of labour expended upon its production

labour power (Marx) this is what the employer buys from the worker; the difference between its use value to the employer and its exchange value (the wage) explains exploitation

legal-rational domination (Weber) the form of authority most appropriate to modern societies, involving bureaucratic organization under the rule of law

lumpenproletariat (Marx) the riff-raff—criminals, the unemployable, etc.—who can be organized by authoritarian leaders

meaning adequacy (Weber) an explanation is adequate on the level of meaning if it tells a coherent, rational story

means of production (Marx) the raw materials and machines used in the production process

mechanical solidarity (Marx) a form of social organization in which there is a minimal division of labour, and the group is united by the *conscience collective*, usually in religious form; evolves into organic solidarity

mode of production (Marx) the basic economic structure of a society, comprising the forces and relations of production

meta-narratives a term used by postmodernists to describe general social theories such as those discussed in this text

objective culture (Simmel) ideas, beliefs, practices which have grown up between people and taken on an objective quality and which then threaten to stifle the life process and the individuality of subjective culture

organic analogy looking at society as if it were a living organism; used by Durkheim

organic solidarity (Durkheim) a differentiated form of society held together by the division of labour and a 'religion of individualism'

overdetermination a concept developed by Lenin and Trotsky to describe the multiple contradictions that create a revolutionary situation

patriarchal authority (Weber) the form of authority in traditional society, based on male heads of households; not to be confused with modern usage, where it means male domination in general

patrimonialism (Weber) authority resting on personal authority and bureaucratic position; develops from the routinization of charisma in traditional settings

peasantry (nearly everybody, but especially Marx) the class of small farmers, according to Marx isolated from each other only to be united by a strong leader

petty bourgeoisie (Marx) the middle class—for Marx, small entrepreneurs and professionals; modern Marxists have included many other groups in the category—including managers and state employees

play forms (Simmel) the point where social interaction becomes an art form; examples of play forms are flirting and sociability

positivism (Comte) a view of social science as empirical investigation aiming to establish general laws of society (*beware*: it has accumulated other meanings during the twentieth century)

pre-notions (Durkheim) common-sense ideas which must be ignored if we are to achieve scientific knowledge

primitive communism (Engels/Marx) a supposed early period of egalitarianism and collective ownership at the beginning of human history

proletariat (Marx) the working class; those who sell their labour power

realism, critical realism a modern philosophy developed by Bhaskar (1978, 1979) which posits a difference between structure and agency and between different (surface and underlying) levels of reality

relations of production (Marx) the crucial relationships between humans and the means of production, which define social classes and modes of production; the two relationships are of ownership and control

social action, meaningful social action (Weber) social action is action directed towards others; meaningful social action is social action to which we attach a meaning. Don't worry about the difference. For Weber, meaningful social action is the proper object of sociology

social currents (Durkheim) sentiments which run through social groups without taking on the solidity of social facts

social facts (Durkheim) social facts have an existence over and above individuals and force themselves upon people—language is a good example

social and system integration social integration refers to principles governing the relationships between individuals, system integration to those governing relationships between parts of a society or social system; such relationships may be complementary or conflictual

species being (Marx) humanity and its defining features

status groups (Weber) a group which shares a particular social esteem, usually involving a similar lifestyle and training; the priesthood is a good example

traditional authority (Weber) *see* **patriarchal authority**

postmodernism the term refers to either or both of (*a*) a new type of society in which traditional boundaries have broken down and which has emerged towards the end of this century or (*b*) various new relativist theories and philosophies which deny the possibility of knowledge

rationality, rational action (Weber) rationality is another feature of the meaningful social action that is the proper object of sociology; it makes social science possible

rationalization (Weber) the process which has dominated the development of the modern world, replacing traditional societies; *see also* **instrumental rationality**

repressive law (Durkheim) law of which the prime purpose is to punish; its dominance is an indication of mechanical solidarity

restitutive law (Durkheim) law of which the prime purpose is to restore the situation as before; its dominance is an indication of organic solidarity

use value (Marx) the (un-measurable) value of a good to the person who possesses it; to be distinguished from **exchange value**

values, value-freedom (Weber) for Weber, our rational lives are bounded by existential (i.e. a-rational) value choices; science is such a value choice, but, once it is chosen, rational value-free investigation is possible within the scientific community

Verstehen (Weber) the rational understanding of people's actions

References

Adorno, T. W., and Horkheimer, M. (1972), *Dialectic of Enlightenment* (New York: Herder & Herder).

Anderson, P. (1976), *Considerations on Western Marxism* (London: New Left Books).

—— (1990), 'A Culture in Counterflow—1', *New Left Review*, 180: 41–78.

Albrow, M. (1990), *Max Weber's Construction of Social Theory* (Basingstoke: Macmillan).

Alexander, J. C. (1982–4) (ed.), *Theoretical Logic in Sociology* (London: Routledge & Kegan Paul).

—— (1988) *Durkheimian Sociology: Cultural Studies* (Cambridge: Cambridge University Press).

Althusser, L. (1969), *For Marx* (London: Allen Lane, The Penguin Press).

—— (1971), *Lenin and Philosophy* (London: New Left Books).

Althusser, L., and Balibar, É. (1970), *Reading Capital* (London: New Left Books).

Anon. (1961), *The Cloud of Unknowing and Other Works*, ed. P. Hodgson (Harmondsworth: Penguin Books).

Axelrod, C. D. (1991), 'Toward an Appreciation of Simmel's Fragmentary Style', in L. Ray (ed.), *Formal Sociology* (Aldershot, Hants: Edward Elgar), 156–67.

Bailey, A. M. (1981), 'The Renewed Discussions on the Concept of the Asiatic Mode of Production', in J. S. Kahn and J. L. Llobera (eds.), *The Anthropology of Pre-Capitalist Societies* (London: Routledge), 89–107.

Barrett, M. (1980), *Women's Oppression Today: Problems in Marxist Feminist Analysis* (London: Verso).

Barrett, M., and McIntosh, M. (1982) (eds.), *The Anti-Social Family* (London: Verso).

Bendix, R. (1966), *Max Weber: An Intellectual Portrait* (London: Methuen).

Benton, E. (1977), *Philosophical Foundations of the Three Sociologies* (London: Routledge & Kegan Paul).

—— (1984), *The Rise and Fall of Structural Marxism* (London: Macmillan).

—— (1993), *Natural Relations, Ecology, Animal Rights and Social Justice* (London: Verso).

Berger, P., and Luckman, T. (1967), *The Social Construction of Reality* (London: Allen Lane, Penguin).

Bhaskar, R. (1978), *A Realist Theory of Science* (Sussex: Harvester Press).

—— (1979), *The Possibility of Naturalism* (Sussex: Harvester Press).

Bion, W. (1976), *Learning from Experience* (London: Heinemann).

Blauner, R. (1964), *Alienation and Freedom; The Factory Worker and his Industry* (Chicago: Chicago University Press).

Blumer, H (1969), *Symbolic Interactionism* (Engelwood Cliffs, NJ: Prentice-Hall).

Bottomore, T. (1990), 'Giddens's View of Historical Materialism', in J. Clark *et al.*, *Anthony Giddens: Consensus and Controversy* (London: Falmer Press).

Bowlby, J. (1988), *A Secure Base* (London: Routledge).

Buck, N., *et al.* (1994), *Changing Households: British Household Panel Survey 1990–92* (Colchester: ESRC Research Centre on Micro-Social Change).

Bunyan, J. (1928), *A Pilgrim's Progress from this world to that to come* (Oxford: Oxford University Press).

Burger, T. (1976), *Max Weber's Theory of Concept Formation* (Durham, NC: Duke University Press).

Bryant, C. A. (1985), *Positivism in Social Theory and Research* (Basingstoke: Macmillan).

Carver, T. (1975), *Karl Marx: Texts on Method* (Oxford: Blackwell).

Chodorow, N. (1978), *The Reproduction of Mothering* (Berkeley and Los Angeles: University of California Press).

Clarke, S. (1994), *Marx's Theory of Crisis* (London: Macmillan).

Comte, A. (1976), *The Foundations of Sociology*, ed. K. Thompson (London: Nelson).

Coser, L. A. (1956), *The Functions of Social Conflict* (Glencoe, Ill.: Free Press).

—— (1991*a*), 'Georg Simmel's Style of Work: A Contribution to the Sociology of the Sociologist', in L. Ray (ed.), *Formal Sociology* (Aldershot, Hants: Edward Elgar), 139–45.

—— (1991*b*), 'The Sociology of Poverty', in L. Ray (ed.), *Formal Sociology* (Aldershot, Hants: Edward Elgar), 231–42.

Craib, I. (1989), *Psychoanalysis and Social Theory: The Limits of Sociology* (Brighton: Harvester Wheatsheaf).

—— (1992*a*), *Anthony Giddens* (London: Routledge).

—— (1992*b*), *Modern Social Theory: From Parsons to Habermas* (Brighton: Harvester Wheatsheaf).

—— (1994), *The Importance of Disappointment* (London: Routledge).

—— (1995), 'Some Comments on the Sociology of the Emotions', *Sociology*, 29: 151–8.

Crook, S., Pakulski, J., and Waters, M. (1992), *Postmodernization: Change in Advanced Society* (London: Sage).

Darwin, C. (1970; first pub. 1859), *The Origin of the Species* (Harmondsworth: Penguin).

Derrida, J. (1995), *Specters of Marx* (New York: Routledge).

Douglas, J. (1967), *The Social Meanings of Suicide* (Princeton: Princeton University Press).

Durkheim, É. (1915; first. pub. 1912), *The Elementary Forms of the Religious Life* (London: Allen & Unwin).

—— (1952; first pub. 1896), *Suicide* (London: Routledge & Kegan Paul).

—— (1953; first pub. 1897), *Sociology and Philosophy* (Glencoe Ill.: Glencoe Free Press).

—— (1957), *Professional Ethics and Civil Morals* (London: Routledge).

—— (1958), *Socialism and Saint-Simon* (London: Routledge & Kegan Paul).

—— (1962), *Moral Education* (New York: The Free Press).

—— (1964; first pub. 1895), *The Rules of Sociological Method* (New York: Free Press).

—— (1969), 'Two Laws of Penal Education', *University of Cincinnati Law Review*, 38: 32–60).

—— (1977; first pub. 1938), *The Evolution of Educational Thought* (London: Routledge).

—— (1979), *Durkheim: Essays on Morals and Education*, ed. W. F. Pickering (London: Routledge).

—— (1984; first pub. 1893), *The Division of Labour in Society* (Basingstoke: Macmillan).

—— (1990), 'Individualism and the Intellectuals' (1898), in Peter Hamilton (ed.), *Emile Durkheim: Critical Assessments* (London: Routledge), iv. 62–73.

—— and Mauss, M. (1963; first pub. 1903), *Primitive Classification* (London: Cohen & West).

Engels, F. (1940), *Dialectics of Nature* (London: Lawrence & Wishart).

—— (1967), 'Socialism, Utopian and Scientific', in *Selected Works*, ed. W. O. Henderson (Harmondsworth: Penguin).

—— 1968; first pub. 1884), *The Origin of the Family, Private Property and the State*, in K. Marx and F. Engels, *Selected Works* (London: Lawrence & Wishart).

Etzioni, A. (1995), *The Spirit of Community* (London: Fontana).

—— (1996), 'The Responsive Community: A Communitarian Perspective', *American Journal of Sociology*, 61: 1–11.

Faught, J. (1991), 'Neglected Affinities, Max Weber and Georg Simmel', in L. Ray (ed.), *Formal Sociology* (Aldershot, Hants: Edward Elgar), 86–105.

Foucault, M. (1973), *The Birth of The Clinic* (London: Tavistock).

—— (1977), *Discipline and Punish* (London: Allen Lane).

—— (1979), *The History of Sexuality* (London: Allen Lane).

Freud, S. (1985a), 'Civilisation and its Discontents', in *Civilisation, Society and Religion* (Pelican Freud Library 12; Harmondsworth: Pelican Books).

—— (1985b), 'Totem and Taboo', in *The Origins of Religion* (Pelican Freud Library 13; Harmondsworth: Pelican Books).

Friedmann, G. (1961), *The Anatomy of Work* (London: Heinemann).

Frisby, D. (1981), *Sociological Impressionism* (London: Heinemann).

—— (1984), *Georg Simmel* (Chichester: Ellis Horwood).

—— (1992), *Simmel and Since: Essays on Georg Simmel's Social, Theory* (London: Routledge).

Fukuyama, F. (1992), *The End of History and the Last Man* (Harmondsworth: Penguin).

Gane, M. (1988), *On Durkheim's Rules of Sociological Method* (London: Routledge).

Garfinkel, H. (1967), *Studies in Ethnomethodogy* (Englewood Cliffs, NJ: Prentice Hall).

Gergen, K. (1991), *The Saturated Self* (New York: Basic Books).

Giddens, A. (1971), *Capitalism and Modern Social Theory: Analysis of the Writings of Marx, Durkheim and Weber* (Cambridge: Cambridge University Press).

—— (1972), *Politics and Sociology in the Work of Max Weber* (London: Macmillan).

—— (1973), *The Class Structure of Advanced Societies* (London: Hutchinson).

—— (1976), *New Rules of Sociological Method* (London: Hutchinson).

—— (1978), *Durkheim* (London: Fontana).

—— (1981), *A Contemporary Critique of Historical Materialism, I. Power, Property and the State* (London: Macmilllan).

—— (1984), *The Constitution of Society* (Oxford: Polity Press).

—— (1985), *A Contemporary Critique of Historical Materialism, II. The Nation-State and Violence* (Oxford: Polity Press).

—— (1990a), 'Durkheim's Political Sociology', in P. Hamilton (ed.), *Emile Durkheim, Critical Assessments, IV* (London: Routledge), 184–219.

—— (1990b), *The Consequences of Modernity* (Oxford: Polity Press).

—— (1991), *Modernity and Self-Identity* (Oxford: Polity Press).

Gilligan, C. (1982), *In a Different Voice: Essays on Psychological Theory and Women's Development* (Cambridge, Mass.: Harvard University Press).

Ginsberg, M. (1956), *On The Diversity of Morals* (London: William Heinemann Ltd.).

Gladis, M. S. (1992), *A Comunitarian Defence of Liberalism* (Stanford, Calif.: Stanford University Press).

Goff, T. (1980), *Mead and Marx* (London: Routledge & Kegan Paul).

Goldmann, L. (1969), *The Human Sciences and Philosophy* (London: Jonathan Cape).

—— (1977), *Lukacs and Heidegger* (London: Routledge & Kegan Paul).

Gouldner, A. (1958), Introduction to E. Durkheim, *Socialism and Saint-Simon* (London: Routledge & Kegan Paul), pp. v–xxvii.

Habermas, J. (1972), *Knowledge and Human Interests* (London: Heinemann).

—— (1974), *Theory and Practice* (London: Heinemann).

—— (1976), *Legitimation Crisis* (London: Heinemann).

—— (1979), *Communication and the Evolution of Society* (London: Heinemann).

—— (1984), *The Theory of Communicative Action, Reason and the Rationalisation of Society* (Oxford: Polity Press).

—— (1987), *The Theory of Communicative Action, II. A Critique of Functionalist Reason* (Oxford: Polity Press).

—— (1990), *The Philosophical Discourse of Modernity: Twelve Lectures* (Oxford: Polity Press).

Hamilton, P. (1990) (ed.), *Emile Durkheim: Critical Assessments* (London: Routledge).

—— (1991) (ed.), *Max Weber: Critical Perspectives* (London: Routledge).

Hall, D., and Gay, P. (1996) (eds), *Questions of Cultural Identity* (London: Sage).

Harding, S. (1986), *The Science Question in Feminism* (Buckingham: Open University Press).

—— (1991), *Whose Science? Whose Knowledge* (Buckingham: Open University Press).

Hartman, H. (1986), *The Unhappy Marriage of Marxism and Feminism*, ed. L. Sargent (London: Pluto Press).

Harvey, D. (1989), *The Condition of Postmodernity* (Oxford: Basil Blackwell).

Hayward, J. E. S. (1990), 'Solidarist Syndicalism, Durkheim and Duguit', in P. Hamilton (ed.), *Emile Durkheim: Critical Assessments* (London: Routledge), iv. 128–44.

Hegel, G. W. F. (1977), *The Phenomenology of Spirit* (Oxford: Oxford University Press).

Held, D. (1980), *Introduction to Critical Theory* (London: Hutchinson).

Hempel, C. (1969), 'Logical Positivism and the Social Sciences', in P. Achinstein and S. F. Barker (eds.), *The Legacy of Logical Positivism* (Baltimore: John Hopkins University Press).

Hindess, B. (1973), *The Uses of Offical Statistics* (London: Macmillan).

—— and Hirst, P. Q (1975), *Pre-Capitalist Modes of Production* (London: Routledge and Kegan Paul).

Hobsbawm, E. (1964), Introduction to K. Marx, *Pre-Capitalist Economic Formations* (London: Lawrence & Wishart), 9–65.

Hochschild, A. (1994), 'The Commercial Spirit of Intimate Life and the Abduction of Feminism: Signs from Women's Advice Books', *Theory, Culture and Society*, 1–24).

Holton, R. J. and Turner, B. S. (1989), *Max Weber on Economy and Society* (London: Routledge).

Horton, J. (1990), 'The Dehumanisation of Anomie and Alienation: A Problem in the Ideology of Sociology', (1964), in P. Hamilton (ed.), *Emile Durkheim: Critical Assessments* (London: Routledge), iv. 145–62.

Jameson, F. (1991), *Postmodernism or the Cultural Logic of Late Capitalism* (London: Verso).

Jones, R. A. (1986), *Emile Durkheim* (London: Sage).

Klein, M. (1957), *Envy and Gratitude* (London: Tavistock).

Lacan, J. (1977), *Écrits* (London: Tavistock).

Lane, C. (1981), *Rites of Rulers* (Cambridge: Cambridge University Press).

Lasch, C. (1980), *The Culture of Narcissism* (London: Sphere Books).

—— (1995), *The Revolt of the Élites and the Betrayal of Democracy* (New York: W. W. Norton).

Leat, D. (1972), Misunderstanding *Verstehen, Sociological Review*, 20: 29–38.

Lee, D., and Newby, H. (1983), *The Problem of Sociology* (London: Hutchinson).

—— and Turner, B. (1996) (eds.), *Conflicts about Class: Debating Inequality in Late Industrialism* (London: Longman).

Lefebvre, H. (1968), *Dialectical Materialism* (London: Jonathan Cape).

Lenin, V. I. (1972), *The State and Revolution* (Moscow: Progress Publishers).

Levi-Strauss, C. (1966), *The Savage Mind* (London: Weidenfeld & Nicolson).

—— (1969), *Totemism* (Harmondsworth: Pelican Books).

Levine, D. N. (1971), Introduction to *Georg Simmel on Individuality and Social Forms*, (Chicago: Chicago University Press).

—— (1991), 'Simmel at a distance: On the History and Systematics of the Sociology of the Stranger', in L. Ray (ed.), *Formal Sociology* (Aldershot, Hants: Edward Elgar), 272–88.

Lobkowicz, N. (1978), 'Historical Laws' in D. McQuarie (ed.), *Sociology, Social Change, Capitalism* (London: Quartet), 120–33.

Lockwood, D. (1958), *The Blackcoated Worker* (London: Allen & Unwin).

—— (1964), 'Social Integration and System Integration', in G. K. Zollschan and W. Hirsch (eds.), *Explanations in Social Change* (London: Routledge & Kegan Paul), 244–57.

Lukacs, G. (1971*a*; first pub. 1923), *History and Class Consciousness* (Cambridge, Mass.: MIT Press).

—— (1971*b*; first pub. 1910), *Soul and Form* (London: Merlin).

—— (1972), *Studies in European Realism* (London: Merlin).

Lukes, S. (1973), *Emile Durkheim* (Harmondsworth: Penguin).

Lyotard, J.-F. (1984), *The Post-Modern Condition: A Report on Knowledge* (Minneapolis: University of Minnesota Press).

McBride, W. L. (1977), *The Philosophy of Marx* (London: Hutchinson).

McLellan, D. (1971), *The Thought of Karl Marx* (London: Macmillan).

—— (1977) (ed.), *Karl Marx, Selected Writings* (Oxford: Oxford University Press).

McLemore, S. D. (1991), 'Simmel's "Stranger": A Critique of the Concept', in L. Ray (ed.), *Formal Sociology* (Aldershot, Hants: Edward Elgar), 263–71.

Mandel, E. (1962), *Marxist Economic Theory* (London: Merlin Books).

—— (1970), *An Introduction to Marxist Economic Theory* (New York: Pathfinder Press).

Mann, M. (1986), *The Sources of Social Power, A History of Power from the Beginning to A.D. 1760* (Cambridge: Cambridge University Press).

—— (1995), 'Sources of Variation in Working Class movements in 20th Century Europe', *New Left Review*, 212: 14–55).

Mann, T. (1961), *The Magic Mountain* (London: Secker & Warburg).

Mannheim, K. (1938), *Ideology and Utopia* (London: Routledge & Kegan Paul).

Marcuse, H. (1969), *Eros and Civilisation* (London: Sphere Books).

Marshall, G. (1980), *Presbyteries and Profits: Calvinism and the Development of Capitalism in Scotland, 1560–1707* (Oxford: Oxford University Press).

—— (1982), *In Search of the Spirit of Capitalism* (London: Hutchinson).

Marshall, T. H. (1973; first pub. 1950), *Class, Citizenship and Social Development* (Westport, Greenwood).

Marx, K. (1964), *Pre-Capitalist Economic Formations* (London: Lawrence & Wishart).

—— (1968*a*; first pub. 1848), *The Communist Manifesto* in *Marx and Engels: Selected Works* (London: Lawrence & Wishart).

—— (1968*b*; first pub. 1859), Preface to *A Contribution to the Critique of Political Economy*, in *Marx and Engels: Selected Works* (London: Lawrence & Wishart).

—— (1968*c*; first pub. 1852), *The Eighteenth Brumaire of Louis Bonaparte*, in *Marx and Engels: Selected Works* (London: Lawrence & Wishart).

—— (1968*d*; first pub. 1845), *Theses on Feuerbach*, in *Marx and Engels: Selected Works* (London: Lawrence & Wishart).

—— (1969; first pub. 1862), *Theories of Surplus Value, II* (Moscow: Progress Publishers).

—— (1970; first pub. 1867), *Capital, I* (London: Lawrence & Wishart).

—— (1971), *Karl Marx: The Early Texts*, ed. D. McLellan (Oxford: Oxford University Press).

—— (1972; first pub. 1865, *Capital, III* (London: Lawrence & Wishart).

Marx., K. (1973*b*; first pub. 1859), Introduction to *The Grundrisse: Foundations of the Critique of Political Economy* (London: Allen Lane and Penguin Books).

—— (1974), *Economic and Philosophical Manuscripts of 1844* (London: Lawrence & Wishart).

—— (1976; first pub. 1847), *The Poverty of Philosophy*, in K. Marx and F. Engels, *Collected Works*, vi. *1844–1848* (London: Lawrence & Wishart), 105–212.

—— (1977*a*; first pub. 1846), *The German Ideology*, in *Karl Marx, Selected Writings*, ed. D. McLellan (Oxford: Oxford University Press).

—— (1977*b*; first pub. 1875), 'Critique of the Gotha Programme', in *Karl Marx, Selected Writings*, ed. D. McLellan (Oxford: Oxford University Press).

Mead, G. H. (1938), *Mind, Self and Society* (Chicago: Chicago University Press).

Meillasoux, C. (1972), 'From Reproduction to Production', *Economy and Society*, 1: 93–105.

Michels, R. (1911/1962), *Political Parties* (New York: Collier).

Miller, R. W. (1991), 'Social and Political Theory: Class, State, Revolution', in T. Carver (ed.), *The Cambridge Companion to Marx* (Cambridge: Cambridge University Press).

Mitzman, A. (1971), *The Iron Cage: An Historical Interpretation of Max Weber* (New York: Alfred Knopf).

Moore, B. (1966), *The Social Origins of Dictatorship and Democracy* (Harmondsworth: Penguin).

Mouzelis, N. P. (1990), *Post-Marxist Alternatives: The Construction of Social Orders* (London: Macmillan).

Nietzsche, F. (1957), *The Use and Abuse of History* (Indianapolis, Ind.: Bobbs-Merrill).

Nisbet, R. (1967), *The Sociologicak Tradition* (London: Heinneman).

Oakes, G. (1984), Introduction to *Georg Simmel: On Women, Sexuality and Love* (New Haven: Yale University Press).

Ollman, B. (1971), *Alienation* (Cambridge: Cambridge University Press).

Owen, D. (1994), *Maturity and Modernity: Nietzsche, Weber, Foucault and the Ambivalence of Reason* (London: Routledge).

Parkin, F. (1982), *Max Weber* (Chichester: Ellis Horwood).

Parsons, T. (1947) Introduction to M. Weber, *The Theory of Economic and Social Organization* (New York: Oxford University Press).

—— (1951), *The Social System* (New York: Free Press).

—— (1965), Introduction to M. Weber, *The Sociology of Religion* (London: Methuen), pp. ix–lxvii.

—— (1966), *Societies, Evolutionary and Comparative Prespectives* (Englewood Cliffs, NJ: Prentice Hall).

—— (1973), 'The Superego and the Theory of the Social System', in P. Roazen (ed.), *Sigmund Freud* (Englewood Cliffs, NJ: Prentice Hall).

Pearce, F. (1989), *The Radical Durkheim* (London: Unwin Hyman).

Pickering, W. F., and Martins, H. (1994), *Debating Durkheim* (London: Routledge).

Popper, K. (1957), *The Poverty of Historicism* (London: Routledge & Kegan Paul).

—— (1959), *The Logic of Scientific Discovery* (London: Hutchinson).

Poulantzas, N. (1976), *Classes in Contemporary Capitalism* (London: New Left Books).

Powers, C. H. (1991), 'In Search of Simmelian Principles: An Alternative Interpretation of Simmel's Work', in L. Ray (ed.), *Formal Sociology* (Aldershot, Hants: Edward Elgar), 353–5.

Ray, L. (1991) (ed.), *Formal Sociology* (Aldershot, Hants.: Edward Elgar).

Rex, J., and Moore, R. (1967), *Race, Community and Conflict* (Oxford: Institute of Race Relations & Oxford University Press).

Rickert, H. (1962), *Science and History* (Princeton: Van Nostrand).

Rose, N. (1996), 'Identity, Genealogy, History', in S. Hall and P. du Gay, *Questions of Cultural Identity* (London: Sage), 128–50.

Rubin, G. (1984), 'The Traffic in Women: Notes on the "Political Economy" of Sex', in R. Reiter (ed.), *Toward an Anthropology of Women* (New York: Monthly Review Press), 157–210.

Runciman, W. G. (1966), *Relative Deprivation and Social Change* (London: Routledge & Kegan Paul).

—— (1972), *A Critique of Max Weber's Philosophy of Social Science* (Cambridge: Cambridge University Press).

—— (1983), *A Treatise on Social Theory, I. The Methodology of Social Theory* (Cambridge: Cambridge University Press).

—— (1989), *A Treatise on Social Theory, II. Substantive Social Theory* (Cambridge: Cambridge University Press).

—— (1995), 'The 'Triumph' of Capitalism as a Topic in the Theory of Social Selection', *New Left Review*, 210: 33–47).

Rustin, M. (1991), *The Good Society and the Inner World* (London: Verso).

Sacks, K. (1984), 'Engels Revisited, Women, the Organisation of Production and Private Property', in R. Reiter (ed.), *Toward an Anthropology of Women* (New York: Monthly Review Press), 211–34.

Sartre, J.-P. (1957), *Being and Nothingness* (London: Methuen).

—— (1963), *The Problem of Method* (London: Methuen).

—— (1976), *Critique of Dialectical Reason* (London: New Left Books).

Sayer, D. (1991), *Capitalism and Modernity: An Excursus on Marx and Weber* (London: Routledge).

Scaff, L. A. (1991), 'Weber, Simmel and the Sociology of Culture', in L. Ray (ed.), *Formal Sociology* (Aldershot, Hants: Edward Elgar), 106–35.

Schutz, A. (1972), *The Phenomenology of the Social World* (London: Heinemann).

Shils, E., and Young, M. (1953), 'The Meaning of the Coronation', *Sociological Review*, 1: 63–81.

Simmel, G. (1950), *The Sociology of Georg Simmel*, ed. by Kurt H. Wolff (New York: Free Press).

—— (1955), *Conflict and the Web of Group Affiliations* (Glencoe, Ill.: Free Press).

—— (1968), *The Conflict in Modern Culture and Other Essays* (New York: Teachers College Press).

—— (1971), *Georg Simmel on Individuality and Social Forms*, ed. D. Levine (Chicago: Chicago University Press).

—— (1984), *Georg Simmel: On Women, Sexuality and Love*, ed. G. Oakes (New Haven: Yale University Press).

—— (1990; first pub. 1900), *The Philosophy of Money* (London: Routledge).

Solzhenitsyn, A. (1968), *Cancer Ward* (London: Bodley Head).

Spencer, H. (1971), *Structure, Function and Evolution*, ed. S. Andreski (London: Nelson).

Swingewood, A. (1991), *A Short History of Sociological Theory* (Basingstoke: Macmillan).

Taylor, C. (1977), *Hegel* (Oxford: Oxford University Press).

—— (1989), *Sources of the Self* (Cambridge, Mass.: Harvard University Press).

—— (1991), *The Ethics of Authenticity* (Cambridge, Mass.: Harvard University Press).

Thompson, E. P. (1965), *The Making of the English Working Class* (London: Gollancz).

Thompson, K. (1982), *Emile Durkheim* (Chichester: Ellis Horwood).

Tonnies, F. (1957), *Community and Association* (London: Routledge & Kegan Paul).

Trotsky, L. (1967), *History of the Russian Revolution*, I (London: Sphere Books).

Turner, B. S. (1992), *Max Weber: From History to Modernity* (London: Routledge).

—— (1996), *For Weber* (London: Sage).

Turner, J. H. (1991), 'Marx and Simmel Revisited: Reassessing the Foundations of Conflict Theory', in L. Ray (ed.), *Formal Sociology* (Aldershot, Hants: Edward Elgar), 47–58.

Walby, S. (1990), *Theorizing Patriarchy* (Oxford: Blackwell).

Wallerstein, I. (1974), *The Modern World System* (New York: Academic Press).

Wallwork, E. (1972), *Durkheim: Morality and Milieu* (Cambridge, Mass: Harvard University Press).

Weber, M. (1930; first pub. 1904–5), *The Protestant Ethic and the Spirit of Capitalism* (London: Allen & Unwin).

—— (1947; first pub. 1922), *The Theory of Social and Economic Organisation* (New York: Oxford University Press).

—— (1949), *The Methodology of the Social Sciences* (Glencoe: Free Press).

—— (1951; first pub. 1915), *The Religion of China* (Glencoe: Free Press).

—— (1952; first pub. 1921), *Ancient Judaism* (Glencoe: Free Press).

—— (1958; first pub. 1921), *The Religion of India* (Glencoe: Free Press).

—— (1965; first pub. 1922), *The Sociology of Religion* (London: Methuen).

—— (1978; first pub. 1925), *Economy and Society: An Outline of Interpretive Sociology* (New York: Bedminster).

Weinstein, D., and Weinstein, M. A. (1993), *Postmodern(ized) Simmel* (London: Routledge).

Winch, P. (1958), *The Idea of a Social Science* (London: Routledge & Kegan Paul).

Wittfogel, K. A. (1963), *Oriental Despotism* (New Haven: Yale University Press).

Woolf, V. (1929), *A Room of One's Own* (London: Hogarth).

Wright, E. O. (1978), *Class, Crisis and the State* (London: New Left Books).

—— (1989), 'Models of Historical Trajectory: An Assessment of Giddens's Critique of Marxism', in D. Held and J. B. Thompson (eds.), *Social Theory and Modern Society: Anthony Giddens and his Critics* (Cambridge: Cambridge University Press), 77–102.

Wrong, D. (1957), 'The Oversocialised Conception of Man in Modern Sociology', in L. Coser and B. Rosenberg (eds.), *Sociological Theory* (New York: Collier Macmillan).

Zaretsky, E. (1973), *Capitalism, The Family, and Personal Life* (New York: Harper & Row).

Zeitlin, I. M. (1968), *Ideology and the Development of Sociological Theory* (Englewood Cliffs, NJ: Prentice Hall).

Index